THE MAKING OF A SAINT

J. H. HUIZINGA

THE MAKING
OF A SAINT

THE TRAGI-COMEDY
OF JEAN-JACQUES ROUSSEAU

HAMISH HAMILTON

LONDON

First published in Great Britain 1976
by Hamish Hamilton Ltd
90 Great Russell Street London WC1B 3PT

Copyright © 1976 by J. H. Huizinga

SBN 241 89275 9

Printed in Great Britain by
Western Printing Services Ltd, Bristol

For

SALLY

who has brought so many joys
into my life

CONTENTS

ILLUSTRATIONS

ACKNOWLEDGEMENTS

My acknowledgements are due to the following publishers for allowing me to quote from the works listed below:

J. M. Dent & Sons Ltd.: *Emile*, by J.-J. Rousseau, translated by Barbara Foxley (Everyman's Library series)
Social Contract and Discourses, by J.-J. Rousseau, translated by G. D. H Cole

Macmillan Publishing Co., Inc.: *Jean-Jacques Rousseau*, by Lester G. Crocker (Copyright © 1968–1973 by Macmillan Publishing Co., Inc.)

Oxford University Press: *Diderot's Letters to Sophie Volland*, translated by Peter France

Penguin Books Ltd.: *The Confessions*, by J.-J. Rousseau, translated by J. M. Cohen (Copyright © J. M. Cohen, 1954)

The Pennsylvania State University Press: *La Nouvelle Héloise*, translated by Judith J. McDowell. Copyright © 1968 by the Pennsylvania State University. Reprinted by permission of The Pennsylvania State University Press

PREFACE

I AM deeply grateful to the following for helping me in the preparation of this book: Sir Isaiah Berlin, who read the essay out of which it grew and who gave me encouragement as well as some valuable insights; Professor Maurice Cranston who read the chapters on *The Social Contract;* Comte Dominic de Grunne who read those dealing with Rousseau's religious thought and helped me with some of the trickier translation-problems; Donald J. Hall and Christopher Sinclair-Stevenson who wrought countless stylistic improvements, and last not least Douglas Matthews, deputy-librarian of the London Library, as knowledgeable as he is unfailingly helpful.

Rather than encumber the narrative with the names of the many biographers and historians to whose works I am indebted and whose authority I have on occasion invoked, I would refer the reader to the select bibliography at the end of this volume.

J.H.H.
London, February 1975

CHRONOLOGY

1712	Rousseau born in Geneva.
1725–28	Apprentice to engraver in Geneva.
1728	Leaves Geneva. Meets 'Maman' at Anneçy, is prepared for conversion to Catholicism in Turin, abjures Calvinism, gets job as lackey.
1729	Returns to 'Maman'.
1730	Travels, sets up as music master, visits Paris.
1731–40	Lives with 'Maman', educates himself.
1740–41	Tutor in Lyon.
1742	Moves to Paris, makes contact with Beau Monde, becomes friend of Diderot.
1742–43	Secretary to French Ambassador in Venice.
1745	Starts affair with Thérèse Levasseur.
1746	Secretary to châtelaine of Chenonceaux. Birth of first child by Thérèse.
1747	Meets Madame d'Epinay.
1749	Becomes friend of Grimm. Has 'illumination' on road to Vincennes. Sets up house with Thérèse.
1750	Academy of Dijon crowns the essay inspired by the 'illumination'.
1751	With publication of the prize-winning essay (on the destructive effect of the arts and sciences on morality) its author becomes fashionable overnight. He 'reforms' by dressing the part of the simple-lifer, 'renouncing all worldly ambition', and 'setting an example' by his conduct.
1752	Scores great success with operetta put on at the Royal Theatre at Fontainebleau. Works on a book, part of which ten years later saw the light as *The Social Contract*.

1754   Visits Geneva, reconverts back to its church so as to regain his status as citizen of Geneva.

1755   Publication of the *Discourse on the Origin of Inequality*.

1756   Moves to the 'Hermitage' on Madame d'Epinay's estate. Starts *La Nouvelle Héloise*.

1757   Meets his *grande passion*, quarrels with Madame d'Epinay and Grimm and is expelled from the Hermitage.

1758   Lionized by the Duke and Duchess of Luxembourg, who lend him a house on their estate. Starts *Emile*. Breaks with Diderot. Incurs Voltaire's enmity by his denunciation of the theatre, as fatal to morality.

1761   Publication of *La Nouvelle Héloise*.

1762   Publication of *Emile* and *The Social Contract*. Warrant for their author's arrest forces him to flee to Switzerland. After expulsion from Bernese territory, settles down in that of Neufchâtel. Replies to denunciation of *Emile* by Archbishop of Paris.

1763–64   Replies to Geneva's condemnation of his 'profession of faith' in *Emile*. Renounces his status as citizen of Geneva. Voltaire publishes pamphlet revealing he had sent all the children Thérèse bore him to a foundling-home. Makes new friend and literary executor of Dupeyrou.

1765   Starts the *Confessions*. Flees from wrath of local populace to Bernese territory. Urged by David Hume to seek asylum in England. On journey there fêted in Strasbourg and Paris.

1766   Fêted in London. Settles down in Derbyshire country house. Hume gets him royal pension. Scandalises his admirers by accusing Hume of treachery.

1767   Returns to France under false name. Guest of King's cousin. Breaks with Dupeyrou. Travels in France.

1768   'Marries' Thérèse.

1770   Resumes own name, returns to Paris.

1771   Gives readings of the *Confessions*.

1772   Starts the *Dialogues*.

1776   Starts the *Rêveries du Promeneur Solitaire*.

1778   Accepts hospitality of Marquis de Girardin at Ermenonville where he dies six weeks later.

PROLOGUE

BEST-SELLING authors have rarely achieved sainthood. Somehow the profession of letters seems to be rather less conducive to the practice of virtue—as distinct from its advocacy—than humbler occupations such as that of carpenter or fisherman. But there has been one member of the literary guild who did win his halo, the great Jean-Jacques Rousseau. No sooner had he died, eleven years before the Fall of the Bastille, than pilgrims of the most diverse plumage, from royalty downward, started flocking to his grave. The luckless Marie-Antoinette, accompanied by a number of princes and princesses of the blood, spent more than an hour under the poplars that had given his burial-place its name: 'Ile des Peupliers'. It was a suitably romantic spot for the worship of the departed, a tiny island in the middle of a lake on the magnificent estate of the Marquis who was the last of his many aristocratic hosts and protectors.

There is no record of what went through the Queen's head as she stood by the tomb of the man some of whose teachings would soon be invoked by those determined to cut it off. But we do have records of many a humbler pilgrim, records showing that they hardly needed the exhortations to piety addressed to them by the lord and master of the hallowed ground who, much like the owners of the Stately Homes of our day though with a less mercenary motive, provided his visitors with a guidebook; 'It is to you, friend of Rousseau, that I address myself . . . let your tears pour out, never will you have wept sweeter or more justifiable tears.' One of these visitors came to the island to commit suicide in the hope of being buried by the side of the tomb. Another deposited a prayer on it comparing its occupant with Jesus Christ. A third, a poet, felt his heart 'filled with religious mourning', when he came to 'meditate in this pious temple'. A fourth relates how he and his young wife 'gathered themselves' as they approached, 'the way you do at the entrance of a temple so as to have a more religious attitude', and how his wife 'pressed her bosom against the sacred marble'.

But the fullest account stems from two friends, a French curate and a Prussian baron, one of whom describes how they spent eight days at the place of their 'pilgrimage'. They, too, felt it necessary to begin by preparing themselves 'so as to approach the sanctuary with the respect demanded by its saintliness and the memory of him whom one reveres'. And so they started by worshipping the saint's relics which the Marquis had apparently put on display and one of which was a tobacco-pouch; 'my fingers touched this box, my heart trembled, and my soul became purer'. The second day they were as 'agitated as Apollo's highpriestess at the approach of the god'. Only on the fourth did they feel ready to traverse the narrow strip of water to the island which 'two virtuous Englishmen, refused passage by the boatman, had crossed by swimming to the sacred ground'. Having set foot on it at last, so their story continued: 'I dropped to my knees . . . pressed my lips on the cold stone of the monument . . . and kissed it repeatedly.' There followed a veritable religious ritual, complete with prayers and vows and ending with the burning in effigy of one of the saint's foremost enemies, except that it was really his blasphemous spirit, expressed in a hostile essay, which they burnt at the stake. 'Both on our knees, each of us holding a side of the infernal libel, we proclaimed in a loud voice: "we offer this expiatory sacrifice on the tomb of the great man, handing over to the flames a libel which the lie claims its own and truth disavows . . . Thus perishes the memory of the wicked and the slanderers".'

Clearly, the saint worshipped on the 'Ile des Peupliers' was unusual not only in the manner in which he had earned his halo, as a literary Jack-of-all-trades, who had written light operas and love-stories as well as sociological, political, religious and educational treatises. He was unique also in the intense hostility he aroused. It was such as to provoke the faithful to outbursts of retaliatory ferocity well illustrated by the words of one of their prominent descendants (for the battle continues to this day), a member of the prestige-laden Académie Française and one-time Minister of Education. About a century after Rousseau's death he described his hero's female detractors as 'viragos who are seized by an epileptic fury at the mere mention of his name; their eyes burn with rage, they go pale and start frothing at the mouth from which there rushes a torrent of curses . . . their voice hoarse with alcohol and madness'.

Indeed, of 'St. Rousseau' (as George Sand did not hesitate to call him) it could be said that one man's saint is another man's Satan. For Diderot, whose 'infernal libel' had been burnt on Jean-Jacques's tomb, he was 'false, vain as Satan, ungrateful, cruel, hypocritical and malicious'. And this erstwhile friend, to whose huge efforts the Age of Reason owed its bible, the *Encyclopédie*, was far from being the only fellow-intellectual who came to see him in this light. Another former friend, Melchior Grimm, who had set up a sort of highbrow news-agency supplying his mostly royal subscribers all over Europe with the latest news from the literary scene in

Paris, found him to be so 'monstrous and odious' that he, too, broke off all relations; 'I shall never see you again and I shall count myself lucky if I can banish the memory of your behaviour from my memory.' Yet another, the soldier-poet the Marquis de St. Lambert, asked him 'to forget my existence . . . I promise for my part to forget your person and remember only your talents'. A woman-friend, the Marquise d'Epinay, couched her goodbye in gentler but no less revealing terms: 'I have nothing left for you but pity.' The Scottish philosopher and historian David Hume, under whose auspices Rousseau came to England, reached the conclusion that he was a 'monster who regarded himself as the only important being in the universe'. Horace Walpole, who called him a 'charlatan', had no more use for him than Voltaire, who called him every name under the sun: 'malicious rascal', 'bastard dog of Diogenes', 'little man bursting with conceit', 'monster of vanity and baseness', 'the most wicked knave that ever dishonoured letters', etc., etc.

But then, the profession of letters has never formed a mutual admiration-society, the members of the intelligentsia have always conducted their particular rat-race with at least as much backbiting, acid-throwing and, when expedient, backscratching as those who compete for the prizes of life in less exalted spheres such as politics or business. And so, against the denunciations of Rousseau's rivals must be set the testimony of humbler men with no axes to grind, like the two who came back from his island-grave feeling morally uplifted. 'It is not in vain,' the couple's spokesman wrote, 'that I made this pilgrimage nor was it idle curiosity that made me undertake it; I did so with the intention of becoming better acquainted with virtue. The benefit I have obtained from it is the firm resolve to get a grip on myself, correct my faults, and try to be a better man. I maintain that no one . . . who makes this pilgrimage can return from it without having taken the same resolution, so redolent is the place with virtue.' That was exactly how great numbers of his contemporaries felt about the writer, regarded by almost all those who came to know him as, at best, the pitiful victim of a self-love so obsessive, so boundless, so all-embracing as to border on self-deification.

It seems odd, all the more so as it is not only the humble who have worshipped at his shrine. So did the great philosopher Kant who credited him with 'a sensibility of soul of unequalled perfection'. So did the great poet Schiller who called him 'a Christ-like soul for whom only the angels of heaven are fit company'. So did the great novelist Tolstoy who in his youth carried a medallion with his image around his neck and, when an old man, said that 'Rousseau and the Gospel have been the two great and salutary influences in my life'.

Odd indeed. And therefore, perhaps, worthy of closer examination.

CHAPTER ONE

Arrival and Departure

'Let us excel, never mind in what . . .'

IT WAS in the brilliant Paris of Louis Quinze—as brilliant for the few as it was brutish for the many—that Jean-Jacques, at thirty-eight still an obscure struggling intellectual, suddenly leapt to fame. Overnight, on the strength of a thirty-page pamphlet, he had become a literary lion, the talk of the glittering salons.

'The position I had taken up,' he recalls in his memoirs, the famous *Confessions*, 'excited curiosity . . . and made me fashionable . . . People wanted to see this odd man . . . My room was never empty of people who came to take up my time, the ladies employed countless ruses to get me to dine with them.' Though the *Confessions* are anything but a reliable historical record, having been partly designed as a public relations campaign at a time when their author's image was badly damaged, there is nothing implausible in the assertion that admirers flocked to his room. For in his day a good part of the reading-public belonged to that upper crust of society whose main occupation was to keep not the wolf but *ennui*, boredom, from the door, aristocrats whose status traditionally excluded them from practically all occupations other than those of the soldier, the courtier and the amateur of literature and the arts.

What is more, Jean-Jacques's account of his sudden emergence into the brilliant light of the salons illuminated by innumerable crystal-held candles, has been corroborated by more than one of his contemporaries. 'Your essay,' wrote Diderot, then still a great friend of his, 'is everywhere praised to the skies, there has never been such a success.' Grimm reported to his subscribers that 'it has brought about a revolution in Paris laying the foundations for the renown of M. Rousseau whose talents were little known up to now'. One of the great ladies for whom Jean-Jacques had worked as a secretary was so carried away that she allowed her enthusiasm to express itself in a somewhat double-edged compliment: 'Why, who would have thought it of you, Monsieur Rousseau!' And according to one of France's foremost literary historians, writing in the nineteenth century, 'neither Montesquieu nor Voltaire ever had such a success'.

Thus, after an unusually variegated career as apprentice to an engraver, lackey, seminarist, music-master, gigolo (of a kind), clerk, tutor, diplomat, secretary, composer and writer, Jean-Jacques, in the year 1750, had at last arrived. And he had arrived, not with a whimper, but with a bang that blew open the doors of all the best houses. Suddenly he was well and truly launched. For it was the salons who made a writer's reputation in those days, not the press, then still a long way from becoming the fourth estate. Limited to three or four weeklies and periodicals, it was despised by the leading intellectuals as 'the grazing ground of the ignorant', 'the ruination of letters', 'the rabble of literature'.

So, what with those countless ladies using all their ingenuity to get the latest literary lion to come and grace their soirées, Jean-Jacques's every dream seemed to have come true. He had been hungering for success, recognition and fame, ever since he had come to Paris some eight years before to try and make his name as a writer and composer. Even 'as a boy', he says in his *Confessions*, he had dreamt of 'the most brilliant fortune', convinced that 'people of rank could not fail to welcome me for my talents and deserts as soon as I became known to them'. The reference to 'people of rank' might sound strangely snobbish in a man whose writings are said to have done so much to foment egalitarian passions all over Europe and who has often been spoken of as a revolutionary and a plebeian. But the fact of the matter is that the same Geneva background to which he owed his taste for the simple life had also left its imprint on him in a keen pre-occupation with his rightful place in the social pecking order. Born into the privileged class of a Republic (where only 2,000 *bourgeois* and *citoyens*, forming barely ten per cent of the populace, were enfranchised), he re-mained throughout his life very class-conscious, looking down upon the *canaille*, as he often called the people, as much as looking up to the grand (however much he might revile them when he chose to put on the dema-gogue's hat from among the many he was to collect in his cupboard). In his youth when he roamed around a good deal, he had hoped to chance upon a château and to become 'the favourite of its lord and lady, the lover of their daughter, the friend of their son and the protector of their neighbours'. And when at the age of thirty-one he got a job as secretary to the French ambassador to the Republic of Venice, his employer found him still painfully obsessed with 'pride of rank'. On one occasion, so the ambassador reported to his superiors in Paris, his secretary had refused to join him in his country residence because that would have meant travel-ling by public transport which he had declared 'fit only for servants'.

But if, therefore, the breakthrough Jean-Jacques had achieved eight years later was such a dream come true, it was also because of another characteristic that had made the years of failure so tormenting: his high opinion of himself. If there was one thing he never seemed to suffer from in a life which, he claims, was 'unparalleled' for suffering, it was an inferiority complex. Admittedly the underlying reality may well have been very different. Indeed, those of his biographers who have tried to unravel the murky complexities of his subconscious have argued, often very persuasively, that he was one of those who boast only from weakness. Plagued, according to them, by a deep sense of inadequacy and worthlessness as well as assorted guilt-feelings, traceable to infancy, he indulged in such orgies of self-praise only to reassure himself. But even if there were hidden elements of an inferiority complex in his psyche, they were hardly visible to his contemporaries. What they saw was that overweening conceit and that self-importance which Voltaire was to mock so mercilessly when he said that 'Jean-Jacques is convinced that one half of the universe is busy erecting his statue and the other half demolishing it'. The ambassador to Venice who called him 'the greatest cox-comb a man could ever have in his service' and who became so annoyed with his 'insolence' that he threatened to have him thrown out of the window, may not have been the most objective of judges. But when one sees how Jean-Jacques describes his shortlived diplomatic career it is difficult not to feel that his former employer may have had some right on his side in the quarrel that led to his secretary's dismissal, or, as Jean-Jacques calls it, his 'resignation'. 'Irreproachable . . . I deserved and won the esteem of the Republic and all the ambassadors with whom we were in contact . . . I did my duty all the time with a zeal, an honesty and a courage which deserved a better reward . . . I also won the affection of the French residents in Venice . . . But for me they would have been unaware that their nation was represented by an ambassador . . . Opinion was unanimous about me from the heads of missions downward.'

Admittedly these lines date from a time when his countless admirers had long since set the head-swelling process in motion. But that Jean-Jacques was not the most modest of men even when he still had reason to be, is clear from the manner in which he wrote about his row with the ambassador at the time. What worried him was not so much the 'monstrous affronts' he had suffered at the latter's hands but 'what the general public will think'. The Foreign Secretary, to whom he addressed his complaint, owed it to him 'to restore in the eyes of the public the honour of an upright man . . . All Venice has seen with indignation the disgraceful treatment he has inflicted on me.'

*

To a man so impressed with his own importance, failure to achieve not only recognition but even to maintain himself in the rank to which he feels entitled by birth, can only have an exacerbating effect; his pride is wounded, starts festering and swells. And until the age of nearly forty Jean-Jacques suffered both types of failure. As a teenager he had at times been reduced to earning his living as a lackey, serving at table, which had been all the harder to tolerate because, like most of us, he 'had marched confidently out into the great world'. And here he was 'dressed in a servant's livery', at the beck and call of a countess 'who never spoke to me except to give orders, who judged me less by what I was than by what she had made of me . . . and saw nothing in me but a servant'.

But much more corrosive were the years of failure and frustration he suffered in his thirties when, thanks to a provincial lady on whose bounty he had lived during most of his twenties, he had been able to equip himself for the intellectual rat-race in Paris. Wounds inflicted on the pride of an adolescent may leave their mark, but they normally heal quickly in the onrush of life of that breathless age. Certainly the injuries his pride had sustained at the hands of the haughty countess were soon forgotten in the boost it derived from his next employer, a count in whose house he 'had won everyone's respect almost by storm' and where his 'general reputation was that of a young man of the highest expectations who was not in his proper place'. And for the next ten years he led a mostly very sheltered existence that safeguarded him from all but sexual humiliations. Kept by a benefactress, twelve years his senior, who demanded only his services in bed as a *quid pro quo*—and that only until a more expert performer took his place—his pride was spared the wounding blows it had suffered in the early struggle to earn his living. Indeed, it could blossom in this new environment which more than met the exigencies of his 'rank', his 'proper place'. For the lady, Madame de Warens, was—or at any rate called herself—a baroness and moved in the best circles of the country-town in Savoy where she had fled from her native Switzerland.

During these long, leisurely years in which he read widely enough to qualify as an eighteenth-century intellectual, spanning the 'two cultures', at home both in the sciences and the humanities, his all-devouring ambition seemed to lie dormant. It was only when, having at last outstayed his welcome, he had to go in search of his fortune in Paris that his fierce desire for recognition reasserted itself, filling him with mounting resentment at a whole series of failures and frustrations.

Yet he had come well-prepared for success. Though largely self-taught —his formal schooling had come to an end at the age of thirteen—he had no difficulty in winning the respect and friendship of such a leading light as Diderot was soon to become. The doors of the literary club that was Baron d'Holbach's house—where the intellectual avant-garde used to foregather every week, lingering five or six hours over immensely talkative luncheons—were wide open to him. He had not come ill-prepared for entry into the salons of the Beau Monde either. For he was sufficiently world-wise to have asked 'Maman', as he used to call the provincial baroness, for introductions, 'first of all to the nobility and people in government . . . next to tradesmen . . . and finally to intellectuals'. Moreover, before he had reached Paris he had collected another batch from the people he met in the house of a high-ranking official in Lyon to whom 'Maman' had recommended him for the post of tutor (a role for which the future author of a famous treatise on education did not appear to be very gifted; 'when my pupils did not understand me I raged, when they showed signs of disobedience I could have killed them').

But far from proving a stepping-stone to the worldly success he craved, his introductions only paved the way to embittering defeats. It was through one of the great hostesses he met that he had obtained the diplomatic appointment in Venice that ended so ignominiously. And before then he had already had more than one sour taste of the treatment her kind reserved for intellectuals who had not yet made the grade. He had been introduced to the lady administering it by a Jesuit priest who had advised him that the only way to get on in Paris was to 'try the women . . . you will never get anywhere without the help of the ladies'. But when he went to call on her, so he relates, 'she proved so full of her illustrious nobility' that she invited him to stay for lunch . . . in the servants' hall. Fortunately, her daughter showed more understanding for the 'respect due to talent', so that things were arranged and Jean-Jacques got an opportunity to impress the company with his talent by reading them a poem of his that 'moved them to tears'.

He had no such consolation with the next great lady he tried and whose house 'was as brilliant as any in Paris', full of 'noblemen, men of letters, beautiful women, dukes, ambassadors, and men with decorations'. But in this case he really had only himself to blame for his discomfiture. Instead of showing insufficient 'respect for his talent', this thirty-six-year-old *grande dame*—whose great-granddaughter was to achieve fame as George Sand—gave him such a welcome that 'I went there nearly every day and lunched there twice or three times a week'. What got him into trouble was the lady's beauty and his own 'lascivious temperament' which overcame his usual timidity. He had fallen 'in love', the moment she had first received him, 'in her dressing room, her arms bare, her hair dishevelled, and her dressing-jacket loose'. If he had not declared his passion then and there it was because it required formidable nerve for someone in his modest position to make a pass at such a distinguished Paris hostess, the châtelaine of the most beautiful château in France: Chenonceaux. Painfully aware that he did not 'cut much of a figure in her surroundings', and so 'not daring to speak but unable to remain silent', he wrote her a passionate letter the effect of which was disastrous. After keeping him in agonizing suspense for two days during which she did not react in any way, she returned the letter 'admonishing me briefly in tones of such coldness that my blood froze'. It was a fearful setback, not so much to his heart, which not for the first nor the last time showed its capacity for instant refrigeration—'my passion was extinguished with my hopes'—as to his career. For 'entry into a wealthy house was an open door to fortune which I dared not, in my position, risk being shut'.

What with the lady's clemency, however, and his own abject begging for it—'I need only feel,' he wrote to her husband, 'that the sight of me is not abhorrent beyond a certain point in order to make a successful effort to become bearable'—he was eventually restored in the household's good graces. Indeed, he found employment there, first as a tutor to the lady's son, later, on his return from Venice, as her secretary and research-assistant, for she was not only a society-hostess but also a writer active in the cause of the emancipation of women. But while this solved the problem of keeping body and soul together, it was hardly calculated to satisfy his hunger for that glory which he felt to be his due and, he later admitted, 'had searched too avidly'.

To win it he tried his hand at one thing after another. The only thing that mattered in those days was to get his foot on the ladder somehow: 'Anyone who excels in something, I told myself, is always sure to be sought after. So let us excel, never mind in what, I shall be sought after, opportunities will present themselves, and my merit will do the rest.' When he had first arrived in Paris he had put all his hopes of 'attaining celebrity which in Paris is always accompanied by a fortune' in a new system of musical notation by numbers which he had worked out while still with 'Maman' but which got no further than a hearing by the Academy of Science where it was rejected as unpractical. (Nor, in fact, was it new, as someone else had already invented it sixty-five years earlier.) Back in Paris, after his abortive diplomatic career in Venice, he switched to composing and writing an operetta from which again he derived little joy. Though a fragment of it was staged in the salon of Paris's best-known female Maecenas of the time (and the whole of it subsequently in the presence of a duke who promised to have it performed at Versailles), the foremost composer of the age, Rameau, accused its author of flagrant plagiarism; he had stolen all the best music from an Italian in Venice and the rest was worthless.

Even bitterer was the disappointment he suffered with his next attempt to make his name as a composer and a librettist. Asked by the duke, who had heard his first effort, to tighten up a musical entertainment knocked together for the Dauphin's wedding by no one less than the great Voltaire and the great Rameau, his contribution not only remained unmentioned on the programme, but was even revised almost out of existence by Rameau. It was such a blow that 'sick at heart, tired out and consumed by grief, I fell ill'. And still his cup was not full. When he had recovered sufficiently to try and interest one of the leading theatres in staging a comedy he had written more than ten years earlier, he once again met with defeat. The bitter resentment he felt in those days as well as the contemptuous lofty self-complacency in which his wounded ego sought refuge, are all in the letter he wrote to a friend shortly afterwards. 'As a true Swiss I had imagined that one needed to merit success to win it, but I have learnt other talents are required which I do not have and do not wish to have.'

But if at the time these years of failure and frustration seemed pure loss, in retrospect they can be seen to have made their contribution to the making of St. Jean-Jacques. They provided him with the beginning of a title to that martyrdom without which no halo is ever awarded and which he only fully attained when the hero of the salons he became at the age of forty, was persecuted as a heretic by the Establishment of the day. His early sufferings, or rather his account of them, helped to create the myth that he was and nearly always had been the 'unhappiest of mortals', as he likes to say of himself when claiming to have 'a heart that has never been open to anything but sorrow', or wailing about 'the grim fate which dogs my footsteps . . . Few men have sighed as I have, few men have shed so many tears . . . My fate is such that one would not dare to describe it for no one would believe it'. His was not an age that indulged in understatement. And it is perhaps because Rousseau's biographers of Victorian times were apt to take these stereotyped laments at face value, that the myth of his life being one long martyrdom has found such widespread and tenacious credence.

But his own contemporaries were taken in by it too. One of his powerful protectors, the chief censor, called him the 'unhappiest of men'. So did Voltaire. And even Grimm, hardly one of his hagiographers, reported that 'M. Rousseau has been unhappy practically all of his life'. Apparently he had a way of talking about his 'chain of misfortunes' that made so deep an impression on his listeners that they took them at face value. 'I still feel moved,' wrote Madame d'Epinay, 'by the simple and original way in which he recounted his misfortunes.'

And yet, that his life-long bondage to an unrelenting fate was a myth, that he was allocated more than his full share of the joys of life, no one has attested more fully than the 'unhappiest of mortals' himself.

CHAPTER TWO

Marche Funèbre with a Light Air

'You think I am unhappy; how wrong you are!'

SUCCESS and its attendant, fame, are not the least of the joys that can fall to a man avid for recognition and glory. Jean-Jacques was to taste them to the full. And though he was not one to count his blessings, there was at least one occasion on which he proved unable to affect disdain for the joy success brought him: 'I surrendered myself completely and unreservedly to the pleasure of savouring my glory.'

It was the kind of evening every writer has dreamt of, but very few live to see. A theatre—and a royal theatre at that, in the Palace of Fontaine-bleau—packed with *le tout Paris* of those flamboyantly glamorous days, the resplendent King and his bejewelled ladies in the royal box, the author-composer in a box 'so placed', he relates, 'as to be seen by all', the stalls and the other boxes full of 'women . . . as lovely as angels and who whispered to one another how 'charming, how delightful' as the orchestra and the singers filled the house with the dulcet tones of his new operetta, *The Village Soothsayer*. No wonder he was 'moved to tears' as were many of the lovely women present, which added yet another ingredient to his exquisite pleasure. For the glory did not so much go to his head as in the opposite direction, acting as an aphrodisiac; 'it was sexual passion rather than author's vanity I felt . . . devoured as I was by the desire to catch with my lips the delicious tears I had evoked.'

That was two years after he had emerged from obscurity with the very different work that had then set the town by the ears, the pamphlet in which he had denounced its elegant, sophisticated society instead of entertaining it. And henceforward he was to go from strength to strength until, as Hume was to say, 'his fame eclipsed even that of Voltaire'. It was no small recompense for the years of failure and frustration. They naturally had seemed long to him. But seen in the perspective of his life as a whole they were but an interlude between a far from unhappy youth and a middle age rich in compensations for the penalties attached to such immense success as he then enjoyed. Though his mother had died within a few days of his birth, in the year 1712, and his father had left him to the care of relations when he was but ten years old, young Jean-Jacques had not had an unhappy childhood. He recalls that 'no royal child could be more scrupulously cared for than I was in my early years . . . I was idolized by everyone around me . . . I was happy'. Where he may be said to have been unlucky was in the 'violent, oafish character' of the young engraver to whom he was apprenticed at the age of thirteen and with whom he not only worked but for three years lodged and boarded as well. It was one of the many occasions on which Jean-Jacques, whose outstanding characteristic was his lack of character, the 'feebleness of soul' as he himself calls it, claims to have become 'another man'. And as usual when the transformation was for the worse, it was not really his fault; 'my master managed to coarsen my affectionate and lively nature . . . his tyranny drove me to vices I should otherwise have despised, such as falsehood, idleness and theft.' It is a theme that recurs throughout his autobiographical writings. His '*peccavi*' is invariably qualified by a '*sed non mea culpa*', the plea of guilty is always followed by that of '*nolle prosequi*'.

*

Hard as the years of his adolescence may have been and much as his class-conscious pride may have suffered during the short period when the haughty countess treated him as a servant, 'by and large,' he says in his autobiography, 'my peaceful youth . . . was pleasant enough without great setbacks or remarkable spells of prosperity'. In fact, there were quite a few spells when life seemed to offer everything he could ask for. There had been happy wanderings in and out of Italy, sometimes with young fellow-adventurers setting out 'with a light purse but a heart overflowing with delight'. There was the winter he spent with the choirmaster who was to make a musician of him and where 'all was song and gaiety'. There was his first trip to Paris 'which I count among the happy days of my life'. There was the 'period of eight or nine years' when he lived with his 'Maman' and when 'my life was as simple as it was pleasant . . . a life of sweet repose divided between work, pleasure and instruction'. And during this period there had been 'four or five years . . . of the purest and fullest happiness . . . I needed a woman-friend after my heart's desire and I possessed one . . . I wanted to live in the country and I did. I could not stand restraints of any kind and I was perfectly free . . . I did only what I wanted to do . . . I desired nothing but that so sweet a condition might continue.' Well might he conclude, looking back on the first three decades of his life, that 'fate had favoured my wishes for thirty years'.

Life had not been without its happy moments either when, after these long, carefree years of 'sweet repose'—not idleness, for it took a great deal of cramming to qualify as a highbrow fit to attend d'Holbach's interminable luncheons—he had to go to work for his living. Within a year of his arrival in Paris the genial, warm-hearted, ebullient Diderot, as hard up as Jean-Jacques himself and like him a struggling intellectual of modest provincial origin, brought companionship of the heart as well as the mind. And even before they became friends the Swiss newcomer, thanks to the Academy of Science's interest in his ill-starred musical invention, had already met 'all the most distinguished literary men of Paris'. The loneliness in the big city suffered by the unrecognized genius, the poet in his garret of romantic tradition, does not seem to have been one of his troubles. Nor—though 'perpetually on the verge of penury'—did he starve. Whatever the origin of his resources in those days, he was able 'calmly to wait for my money to give out' and spend his afternoons 'playing chess at the Café Mougis on the days I did not go to the play'.

That something always turned up to keep him from starving is clear from his statement that 'the last time in my life I knew hunger and want was at the age of nineteen'. (That was during a journey away from 'Maman's' home, some ten years before he came to Paris.) When he was calmly waiting for his money to run out it was a Jesuit priest who came to the rescue, introducing him to the great ladies one of whom got him his job in Venice. And there, too, he was far from being the unhappiest of mortals, though he found his master as insufferable as the latter found the bumptious Jean-Jacques 'insolent'.* He derived great satisfaction from his (somewhat doubtful) diplomatic status, as well as enjoying the pleasures the town had to offer outside office hours. 'I have adopted,' he wrote in a letter, 'the local way of life. I promenade around the Piazza and the shows in my mask and domino as cocky as if I had spent my whole life in that costume.'

Back in Paris, the new job as secretary and research-assistant to the châtelaine of Chenonceaux brought him an assured though meagre income as well as a new friend, the cultivated man-about-town who was his employer's stepson. It was through him that Jean-Jacques had his first taste of château-life when his new friend took him to visit his mistress, the Marquise d'Epinay, who was to play such a fateful role in days to come. 'Franceuil,' she recorded in her memoirs, 'brought a poor devil of a writer who is as destitute as Job and fantastically intelligent and conceited . . . When you see him and listen to him conversing he appears to be handsome, when you think about him in retrospect he always seems

---

* If the ambassador paused for a word when dictating, so he reported to Paris, Jean-Jacques 'would pick up a book or look pityingly at me'.

ugly.' Perhaps she only saw ugliness in retrospect because by then she had come to detest him. But he must certainly have seemed poverty-stricken by her standards, especially if she had been told of the stratagem Jean-Jacques had resorted to when Franceuil had invited him to the Opera. Profiting from the crush at the entrance, where the two friends became separated, he had promptly cashed in his ticket at the box office and slipped away, leaving his host to indulge his expensive tastes by himself. It is by no means the only time his *Confessions* reveal a cunning, sometimes endearingly impish and naïve as in the present case, sometimes so low and cold-blooded as to be far from endearing.

*

Even if, during the early years in Paris, he suffered more from his poverty than he himself admitted, there were interludes when he lived in the lap of luxury. His smart friend's mistress was not the only great lady whose hospitality he enjoyed when, as far as the Beau Monde was concerned, he was still a nobody. Three years before he broke through its barriers to fill the heavens with the thunder of his name, he had spent the autumn with his employer at Chenonceaux, a former royal mansion. 'We greatly enjoyed ourselves in this lovely spot,' he recalls, 'and we lived very well. I became as fat as a monk. We had a great deal of music. I composed several trios for voices . . . We acted comedies and I wrote one . . . I composed some other little things there including a play in verse.'

The contrast with life in his humble lodgings back in Paris must have been stark indeed. Yet this life, too, was not without its gaieties. In addition to the weekly meetings with his highbrow friends at the affluent baron's table there was the almost daily midday meal in the rather different but no less 'giddy and brilliant company of young Guards and Musketeer officers . . . merchants, financiers and provision-dealers'. They had formed a sort of luncheon club where the conversation was 'very gay . . . with no lack of tales about girls', since around the corner there was a dressmaker's shop 'employing some very pretty ones with whom our gentlemen would go and chat'. If he himself did not join in these 'chats' it was partly because by this time the problems caused by his 'lascivious and ardent temperament' had found another solution. It had materialized in the shape of a semi-literate young woman who worked as a waitress and laundress in his boarding-house. Things had worked out so well, in the course of three years Jean-Jacques and his Thérèse had come to feel so strongly they were 'made for one another', that they decided to set up house together, helped to do so by his employer who gave him an increase in salary as well as some money to buy furniture. And there they would have lived happily ever after, perpetuating the bliss of 'those six or seven

years when I enjoyed the most perfect domestic happiness that human
frailty permits', had not the fate that had 'favoured my wishes for thirty
years opposed them for the next thirty'.

In actual fact, it did nothing of the sort. Not only did it shower fame
and glory upon him beyond any writer's wildest dreams, one also has his
testimony for it that he continued to have his happy moments, and many
of them, even when made to pay the penalties of success and suffer the
corrupting effect this heady brew had on his 'feeble soul'. His stay in the
rural retreat lent to him by the marquise, who then still found him handsome as well as fantastically intelligent, may have ended in disaster or, as
he put it, proved the beginning of 'a terrible and fatal epoch in a life
unparalleled among human kind'. But for some eighteen out of the
twenty-one months he spent at the 'Hermitage', he found it 'delightful to
be the guest of my friend in a house of my own choice she had built
expressly for me . . . I cried in my rapture; "at last all my wishes are
fulfilled" '.

What more indeed, except better health, could he have asked for? He
had a comfortable and rent-free roof over his head. His different bodily
needs were looked after by Thérèse and her mother, just as his intellectual
needs were met by the cultivated company he frequented at his landlady's
château. He could earn his keep with the copying of music at so much per
page which he had adopted as his trade, once he had become fashionable
enough as an eccentric man of letters to be sure of all the custom he
needed. And even if he should ever want to give all his time to literature
he need have no short-term money-worries; 'the 2,000 francs that
remained over from the profits of the *Village Soothsayer* and my other
writings left me sufficient reserves not to be pushed for money.'

But there were other and vastly greater joys than these lowly material
comforts. There was the warm friendship that sprung up between him
and the marquise. It was of a depth of feeling well illustrated by his
reaction to a present she sent him, 'an under-petticoat which she informed
me she had worn and out of which she wanted me to make myself a
waistcoat . . . It was as if she had stripped herself to clothe me . . . In my
emotion I kissed the note and the petticoat twenty times in tears'. There
were the 'sublime' moments he owed to having fallen in love with her
sister-in-law. And though the quarrels that supervened left him not only
homeless, sent packing by the marquise, but also 'cured of the vain dreams
of friendship, detached from everything that made me love life', it was
not long, seventeen months, before once more he found himself in an
'earthly paradise; I lived in heavenly innocence and tasted something of
the pleasures that go with it'. The place of the jumped-up marquise—for
she really had as few quarterings as her husband—was taken by a duke

and duchess of the bluest blood, friends of the King. They had provided him with an 'enchanting abode' where he occupied 'perhaps the best and most comfortable apartments of any private individual in Europe' and 'in delightful solitude, amongst woods and water, to the sounds of birds of every kind, amidst the perfumes of orange blossoms', worked on a new book 'in continuous ecstasy'. And as if that were not enough his new hosts also met his craving for tender friendship, never stopped telling him how much they loved him; 'the duchess embraced me ten times a day.' Much as he liked being pitied—'if only you'd feel some pity for me,' he used to lament to a lost love—this was a time when he had no use for it. 'You think I am unhappy,' he wrote to a friend, 'how wrong you are!'

When he was forced to flee from this paradise because of the wrath he had aroused with his unorthodox religious writings, the years of exile that followed were once more hardly such as to qualify as a 'terrible and fatal epoch in a life unparalleled among human kind'. What was perhaps unparalleled were the offers of hospitality that were pressed upon him and that made him the most pampered refugee, the most cosseted martyr, in history. While he lamented that 'I have nowhere a stone on which to lay my greying head', or described himself as 'a poor invalid without asylum and bread', reigning monarchs like Frederick the Great and the Duchess of Saxe-Gotha, members of the French royal family like the Prince de Conti, nobles like the Scottish Earl Marischal, the Marquis de Mirabeau or the Marquis de Girardin, owners of stately homes like Mr. Davenport and Mr. Malthus, rivalled with old friends in his native Switzerland in showering invitations on him. And the result was that only once during the first three years, in which he was made to move three times by the different Swiss authorities with whom he had sought refuge, did he pass seventy-two hours in the sort of lodging the ordinary refugee usually has to put up with; 'a wretched little third floor room at the back of a house looking out upon a courtyard with as only view the display of stinking skins belonging to a leather dresser . . . So miserable was my lodging I felt liable to die of melancholy within a very few days.' All the rest of the time he was comfortably and often luxuriously housed.

His first stay, with an old Swiss friend—after his precipitate flight from France in a carriage provided by his ducal host who had been tipped off by a member of the Royal Family—was 'so pleasant' that he would have remained there indefinitely had the local authorities allowed it. His next halting place, where another Swiss friend had lent him 'a fully furnished house', again proved 'so very pleasant' he decided to end his days there if he 'could afford it', for 'living in that district was fairly expensive'. But in fact, unlike most refugees, he had no real money worries. He had come away with 'a little capital' that would last him 'two or three years'. Writing to a friend about the 'delicious carefree days I spend wandering in the woods', he added: 'As for my material resources, I have all I need, even in abundance, and shall not run short for quite a while.' He had all the less reason to worry on this score, as he had long since forsworn worldly glory and its expensive trimmings. Just as two centuries later a very different type of hero, who wrote about himself in the third person, ruthlessly pursued *'une certaine idée de la France'*, so Jean-Jacques, grown equally contemptuous of the fleshpots, had come to devote his life to the single-minded cultivation of a certain equally exalted idea of himself, as the image of man's natural goodness, cleansed of all the layers of dirt and varnish and overpainting with which, according to his theory, life in society had covered it. All he needed in the way of money was the means of subsistence. And apart from his earning-power, both as a music copyist and as the world-famous writer he had now become, he was deluged with offers of help, pensions offered by kings, annuities pressed upon him by friends, contracts for his collected works offered by publishers, as well as gifts of every kind sent to him by private admirers, pheasants and herring and butter for his larder, wood to burn in his stove, under-petticoats to clothe him.

It is true that he usually refused them, often abusing those who had made such offerings to the point where they felt compelled to offer grovelling apologies instead. And this self-imposed austerity was another element, like his martyrdom, of which his halo would be made. But his motive for refusing gifts was not mortification of the flesh; it was the fear of being beholden to his friends and admirers, of becoming 'enslaved' to them, as he called it. Nor was it poverty he sought. He refused help only when he could do without it. 'For heaven's sake,' he wrote to one of the countless highborn ladies who at one time or another offered to subsidize him, 'do not bother me, I shall let you know when and if I need it.' 'You will agree,' he wrote to another, 'that it would hardly do for me to accept your offer of help before I am in need of it.'

'Very pleasant' as were the first three years of his exile—though in addition to the usual bouts of ill-health he had a lot to put up with from importunate admirers as well as relentless foes—the next seven weeks were positively idyllic. Spent on an island in a Swiss lake, he remembers them—his self-pity getting the better of his memory—as 'the first pleasant experience of my life'. And just as this first experience had had any number of predecessors so there were many more to come. The fame he had hungered for might have brought him more sorrow than joy, the triumphant reception that awaited him in London, where royalty came to visit him, might no longer make him 'savour his glory', whose taste, he said to a friend, had turned 'bitter'. But its dividends in the form of more offers of hospitality than he knew how to choose from, enabled him to go on living the kind of retired life he now most wanted and in which, again and again, he found contentment. 'I am offered country-houses,' he said in one of his letters, 'in every county of England.' And when he had settled for a stately mansion in Derbyshire he reported that it was 'comfortable, agreeably remote; the owner has seen to everything, I lack nothing'. Six weeks later things were better still: 'I've never lived more at my ease.' And again six months later: 'I am as nearly perfectly happy as one can be in exile, only a few things are lacking to fulfil all my wishes; better health, a softer climate, fewer clouds in the sky and above all more open hearts.'

So it continued till the end. For he was as capable of enjoying himself in the small fifth floor flat in Paris where he spent all but the last six years of his life, as in the châteaux and manor-houses of his wealthy admirers. 'Though very small,' he told a friend when he had moved in, 'it is very cheerful and agreeable, it's thought charming by all who come to see me, I have never lived anywhere that I liked better . . . Even if I had 100,000 francs a year I would not want to be housed, fed or clothed in any other way.'

*

As already indicated, this life-long ode to joy—'Oh,' he once exclaimed, 'Oh, if only the whole world could have enjoyed a destiny like mine'— has as counterpoint an equally unceasing lament, a wailing and moaning fit for an Irish wake. From the Swiss village where, until the last few months of his three-year stay, things had been 'so very pleasant', he wrote to a friend: 'I know very well that I shall never lack bread but I will eat it soaked with my tears. I knew only one happiness in life, friendship, and there is not a corner of my heart that has not been torn by some attachment leaving wounds that will bleed till the last hour in the heart of the unhappiest of mortals.' Two months later, thanking the ruler of Saxe-Gotha for her invitation, he motivated his rejection with the words: 'I am not made for happiness . . . I am too much at the mercy of my ills, of fortune and of men, ever to be able to do what would be agreeable to me.' When a friend of his dared to bewail his own fate as equalling that of Jean-Jacques, the latter indignantly asked, 'What could your miseries have in common with mine? My situation is unique, unheard of since the beginning of time and, I am sure, never to be paralleled.'

There had been a time when these wailings served a purpose. That had been the case when as a young man he had tried to bolster the always shaky finances of 'Maman's' household with a letter to the Governor of Savoy, backing up his petition for a royal pension with a tear-jerking and highly imaginative life story. Describing himself as 'afflicted by a fearful disfiguring malady', he ended with the assurance that, if his request were granted 'and I am thus assured of the earthly support required for the few days that remain to me, I would compose my spirit and my conscience to find peace with God, to begin with courage and determination the long voyage to eternity and to pray God for the perfect prosperity and the most precious preservation of Your Excellency'. On another occasion 'languours and sickness' that left him 'dragging out the miserable remnant of my life, a burden to others and myself as since I no longer have the strength to move or stand on my feet', were mobilized in the effort to lay his hands on the share of his mother's estate that should have gone to his brother, who had disappeared twenty years before and whom he therefore presumed dead.

But the opportunism that accounts for the wailing and the moaning of the unscrupulous scamp he was in his youth, cannot explain its continuation once he had found his true vocation as an 'example to mankind' who had turned his back on the world and its fleshpots. Other explanations are needed for that strange counterpoint that went on till the end of his days and makes him sound like a pianist playing the 'Marche Funèbre' with his left hand and a polka with the other. Of course, if the contrast between the sentiments expressed is so striking, it is partly because of the declamatory style fashionable in his age when no self-respecting person would admit that Cupid's arrows could be less than fatal and every one was always 'dying' of love or joy or sorrow. And none, of course, did so more wholeheartedly than men of letters, inclined as they are to embellish their feelings, to present the public not so much with the raw material of their sentiments as with the literary end-product thereof, or, as one might say, emotion inflated in tranquillity. Certainly Jean-Jacques, that master of swollen rhetoric (as well as the simple, natural language that earned him his literary reputation), will rarely have been as blissful or as miserable as his ritual raptures or his lachrymose lamentations might make one think.

Even, however, when one allows for the magnifying effect of art, Jean-Jacques's ability to be the unhappiest of mortals and as pleased as Punch, at practically the same time, remains puzzling indeed. Here is a typical example. Writing to a friend when in the latter condition, he reported: 'I find myself in very agreeable circumstances here . . . nothing to worry about and nothing to wish for . . . I play chess with my guest who is now on the mend . . . I grow lazier every day . . . I practise *carpe diem* without counting the days that remain to me, without remembering yesterday or making plans for tomorrow.' But two days later he exclaims in a letter to another friend: 'May God preserve you from ever knowing so cruel a position as mine . . . I have never known any [duties] as hard, as cruel and as sad as those I have fulfilled without a moment's respite for the past two months' (during which he helped to look after the 'guest now on the mend'). Likewise, but within an even shorter space of time, twenty-four hours instead of forty-eight, he told one correspondent, 'I have spent delicious days without cares or plans, wandering about in the woods and climbing rocks', while informing another, 'I have been a prey to continual suffering, I cannot possibly have a moment's health here.'

In actual fact, apart from an inconvenient and often painful ailment of his bladder (or its functioning, for medical opinion differs about its origin, nervous or organic), he enjoyed reasonably good health by the standards of the age. And, indeed, at one point in his autobiography he goes halfway to admitting it: 'I have never had any serious illness in the country [where he spent at least half his life]. I have often been in pain there but never confined to bed.' Yet, elsewhere he calls himself 'an unfortunate wretch worn out with illness . . . struggling every day of my life between pain and death . . . I have practically not been able to sleep for thirty years'. And the better his health the more he suffered: 'When I might have been enjoying the delights of life my decaying physique prevented me . . . Later when, despite my declining years and very real and serious maladies, my body seemed to have retained its strength it was only the better to feel my sufferings . . . Racked by pain of every description I feel more strength and life in me with which to suffer than I had enjoyment when I was young.' He was the victim of a fate as deliberately cruel as it was cunning; 'Nature, which has shaped me for suffering, has given me a constitution proof against pain in order that, unable to exhaust my forces, it may always make itself felt with the same intensity.'

*

The self-pity that was one of the few constants of his emotional make-up found typical utterance when he reproached Diderot with 'caring as little for my tears when you cause me pain as about my life and my health . . . If you could correct this fault in you I would be a less pitiable person.' It was this luxuriant self-pity that provided the main theme for the dirge sung almost simultaneously with the ode to joy. What accounts for the strange counterpoint they form is the extreme inconstancy of his heart, his 'feebleness', as he himself calls it. 'A chameleon or a woman are less changeable than me,' he wrote when, still a literary nobody, he tried his hand at journalism; 'no two people will have the same opinion of me.' At the time he was being only half-serious. But some thirty years later, when his ego could afford the supreme luxury of referring to oneself in the third person, he was in dead earnest. 'Jean-Jacques,' he then wrote in the bizarre concoction entitled *Rousseau judge of Jean-Jacques* but usually referred to as *The Dialogues*, 'goes from one extreme to another with incredible rapidity without even being aware of the change . . . nor remembering what he was like the moment before.' That is why the real agonies he suffered when in the throes of his persecution mania were of short duration. The fullest account of them, the 300 pages in which he writes about himself in the third person and which make it seem as if during the four years he devoted to this work the oppressive cloud never lifted from his poor tortured spirit, is highly deceptive. For as he explained in the introduction, the endless and heartbreaking lament is really only a description of what he felt in the 'very short moments' which alone he could 'bring himself to devote to so painful a task'. And in the text itself he repeats that he 'feels his ills very strongly for a moment but forgets them the next'.

Hence his heart's capacity for that instant refrigeration which has already been noted and which it demonstrated most convincingly on the occasion of his last recorded meeting with the *grande passion* of his life. Though by then he had had to resign himself to it being a hopeless one, he had 'trembled' at the thought of seeing the lady again after several months of separation, as well he might for he had felt a passion for her 'perhaps greater than any man had ever felt before'. He feared he would make a 'spectacle' of himself at the luncheon party where they were to meet. And so he nearly did, only to find that by the time lunch was over he no longer cared tuppence; 'although the first sight of her set my heart beating so fast that I nearly fainted, I gave her hardly a thought on leaving.' As he had written of himself in the *Dialogues*: 'The activity of his soul is as short-lived as it is intense, the ardour of his passions devours them, after forcefully exploding they burn themselves out at once.'

It seems only another way of saying that his was essentially a superficial, frivolous, weathercock nature. Therein, in this emotional instability, this self-confessed 'feebleness', lies one of the explanations, not only of the counterpoint in his autobiography but also of the chaotic incoherence that characterizes nearly all his writings. For his head tired as easily of its passions as his heart, witness again his own testimony: 'there is nothing grand, beautiful and generous that he is not capable of by fits and starts, but he tires quickly relapsing into inertia'. So striking are the resulting contradictions that one begins to wonder whether he even remembered what he had said a few pages or chapters earlier, whether he forgot as 'incredibly' quickly what he had written as what he felt the moment before. Thus in one and the same book he describes his life-companion as the 'woman I loved' and as someone for whom he 'never felt the least glimmering of love'. In one and the same chapter he says of his *grande passion*, 'in my heart I have committed the crime of seducing her a hundred times over' and 'I loved her too much to want to possess her'. On one and the same page he glories in his 'noble pride' and calls it 'silly'. And, indeed, he himself admits that 'once I have written a thing down I cease to remember it'.

But it was not only this forgetfulness that rendered him singularly ill-equipped for the role to which he devoted the greatest part of his energies, that of a thinker writing on ethics as well as sociological, political, theological and educational subjects. As, again, he has said himself, he was not 'born for study; continuous application so wearies me that I am utterly unable to devote half an hour on end to a single subject, especially when following someone else's train of thought'. Intellectual discipline was as irksome to him as any other form of restraint; 'To proceed in an orderly and methodical manner is beyond my powers . . . All the thoughts that come to my mind are isolated from one another . . . I find it difficult to link my ideas together . . . I jot down my scattered and unconnected ideas on bits of paper and then try and sew them together as best I can . . . I get quite a lot of ideas but without ever seeing the consequences; order and method I abhor . . . Thinking is very painful to me . . . It is only when I let my ideas take their course without constraining them in any way that I sometimes enjoy it.'

None of this means that he was incapable of close reasoning. Far from it. He was a logician and often a fearful logic-chopper of the first order as well as a highly impulsive, emotional dreamer. If he so often seems hopelessly contradictory, it is partly because the premises, not to say the dreams from which he starts reasoning, vary with and are indeed inspired by the ever-changing feelings of the moment. Thus he could go on record with utterances showing him to be a revolutionary and a reactionary, an individualist and a collectivist, a rabid nationalist and a fervent European, rationalist and romantic, Christian and deist. But there is also another explanation for their bewildering variety, and one that seems to become inescapable when one sees how much trouble he took over his writing, drafting and re-drafting; haughtily indifferent to criticism he simply did not care how much he contradicted himself. And for this explanation, too, his own authority can be invoked: 'I say naïvely what I feel and I think, however bizarre and paradoxical . . . I do not try to persuade anybody, I only write for myself.' Hence the great difficulty indeed, the impossibility, of doing him justice, as a human being or as a writer and thinker. Whatever you make him say by quoting from his writings, whether about society or religion or morality or his favourite subject, himself, you can nearly always make him say the opposite, too. Never was there an author who had so much reason to protest against selective quotation, 'that odious practice of cutting a work up in little bits . . . and judging it by shreds picked up here and there'. Never was there a man of ideas—and sentiments—who could so confidently offer his stock in trade with the defiant challenge: you name it, I have it. Never, therefore, was there an intellectual of immense renown whom it is so difficult to take seriously. Yet few writers have been the object of such painstaking study. Few have kept and are still keeping so many erudite scholars at work analysing and interpreting the maestro's every word; putting the most ingenious constructions on his chaotic incoherence so as to 'unify his thought'; annotating his thousands of letters so as to reveal that words like 'I have a cold' in a first draft were replaced by 'I have a bad cold'; digging out yellowed documents so as to acquaint the world with the details of the great man's laundry bills (which—believe it or not—fill twelve pages in the latest edition of his collected works); founding societies such as the one that was established in 1905 and still publishes a new volume of studies every year or so. 'Generations of serious scholars,' so wrote one of them in recent years, 'spend their precious years scrutinizing the minutest aspect of his work. Men of every nation . . . devote their lives to the study of Jean-Jacques Rousseau.' It is, of course, partly because a reputation, once established at the level where its beneficiary attracts the interest of scholars, becomes both self-perpetuating and self-expanding. The more the great man is made the object of study, the more library shelves are filled with books on his life and works, the greater he seems and the more scholarships he attracts, compelled to mine ever deeper and poorer seams that yield little but trivialities or fanciful interpretations, *ad infinitum risumque.*

*

Thus yet another of Jean Jacques's fondest dreams has come true. When in his gloomier, paranoid moments he felt that the whole world was out to malign him, he had looked forward to finding consolation in the hereafter, convinced that 'posterity will honour me and bless my memory . . . because that is my due . . . and posterity is always just'. He has not been disappointed. Posterity may not always have uttered only benedictions. But as he would doubtless agree that bad publicity is better than no publicity—'I would rather be forgotten,' he has said, 'than to be thought an ordinary man'—one cannot help but feel that his spirit must be revelling in the spectacle of the Rousseau-industry, nearly two centuries after his death, still busy honouring his memory, still perpetuating the power and the glory of his name.

CHAPTER THREE

Bull in the China Shop

'I am uncouth, disagreeable and impolite on principle.'

WHEN Jean-Jacques had first caught the public eye, he did so, not so much by the originality of his ideas as by his manner of giving expression to them. The thesis he defended in an essay he entered in a literary competition set by the Academy of Dijon, which had posed the question whether 'the restoration of the arts and sciences had a corrupting effect on morality', was far from novel. In denouncing the artifices of civilization and singing the praises of 'the simplicity which prevailed in earliest times . . . when men were innocent and virtuous', he had taken up a nostalgic theme as old as civilization itself. Antiquity had resounded with lamentations for the good old days before men's minds and morals had become tainted by the pursuit of knowledge. Horace had sung the praises of the barbarian Scythes as Tacitus did of the Teutons. And some two centuries before Jean-Jacques bemoaned the debilitating effect of the arts and sciences on the martial virtues, Montaigne had made exactly the same point. 'History,' he wrote, 'teaches us that the study of the sciences saps rather than strengthens courage and renders effeminate.' He had admired uncivilized man, 'all naked, simply pure in Nature's lap', just as Dryden was to glorify him as 'the noble savage'. Even in Jean-Jacques's own forward-looking epoch with its belief in the perfectibility of men and institutions through the power of Reason, the old backward-looking dream of a lost golden age, whether of earthy bucolic bliss or other-worldly, apostolic purity, had by no means lost its hold on the imagination. Travellers' and missionaries' accounts of the allegedly happy societies they had found among savages, had furnished numbers of writers and dramatists with the theme for their works. Indeed, the very choice of subject for the competition Jean-Jacques won is enough proof that the Age of Reason was not as sure of itself, as besotted with its faith in progress, as is often imagined.

What was novel in the prize-winning essay was the author's wild overstatement of his case, the hyperbole, the defiant, not to say offensive, tone of his contribution to the discussion. At a time when polite society made a veritable cult of elegance in argument, this alone sufficed to attract attention. The salons were fascinated by a newcomer who had the effrontery to introduce himself as an 'honest man who is aware of his ignorance but thinks himself none the worse for it'; a man who in one fell swoop dismissed 'astronomy as born of superstition . . . geometry of avarice, physics of idle curiosity and all sciences, even moral philosophy, of human pride'; a writer who exhorted the rulers of Europe 'to banish the dreadful art of printing from their dominions' and offered up the prayer: 'Almighty God . . . deliver us from the fatal arts and sciences of our forefathers, give us back ignorance, innocence and poverty which alone can make us happy.'

One only needs to read Jean-Jacques's own description of the atmosphere reigning in the *bonne compagnie* of his day to appreciate how inevitably these bull-in-the-china-shop manners set the tongues wagging. 'The tone of conversation is smooth and natural, neither weighty nor frivolous, knowledgeable without being pedantic, gay without being boisterous . . . No one hotly attacks the opinions of others nor stubbornly defends his own. One argues to enlighten one another and stops before reaching the points of dispute.' It is wholly borne out by another witness, that most illuminating memorialist, the Comte de Ségur: 'one argued gently and hardly ever quarrelled, one avoided boredom by never going too deeply into anything'. Not so the newcomer, proud of what he called the 'somewhat uncouth' style of his native Geneva.

But what was perhaps even more intriguing than the polemical violence of Jean-Jacques's old-fashioned diatribe against intellectual civilization, was his attack on its moral counterpart, that very elegance and stylized gentleness cultivated by the salons which, not for nothing, were invariably presided over by the weaker sex. To Jean-Jacques rudeness was all: 'the urbanity for which we are indebted to the enlightened spirit of the age' was no better than a 'uniform and deceitful veil of politeness' behind which there lay only 'jealousy, suspicion, fear, coldness, reserve, hatred and fraud . . . We no longer dare seem what we really are but lie under a perpetual restraint'. How much better things had been 'before art had moulded our behaviour and taught our passions to speak an artificial language, when our morals were rude but natural . . . and men could see through one another'.

This denunciation of the manners of civilized society was, of course, again but the expression of one of its perennial, inbuilt discontents, caused by its demand for self-restraint and thus, in a sense, a measure of self-falsification. Jean-Jacques's attack on the 'Good Form' of his day was in essence inspired by much the same rebellious sentiments as harboured by those who today, in the sacred name of 'authenticity', demand the right to recognize no higher moral imperative than to be honest with themselves. There is nothing surprising in his having taken up this attitude. Being what he was and where he was, he could hardly help but feel that the civility, which, Erasmus said, 'arouses love or at least softens hatred', (or, in Hume's words, 'leads us to curb and conceal the presumptuousness and arrogance natural to the human mind') was too dearly bought; that in terms of sincerity the price of the social lubricant was prohibitive; that, as he put it, 'concealment of sentiments by good manners is contemptible falsity'. Ambitious, snobbish in the sense of being full of 'pride of rank', insecure, out of his depth, ill at ease in the great world that had so suddenly clasped him to its bosom, he not unnaturally came to resent a style and social graces to which he could not adapt. Afraid of the malicious wit its native-born inhabitants prized so highly, his congenital suspiciousness made him see, under 'the deceitful veil of politeness', offence, mockery and worse even where none were intended. And at the same time the reverse side of his readiness to think the worst of people, the self-complacent conceit that was one of the *défauts de ses défauts*, enabled him to feel he himself had no need of manners. 'I know,' he wrote to a lady who learnt to regret his lack of them, 'I know that in the great world they have taken the place of sentiments, but my sentiments are such that they need not and must not be disguised.' His heart was such, he told another, 'as to dispense me from being polite'. He was, he declared publicly, 'uncouth, disagreeable and impolite on principle; I do not give a damn for all you courtiers, I am a barbarian'. And he had rationalized this principled rejection of civility with a theory which saw it not as 'a workaday reflection of morality' as it has been aptly called, but as born of rivalry and pride, jealousy and conceit. When the noble and happy savages had first settled in communities, when they had thus become aware of one another's existence and hence—so ran his theory—all started vying for recognized pre-eminence, 'it became impossible to refuse esteem without impunity; thus arose . . . civility even among savages'.

*

Just as Jean-Jacques was not the last to raise the banner of revolt against civility so he had not been the first to be provoked by a social style that in his day had indeed become so artificial, so stereotyped, so insistent upon the observation of trifling ritual, as to merit some of his strictures on its 'servile and deceptive conformity'. Before him Montesquieu had already mocked its 'false politeness'. In his own day the writer Duclos, who rose to become secretary of the Paris Academy, had called it 'false, vile and ridiculous'. He had laid his finger on the 'immoderate desire to please and to amuse that leads men to speak ill of absent friends . . . the desire to make oneself agreeable at all costs that has become a sort of epidemic among us and which is all people care about . . . What constitutes "Good Form" [Bon Ton] is to talk pleasantly of trifles and never to say anything sensible unless it be redeemed by the graciousness of its expression . . . This so-called Good Form . . . gives rise to unintelligible jargon . . . that makes fools laugh and outrages Reason, disconcerts honest or timid people and makes society unbearable.' His sentiments were echoed by the first of Jean-Jacques's many château-dwelling hostesses, Madame d'Epinay, who, in a letter to her son, attributed 'the habit of praising those who are present while reserving blame and criticisms for the absent' to the 'depravity of our manners and also the immoderate taste for society which is so necessary to the idle'. Like Jean-Jacques, she was repelled by the fatuous insincerity rampant in polite society, the effusions, 'the liveliest demonstrations of friendship which the heart has never felt', the putting on of acts at which her own sex excels to this day. And even the Comte de Ségur who praised the conversational good manners of the Beau Monde had to admit that the insistence upon Good Form was not without its price; 'the rules of what are called Bon Ton . . . compelled everyone to submit his taste, opinions, speech and way of life to a mono- tonous uniformity.'

Again, therefore, Rousseau's critique was original only in its vehemence and its sweeping character. Not for him the careful balance preserved by Duclos who, far from denouncing civility as such, called it 'the expression of social virtues that make us useful and agreeable to those with whom we have to live' and who only denounced its excesses. Not for Jean-Jacques the recognition that 'offensive truthfulness' is not necessarily morally superior to 'polite feigning' or that his strictures on society's manners and morals only applied to that tiny section of it formed by 'the opulent and the idle'. For him only splendid, resounding generalizations would do, such as that 'the sweetness of disposition and urbanity of civilized peoples' gave them the 'appearance of all the virtues without being in possession of even one of them . . . sincere friendship, real esteem and perfect confidence are banished from among men'.

Whether or not Jean-Jacques's fierce attack on culture and civilization was a deliberate essay in the highly rewarding art of '*épater le bourgeois*', it certainly proved eminently successful in dazzling the countesses and marchionesses who could make or break a writer in those days. Nor was it only the ladies who applauded the newcomer. Several professionals, critics and fellow-writers, joined in the chorus of praise, complimenting him on what Grimm called 'his masculine eloquence, fire and vigour such as one has not yet seen in an academic discourse'. Another critic, Marmontel, spoke of 'the perfect virility and astonishing fullness of his writing', while yet another, La Harpe, hailed him as 'one of the most eloquent writers of the eighteenth century'. It was partly because to an age which prized the irony, wit, grace and finesse of a Voltaire as the model for all, Jean-Jacques's passionate, sweeping statements and thundering denunciations had all the appeal of freshness and spontaneity. As a leading literary historian has said, there had hardly been a single page in the French prose of the first half of the century by a writer 'who had let himself be carried away, afraid neither of worldly convention, nor of ridicule or established opinion'.

But if Jean-Jacques's display of this type of eloquence—perilously close to the art of the sloganeering demagogue he was to show himself later—gained him the esteem of his fellow writers, they were far from being impressed with the substance of his argument. No less than sixty-eight contemporary articles defending the arts and sciences against his onslaught have been unearthed by the Rousseau-industry. What is more, so perverse and outrageous seemed his wholesale denunciation of civilized society and its works that, among two hundred writings of the period, not one was found whose author was prepared to believe he had been in earnest. The general attitude was pithily expressed by Dr. Johnson, when at a later stage he said, 'a man who talks nonsense so well must know that he is talking nonsense'. And the enemies his success promptly and inevitably gained him owed to his native arrogance a weapon they were not slow to use. For he had not been content to denounce 'the labours of even the most enlightened of our learned men' as of 'little utility', and to express his contempt for 'that numerous herd of obscure writers and idle littérateurs who devour the substance of the State'. He had gone on to hurl the very accusation at them to which he was dangerously vulnerable himself; that of being show-offs, charlatans out to catch the limelight with provocative challenges to established values: 'What extravagances', he exclaimed, 'will not the rage to be different induce men to commit.' It was simply asking for the rejoinder: 'Look who's talking!'

*

How much of the vitriolic scorn he poured on the values, the manners and the morals of his age was heartfelt? What was the driving-force that had made him set himself up, as he defiantly proclaimed, 'against all that is nowadays most admired'? Nothing is easier than to make out a case for the cynical answer of his detractors. For within a year he had written another essay—though leaving it unpublished—in which he took on many points the opposite line to that adopted in the first, and, in particular, hailed the arts 'in all their splendour'. But easy and simple answers to questions about the motivation of so complex and 'incredibly mercurial' a man are hardly likely to do him justice. Doubtless he had adopted his iconoclastic line and provocative tone partly in hopes of 'the universal outcry' which he confidently predicted in the preface of his essay. If he denounced the works of civilized society, resentment at his repeated failure to achieve recognition of his own contribution to them was not wholly foreign to it.

But what above all drove the soured, ambitious Jean-Jacques of those days to lash out wildly at the world he had failed to conquer as a composer and a man of letters, was his newly discovered vocation as a moralist whose aim, so he proclaimed, was not so much to attack science as 'to defend virtue'. It had come to him in a blinding flash, much like St. Paul's on the road to Damascus. Reading a paper as he walked along the road to Vincennes his eye had chanced upon the question framed by the Academy of Dijon. 'The moment I read it,' he recalls in his *Confessions*, 'I became another man . . . all my little passions were stifled by an enthusiasm for truth, liberty and virtue.' He had known in advance, he told a friend at the time, how much opposition he would meet. But he would use only two words in reply: 'Virtue, truth! I will cry increasingly, truth, virtue!' So violent, he told another friend later, had been the 'agitation bordering on delirium' he had suffered in the moment of illumination that when, after half an hour spent under a tree, he re-covered his composure, his waistcoat proved 'soaked with tears I had shed without even being aware of it'.

One can well believe it (even though allowance should be made for the element of 'literature' in these testimonials to the productivity of eighteenth-century tear-ducts). For it was indeed a dramatic trans-formation, as until then he had never shown any promise as a budding saint. There is precious little in the record of his first thirty-nine years to indicate that the moral teaching he had received during his childhood in Geneva had taken firm root, let alone borne fruit. What the record does seem to show is an insatiable need for recognition, a passionate desire 'to excel, never mind in what'. Perhaps, therefore, it was his failure to do so as a composer and a man of letters that helped to make him opt for the demanding career of an 'example to mankind'. 'Failures,' D. H. Lawrence has said, 'are usually the most conceited of men.' Perhaps it was a case of virtue being the last resort of the unsuccessful. What better way to make up for the lack of public esteem than to cultivate self-esteem by devoting oneself to the pursuit of virtue? What better consolation for the disdainful silence of the world than the applause of one's conscience? And whose congratulations were more readily available? They constituted the only form of recognition he knew he could count on: 'Whatever my apparent success,' he said in the prize-winning essay, 'there is one reward which cannot fail me, I shall find it at the bottom of my heart.'

The pursuit of the elusive bitch-goddess having proved unproductive of the applause so necessary for his happiness, nothing was more sensible than to dedicate one's life to the pursuit of virtue instead. 'Why,' he asked in his closing paragraphs, 'should we build our happiness on the opinions of others when we can find it in our own hearts? Virtue, sublime science of simple minds . . . are not your principles graven on every heart? We need do no more than . . . listen to the voice of conscience . . . without envying the fame of those celebrated men whose names are immortal in the republic of letters.'

*

It would be over-simplifying, however, to suggest that he 'became another man' only from self-regarding motives whether conscious or subconscious. In his new preoccupation, not to say obsession, with morality, he was very much a child of his age. Virtue, or rather to wax lyrical about it, was all the fashion. Diderot was as voluble on the subject as Jean-Jacques. Even the sprightly Voltaire felt obliged to assure an early love of his, 'I love your virtue no less than your person.'

It was not because virtue was, as always, more honoured in the breach than in the observance that people talked about it so readily. As civilized societies go, that of the Ancien Régime was not a particularly dissolute one. Indeed, in the view of a well-known historian of Western morals,* even its upper crust, the court-nobility living in the debilitating, hothouse atmosphere of Versailles, toadying to the King and currying favour with his Ministers, 'looked pretty Victorian' compared with the privileged classes of imperial Rome or Renaissance Italy. Sexual morality in particular was far from being permissive in the modern sense of the word. It is true that in the sybaritic salons of Paris—though much less in the countryside with its mostly staid and impoverished gentry—marital fidelity was so little in fashion that one exposed oneself to ridicule by professing to love one's wife (this 'untogetherness' had its compensations; 'if morals lose by it', said one of the great ladies of the day, 'society was infinitely the gainer; without the annoyance and dullness caused by the husband's presence the coquetry of both men and women greatly contributed to social vivacity'). But though the prevailing code permitted young bloods to emulate the exploits of Casanova or, nearer home, the Duc de Richelieu, grand-nephew of the cardinal-statesman and, when young, the most fashionable man about town, the ladies were certainly not expected to

* Crane Brinton.

model their conduct on Messalina. Not only did they take great pains to keep up appearances, but if they were to remain respectable they could barely afford more than one extra-marital affair in the course of their life. As the author* of one of the most balanced nineteenth-century appreciations of Jean-Jacques's age has said—and as doubtless could be said with equal validity of our own time—there was much more libertinage in theory, in speech and writing, than in practice. That the society of the Ancien Régime has acquired the popular reputation of being thoroughly debauched was largely due to the efforts of those who overthrew it and who naturally painted it in the most lurid colours. But there is also another explanation suggested by the critic La Harpe when he warned, without much success, against the danger of taking a book like *Les Liaisons Dangereuses* as a reflection of the morals of the age, while it was in fact only the 'story of a couple of dozen fools and strumpets'. Moreover, then as now, wickedness of every kind seemed much more prevalent than it was in reality, for the simple reason that only wickedness is news, makes good reading.

If the intellectuals of the period were so much concerned with questions of morality, it was not, therefore, in reaction against an amoral society; it was rather because with the loss of belief in the revealed truth of Christian dogma the moral code had been cut loose from its religious mooring, deprived of its divine authority as well as its ultimate sanction. The Christian ethic, whose essence the thinkers of the Age of Reason continued to cherish, could no longer be taken for granted, as in the days when it was still held to be part of the divine, preordained order of things. And that is why it was felt to be all the more in need of voluble reaffirmation, particularly by those—still, after all, but a small and controversial *avant-garde* of intellectuals—accused of immorality because of their attacks on religion. 'We must show the theologians,' Diderot said, 'that philosophy makes more good men than does grace.' And there was also something else. Original Sin being 'out', discredited, while the worship of 'Nature' was very much 'in', society had more need than ever of a curb on man's natural passions. And so even those who were inclined to throw out the baby of the Christian ethic with the bathwater of Revelation, had to fall back on the traditional concepts of virtue dictated by social necessity, enlightened self-interest.

No wonder, therefore, the time proved far from unresponsive to the type of moralizing Jean-Jacques made his own. On the one hand it was common practice among the intellectuals of the day. On the other his old-fashioned exaltation of virtue as 'the sublime science of simple minds', and his taunting allusion to the 'celebrated men that need not be envied',

* Saint Marc Girardin.

were well designed to strike a chord also with those ordinary folk who had remained untouched by the Enlightenment or who regretted its destruction of the old certainties, who felt lost, as an American scholar has well phrased it, 'in a world that man had not dared to conceive of before'.

Finally, there is one other thing that could help to explain how so feeble an intellectual charge as contained in Jean-Jacques's prize-winning essay could prove so successful in firing him into orbit. Looking back on it later in life, Jean-Jacques himself dismissed the essay as 'completely lacking in logic and order', 'the most feebly argued' of all his writings—a judgment in which most of his biographers have concurred. And perhaps, therefore, it would not be altogether inapposite to suggest that his 'take-off' was helped by the docility of the public echoing the hosannahs of the pundits. For in his time, as in ours, literary comrades-in-arms were not unknown to indulge in a *commerce d'encens*, as one of their critics called the workings of the mutual admiration society Jean-Jacques then still formed with Diderot: 'each extolled the other as being worthy of a place next to the greatest of the day, Voltaire' (who himself, incidentally, said he had no time to read 'schoolboy-essays').

No one has better characterized this process of reputation-making than Duclos: 'The majority of men dare neither blame nor praise on their own; they acquiesce in prejudice from sheer timidity . . . Fashion reigns supreme . . . Often the public, puzzled by certain reputations it has made, searches for their cause and, unable to find it because there is none, only feels all the more respect for the phantom it has created.' And nowhere, according to one of Duclos's contemporaries, was this process more effective than in the France of their days. 'Our country alone,' he wrote, 'is ruled by a supreme power called fashion that derives its empire from the lack of critical spirit, the readiness to embrace things and the proclivity to imitation.' It was a power whose 'tyranny' (Duclos's word for it) some found difficult to bear. 'To the shame of our century,' wrote a well-known naturalist of the time,* 'Rousseau has shown what a brilliant reputation one can make for oneself with mere paradoxes. The Frenchman will always fall for anyone who can string words together harmoniously.' Posterity was to be even more severe, with one of the 'immortals' enthroned in the Académie Française† around the turn of our century, calling the 'noise' created by Jean-Jacques's blast-off 'one of the strongest proofs ever given of human stupidity'. But such, stupid or not, is the power of fashion, so firmly had it established him, that ever more and more palatial doors went open to him during the long years, no less than ten of them, that elapsed between the appearance of the 'schoolboy-essay' which put him into orbit and the first of the books that were to keep him there for eternity.

* Charles Bonnet.　　　　　　† Jules Lemaître.

CHAPTER FOUR

In the Swim

'The ladies employed countless ruses to get me to dine with them.'

IF JEAN-JACQUES'S first great success seems somewhat out of proportion to the occasion it should be remembered that in his day fame was a good deal easier to come by than in our time. For one thing the reading public was infinitely smaller and more compact, though estimates vary widely. Voltaire at one time spoke of two or three hundred, at another of thirty thousand, and, in what was clearly only a *boutade*, of 'forty or fifty for a serious book, four or five hundred for a pleasant one and twelve hundred for a play'. Perhaps the nearest approximation to reality could be found in the circulation of the *Mercure de France*, the most widely read paper of the time, appearing weekly and selling some seven thousand copies all over Europe. But whatever the size of the public, to the writer in search of renown there was only one section of it that mattered: Parisian society. Though the provinces were by no means without educated circles (from which no less than forty 'Academies' were recruited), they could be trusted to take their cue from Paris, as did, indeed, most of Europe. And its Beau Monde was not only very compact but also almost exclusively reliant on men of letters for help in their never-ending struggle against that boredom that Jean-Jacques called 'the tyrant that makes them pay so dearly for their immunity from work'.

But while fame was more readily available, it was in some ways, though not in all, much less profitable. Even best-selling authors rarely made any money to speak of. Voltaire, with his country mansions, may have lived in state, but what enabled him to do so was not so much his literary talent as his gift for sniffing out and conducting highly profitable if sometimes rather shady business operations. In fact, true to the tradition of the seventeenth century, in which the grand old man of French literature was born and which thought it undignified for writers to sell their brain-children, he usually renounced payment. Other literary lions, men like Montesquieu, Buffon, Helvétius or d'Holbach, owed their affluence to their aristocratic origins, while Duclos—a man of simple tastes judging by his definition of paradise as 'bread, cheese and any woman that happens along'—owed his to the hard work and thrift of his bourgeois parents. But those who had to live by their wits, leading lights of the age like Diderot, the mathematician d'Alembert and Jean-Jacques himself, remained in pretty modest circumstances even after they had become the idols of the Beau Monde. In order to provide his daughter with a dowry Diderot was reduced to selling—to Catherine the Great—his library (though keeping the use of it till his death). D'Alembert spent twenty-five years of his life in one dark, airless room over a glazier's shop. And there were times when Jean-Jacques, the most successful of them all—in terms of sales—needed the subsidies and annuities his admirers pressed upon him to maintain his simple standard of living.

It was partly because writers enjoyed very little protection of their copyright. A best-selling novel like Jean-Jacques's great love-story, *La Nouvelle Héloise*, was pirated all over the place the moment it was published. But they also had another complaint and one which authors still voice as frequently today; 'the greediness' (as Molière had already called it) of publishers, who in those days only paid their authors a lump sum and never any royalties. For Diderot they were 'men whose fortune we make but who condemn us to chew laurel-leaves'. An anonymous pamphleteer of the time asked why 'publishers, who are only tradesmen, should get all the profit while the author, who is a thinker, gets practically nothing out of it'. And Jean-Jacques, too, sounded a familiar note when he spoke bitterly of the publisher of his prize-winning essay: 'Every time I ask him how it is doing, all he says is: "so so".'

There is much else in his correspondence with his publishers that will strike a chord in the heart of modern authors. They may not always harbour the sentiment that made Jean-Jacques end his letters with the formula, 'I embrace you with all my heart.' But they will recognize and approve of the spirit in which he protested against emendations introduced in his manuscript by the publisher's office: 'Am I supposed to be an author you are going to publish or a schoolboy in need of correction. . .? I am prepared to admit to your editor's superior knowledge when questions of fact are at issue, but in matters of style I insist on being left to make my own mistakes.' How perennial, too, is the complaint of 'galley-proofs full of horrible misprints', the impotent anger at delays that 'drive me to despair because the book is highly topical and will lose all its point if it does not appear straight away', and last not least the charge of underpayment: 'I could easily have got twice as much as you have paid me for every book of mine you have published . . . In future you will pay me what my work is worth or it will never see the light of day.'

What modern author, finally, does not on occasion long to get as tough with his publisher as Jean-Jacques could eventually afford to be, demanding no less than sixty presentation copies or taking a high and mighty line like: 'I haven't replied to your letters because they are so senseless as to merit only silence,' or, 'forgive me for saying so but you really are the most hare-brained man I know'.

But if one can sympathize with many of his grievances there are moments when even a fellow-writer cannot help feeling sorry for his publisher. For there is no denying that Jean-Jacques could be very difficult and that the man with whom he did most of his business, a Swiss established in Amsterdam and called Rey, showed remarkable powers of forbearance. Thus there was the occasion when he wrote to Jean Jacques's concubine, Thérèse, to say that, by way of a present, he was sending her a dress. It is not every publisher that has such charming attentions for his author's mistress. And it was all the more commendable since at that time Jean-Jacques had not yet become a literary property whose cultivation warranted such investments. But all the thanks Rey got was a reprimand: 'I must scold you for the letter you sent her; if it had passed through my hands she would never have seen it.' For as already indicated, Jean-Jacques was exceedingly touchy on the subject of gifts, which he saw as attempts to 'enslave' him or resented as insults to a man who—not unnaturally after having scrounged on 'Maman' for so long—took a fierce, umbrageous pride in being independent and self-supporting at last. It was hard luck on Thérèse who more than once had to pay the price of his principles, as she did again some years later when an admiring duchess committed the same offence as Rey.

Whether or not it was because Rey knew he was on to a good thing, he refused to be deterred by his author's somewhat grumpy manners. And so five years later, when Jean-Jacques had indeed become a highly valuable name on his list, he had another idea that too rarely occurs to publishers of our day. He would give his author's lady-friend not just a dress but an annuity payable after her master's death. And though this time he ultimately triumphed over the latter's principles there was again quite a bit of trouble and unpleasantness before it was all settled. To begin with, Jean-Jacques said he preferred payments, even though on a somewhat lower scale, to start straight away, 'as I somehow don't like the idea of my continued sojourn on this earth, where I am no longer of any use, standing in the way of Thérèse's enjoyment of your benefaction'. However, as Rey was nothing if not accommodating, this presented no problem. He would do as Jean-Jacques wanted except that he would not hear of scaling down the annual payment. All that remained was to draw up the document for which, he added somewhat mysteriously, 'I need

some particulars I don't know'. What, Jean-Jacques wondered, could he
mean? If he wanted to know how to phrase the preamble which had to
motivate the annuity, that was easy enough; you simply say that 'you
wanted to show your gratitude for the advantage you have derived from
my having chosen you as my publisher'. Or had he meant something
quite different? Was he obliquely trying to find out whether to credit the
rumour about his having married Thérèse? And was he perhaps insinuating that 'though not wishing to accept any gifts from you I was not averse
from receiving them . . . through her? . . . If that is what you think you
can keep your gifts.' The squalid and ambiguous little episode would
hardly be worth recalling if it were not for the fact that Rey's mind-
boggling response offers a striking example of the reputation for pristine
virtue Jean-Jacques had achieved in his eyes. Indignantly denying the
imputation he attributed the rumour about the marriage to 'men having
become so corrupt that they cannot imagine one can live with a female
without enjoying her favours', which, once one has straightened out the
tortuous logic, turns out to mean: the wicked world argues that, as you
live with her you must sleep with her and, therefore, you must be married
to her, whereas to me the fact that you live with her only proves that you
do not sleep with her since otherwise you would, of course, have married
her.

Alas, the worthy publisher was poorly rewarded for his trust and forbearance. Long treated as a friend he was eventually relegated to that
'impenetrable outer darkness' where the whole of mankind, as poor Jean-
Jacques in his paranoid days came to see it, was busy blackening his name.
Rey, too, had been 'recruited by the conspiracy' to which he had made his
contribution by publishing 'the most cruel falsification' of Jean-Jacques's
works. It was hard indeed on the man who all these years had tried his
utmost to emulate the indulgence and understanding shown by another
figure professionally involved with the prima donna-ish breed of authors.
That was the official Voltaire called 'Minister for Literature', Malesherbes,
whose main function was that of chief censor. Being of a liberal disposition, he acted more as a friend in need and a trouble-shooter for
his charges than as a meddling oppressor. When Jean-Jacques poured out
his bitter complaints to him about the intolerable slowness of his publishers he would try to pacify him with sympathetic and soothing noises:
'I have never yet seen a publisher who has not incurred these reproaches . . . It greatly distresses me to see you so upset, nothing could
be more natural in an author.' Or he would tactfully point out that,
perhaps, there would be fewer delays if Jean-Jacques would try to be less
of a perfectionist: 'If you would not make quite so many changes.' And
when the latter flew into high dudgeon, as he often did, giving vent to his

extreme touchiness, he would make allowances for 'the outbursts and fits
of temper to which men of letters are liable' and which he regarded as an
inevitable occupational disease, 'little defects inseparable from their
talents'.

*

Meagre as were the rewards of fame, the profession attracted hardly
fewer practitioners than in our day when fortunes are to be made by the
elect. 'The success of a few,' regretted Duclos, that astute observer of the
contemporary scene, 'has induced many young men, thinking themselves
geniuses, to make the mistake of going in for a literary career.' And this
they did in spite of the fact that it was by no means without its hazards.
Voltaire was far from being the only one who experienced them during
his eleven months in the Bastille. So did Diderot, in the fortress of
Vincennes where the three weeks' solitary confinement with which his
sentence began were enough to make him promise to publish no more
without official sanction. And many lesser lights, an average of ten per
year, enjoyed the distinction of becoming literary jailbirds. However,
inasmuch as the publicity and the martyrdom often stood them in good
stead, it was more than a distinction, a piece of good luck. 'I saw the walls
of my prison light up in the rays of my literary glory,' wrote one of them,
'Persecuted, I would be better known . . . my career opened up before me.
These months in the Bastille would make my fortune.' As one of Diderot's
colleagues on the *Encyclopédie* said at the time, 'the result of persecuting
writers had often been to gain them a reputation beyond their deserts'.
And it was not only the 'progressive' intellectuals who enjoyed these
fringe-benefits of incarceration. Some of their ideological opponents, men
like the 'reactionary' Fréron, also got to know the Bastille, even though
they had done nothing to incur the wrath of the Establishment. If they
went 'inside' it was because it was by no means difficult, if you had connections, to get your pet aversion put away for a while; all you had to do
(as Voltaire is said to have done for Fréron) was to wangle or bribe a blank
lettre de cachet out of the hands of an official, and fill in the desired name.
Fathers—Mirabeau's was a case in point—were not unknown to make use
of this ploy to make unruly sons see reason, nor wives to get a holiday
from their husbands.

By and large, however, the Establishment made up of—or rather
divided between—the King, his Ministers, the Bishops, the theological
faculty of the Sorbonne, and the top layer of the judiciary, known mis-
leadingly as the 'Parlement de Paris', was a good deal less severe in
practice than in theory. On the paper of a law of 1563 exhumed after an
attempt on the King's life in 1757, writers and printers faced the death

penalty for 'attacking religion, stirring up the people, impairing our authority and troubling the calm of our estates'. But in spite of the intelligentsia's massive attack on the Church and its faith, carried on under Voltaire's famous battle-cry *'Ecrasez l'Infâme'*, the worst any of their members suffered was self-chosen exile or a short and often quite comfortable spell behind bars. It was partly because the throne, the major pillar of the established order, felt it had little to fear from the intellectuals since they remained as yet loyal and, indeed, ardent supporters of the monarchy, reserving their animosity for its ancient rival, feudalism. And as the King was less inclined to curl up with a good read than with the eighteenth-century equivalent of call-girls, he might well have missed Diderot's prophetic warning that 'once men have turned menacing glances towards the majesty of heaven they will not fail a moment later to direct them against the sovereigns of the earth'.

Of course, there was preventive censorship; no book could be published without official sanction. But it was easy to evade by the simple process of having one's works printed in London, Amsterdam or Geneva. Provided the author did not put his name to his brain-child it was usually allowed into the country. Moreover, even when its import was banned there were plenty of opportunities for smuggling it in while there was also no lack of clandestine printers operating in France itself. Better still, officialdom won over to the cause of the intelligentsia, often connived with it. The *Encyclopédie*, that handbook of the New Age, had been launched with the help of the Chancellor and the Minister of War. When after the appearance of its first volume it was banned, publication could soon be resumed by virtue of a subsequent decision to forbid only the public sale of the great work; subscribers had to collect their copies from the printers. And at the height of this bit of trouble, when Diderot's rooms were being searched for incriminating papers, it was the chief censor, of all people, who had hid them for him, just as later he was to be in league with Jean-Jacques when he, too, fell foul of the Establishment.

So, as long as writers played the game according to the rules of the Ancien Régime, as long as they agreed to forego the pleasure of seeing their name in print, they enjoyed a good deal more latitude than allowed to dissidents by many a Nouveau Régime of our century. Nor was obligatory anonymity a great price to pay. As it was customary for a writer to read his latest product to the company frequenting one or the other of the great salons, the grapevine could be relied upon to do the rest. It is, incidentally, a tribute both to the intellectual curiosity and the sheer physical staying power of these assemblies that such readings often went on for an unconscionable length of time. Thus one of those present when towards the end of his life Jean-Jacques gave a preview of his *Confessions*, reported to a friend: 'We met at 9 a.m. and only broke up at three the next morning, with the reading only being interrupted for meals.'

*

While success in the profession of letters hardly opened up a long vista of square meals it did usually provide the writer with the next best thing, a meal-ticket valid at any number of great houses. As already related, Jean-Jacques had no sooner arrived on the literary scene than the hostesses of the day vied with one another for his presence at their tables. It was not long, however, before he came to the conclusion that all this hospitality, whether in Paris or in the neighbouring châteaux, was a mixed blessing. It was not only that he felt ill at ease in the Great World. As many a poor but fashionable young man had found to his cost, the inescapable tipping was apt to be more than the free meals were worth; 'Although I limited my gratuities to the places where I stayed frequently, they were nevertheless ruinous to me.' Even the raptures he had known in the days of his *grande passion* had not obliterated the memory of its expense: 'I am quite certain,' he wrote fifteen years later, 'I paid out a good 25 crowns at Madame d'Houdetot's' (the lady who had inspired him with 'perhaps the greatest passion man had ever felt'). Moreover, his stomach suffered as much as his purse from having become such a social catch. When, having fallen out with Madame d'Epinay whose rural hospitality he enjoyed for a year and a half, he wrote a letter listing his grievances so as to prove he owed her no debt of gratitude, the last in this list was 'the sad indigestion' he had suffered at her opulent board while 'sighing for homely fare'. It was perhaps not the most gracious bread-and-butter-letter ever written. But that regular attendance at the tables of the rich must indeed have been a strain can hardly be disputed. Already at Chenonceaux the fare had been such as to make him grow as 'fat as a monk'. At Madame d'Epinay's, too, it had been sumptuous, witness the enthusiastic account Diderot gave to his lady-love: 'We dined magnificently, gaily, lengthily. Then there were ices. Oh my dear, what ices! You should have been there to taste them, you who like good ices.' And, of course, things were no different in Paris where, as Montesquieu had said, 'supper kills one half of society and lunch the other half', to say nothing of Versailles where, according to an ex-Minister, 'mesdames de France [Louis XV's daughters] have their cupboards always stocked with hams and sausages and stews to which they help themselves, locking the door of their room, at all times of the day'.

Even for the dyspeptic, however, High Life and particularly Château-life had its attraction none the less, both aesthetic and intellectual. Though Jean-Jacques appears to have been singularly unsusceptible to architectural décor—in all his letters from Venice he never once refers to its beauties—his grandee admirers offered him at least an escape from the cramped quarters of his Paris lodgings and from the even more restricted scope of Thérèse's conversation, narrowly confined as it was to housewife-gossip. Not that the talk and the wit of the Beau Monde were invariably on the high level indicated by Diderot when, staying at Baron d'Holbach's château, he wrote to his mistress: 'We talked of art, poetry, philosophy, love, of the greatness and vanity of our undertakings . . . of space and time, of death and life.' There were also occasions when the guests amused themselves with some pretty elementary high jinks. Such, for instance, was the case one evening after a supper at which they had 'gorged themselves, especially the women' and one of the latter, the baron's mother-in-law, 'tempted by the broad rump' of an abbé who was leaning over a table, climbed on his back, 'sitting astride him with her legs dangling, kicking her heels into him . . . and he meanwhile whinnying, bucking . . . and all of us laughing and the lady laughing still more and holding her sides with laughter and finally shouting "Help, help, I can't contain myself, it's coming . . ." and the abbé being drenched with a flood of warm water . . . and shouting out in turn "Help, help I'm drowning", and all of us collapsed on the sofas, choking with laughter.' Fortunately for the victim of the lady's incontinent sense of humour she was 'a decent woman' . . . the next morning she gave orders to buy him a new outfit.

It was all part of a way of life that often made the lot of the successful writer far from unenviable. Here again is Diderot describing how he was installed and passed his days at the baron's château—as glad to escape from his shrewish Nanette as Jean-Jacques from his Thérèse: 'They have put me in a small, separate apartment, quiet, cheerful and warm. It is between Horace and Homer and a portrait of my sweetheart that I spend hours reading, thinking, writing and sighing. That is my occupation from six in the morning till one . . . We lunch well and at length. The table is served here as in the city and perhaps even more sumptuously . . . After lunch the ladies sew, the baron dozes on a couch and, as for me, I do what I please. Between three and four we go for a walk, the women in their direction, the baron and I in ours . . . We talk of history, politics, chemistry, literature, physics or morals. Sunset and the freshness of the evening brings us back to the house . . . The women have already returned and are already changed. There are lights and cards on the table . . . We begin a game of *piquet* . . . Ordinarily supper interrupts our game. On leaving the table we finish it. It is ten-thirty. We chat until eleven. At half past eleven we are all sleeping—or should be. The next day we begin again.'

And Jean-Jacques had done at least as well, first at Chenonceaux, later at Chevrette, Madame d'Epinay's 'gloomy but magnificent mansion'. What is more, he had enjoyed rather more sophisticated entertainment than that provided by the baron's giggly mother-in-law. He had taken part in the amateur theatricals hosts and guests were fond of devising, writing their own scripts, composing their own music, putting on their own shows in the private theatres attached to some of these great houses. However, being the kind of man he was, his letters describing such visits lack the charm of Diderot's: 'As the mistress of the house is very charming and leaves me free to do as I like and as the food is very good and the house and the walks delightful, I have not yet regretted coming out here though I shall leave for Paris the moment I get bored.'

But what perhaps did most to make the lot of the successful intellectual by no means an unhappy one was the immense prestige they enjoyed. To a foreigner, like David Hume, who spent some time at the British Embassy in Paris, the contrast with the Breed's relatively modest status on the other side of the Channel, was such as to elicit cries of rapture. 'Here,' he wrote to a friend, 'I only feed on ambrosia, drink nothing but nectar and breathe incense only.' The truly royal reception that a wildly cheering populace gave Voltaire, on his return to Paris after his long exile, is well known. 'Scarcely,' says Carlyle, 'could the arrival of the Grand Lama of Tibet have excited greater ferment . . . few royal progresses, few Roman triumphs have equalled this long triumph of Voltaire.' The mere sight of him, a contemporary relates, was enough to make 'young women get emotional, grow pale, even begin to feel ill; they throw themselves into his arms, stammer, burst into tears'. And it was by no means only the Grand Old Man who was revered to the point of having ships named after him. Jean-Jacques, too, was so honoured, as were d'Alembert and even lesser figures like Marmontel. Another form of tribute, so Grimm reported, was that paid by foreign potentates who, when in Paris, always made a point of seeing the leading men of letters, a custom that had almost obtained 'force of law'. On one such occasion Gustavus III of Sweden went so far as to call himself 'singularly honoured' by Jean-Jacques's willingness to call on him. And long before then, when the latter had only just made his first breakthrough, he had already found royalty keen to engage in debate with him—with the King's father-in-law taking up his pen in defence of the arts and sciences.

If the monarch himself showed little interest in the literary lions of the day his colleagues more than made up for it, with Frederick the Great cajoling Voltaire to come and live with him ('I hope you will not exclude me,' he had written when still the Crown Prince of Prussia, 'from those whom you find worthy of instruction'), and Catherine the Great doing the same for Diderot. Moreover, the Comte de Ségur recalls in his memoirs how 'even intellectuals of the second or third rank were often treated with more consideration than the provincial nobility . . . Only the court maintains its usual superiority. But as French courtiers are even greater slaves to fashion than to their princes they deemed it expedient to curry favour with public opinion by paying tribute to d'Alembert and his like.' Though de Ségur was referring to conditions under Louis XVI, who acceded in 1774, four years before Rousseau's death, things had been hardly different under his predecessor. 'Even those among the grand, who do not really care for intellectuals,' Duclos had written, 'pretend they do because it is the fashion.'

No wonder there were those among the latter who could not take it, who abused, so another memorialist reported, 'the veneration with which many regarded the sort of priesthood men of letters had become . . . spoke only in lofty tones to the grand that felt honoured to be receiving them in their midst or paid for their dinner with insolence, all of which only increased the respect that was felt for them'. And no wonder either that no one was to earn these strictures more fully than so feeble a soul subjected to so intense a barrage of adulation as poor Jean-Jacques.

CHAPTER FIVE

Off the Soap-box and into the Pulpit

'I became intoxicated with virtue, I was truly transformed.'

As is well known, nothing succeeds like success. Once the public have been induced to invest heavily in a new literary or artistic discovery they are usually disinclined to sell out at a loss, however disappointing its subsequent performance. Better still, success often proves retroactive as it did with Jean-Jacques, one of whose earliest efforts, a comedy written at the age of eighteen and, not surprisingly, rejected for production when he had hawked it around as a thirty-seven-year-old nobody, was now suddenly discovered to merit the public's attention.

Meanwhile his name had been kept before the public eye by the controversy he had aroused with his prize-winning essay, 'the universal outcry' he had so correctly anticipated, rather than by any new bombshell dropped into the millpond of civilized society. Challenged by the latter's defenders he provoked them to keep up and intensify their attacks by displays of arrogance and conceit that at this stage, when the head-swelling process had only just begun, occasionally still sound impressive in their cool effrontery but later become so breathtaking as to be comical or, more compassionately, the stuff that tragi-comedy is made of.

Here are some samples of what the most prominent of his adversaries, the exiled King of Poland who was Louis XV's father-in-law, called 'the brusque tones and disdainful cutting airs' Jean-Jacques felt obliged to adopt from the start. 'A very large number of writers have tried to refute my thesis . . . If once again I parry their blows it is more to honour myself than to defend it and lend it a support of which it has no need . . . It is only the love of humanity and of virtue that make me break my silence . . . Concerned to earn self-esteem I have learnt to do without that of others. It's immaterial to me what they think.' Nor was he prepared to give an inch in the argument itself. Quite the contrary. If he had laid it on pretty thickly when he first denounced civilization and all its works he now used an even bigger trowel. He had 'shown that morals had degenerated wherever in the world people had developed a taste for study and

literature . . . This taste was destructive of our love of duty . . . softens up
the body as well as the soul . . . exhausts the spirit, unnerves courage' etc.,
etc. To those who objected that primitive Africa appeared to be no
paradise of innocence he answered that if this was so it was all the fault
of the civilized world: 'If I were the chief of an African tribe I would hang
every European daring to enter as well as any African trying to leave.'
Or again, if it was argued that among a hundred barbarian peoples you
would find at most one that was virtuous, he replied that 'that would still
be one more than you would ever find among people cultivating sciences'.
He did not hesitate to claim it was strictly impossible to prove him wrong,
for the simple reason that 'the truth cannot be refuted'. Even when the
refutations with which he was 'overwhelmed' seemed conclusive, this only
proved that he 'had not made himself clear; they may have disposed of
what I have said but not of what I wanted to say'.

*

It is in his polemical writings of this period that he first reveals those
characteristics that enabled him to be all things to all men, furnishing the
revolutionaries of the future with as many rousing slogans as their opponents with reasoned refutations thereof. For after he had drawn out all
the registers in his blast against the disastrous effects on morality of
intellectual and artistic pursuits he ended the ensuing argument on a very
lame note. Challenged to say whether these wicked pursuits should be
banned his answer was: 'No . . . though they destroy virtue . . . the
institutions of learning can at least help to offer men some diversion from
wickedness.' There was no point in doing away with them, he argued,
since they had destroyed virtue beyond repair. Of course, he did not say
it as simply as this, he had to put it with that theatrical bombast which the
age, apparently humourless in this respect, seemed to glorify as eloquence.
'It is with sorrow that I am going to pronounce a great and fatal truth . . .
One has never seen a people return to virtue once it has been corrupted . . .
Let us, therefore, allow the arts and sciences to alleviate somewhat the
ferocity of the men they have led astray.' Having opened the debate with
such a bang it was indeed closing it with a barely audible whimper.

   No wonder, therefore, it was seized upon by his enemies as proof that
he owed his sudden fame to a mere publicity stunt, that he had only been
out to shock. It was a suspicion for which plenty of confirmation could be
found in his later writings where again and again his revolutionary
trumpet ends up by giving a very uncertain sound, once he has stepped
off the soap-box. As a far from unsympathetic biographer* has expressed
it, he was a past master in the art of collecting an audience by firing off a

* Saint Marc Girardin.

gun in the street and then treating the bystanders to anodyne homily.

There are many good reasons, however, for acquitting Jean-Jacques of the charge that he was simply out to attract attention. Other things can account for his having gone out on a limb and then cutting it off, as he was to do practically every time an idea hit him. One has already been indicated: the self-admitted lack of intellectual discipline which in the eyes of one scholarly student* of his writings makes him 'an emotional enthusiast who spoke without reflection, an irresponsible writer with a fatal gift for epigram', or as another has put it, 'someone who seriously says things that are not serious'.

Another reason can be found in that prosaic, down-to-earth common sense of the cautious, shrewd Swiss which reasserts itself after the resentful outsider in the great world of Paris, enjoying and revenging himself in his newly found role of its Cato, has blown off steam. A third explanation lies in that congenital 'timidity' and 'laziness', to which he admits as often as to the general 'feebleness' of his will and the evanescent character of his 'great and generous impulses', all of which combine to make him as much of a conservative as these passing impulses inspire him with revolutionary fervour.

It was this inconsistency which made it so easy for his enemies to accuse him of playing to the gallery. 'My adversaries,' he wrote at this time, 'have spared me neither abuse nor falsehoods, they claim that I do not believe a word of the truths I have put forward.' Not without reason was he so often to bewail the moment when he had taken up 'the sad profession of letters . . . From the moment I began to publish I have known only sorrow, anguish and affliction . . . Cruel poverty is less hard to bear than a literary reputation . . . As soon as my essay appeared the champions of literature fell upon me as of one accord.' And though he treated them with his usual haughty disdain—'I crushed their little witticisms with my observations as I might crush an insect between my fingers'—the venom with which he described them as 'poisonous insects buzzing around my legs' indicates clearly enough that they had penetrated the armour of his conceit.

But what made him most bitterly regret that he had taken to the pen—'cursing every day of my life the stupid pride that made me do so'—was that his use of it gradually alienated him from all those friends he used to meet at Baron d'Holbach's marathon luncheons (though in fact, it was not so much reading him as getting to know him that made one after the other 'cool off' as, with saddening regularity, he reports in telling the story of his life). The final rupture was not to come until eight years after his first great success had established him as a member of the 'Progressive

* F. J. C. Hearnshaw.

Party' of the day, that coterie of men of letters and of science, known as the Philosophes, who had come together as comrades-in-arms in the battle for the 'Enlightenment'. But the germ of the ideological conflict envenoming the personal antagonisms that developed as the years passed, was already visible in Jean-Jacques's earliest writings of this period. It was not so much that he had gone against the grain in dethroning Reason and putting Conscience in its place, vilifying the intellectual sophistication of 'celebrated men' and glorifying virtue, as the 'sublime science of simple minds'. Nor was it because of his rudeness to these men, 'the mounte-banks', that his friends turned against him. They seemed to have taken it all in good spirit, perhaps because he had been careful to put his insults in a context enabling the leading lights of the day to ignore them, as meant only for the lesser fry. However this may be, far from having given offence to his luncheon companions *chez* Holbach, he had, so Grimm reported, 'converted nearly all the philosophers . . . among others Diderot and d'Alembert'. Grimm himself found this 'very strange'. But as already indicated (and convincingly demonstrated in Peter Gay's illuminating study *The Party of Humanity*) its leaders were far from inaccessible to doubts about the omnipotence of Reason. Nothing could be wider off the mark than the popular conception of the Philosophes as out-and-out rationalists, with a naïve utopian belief in the perfectibility of men and the inevitability of moral progress. Rather than it being strange that Jean-Jacques's diatribe against the glorification of Reason struck a chord among his fellow-intellectuals, to say nothing of the ordinary reading public, it would have been surprising had it failed to do so. For as one of the most distinguished among Rousseau's countless biographers, the Catholic P. M. Masson, has said, 'from Montaigu to Pascal too many moralists had deprecated Reason, warned against pride of spirit for French thought to have become unresponsive to these teachings'.

But if, therefore, Jean-Jacques had not really been guilty of violating the party-line or letting down the side with his disparagement of intel-lectualism—in a piece which anyhow was indulgently regarded as not much more than a clever *boutade*, a bit of a dialectical lark—it was quite a different matter when he started up-grading religion. That was felt to be little short of treason by the Philosophes, who were as united in their abomination of '*l'Infâme*', with its bloodstained history of fanatical, warring sects, as in their contempt for its anthropocentric conception of the universe, its dogma of the Fall and its promise of Redemption. Though only some of them were full-blown atheists and many more were deists, professing belief in a supreme but not benevolent, man-orientated Being or Intelligence, while yet others worshipped 'Nature' as the all-good all-wise divinity of traditional belief, they closed ranks against the guardians of the old Theology, whether they were Jesuits, Jansenists (the 'puritans' of the Catholic Church) or Protestants. It was Jean-Jacques's breaking of these ranks that did as much to make his old friends 'cool off' to freezing point as the squalid or petty personal quarrels that broke out. Not that he ever went over to the enemy. What he did was to take up a position in the ideological no-man's-land between the two camps, attacking both the old faith and the new. And though another ten years were to pass before he finally left the trenches where at one time he had seemed to stand shoulder to shoulder with men like Diderot, to whom Christianity was an 'abomination', there had already been indications of his inability to go on fighting for the brave new cause at the time he first caught the public eye. 'In what way,' he had asked, 'has religion benefited from the literature and the arts? . . . The divine book, the Gospel, is the only one a Christian needs . . . No man needs any books other than those of religion.'

That such unfashionable sentiments did not get him into serious trouble with his 'Party' then and there, was doubtless due to the fact that as yet he did not feel very strongly about them nor stood up for them with much vigour when challenged. 'I spent my days,' he recalls, 'with modern philosophers . . . who had shaken my most fundamental beliefs, for being fervent missionaries of atheism and domineeringly dogmatic, they got angry with anyone who dared to differ from their way of thinking. Taking no pleasure in disputes and not being very good at arguing I usually defended my views rather feebly . . . But I never accepted their dreary doctrine.' There was one famous occasion, however, when he did speak up forcefully, very much the lone wolf. That was at a dinner party where the talk became so blasphemous that he exclaimed: 'If it is cowardice to allow people to speak ill of an absent friend it is surely a crime to allow people to speak ill of God when he is present; well, gentlemen, I believe in God and I shall leave if you say another word.'

*

Though from the beginning he had been made to pay the penalties of success in full measure, suffering the slings and arrows of outraged envy as well as sensing the approach of the gathering storm with his friends, yet these first few years of fame were far from being as full of sorrows as one would think from his repeated complaints that he had become 'the most miserable of creatures the moment he had made a name for himself'. To be sure, fêted by the Beau Monde he had so ardently longed to conquer, 'in the whirl of high society, at luxurious suppers, amidst the glitter of the theatre, in a cloud of vainglory', there were moments when he longed for 'the woods and streams and solitary walks in the country'

such as he had known in his years with 'Maman'. But that did not stop
him from savouring a glory whose taste was still far too fresh to have
turned sour.

It was all the sweeter as in those early days he was getting the best of
both worlds, the applause of those ladies as lovely angels whose tears he
had wanted to catch with his lips on that unforgettable evening at
Fontainebleau, as well as the congratulations offered by the voice of his
own conscience. Better still, he could feel that both were equally well
merited. On the one hand, 'the public's delirious enthusiasm', as he was
to say later, 'was proof enough of the sublime quality' of his operetta. On
the other hand, two years before he had thus earned the esteem of the
highest in the land (the King had been so taken with one of his songs that
the day after the performance he never stopped singing it 'in the vilest
voice in the Kingdom' and Madame de Pompadour had arranged for two
further performances at her country place), he had taken a further step
in his campaign to earn the applause of his conscience by dedicating
himself to the full-time pursuit of virtue. No longer content with just
preaching he had decided to practise what he preached. He had renounced, so he put it in the *Confessions*, 'all plans for fortune and advance-
ment, determined to spend the little time I still had to live in independence
and poverty . . . courageously doing what seemed right without in the
least worrying about what people might think . . . trampling underfoot the
senseless opinions of the vulgar herd of the so-called great and so-called
wise'. In short, as he summed it up later in a letter to his friend and
protector, the chief censor, he had decided 'to set an example to mankind,
showing men how to live'.

Even the most demanding conscience could hardly ask for more.
Delirious enthusiasm in that quarter, too, would therefore have been
fully assured, had it not been for one niggling little question: how to
square this selfless dedication to truth and virtue with the writing and
composing of a theatrical entertainment that not only brought him 'completely into fashion, no man was more sought after', but also enough
money 'to enable me to subsist for several years'. Somehow it did not
quite seem to fit the role of the new Savonarola he had adopted when,
after having denounced the corrupting effect of the arts (as he was to do
again, concentrating all his approval on the theatre eight years later), he
had set up in business as a practising moralist, a saint, determined to
'reconcile my actions to my principles'. That had been no small step
forward on the road to holiness: 'Until then I had been good, from that
moment I became virtuous or at least intoxicated with virtue . . . I was
truly transformed. My friends and acquaintances no longer recognised
me.' And yet, here, two years later he was very much back 'amidst the

glitter of the theatre', vastly enjoying the 'cloud of vainglory' on to which 'high society' had lifted him.

True, he had given an earnest of his decision to set an example to mankind by the time-honoured method of dressing the part of the prophet in the wilderness: 'I began my reformation with my dress, I gave up gold lace and white stockings and wore a round wig. I gave up my sword and sold my watch.' And perhaps that was why his friends no longer recognized him, which had become all the more difficult as he had also gone in for the hairiness that so often goes with the profession. Few of its members, however, have ever had occasion to show the courage of their sartorial and capillary convictions with as much bravery as Jean-Jacques displayed in the royal theatre at Fontainebleau, it was all the more impressive as, by nature timid, it cost him a considerable effort. At first, he relates, he had felt proud that he had dared to come 'dressed in my usual careless style with a rough beard and ill-combed wig'. But as the theatre filled up and 'I saw myself dressed like that in the middle of an overdressed crowd, I began to feel ill at ease'. It took quite a little arguing with himself before he had come to the conclusion that he had been right to defy convention: 'If I begin to pander to opinion over one matter I shall pretty soon be doing so over everything.' And anyhow, what was wrong with a beard? 'It is a gift of nature . . . Let them think me ridiculous and offensive. What is that to me? I must know how to bear ridicule and censure provided they are undeserved.'

But even a hairy, ill-dressed and ill-combed composer of profitable light opera can hardly claim to be selflessly concerned with furthering the stern cause of truth and virtue. Clearly he had strayed off the straight and narrow path he had so recently mapped out for himself. He had once again 'become another man', but this time in reverse. Only, just as with that earlier pejorative metamorphosis, that transformation for the worse the young engraver's apprentice had suffered at the hands of his bullying master, it was not really his fault. His friends were to blame. 'If I had shaken off the yoke of friendship . . . I should have accomplished my purpose, the greatest perhaps, or at least the most serviceable to virtue ever conceived by mortal man. But I allowed myself to be enslaved and led like a child by so-called friends who were jealous of seeing me strike out alone down a new road . . . It was not so much my literary celebrity as the change in my character . . . that evoked their jealousy. They would perhaps have forgiven me for my brilliance in the art of writing but they could not forgive me for setting an example by my conduct.'

And so, it seems, they had resolved and somehow managed to make him forget his new role of holy man and resume, this time successfully, that of practitioner of those arts that had become morally harmless, indeed beneficial, because they had long since proved fatal to morality. Nor was the work with which he scored such a triumph at Fontainebleau and which six months later was presented to the general public by the Paris Opera, in whose repertoire it remained for many years, his only lapse. Towards the end of the same year he created yet another sensation in the salons, where already the eccentricity of his 'Reform' had enhanced his value as a social catch. Once again forgetting all about his new love, virtue, to return to the old, the arts, he took sides in a violent quarrel about the relative merits of French and Italian music, which was then the main subject of heated conversation in the salons 'whose excitement was greater than if they had been divided over politics or religion'. So rude was he about French music—though, typically, having defended it barely two years earlier—that he was burned in effigy by the Opera's orchestra, roused to fury by such remarks as that 'French singing was a continuous yelping unbearable to any unprejudiced ear'. Possibly he may have indulged his congenital dislike of understatement somewhat when he described the effect of his pamphlet as 'worthy of the pen of Tacitus . . . such was the outburst it provoked that the nation has never quite re-covered from it'. But Grimm, too, reported that 'it kicked up a fearful shindy'.

*

What was one to make of it all? Who was the real Jean-Jacques, the stern moralist or the entertainer? In which of the many simultaneous roles that caught the public eye was he really himself? What did he really believe in, this man who had abjured his native Calvinism to become a Catholic at the age of sixteen only to reconvert back again, for equally practical reasons and after several years of siding with the unbelievers. When was he really serious? Denouncing civilization and its works or defending them? Attacking the arts or practising them? Condemning the theatre or working for it? Praising French music or reviling it?

It was hardly surprising that this mystifying versatility made him so intriguing to a society, ever hungry for diversion, that within two years of his arrival on the scene, when as yet he had barely more than a thirty-page pamphlet and his operetta to his credit, his portrait, executed by one of the most fahionable painters of the age, had already found its way into the famous Paris 'Salon'. Nor is it as strange as it might seem that the only constant in his public behaviour, the arrogance and conceit he displayed even in these early days, added still further to his fame. For as Duclos pointed out in his shrewd observations on the process of reputation-making, self-praise is not always counter-productive: 'Some people owe their renown to impudence, they vaunt their own merits and do it so often that in the end the public is taken in by it, one does not recall any more where one has heard about them and so one begins to believe what one has heard, it gets repeated and spreads like a rumour all over the town.' It fitted Jean-Jacques like a glove. Except that in his case the renown was to spread all over Europe and still finds zealous defenders today.

CHAPTER SIX

Rebel, Reformer and Drop-out

'A chameleon or a woman is less changeable than I.'

'It is hardly in me to subject myself to restraint . . . I cannot stand any kind of obstruction . . . Even the most trifling social duties are unbearable to me.'

FEW writers were ever less well equipped to face the perils of the literary game than Jean-Jacques. On the one hand his incorrigible arrogance and boastfulness—even if they were only the product of a deep-seated inferiority complex—could not but provoke his critics to redouble their efforts. On the other hand, his feeble soul, so sensitive and thin-skinned as to make him suffer every pinprick as it were a thrust to his heart, rendered him as painfully vulnerable to his adversaries as to his admirers whose worship, by swelling his easily inflatable head still further, only had the result of making him offer still more provocation. 'If,' one of his critics wrote in the early days of his rise to fame, 'if contempt for others and esteem for oneself carried to the point of indecency, are the things that make a philosopher, then Jean-Jacques is a very great philosopher indeed.' It was the sort of jibe he practically asked for every time he put his polemical pen to paper. Never was there a writer who begged for more punishment from his rivals.

Hence his recurrent expressions of regret that he had allowed himself to be caught up in the literary life and hence his decision to retire from the Paris scene. 'Life among pretentious people,' he recalls in the *Confessions*, 'was so little to my taste, the cabals of men of letters, their shameful quarrels, the lack of honesty in their books, the important airs they assumed, were so antipathetic to me . . . that in my disgust for that turbulent life I began to long ardently to live in the country.' Strangely, Voltaire, his total antithesis and future chief enemy, has expressed himself in almost identical terms in his memoirs. 'I was tired of the idle and turbulent life of Paris, the crowd of second-raters, the bad books, that got official approval, the cabals of the literary crowd, the meanness and dishonesty of the wretched people who dishonour literature.'

Both men, however, had other reasons besides distaste for the seamy side of literary life to flee the capital. Voltaire, with eleven months in the Bastille and three years of exile in England behind him, had had little choice. In the case of Jean-Jacques ill-health, the embarrassment he suffered from his need for frequent and often painful micturition, played its part in his growing aversion from High Society. 'I still shudder to think,' he once wrote to a friend, 'of myself in a circle of women, compelled to wait until some fine talker has finished . . . When at last I find a well-lit staircase there are other ladies who delay me, then a courtyard full of constantly moving carriages ready to crush me, ladies' maids who are looking at me, lackeys who line the walls and laugh at me. I do not find a single wall or wretched little corner that is suitable for my purpose. In short, I can urinate only in full view of everybody and on some noble white-stockinged leg.' Another reason why he was longing to get away from it all was the fearful nuisance his admirers made of themselves. What these idle-rich lion-hunters may have lacked in number, compared with those who afflict the popular celebrities of our day, they more than made up for by the amount of time they could devote to the pursuit of their prey; 'as bored as they are boring,' their victim complained, 'they waste other people's time because they do not know what to do with their own.'

But perhaps the most important factor in his decision to leave the capital was hurt pride. His retreat from the Great World was in a sense an admission of defeat as a socialite. For by nature he was far from unsociable, anything but a born hermit: 'I should have liked society as much as anybody,' he admitted in the *Confessions*, 'if I were not sure of always showing myself at a disadvantage.' Six years of fame, during which 'no man was more sought after', had been more than enough to make him realize his inability to shine in the world of the salons, where fellow-intellectuals like Duclos or d'Alembert (to say nothing of the sparkling Voltaire) had made their name as much by their conversational as by their literary talents. In spite of the polish the watchmaker's son from Geneva had acquired under the tutelage of his pseudo-baronial 'Maman'—who was after all only a Swiss country-bumpkin herself—he had never, so d'Alembert said, 'learnt to adapt himself to the manners of Paris society'. Nor, judging by the account of Madame d'Epinay, did he avoid the most dangerous pitfall awaiting the social climber, that of trying too hard: 'He is a great payer of compliments, but he is not, or at any rate does not appear to be polished, he does not know the ways of the world.'

Once he had turned his back on it he was perfectly willing to admit his lack of talent for its wicked ways, his inability to master those social graces that only drew a 'deceitful veil' over every kind of moral mischief. 'I can think of no greater torture,' he wrote in the *Confessions*, 'than to be obliged to speak . . . without a moment for reflection . . . I infallibly say something stupid. But what is even more fatal is that, instead of keeping quiet when I have nothing to say, it is just at these moments that I have a furious desire to chatter . . . So anxious am I to conquer or to hide my ineptitude that I rarely fail to make it apparent . . . Though not a fool I am often taken for one.' It was hard to bear for someone so convinced of his superior merits. How maddening it was to hear oneself talk as 'an awkward schoolboy at a loss for words instead of a forceful thinker full of new ideas and expressing them with precision'. How he had resented it, 'knowing what he is really worth', so he put it in the *Dialogues*, 'his seeming and hopeless ineptitude often makes him angry not only with himself but sometimes also with those who force him to reveal it'.

At one time it had driven him to try and revenge himself on the world in which he felt so ill at ease by defying its manners just as he had defied its sartorial conventions. 'I decided to adopt manners of my own.' It was the discovery of his vocation as 'an example to mankind' that had given him the courage 'to trample all courtesies underfoot . . . I ceased to be that shy creature . . . who was put out by a joking word and blushed at a woman's glance. Bold, proud and fearless, I now carried with me where ever I went a self-assurance, which . . . dwelt in my soul rather than my bearing. The contempt which my deep reflections had inspired in me for the customs, the principles and the prejudices of the age made me insensible to the mockery of those who followed them . . . What a change! All Paris repeated the sharp and biting sarcasms of that same man who two years before . . . could never find the right thing to say.'

Whether or not all Paris really did take quite so much notice, he had indeed once again become another man. 'Until then,' Grimm reported, 'he had been lavish in his flattery, gallant and affected not to say obsequious and so convoluted as to be tiring. Then suddenly he put on the mantle of the uncouth cynic.' Nor did he confine himself to sarcasms and cynicisms, he also went in for plain rudeness, as on the notorious occasion when a duke asked him if he might congratulate him on the success of his operetta, and he replied, 'if you wish, but make it short.' It was a time, he recalls in his memoirs, when he exalted 'rudeness into a dauntless virtue' which, the world of fashion being what it is, made him all the more sought after: 'the ruder I was to people the more they insisted' (on asking him to dinner).

*

There came a day, however, when he tired of this attitude (than which, he now decided, 'nothing could be more contrary to my true nature') and longed only for the peace and quiet of life in the country. It was a

preference so incomprehensible to his fellow-writers that it made him even
more suspect, as a *poseur*, just as it rendered him still more interesting, as
an eccentric, to his society friends. And it was thanks to one of the latter,
the thirty-year-old Marquise d'Epinay who had given him his first
glimpse of château-life when he was still an unknown quantity to her
world, that the literary lion he had now become could fulfil his latest
dream. Remembering that he had once admired a tumble-down cottage on
her husband's estate she had had it put in order and some months later
offered him, by way of a surprise-present, the indefinite loan of it: 'Here
is your refuge, Mr. Bear, you chose it yourself, it is offered to you out of
friendship.'

Suspicious and umbrageous as always when his friends wanted to
render him a service, he started by living up to the affectionate nickname
she had bestowed on him. 'I am not for sale,' he growled, 'how little you
understand your own interests in wanting to make a valet of a friend.'
What had aroused his ire to such a point was that she had dared not only
to offer him the use of the five-room cottage, known as the Hermitage,
but also to help him make both ends meet should he be short of money,
which he was not at the time; 'I had a name and talents, I was temperate
and had rid myself of my expensive wants . . . With my trade of music-
copying . . . I could earn enough to live on. And the two thousand francs
which remained over from the profits of the *Village Soothsayer* and my
other writings left me with sufficient reserves to prevent my being
pushed for money.' And so he could afford to set out his terms for
accepting his friend's hospitality with brutal frankness. They boiled down
to the demand that he was on no account to be bothered: 'I do not want
to be subject to any duties . . . I shall never mortgage any part of my
liberty.'

It was the first intimation the Marquise had of his original conception
of friendship as a 'mingling' and 'mutual outpouring of loving hearts'
involving no obligations of any kind. One must not forget, however, that
in his day members of the intelligentsia had reason to be somewhat on
their guard with those in high society who befriended them. Open as this
society was to men of talent, however humble their origin, much as it
might lionize them, the friendship its grandees offered was neither always
wholly disinterested nor wholly without condescension. Especially the
small fry among the men of letters were often made painfully aware of it.
'Now that the fashionable thing is to have writers in your employment,'
wrote a contemporary, 'their position [on the payroll of some blue-
blooded dunderhead] is often truly agonizing . . . obliged to applaud the
dreary talk of their master and the bad taste of his wife.' Even Voltaire,
as a young man, had learned on the occasion of his famous quarrel with

the Chevalier de Rohan who had him beaten up by his servants, that his grand friends would leave him in the lurch when it was a question of choosing between him and a member of their own class. True, that was at a time when intellectuals were not yet idolized by the Beau Monde as in Jean-Jacques's day and Voltaire's own old age. But judging by the Comte de Ségur's account, things had not really changed all that much even then. 'The men whose talents should have placed them in the top-drawer of society but whose birth had placed them in a lower one, still showed signs of a chip on their shoulder. Even fame . . . never quite cures them of a certain touchiness, still leaves the germ of the discord that has always existed between patricians and plebeians; the radical vice of the former is ridiculous disdain, that of the latter equally ridiculous envy.'

It was not surprising, therefore, that someone so pathologically distrustful and touchy as Jean-Jacques—and so reluctant to incur any of the ordinary obligations of friendship—should have hesitated to accept the Marquise's offer and suspected her motives. Fully aware that for these grand ladies he had become a social catch, which they were the more anxious to show off to their friends—'as a performing bear kept on a leash'—the more eccentric his conduct had become, he could not help but wonder what he might be letting himself in for by accepting the loan of the Hermitage. He had all the more reason to do so as Madame d'Epinay, who went in for writing herself, liked nothing better, he said, than to 'read her efforts to a favourable audience', and he was as disinclined to provide one as he was uninhibited in inflicting his own works on his friends (as Diderot learnt to his cost when Jean-Jacques went to stay with him to get his comments on the draft of *La Nouvelle Héloise* and, after treating him to some forty hours of it, declared himself too 'sleepy' to help his friend with one of his writings).

However, having made it clear on what terms he was prepared to accept the Marquise's hospitality and in particular having obtained a promise that he would never be expected to join her at her neighbouring château when she was entertaining more than one or two friends, his fears were apparently set at rest. And so he could abandon himself to the joys of a friendship that, he assured her, was 'more precious to him than life itself'. They were the days when she sent him the underpetticoat he kissed so fervently and so tearfully that Thérèse, not altogether surprisingly, 'thought I had gone mad'. Whether she also thought there might be more behind the gift and his reception of it than met the eye, he does not record. There are indications in his letters of the period that for a time he may perhaps have aspired to even more intimate favours than presents of his hostess's underwear. But if one is to believe his autobiography (written, it should be remembered, long after he had fallen out with her, which accounts for the doubtful taste of his comments on her vital statistics) she was not his type: 'Her chest was as flat as my hand and that alone was enough to freeze me, as neither my heart nor my senses have ever been able to think of one without breasts as a woman.' His account of their relationship also shows that even the temperature of his platonic sentiments was not, fortunately for Thérèse's belief in his sanity, maintained at the level of overheating caused by the arrival of the under-petticoat. That was 'literature', a typical case of emotion inflated in tranquillity. For the thank-you letter he wrote at the time is singularly lacking in lachrymose and osculatory raptures. Real life with the Marquise was rather more as we all, not excluding the greatest writer, know it, with long stretches of emotional calm so flat as to be beyond ruffling even by the somewhat unusual methods to which Jean-Jacques had recourse; 'her conversation though pleasant enough in company was dull in private and mine, which was no more brilliant, was of no great assistance to her. Ashamed of the long silences, I strained every nerve to enliven them . . . I gave her the most fraternal of little kisses which aroused her sensuality as little as they did mine.'

*

As will have become evident, the Age of Reason was also the Age of Sentiment. Or rather—for there is precious little reason to think Enlightened Man knew a greater intensity of feeling than Renaissance or Medieval or, for that matter, Biblical Man—it was the Age of Gushing. Men as well as women made a cult of sentiment, prided themselves on their sensibility, demonstrating it with endless talk about the delights of friendship, the transports and the sorrows of love, the beauty of virtue. Contradictory as it may seem, the Cult was as much a reaction against the spirit of the Enlightenment, with its stress on the primacy of cold, calculating Reason, as it was a product of this spirit. By dethroning Revelation, taking its place as the source of all truth, clearing man of the stain of Original Sin and glorifying or even deifying Nature, Reason had vindicated man's passions. Emotion, so long distrusted and kept under severe surveillance as belonging, except for its religious variety, to the darker side of man, restrained and stylized when the aristocratic conception of the good life, a texture of classical, Christian and knightly ideals, held the field, was at last liberated and, once freed, turned against its liberator, advancing the claims of the unruly heart against those of the head. As early as the turn of the century one of the great salons had acted as the centre of this movement and its presiding genius, the Marquise de Lambert, was complaining that, while there were schools for the training of the intellect, there was none devoted to the faculties of the heart.

Reason's own torch-bearers, the very men who had replaced the authority of Holy Writ with that of the new scientific age, joined in the exhaltation of sentiment. No one wore his heart more firmly pinned on his sleeve than Diderot, talked more effusively about its contents, wept more freely; at the mere thought of 'a beautiful action my heart expands within me . . . I can scarcely breathe . . . my eyes are filled with tears'. When he met Grimm after only a fortnight's separation, he wept on his waistcoat, sobbing 'my friend, my dear friend'. Writing to his mistress at the time Grimm was going blind he begged her not to be jealous that he had 'kissed those poor eyes over and over again'. Grimm, himself, though a very different character from the emotional, warm-hearted Diderot, achieved fame as an inconsolable lover by the display he gave of a broken heart when jilted by an actress he fancied. And even the astringent Marquise du Deffand, a friend of Voltaire and Walpole whose side she took in her detestation of the gelatinous sentimentality of *La Nouvelle Héloise*, sometimes spoke in the tones of the cult. 'I am glad to be old and hideous,' she wrote late in life, 'incapable of anything but the purest and most sacred friendship. But friendship I love to distraction. My heart was made for it.'

Clearly, therefore, Jean-Jacques had by no means initiated the Age by whose standards the open tear-duct rather than the stiff upper lip marked the man of fashion. What he did do was to adapt the cult to his own requirements by devising a theory of love and friendship that enabled his heart to wallow in these expensive emotions at no cost whatever. Necessity had been the mother of invention. For he had come into the world with two qualities that were irreconcilable and thus threatened to make his life a misery if he did not find a way out of the dilemma. One of them was his craving for love and friendship: 'I have never known any other happiness,' he wrote to a friend towards the end of his life, 'than to love and be loved.' Finding such happiness should have posed no problem as he had a genius for friendship; 'Heaven made me for it . . . I was born to be the best friend that has ever existed . . . I have a very loving heart . . . it only needs to be loved . . .' No one had more talent for loving. 'The person who could love me as I can love is still to be born.' And when once a friend angered him by suggesting that he was perhaps a tiny bit quarrelsome, he exploded: 'Show me a better man than me, a heart more loving, more tender, more sensitive, more captivated by the delights of friendship, more susceptible to the good and the beautiful.'*

* If he evoked such a glowing response in Tolstoy it was doubtless because in this respect the two men were birds of a feather. For the great Russian, too, was much impressed with his own innate goodness: 'I have not yet met,' he said at the age of twenty-five, 'a single man who was morally as good as I am'. And he, too, suffered from the inability of his fellow-men to love as he could love; all his

But as ill-luck would have it Jean-Jacques's craving and genius for friendship coincided with an unconquerable dislike of putting himself out in the slightest degree, suffering the most trifling inconvenience. He was happy only in 'loving and being loved' as long as it did not involve him in any fuss or bother. 'My idea of happiness,' he told Malesherbes, 'is not so much to be free to do as I like but never to have to do anything I don't feel like doing.' That was yet another reason why he had buried himself in the countryside; 'even the most trifling duties of social life are unbearable to me.' His autobiographical writings as well as his correspondence are full of admissions that 'it is hardly in me to subject myself to restraint . . . I cannot stand any kind of obstruction . . . in all matters constraint and compulsion are unbearable to me'. His oldest Swiss friend, with whom he had first sought refuge when he had to flee from France, read in a letter announcing a further visit: 'I must ask you most pressingly to leave me completely free . . . not to oppose my wishes in any way, whether I want to stay a day, half a day or even only an hour with you . . . I swear that if you cause me the slightest annoyance you will never see me again.'

As he saw it there was nothing childish in this insistence on having everything his own way that made him 'incapable of the restraints necessary to live in society'. Though he admitted in another connection that he had never really grown up—'in many respects I am still a child'— he attributed his 'invincible distaste for ordinary human intercourse' to his 'indomitable love of freedom and independence'. He was willing to agree, however, that one might also call it his 'incredible laziness'. He was 'frightened of the most trivial social duties; to have to say a word, write a letter, pay a call is torture to me'. And towards the end of his life, when he had moments of seeing himself as he really was, he recognized that at the bottom of it there was once again that 'feebleness' whose all-pervasive, paralytic quality he highlighted in the breathtaking avowal that he was too weak, not only to do things he should do but did not feel like doing, but even to act in accordance with his own will: 'When I must do something against my will I do not do it, whatever happens. I do not obey even my own will, for I am feeble and so I abstain from action.'

*

For a man so constituted the satisfaction of his craving to be loved

colleagues on the editorial board of a literary magazine 'disgusted' him because 'I want affection and friendship but they are incapable of it'. In what Edward Crankshaw calls Tolstoy's 'obsessive insistence on his own total sincerity and goodness as opposed to the insincerity and venality of almost everybody else', he is a carbon copy of the man whose medallion he wore around his neck. Except that, in view of the vastly greater treasures his writings have to offer, it would be more apposite to call him the rich man's Jean-Jacques.

presented obvious problems. Jean-Jacques tried to solve them by elaborating a theory that conceived of friendship as a permanent, reciprocal 'unburdening' of 'loving hearts', accompanied whenever possible by the 'delight of weeping together' but involving no obligations of any kind and specifically ruling out that of gratitude for services rendered. 'Intimate friendship,' he told Malesherbes was as 'precious' to him as ordinary human intercourse was 'odious', because the former knew no duties, 'one follows one's heart and all is done'. As he had already warned his hostess at the Hermitage when he set out the terms on which he consented to accept to be her guest, friends 'have all sorts of claims on my heart, none on my liberty'. He was determined, so he told another lady, 'to preserve my freedom in my attachments . . . I want to love my friends for the pleasure I get out of doing so . . . the moment they demand gratitude for services rendered . . . pleasure vanished'. In fact, so he explained to yet another, 'gratitude and friendship cannot coexist in my heart'. That was capable of logical demonstration. Since feeling was all that mattered and he was of all men the most loving, it followed that his friends however generous with their presents, were at all times indebted to him: 'friendship does not reckon services and the one who has loved the most is the real benefactor.' The more his friends did for him, the greater their indebtedness became. It was partly because to give was not just more blessed than to receive, it was to demand a painful sacrifice from the recipient; 'When I give way to prolonged pressure to accept an offer repeated a hundred times over, I suffer for the sake of peace and quiet, rather than gain an advantage; however much it may have cost the giver, he becomes my debtor as it costs me more.' The other reason was that his friends hardly ever reciprocated his gifts in the only currency he recognized and which he lavished so profusely on them out of the inexhaustible supply in his heart. 'My friends are always ready with money and services . . . the only thing they withhold is what would really gladden me. A gentle sentiment, a tender unburdening . . . It is as if they squander their fortune and their time on me so as not to have to draw on their hearts . . . What I demand of friendship is [not] . . . a thousand services I do not care for and which are a burden to me, because there is something patronising about them that displeases me . . . Only their caresses can make me support their benefactions.' And he had to have their caresses even when he was being tiresome; 'If I take criticism badly, fly into a temper without reason, I don't want my friend to reply in kind. I want him to caress me tenderly, to embrace me, in other words, to begin by appeasing me which will not take long . . . Then, when I am soothed and made tender and contrite, let him tell me where I was wrong and he will certainly not find me obdurate.'

Though he was 'born for friendship' it had to be friendship on his own terms. Those who ignored them, so he warned a fellow-countryman who had been so foolhardy as to send him a gift of some apricot jam made by his wife, did so at their own risk and peril. Out of 'respect' for the good lady, Jean-Jacques wrote, he would accept the jam. But he wanted to make it clear 'for the last time' that if there were ever to be a repetition of the offence, that would be the end of their relationship. He saw 'more vanity than true friendship' in such gifts and he was 'determined to shake off any yoke' people might try and impose on him'. 'Presents were an agreeable little friendly exchange when they are reciprocated. But to do so demands care and trouble from both sides and these are the bane of my life; I would rather have half an hour of idleness than all the jam in the world.'

Embarrassingly infantile as was his conception of friendship, it might perhaps have been acceptable if he had been willing to practise what he preached, ready to show the same loving tolerance to others that he demanded for himself. But of that there was no question: 'I demand a good deal more of my friends than they must demand of me', so he concluded the exposition of his ideas on this subject. And he felt entitled to do so for three reasons. 'Living the life of a solitary I am more sensitive than others. If I hurt a friend who lives in the Great World a thousand distractions will help him to forget it straight away ... But nothing comes to my aid if he grieves me, my heart has not a moment's respite.' Next there was his health: 'As a sick man I have a right to the indulgence humanity owes to a man who suffers.' And finally there was his poverty: 'I am poor and it seems to me that on this account too I merit special consideration.'

*

'How could it be,' Jean-Jacques asked at a time when he had long since alienated nearly all of his dearest friends, 'how could it be that someone so made for friendship as I am, should never have found ... a single true friend?' To the reader of his autobiography the answer might well seem only too obvious. The face looking out from the self-portrait that was meant to seduce posterity is so covered with warts and worse that the wonder is not so much its owner lost all his friends as that he ever had any to lose. It raises the question how such a man could have gained the affections of so generous, warm-hearted, good-natured a person as Diderot, so stern and upright a figure as Grimm, so attractive a character (by almost common consent) as Madame d'Epinay, so delightful a creature (by unanimous consent) as her sister-in-law (yet to appear on the scene) and many more, men as well as women.

There are a number of different explanations. One is that in real life he was by no means always as unlovable as would appear from his self-portrait. If he often seems so horrific it is partly because his autobiographical writings mostly date from a time when he lived in the nightmare world of the paranoid. Moreover, the whole of the picture he paints of himself in the *Confessions* and the *Dialogues* is distorted by a *vitium originis*. Telling the story of his life at an age—over fifty—when he had long since become persuaded that he was the embodiment of man's 'natural goodness', he automatically credits the young scamp whose raffish adventures he relates in the first half of the book, with the loud-voiced moral conscience that seems to make such a sanctimonious horror-comic of him but which he had not really begun to develop and cultivate at the time.

Another thing that helps to explain his ability to make friends—and to keep one like Diderot for sixteen years—is that some of his less attractive habits, like the whining and the boasting, were not nearly so off-putting to his contemporaries, who themselves were not disinclined to indulge in them. Take for instance the voluptuous wallowing in self-pity: 'It seemed to me fate owed me something she had never given me . . . This consciousness of my internal worth gave me a feeling of injustice which afforded me some form of compensation and caused me to weep tears that pleased me as they flowed.' It is not the sort of thing Kipling or Hemingway would have said nor would it have commended itself to their respective readerships. But in the Age of Sentiment such lachrymose literary larks were all the fashion. It had not been inaugurated by Jean-Jacques. As so often his contribution was to overdo it. Even so reserved a character as Grimm would exclaim, 'Oh, how I am to be pitied,' when bemoaning the absence of the woman he loved.

It was much the same with the boasting and the bragging. To be sure, Jean-Jacques's type of eloquence, unimpeded by a vigilant sense of humour, enabled him to produce examples outstripping the best efforts of his contemporaries. Describing how he had felt when writing his treatise on the *Origin of Inequality*, in which he 'demolished the petty lies of mankind', he recalled that, 'exalted by these sublime meditations, my soul soared towards the Divinity and from that height I looked down upon my fellow-men pursuing the blind paths of their prejudices'. More modestly, he was not quite sure, he only 'doubted whether any philosopher had ever meditated more profoundly' than he himself. But he had no doubt about the 'inimitable eloquence' of his writings in which he had set out his philosophy 'with such luminous clarity, such charm and such persuasive truthfulness as no wholesome heart could resist'.

If his readers and his friends did not seem to be unduly put off by this sort of thing it was partly because men of letters were like that, one just has to take their boastfulness into the bargain. According to the rather less tolerant Madame du Deffand, 'our writers make one sick with their conceit and their bragging'. Her adored Horace Walpole liked them no better: 'The authors one meets everywhere are worse than their books . . . generally their talk is solemn and pedantic.' That even the likeable, ebullient Diderot indulged in the same type of uninhibited self-praise as Jean-Jacques, if not to the same degree and in a rather more attractive context, is clear from his letters to his mistress. 'I came into the company here full of the tenderness you had inspired in me . . . It shone in my eyes and gave warmth to my speech . . . To the others I seemed extraordinary, inspired, god-like. Grimm was all eyes and ears for me. Everyone was amazed.' And Diderot, too, relied on posterity to make up for the injustice suffered at the hands of his contemporaries: 'O posterity, holy and sacred, support of the oppressed, thou who are just, incorruptible . . . do not abandon me!'

The age apparently saw nothing comical in self-praise. Not only writers but people in general were disarmingly ready to speak well of themselves, to acknowledge the pleasant facts revealed by the mirror or by the contemplation of their soul. Voltaire did not hesitate to say: 'I have accomplished more in my day than either Luther or Calvin.' When Boswell begged to be received by the Great Man Jean-Jacques had then become, he introduced himself as 'a man of incomparable merit'. In a pen-picture Madame d'Epinay gave of herself she claimed to be 'very well made . . . I have a noble, lively interesting look . . . I am not lacking in vivacity or courage . . . I have a tender sensitive heart'. Many of Jean-Jacques's correspondents appeared to be hardly less enamoured of themselves than the holder of the world-record himself. 'If you had known me you would have loved me,' wrote an English country gentleman after he had had to give up all hope of ever meeting the maestro. 'If I were ever to have the happiness,' wrote a German prince, 'of being able to show you my heart you would find that nothing that is not virtuous and humane holds any charm for it.' Yet another of the innumerable admirers who pestered him with their letters made the same point more simply: 'You will not regret becoming acquainted with me, for I am good.' But the most persistent of all approached the situation more tactfully, softening up her prey's defences by extolling his merits before starting on her own. 'You have the most beautiful genius in the world, I have the best heart in the world.' Considering the pride Jean-Jacques took in his own loving heart, the strategy was not without risk. And perhaps that was why she added other inducements: 'I have just the right amount of embonpoint . . . My face is a perfect oval and offers an agreeable profile . . . My nose . . .

though not aquiline . . . nonetheless helps to make me look like an eagle . . . my teeth are healthy, white and neat . . . My arms, hands, fingers and my nails, even, are as a painter would have dreamt them.' Alas, poor lady, in spite of all these alluring attributes including a *'regard accueillant'*, which it is tempting though anachronistic to translate as a 'come-hither look', she never really 'made it'.

*

It would, of course, be absurd to suggest that Jean-Jacques only succeeded in making a considerable number of worthy friends because they were just as vain as he was. There are many witnesses to the fact that he could and often did show himself so unlike his unappealing self-portrait as to be perfectly capable of inspiring affection. Even when his admirers had completed the fatal head-swelling process he was by no means always blowing his own trumpet. Hume, who only made his acquaintance at this time, positively raved about his charms: 'He is very amiable, always polite, sometimes gay, generally sociable . . . gentle, modest, affectionate, disinterested, exquisitely sensitive.' Another contemporary who knew him in his old age described him as being 'of a rare simplicity . . . with the ingenuousness, gaiety, goodness and especially shyness of childhood', though he added that this only applied when 'he was himself'. A third who saw a lot of him in Switzerland also found him 'gay in company, polite . . . amiable'. And a fourth even credited him, as had Hume, with that most becoming of virtues in which Jean-Jacques so often seemed sadly lacking: modesty. 'Who would believe,' he wrote in his memoirs, 'that this man, so notorious for his explosions of conceit, when he talks of nothing but the statues and altars he merited . . . was with us the simplest, gentlest and most modest of men . . . He argued without ever becoming acrimonious or obstinate . . . his tone was never cutting.'

Clearly, the author who so provoked his fellow-intellectuals with his abrasive insolence, appeared to be essentially soft-centred when away from his writing-desk. Nor does one have to take his contemporaries' authority for it that he did not always credit his works with 'inimitable eloquence' and other forms of perfection. His letters to his friends are full of intellectual self-criticism, dismissing his great novel as 'miserable, dull and boring', and the educational and religious treatise *Emile*, which did even more to win him his halo, as mere 'scribbling' and 'twaddle'. But, so contemptuous does he show himself of writings he always claimed to admire profoundly when referring to them in public, that one cannot but suspect there is an element of false modesty in it, showing off.

As Hume and others had remarked, there was a childlike quality about him which, 'combined with his extreme sensitiveness', so the Scotchman

said, 'made it easy for his friends to manage him'. He was soon to find out,
as had Diderot, Grimm, Madame d'Epinay and many others before him,
that the soft-centred, easily manageable child could turn very nasty
indeed and then became wholly unmanageable. But until they discovered
this aspect of his lifelong emotional immaturity, its disarming side, his
readiness to throw himself into the arms of anyone seeming to offer
friendship, had helped considerably to endear him to them. So did, as far
as the women were concerned, the strong feminine streak in his make-up.
To it he owed not only his supremacy in the art of gushing but also a
genuine interest in women and their concerns, in matters of domesticity
as well as of the heart, about both of which he would write at great length
in *Emile* and *La Nouvelle Héloise*. At the same time he was good-looking
enough—'very well proportioned', a fellow-writer said of him, 'dark-
complexioned, with a little red in his cheeks, a beautiful mouth, well-
made nose, a high forehead and eyes full of fire'—to appeal to his female
admirers as a man. Though according to some of his biographers he had
homosexual leanings, he showed no outward sign of it, sought the outlets
for what he calls his 'lascivious temperament' exclusively among members
of the opposite sex.

Shyness, finally, was another characteristic that helped him to win the
indulgent affection of those Parisians who first became his friends. In
those early days, when fame had not yet encouraged him to display his
native conceit, it remained in hiding, sought refuge behind the mask of
taciturn or sulky timidity. That it was only repressed is evident from the
observations of a neighbour who had seen a great deal of him when he
lived with 'Maman': 'he had an innate contempt for all men, a marked
tendency to condemn their faults and weaknesses and an unshakeable
suspicion of their integrity.' To vent such sentiments, as he did so freely
once he had despaired of making the grade as a composer and man of
letters and instead had set up as a moralist, was more than he dared risk.
And so, knowing also how ill-equipped he was for verbal duelling in the
elegant style of the salons, he was inclined to remain silent: 'I was
generally reckoned a complete cipher', he recalls, 'not only in Madame
d'Epinay's society but in Madame d'Holbach's too.'

Not that he always took a conversational back-seat in those days. Suitably provoked he could fascinate, not by the sparkle of his talk for he had
little humour and less wit, but by its fiery impetuosity. 'While his conversation was usually as commonplace as could be,' d'Holbach has
reported, 'it became sublime or mad the moment you contradicted him
which, I must confess, I have done too often, just to see this momentary
brilliance.' And another contemporary tells much the same tale: 'While
always modest, always withdrawn, retiring and only joining in the

conversation and the various amusements of society with infinite reserve, I have occasionally seen him full of charm. It was only a question of getting him interested.' But these occasions were the exceptions that confirmed the rule. Normally, so recalls one of his regular companions at d'Holbach's table, his attitude was one of 'timid politeness sometimes bordering on obsequiousness and humility'. He seemed so awkward and slow-witted that they could hardly see a potential rival in him. And so, though 'beneath his shrinking reserve' they saw 'mistrust', he was nevertheless 'welcomed' and, 'as he was known to be touchy, anxious, sensitive, easily wounded, he was handled with the sort of circumspection and delicacy as one might use with a pretty woman, capricious and vain'.

CHAPTER SEVEN

Typecast in the Wrong Role

'From that moment I was lost, all the rest of my life and of my misfortunes followed inevitably.'

THOUGH in his memoirs Jean-Jacques recalls half a dozen occasions
on which he 'became another man', the one that proved fatal, and from
which he himself dates the 'beginning of my chain of misfortunes', was
under the tree on the road to Vincennes where, in floods of tears, he
discovered his vocation as a moralist. It was fatal in that he was even less
well-equipped for this exacting role than for that of the ordinary man of
letters content with the company of the Muses rather than the Saints. The
self-effacement or self-transcendence, the single-mindedness and the
force of character required to achieve stardom in the part he had chosen,
were not among his strong points. Not that this prevented him from scor-
ing a huge, Europe-wide success. But the more firmly the outside world at
large pressed the halo on his brow, the more painful and the more mad-
deningly incomprehensible became the refusal of so many of his former
intimates to join in the hosannahs. In this sense it was indeed a fatal
turning he took on the road to Vincennes, the beginning of what is even
more searing than tragedy, even more effective in activating the bowels of
compassion: tragi-comedy.

Whose fault was it? Was he destined to play the part for which he was
so singularly ill-fitted? Was it an inner compulsion, a reawakening of his
native predilection for sermonizing (as a boy, he recalls, 'I fancied myself
as a preacher'), a resurgence of his moral nature triumphing over worldly
ambition? Or was it determination to 'excel, never mind in what', hunger
for fame, that made him renounce the World, raise his sights and go out
for the conquest of Heaven?

Whichever of these concurrent motives was mainly responsible for
landing him in the tragi-comedy, the ultimate responsibility may well
have lain with something outside of himself, that arbitrary power which
plays so large a part in every life and which is commonly called Fate or,
less pompously, hazard, simple and stupid accident, pure chance. Just as
a whim of the gods had equipped Helen of Troy with a face (and pre-

sumably a figure) that launched a thousand ships, so it had made Jean-Jacques's eye fall upon the question posed by the Academy of Dijon without which, who knows, he might never have 'beheld another universe, become another man'. Again, what was it but pure chance that he should be on the way to Diderot when the lightning struck or that Diderot encouraged him to 'give my ideas wing and compete for the prize' (or even—as has been maintained, though not plausibly—persuaded him to deal with the Academy's question in the provocative spirit of a latter-day Savonarola)? Since he was 'easy to manage by his friends', as Hume said, 'quickly tiring' of even the noblest impulses, as he said of himself, who can tell whether without Diderot's intervention he would have taken the 'dangerous corner' J. B. Priestley called those moments when one chance word or trifling action can alter the whole course of a man's life, set it irretrievably towards triumph or disaster. That is how, in retrospect, Jean-Jacques saw the meeting with Diderot: 'From that moment I was lost, all the rest of my life and of my misfortunes followed inevitably from that moment of madness.'

It is, of course, a typical bit of imaginative self-dramatization. For, however large a part the encounter may have played in making Jean-Jacques adopt the role for which he was so disastrously untalented, the help of two further outside factors were needed to make him persevere in it. One was the Academy of Dijon; had it not been for its decision to award his essay the prize he would probably never have opted for the career of holy man. For we have it on his own authority that by the time the award was announced he had forgotten all about it: 'I had given up thinking about my essay* . . . the news reawakened all the ideas . . . and set that first leavening of heroism and virtue working in my heart that my father, my native land and Plutarch [his favourite reading as a boy] had implanted there in my childhood'.

The other outside factor that helped him become a moralist was the public. It was its readiness to applaud him in this role that proved his undoing. Indeed, one could say that by its insistence on singling out his moral teaching from among his writings on a wide range of subjects, the public did more to cast him in the role of a saint than he had done himself.

---

* The passage affords one of the many examples of that forgetfulness of his and that extraordinary carelessness as a writer that does so much to help one separate the 'literary' chaff in his memoirs from the factual corn. For it corrects the impression created only four pages back where he would have one believe that the illumination on the road to Vincennes did for him what its counterpart did for St. Paul on the road to Damascus: 'all my little passions were stifled by an enthusiasm for truth, liberty and virtue' that 'worked in my heart for more than four or five years as intensely as perhaps it has ever worked in the heart of any man on earth'.

Like an actor condemned to a lifetime of playing the character in which he had first caught the public fancy, Jean-Jacques was typecast as the moralist he had been when he made his début. His sociological and political writings, like the *Discourse on the Origin of Inequality* and the *Social Contract*, were left largely unread by the public of his day. Of the former he says in his memoirs that 'nowhere in Europe did it find more than a few readers who understood it and not one of those chose to speak of it'. As regards the famous *Social Contract*, only one copy of it was found by the literary historian who examined five hundred private libraries of the period. And even when the Revolution seized on it and Marat read it to crowds in the street, it was not as a political theorist but as a moral hero that its author was worshipped.

*

To make a career of virtue would not have been such a tragic mistake, even for so weak a character as Jean-Jacques, had Providence compensated his weakness of will with meekness of heart, had the passions he was so unable to resist been those of the born saint, or even if he had come into the world no better and more self-effacing than one of 'nature's gentlemen'. But a witch rather than a fairy had stood at his cradle and cursed him not only with an ego of elephantine proportions and infantile ruthlessness, but also with what can only be called a nasty nature that showed the moment an ill wind blew. That was why one of the doctrines of the Age, that at first sight seemed tailored to the need of the weak-willed, proved of little help to Jean-Jacques. Its first tenet was that, Original Sin being a wicked myth invented to oppress men and Nature being wholly good, man could follow his inclinations without any prejudice to his virtue which, as Montesquieu had said, 'was not something that should cost us an effort'. All was for the best in the best of worlds because, according to the doctrine's second tenet, society had nothing to fear from legitimization of man's passions as nothing came more naturally to him, no stronger passion stirred in his bosom than the love of his neighbour. It was in this optimistic spirit that Diderot could exclaim: 'Enjoy without fear ... be happy ... Dare to liberate yourself from the yoke of religion ... Return to nature, she will comfort you, dispel from your heart all those fears that weigh on you.'

But Diderot, though no saint, was blessed with the kind of nature that could indeed indulge itself at no great cost to virtue; generous, warm-hearted, capable of remarkable unselfishness in the service of friends. What is more, he was no moral defeatist. As emotional as Jean-Jacques he did not invoke his sensibility as an excuse for self-indulgence. 'If ever Nature moulded a soul characterised by sensibility,' he said, 'it is mine'.

But to him a man who had 'received such a disposition from Nature will concern himself ceaselessly with trying to weaken it, dominate it, make himself master of his movements'. No wonder he eventually fell out with poor weak-willed Jean-Jacques for whom even the most trifling of social duties were 'unbearable', whose natural inclination was to suit himself at all times and at all costs, and whose nature was as sadly pockmarked by the lesser vices as the faces of so many of his contemporaries were disfigured by the disease itself. For Jean-Jacques the comforting assurance that virtue comes naturally and should require no effort was a bitter mockery. In love with virtue—or with the glory and self-esteem the reputation for virtue had brought him—but congenitally incapable of the effort required to overcome the huge obstacles that, in his case, stood in the way of practising it, he had to find a scapegoat on which to pin such conduct as might seem less than virtuous.

And here the doctrine of the Age did come to the rescue. For if, as nearly all his fellow-intellectuals had been arguing for thirty years, man was not born sinful, it followed that Jean-Jacques could not possibly be anything but good at heart and that somebody or something else must be at fault when, like all men, he added his mite to the wickedness of the world. What that something was he had first suggested when he had denounced the corrupting effect of civilization on morality. But if this were true, he, composer and playwright, had been doing quite a lot of corrupting himself. And so, giving the matter further thought, he decided that the real, the ultimate and the original corrupter was society itself; the noble savage had become ignoble, not so much because he had eaten from the tree of knowledge, but because the fruit he had garnered there had enabled him gradually to exchange the solitary existence of the brute for communal or social life with his fellow men. The ever-growing interdependence of men was what had made them wicked. He had 'fatal proofs' for the strange theory that men would have been far better off had they 'stuck to the . . . solitary manner of life which nature prescribed'; that 'men become unhappy and wicked in becoming sociable'; that 'so long as they undertook only what a single person could accomplish . . . they lived free, healthy, honest and happy lives'; that 'the bonds of servitude are formed by mutual dependence of men on one another'.

It was this stress on the moral advantage primitive man had derived from minimal contact with his fellows, that formed his personal, highly original contribution to the popular conception of the golden age. As regards the nature of the noble savages that had so happily disported themselves in this lost paradise, he had nothing very new to say, though, as usual, he offered a wide choice of assertions. He had not only shown (he was always 'showing' and 'proving') that 'man was naturally good . . .

bearing in his celestial and majestic simplicity the imprint of his divine
Author', but also—and more sensibly—that 'in a state of nature, having
no moral relations, he could neither be good nor bad' and was, in fact,
'brutish'. Under the weight of the many reasoned refutations of his prize-
winning essay, he had shifted his ground so as to declare the savage no
longer possessed of every virtue, but only of a nature capable in the right
environment of becoming virtuous. But when, several years later, he
became involved in an argument with the Archbishop of Paris he was as
defiant as ever in crediting Man with 'a heart that was originally free of all
perversity, loving justice and order, good by nature' though in his 'Profession of Faith', the religious treatise that belongs among his most
famous and influential writings and dates from the same period, he all
but debits him with Original Sin.

There was really only one constant in his attitude towards this question
of the nature of man that was such a burning issue in his time. Whether
Man was born sinful, as the Church taught, or innocent as Diderot and
his supporters maintained, Jean-Jacques never had any doubt that,
whatever might be the truth of the matter for the rest of mankind, his own
heart was free of all evil. It was, in fact, from its examination, rather than
from the study of savages, that he had derived the certainty that man was
born innocent: 'I have the happiness,' he said in one of his early writings,
'of *feeling* that man is naturally good.' And it was because in the course of
time he came to persuade himself that in no other heart had the original
goodness of man survived corruption by life in society or, rather, that no
other heart had been enabled to shake off its deleterious effects so
thoroughly, that he felt justified in calling himself 'on the whole the best
of men'. Nor was that all he claimed. In writing his memoirs he had also
performed the unique 'service' of giving his fellows a 'picture of natural
man'. He alone had been able to do this because he had led 'a solitary life,
had a taste for contemplation and rêverie and the habit of withdrawing
into himself . . . to seek there the original characteristics [of natural man]
that had been lost to the multitudes'. He had given the world his *Confessions* 'because it was necessary that a man should paint himself to show
us primitive man'*

Unfortunately nothing throws a clearer light on the real quality of his

* Masson suggests that perhaps he derived the idea of adopting the profession
of 'natural man' on reading a treatise published and much in vogue when he was
in his early twenties. Certainly the attitude he took up bears a remarkable resemblance to that glorified by its author: 'From time to time a privileged soul is
born to keep alive in the world the idea of what human nature was in all its purity.
Ha! How glorious it would be to have a soul such as to make people say one is
charged from On High with the task of showing by one's virtue how things were
in earliest times.'

soul than this very theory of life in society, according to which human interdependence is fatal to morality. For its premise is that one cannot come into close and regular contact with one's fellow-men without wanting to outshine them and hating them when one fails to do so. The human heart, he argued, cannot hope to remain free from such corruption when men are no longer 'content with their rustic huts' and no longer 'confine themselves to such arts as do not require the joint labour of several hands . . . but begin to stand in need of one another'. The more 'social relations develop, ideas progress . . . and society is drawn closer together by mutual needs', the more men begin to 'compare' themselves with others until they are 'filled only with the desire to rank everyone below themselves . . . And once the heart has taken on this habit of making comparisons it becomes impossible not to feel aversion for anything that surpasses us, lowers us, restricts us, anything that by simply being there prevents us from being everything'.

It is one of those avowals that do more to put Jean-Jacques in the dock, as the supreme egotist, than all his breast-beating *Confessions* put together, one of the many passages he wrote wholly unaware of the damaging self-revelation they contain. For though presented as an objective description and, indeed, condemnation of self-love observed in others, he is, of course, crediting them with the unique all-consuming solipsistic variety of it he felt in his own breast. Never did he speak a truer word than when he admitted in his *Dialogues* that his theory really formed part of his autobiographical writings: 'It may be false but at any rate in developing it he has painted such a characteristic, such a true picture of himself, that there is no mistaking it.' It is the picture of a man unable to conceive of fraternity, or even of friendly rivalry. A man unable to see human intercourse as anything but a source of hatred: 'Society necessarily leads men to hate one another as their interests clash.' A man so cynical as to doubt whether 'there was any well-to-do person whose greedy heirs and perhaps even his children were not secretly wishing for his death'. A man so filled with contempt for his fellows as to let it boil over in childish abuse, such as the statement that what 'the heart of every civilized man secretly aspired to' was to end up a career of brigandage 'by cutting every throat till he finds himself at last sole master of the world'.

But, of course, it is a picture only of the chameleon temporarily turned a fiery red, the timid, conservative, soft-centred Jean-Jacques sounding off on the soap-box. Stepped down from it, he himself supplies the obvious objection to his glorification of the mythical 'youth of the world' when men were not yet corrupted by interdependence; in such a state 'each one of us would have remained isolated, thought only of himself . . . there would have been neither kindness in our hearts nor morality in our actions.' Once having blown off a great deal of scalding steam, with his thesis that men 'become unhappy and wicked in becoming sociable,' he is quite willing to comfort his readers with the usual Sunday school homily. Just as the wicked arts and sciences should not, after all, be interfered with, so there was no need to go back to those 'rustic huts', where the noble savage lived. 'We should not think that there is neither virtue nor happiness for us and that Heaven has abandoned us . . . The art of living together can, as it develops, repair the evils which, in its initial stage, it caused to human nature.' All that was needed was to 'enlighten man's reason . . . with new knowledge, warm his heart with new feeling', as a result of which he and his fellows will live happily ever after, 'become good, virtuous and compassionate.'

*

There had been a time when, 'intoxicated with virtue', he had felt called upon to undertake this great task himself, 'the most serviceable to virtue ever conceived by mortal man'. But after 'nearly six years' at it he had come to the conclusion that he had been 'deluded in thinking I was born to destroy . . . all the foolishness and the error in the doctrines of our sages and the misery of our social order', and that 'no state of being could be more contrary to my true nature'. It sounds as if he had suffered an attack of modesty, realized his unfitness for the role of moral teacher. But it was nothing of the sort. What he had recognized as being contrary to his true nature were those biting sarcasms, the sharp tongue. His conviction that he was 'doomed to be an example to all' remained as strong as ever, indeed, gradually grew into a vision of himself as a new Messiah. Only, having 'felt' that his heart was the best proof of man's natural goodness, intellectual bitchiness, such as he had practised with such success in the first flush of glory, could not long seem the most appropriate or effective way of helping his fellow-men to disinter the goodness in their own corrupted hearts. If he were to remain true to his vocation as an example, he would clearly have to find or create conditions more conducive to the re-emergence of the natural man within him, than were to be found in the salons of Paris. And therein lay yet another reason for his decision to become a drop-out.

But perhaps an equally pressing one was that for a moralist so determined to suit himself, so unable to resist the inclinations of a far from helpful heart, the less he exposed himself to the demands of life in society, the more his environment could be made to approximate that of the noble savage, free 'to think only of himself', the better it would be. In this sense the flight from Paris was as much an admission of moral defeat as of social failure. Jean-Jacques himself knew it perfectly well. For if there was one thing he had no illusions about, it was his weakness of will. The ordeals of his life had enabled him to display 'every virtue except strength of character'. He was 'always wavering between weakness and courage, self-indulgence and virtue'. He was 'the slave of his inclinations, guided only by his heart, never his duty'. He was 'incapable of mastering his passions'. Of course, none of this made him any less 'the best of men', as 'nature had made him good' and his heart was as incapable of 'vile inclinations' as his will of mastering them. That was why it did not matter that 'the most sublime of virtues, forgiveness of enemies' was way beyond his strength; 'his peaceful, loving nature' had never had to 'fight the temptation to hate'. He was not virtuous 'because he had no need to be'.

Even so, to make assurance doubly sure, he 'preferred to flee from temptation rather than to have to resist it'. And that meant avoiding 'the tumult of society', with the 'cruel moral necessity' it so often imposed on its members 'to do the opposite of what they want'. His 'great moral maxim' was to avoid being confronted with 'difficult duties . . . avoid situations in which our duties are opposed to our interests' and in which he would, therefore, have to fight 'dangerous battles' with himself. 'If others think themselves too strong, too virtuous, to fear such conflicts, good luck to them. But do not let us blame poor Jean-Jacques for not daring to trust his strength.' As one of his biographers has said, his 'great moral maxim' really meant replacing the Christian injunction, 'Love thy neighbour as thyself', by, 'Avoid your neighbour like the plague.' And, indeed, Jean-Jacques himself admits it; to live by his maxim in all its fullness 'one must withdraw from society altogether.'

If only he had done so, become a true hermit instead of a guest at the Hermitage, he would have saved himself a great deal of misery. As it was, he had escaped from the Parisian society that had put such a strain on his moral resources, only to find himself trapped in the even greater 'human interdependence' of country life, with a friend and benefactress whose demands on his time and heart soon became more than he had bargained for. 'I found that courtesies which at first had cost me nothing but which I had not reckoned on, very much upset my other activities . . . She was very fond of her friends . . . and since she spared neither time nor trouble on their behalf she certainly deserved some attention in return. Hitherto I had performed that duty without thinking of it as such. But now I realised I had hung a chain around my neck.' What made matters worse was that a stratagem he had employed to lighten the chain's weight had badly misfired. Pleading his dislike of parties, he had asked to be excused whenever she had more than a very few friends at the château. But 'she took advantage of this to make me a proposition which appeared to be in my favour but was even more favourable to her; that was to send me a message whenever she was alone or nearly so. I fell in with this idea without seeing to what I was agreeing'; which was, of course, that 'I no longer called on her at my convenience but at hers'.

Though he claims he had 'submitted to this yoke with fairly good grace for one who so loathes dependence', a letter he wrote to a Swiss friend shows he was in fact contemplating a quiet get-away. 'I might fold my tents and steal away in the night . . . for that is the only way of getting out of here . . . I have not said anything about it . . . to our friend. You must keep it a secret so don't write to me care of her, just address your letter to the Hermitage near Montmorency.' As already indicated the warm, indeed ecstatic feelings with which his hostess had inspired him only eight weeks earlier, when she had made him a present of her under-petticoat, as well as some salt, were only dreamt up when he wrote his memoirs. For far from bearing the watermarks of grateful tears he then claimed to have shed, his thank-you letter was in the style he usually employed when reprimanding friends for their selfishness in inflicting presents on him: 'The underpetticoat is one thing, but, really, the salt! . . . you will end up by making me cross . . . have not you done enough for yourself? Now do something for me and let me love you in my own way.'

Though Jean-Jacques's hagiographers, taking their cue from him, make much of his great moral progress, from the early days when he lied and stole and bore false witness, to the saintliness of his mature age, the handling of his relations with Madame d'Epinay is by no means the only example of a duplicity he never conquered for the simple reason that he never even recognized it as a blemish on his 'natural goodness'. Thus he relates, not as a confession but rather as something doing credit to his sage prudence, how in the one and only great love-affair of his life he had 'taken the precaution' of making his love letters so explicit that their recipient could not possibly use them to compromise him without com-promising herself. (It recalls the comment of one of his companions at Baron d'Holbach's table that Jean-Jacques 'always remained on the reserve, treating his friends as future enemies'.) Thus too, he tells with relish, as if it were an anecdote reflecting no discredit on him, of the tactics with which he had tried to regain the favours of a duchess with whom he had been 'rapidly losing ground' owing to a young priest who had 'utterly routed me in her affection'. As the latter now had her ear it was obviously advisable to 'do something to win his friendship'. So when he painted a 'horrible portrait' of the duchess which displeased her because it was indeed 'not at all like her . . . I like a fool and a liar said it was a good likeness. I wanted to please the priest. But it did not please the lady who noted it against me . . . my clumsy attempts to win him, finally undid me with the duchess. I learned from this ill-success not to try and play the flatterer again since I had no talent for it'. At the age of fifty it is still the same Jean-Jacques who as a young man had made a 'delightful journey' with a friend who 'so captivated me that I could not do without him'. But as he feared this friend would not be welcome at 'Maman's' whence he was returning for the food and shelter he required, he started shaking him off in good time: 'I prepared him for the separation by treating him with some coldness on the last day.'

It would be comical if it were not so sad; the man who devoted the last ten years of his life almost exclusively to the study of himself, writing about very little else, never even began to see himself as he really was. Criticizing his fellow-Genevans—'vanity is their dominant vice, it shows through everything all the more easily as it is clumsy'—he appears to be wholly unaware he is describing himself. The man who sought the honour which he felt posterity owed him, by painting his self-portrait 'warts and all', as no one had ever done before, was as blind as a bat to the ugly sores he revealed, far more disfiguring than the warts to which he so proudly admits. The writer who believed himself the embodiment, indeed the last remaining example of the natural goodness of man, remained wholly unaware of the kind of nature he had been cursed with. Though towards the end of his life he did recognize its morally debilitating weakness and though there are one or two fleeting moments when he seemed to admit to haughty conceit and degrading distrust, there are infinitely more when he shows himself as blissfully unaware of their dominating presence in his make-up as of the craftiness and the many other unappealing characteristics he unwittingly paints into his self-portrait. As Hume said, once his honeymoon with Jean-Jacques had ended in the usual bitter disillusionment, 'no one knew himself less'. Just as he was convinced that his heart was 'transparent as crystal', and that no one had 'such a horror of dissimulation', so he never stopped telling the world and himself that his heart was incapable of hatred and vindictiveness.

'No hateful, envious or vindictive sentiment,' he wrote to a friend, 'had ever approached my heart,' and again, to another: 'Never have I known the hateful passions, never did jealousy, wickedness, vengeance enter my heart. I get carried away by anger sometimes but am never crafty, never bear grudges.' 'Of all the Christian virtues,' he told a third, 'none costs me less effort than forgetfulness of injuries.' He does not hate, he says in the last of his autobiographical writings, 'because I would not know how to . . . and I feel too superior to hate . . . I love myself too much to hate anybody'. He had 'fled the society of men,' he wrote in the *Dialogues*, 'because they merited his hatred and he was made to love men . . . his heart did not know hatred,' which, he had already stressed in the *Confessions*, 'had never gained a foothold in it'. One of his 'happy characteristics', so one learns there, was that he had 'never known that vindictive feeling that is kept boiling in a resentful heart by the continual memory of insults received'.

All this and more in books, many pages of which are sizzling with hatred and curdling with vindictiveness. Pages not so much looking back in anger as in rancour, detailing the misdeeds and the insults of his diplomatic employer of twenty-five years ago. Pages in which he admits that 'I cannot help hating Grimm', just as he told Voltaire in a letter, 'I hate you,' and a friend that, 'I would hate him more if I despised him less.' Pages, no less than ten of them, filled with such petty grudges and venomous tittle-tattle about a former friend that they inspire only pity for their author, pity tinged with that mixture of revulsion and vicarious shame one is apt to feel when some wretchedly ugly creature, believing itself unobserved, allows its deformities to be seen in all their sorry nakedness. 'When Grimm arrived,' so he wrote in the *Confessions* about one of his visits to the château of Madame d'Epinay, 'he succeeded in making my stay unbearable by such conceited behaviour as I had never seen in anyone before . . . I was moved from the favourite room I occupied . . . and it was got ready for Grimm . . . He scarcely condescended to return my bow . . . He took precedence everywhere and always seized the best place without paying any attention to me . . . although I was his senior and in poor health and although I was an older friend of the house than he, having in fact introduced him there whereas, as the lady's favourite, he should really have done me the honours . . . I lent him money and he never lent me any . . . I had introduced him to all my friends and he had never introduced me to any of his . . . He had an upstart's conceit . . . He looked on me as a nonentity . . . He made himself absurd by his continuous insolence . . . He proceeded to humiliate me by proving how much our common friends preferred him to me . . . He was as fatuous as he was vain, with his huge, dull eyes and his flabby face. He fancied himself with the ladies . . . Everyone knew that he made up . . . I found some pots of cosmetic on his dressing-table . . . and discovered him brushing his nails with a little brush . . . I concluded that a man who spends two hours every morning polishing his nails, may well spend a few moments filling the wrinkles in his skin with make-up.' And so on, *ad nauseam*.

To get the full flavour of the pettiness, the spitefulness, the sheer nastiness, one has to read every line of these pages, surely the most shaming ever to form part of a literary work that was to become a seminal

classic. Nor are they the only ones pervaded by this spirit. There is hardly
a chapter untainted by it. The more attentively one reads and re-reads,
the deeper one delves into this work, the more layers of ignominy become
apparent. And on top of that, most pitiful of all because written when his
paranoia had allowed his hatred to luxuriate out of all control, there is that
bizarre document the *Dialogues*, a whole book devoted to accusing '*ces
messieurs*' as he invariably calls his enemies, of every conceivable and
inconceivable villainy devised to make him the 'unhappiest of mortals',
'bury him alive', 'drive him to suicide', etc., etc. Filling page after page
with lurid descriptions of the pleasure they take in 'watching him suffer
and seeking out a corner in his ravaged heart where they have not yet
plunged their dagger in', he remains as unaware as ever of the quality of
heart he reveals in doing so. Once again it would be comical if it were not
tragic; in the very process of pouring out the vials of his hatred for '*ces
messieurs*', held capable of the most diabolical 'cruelty and duplicity', he
congratulates himself on his heart which is 'hurt even more by the
spectacle of their hatred than by its effects'.

*

Small wonder that a man in so many ways so ungifted for sainthood
suffered every kind of frustration and discomfiture, ever since that
unhappy moment on the road to Vincennes when he discovered his
vocation for it. And yet, in a way his very lack of talent for the career he
then adopted helped him to make a success of it. Hopelessly miscast in
the role which an inextricable interlacement of ambition, hurt pride,
Calvinist conscience, hazard and the whims of fashion had forced upon
him, he amassed a capital of suffering that needed only proper handling to
be accepted by the outside world as a valid claim to martyrdom. And
proper handling, in the sense of advertising, it certainly got. Just as he
had first won Madame d'Epinay's heart with the moving story of his
sufferings at the hands of his early employers, so the sufferings she and
Grimm and Diderot inflicted on him when, having found him less than
saintly, they broke off relations, were equally turned to good account.
Together with the bouts of ill-health—at times a cause of real misery, as
doubtless was the 'cooling off' of so many of his friends—the wicked
calumny indulged in by rivals like Voltaire and the persecution by one
established authority after another, it all added up to a respectable amount
of unhappiness. It needed only Jean-Jacques's powerful pen—never more
eloquent than when diluting its ink and blotting the paper with the tears
of self-pity—plus his lawyer's talent for exculpating himself from any and
all responsibility for his misfortunes, to present them as an unanswerable
case for the award of the halo. 'I have borne unhappiness,' he said in a

letter typical of the theme song of his later days, 'now I must learn to bear the derision, contempt, obloquy that are the normal lot of the virtuous among the wicked . . . I hope that one day people will see what I really was from what I have learnt to suffer.'

CHAPTER EIGHT

Don Juan Jacques

'I am sorry to show so many girls in love with me.'

JEAN-JACQUES had reached the age of forty-four, when he fell victim to what is vulgarly known as the seven-year itch, though in his case this distressing complaint did not manifest itself until nearly twice the period had elapsed since he had found an outlet for his ardent and lascivious temperament in the arms of Thérèse. Hence no doubt the intensity of the attack and the disastrous nature of the train of events it set in motion. To see them in proper perspective, however, the patient's case-history must first be sketched in. Unfortunately the only source of information about his earlier sex-life, the *Confessions*, is of doubtful value. A hotchpotch of lyrical passages of evident sincerity and admirable artistry, out-pourings of equally evident malevolence, breast-beatings of gorilla-like absurdity and moral posturings of pitiful transparency, defiantly outspoken on some subjects, prudently silent on others, his autobiography bears all the marks of the mixed motives that drove Jean-Jacques to compose this work, like the curate's egg, very good in parts and appalling in the rest.

One of these motives, the predominant one according to the author himself, was to polish his public image. By the time he had set to work on the *Confessions* he had made so many enemies, some of whom like Voltaire were not above calumny while others were suspect of betraying guilty secrets entrusted to them when they were still friends, that he had good reason to embark on a public relations campaign, to write a book which, he said, was 'meant only for his personal defence'. Hence the prudent silences and the distortions as well as the flatulent self-praise. A second motive had doubtless been the sheer pleasure a natural writer obtains from practising his skill on the evocation of the happy years of his youth. Hence the lyrical passages that constitute his foremost claim to a place in the history of literature. A third motive was derived from the strange fancy, gradually grown into an *idée fixe*, that his heart was the repository of man's natural goodness and that he only need exhibit it to enable his fellow men to see both how wicked they were by comparison and how good and happy they could become if, like him, they turned their back on society with all its corrupting conventions and works: 'I can see a new service I can render my fellow men; offer them a faithful picture of one of them so they can learn to see themselves for what they are.' He himself had got rid of 'the prejudices and artificial passions that blind other men's eyes to the qualities of natural man'. Those qualities 'were still present at the bottom of their hearts but they would never show themselves again if he had not revealed them'.

Hence the defiant outspokenness. But this moral exhibitionism to which we owe what he himself calls 'the indecent and puerile details' of his sex-life, as well as the revelations of his early misdemeanours, was motivated by other things besides his desire to 'render a new service to mankind'. If he let his breeches as well as his hair down, flouted the conventions of an Age which had not yet advanced to our enlightened recognition that sexual reticence is dreadfully philistine and petit-bourgeois, it was also owing to that irrepressible tendency to show off, to shock, to be different, which he had displayed from the beginning and to which he had admitted when he said that he would rather be forgotten by the whole human race than to be thought an ordinary man. If he endangered the success of his public relations campaign by revealing discreditable episodes in his life that were grist to the mill of his enemies, it was again partly from that vanity which the great Tory orator Edmund Burke, in a magisterial denunciation of Jean-Jacques, was to characterize so pointedly as 'the worst of vices and the occasional mimic of them all. It makes the whole man false . . . his best qualities are poisoned or perverted by it and operate exactly as the worst . . . It is omnivorous . . . it is fond even to talk of its own faults and vices as what will excite surprise and draw attention and what will pass as at worst for openness and candour.'

In actual fact, his frankness was by no means as incompatible with the primary aim of the *Confessions* as one might have thought. For one thing it was selective frankness largely limited to the public revelation of peccadilloes which were already known to his enemies (and which, he was always careful to explain, were 'not really his fault'). For another— as these enemies were not slow to point out—the more sins he confessed the more credence he could hope to gain for the virtues he laid claim to in such abundant measure. Finally, self-accusations would also help to legitimize and validate the charges he brought against others. It was a tactic which Diderot denounced as that of someone who 'paints himself in odious colours to give his unjust and cruel imputations a semblance of verisimilitude'.

*

Enough has been said to show that the *Confessions*, which alone throw some light on his amorous adventures, can hardly be regarded as a reliable source of information, to say nothing of their incoherence, the chaotic disorder and contradictions of the narrative. Thus within the space of five pages young Jean-Jacques appears as an adolescent of robust, undiscriminating appetite but also as an innocent abroad who, after three years spent in the presumably none too mealy-mouthed company of his fellow-apprentices, was still wholly ignorant of the facts of life. Both the experiences he relates date from the few weeks spent in a hospice at Turin, where at the age of sixteen he was being prepared for the abjuration of his native Calvinist faith that had become too costly an encumbrance when he had fled from Protestant Geneva to seek his fortune in Catholic Savoy. The 'sister-converts' he met there were 'the greatest set of sluttish, abandoned whores that had ever contaminated the Lord's sheepfold'. But on the old principle of any port in a storm, he longed to conquer one of these deplorable creatures. Or so one must infer from the regret he expresses at his failure to make any progress with her: 'One of them struck me as pretty . . . and she had a roving eye that occasionally caught mine. This inspired me with some desire to make her acquaintance. But . . . it was absolutely impossible for me to approach her, so rigorously was she guarded by the pious missioner who worked at her conversion.' Perhaps it was as well. For the encounter would hardly have proved a success if, in fact, he was still as painfully innocent as would appear from the story he tells of another experience, this time with a brother-convert. 'He frequently kissed me with an ardour which I found most displeasing . . . he wanted to come into my bed . . . and finally took the most revolting liberties and, by guiding my hand, tried to make me take the same liberties with him.' Though Jean-Jacques refused to co-operate, he was not 'indignant or angry for I had not the slightest idea what it was all about'. And when the brother-convert achieved his pleasure nonetheless, his unwilling partner still 'could not understand what was the matter with the poor fellow; I thought he was having a fit of epilepsy or some other seizure even more terrible'.

As he felt obliged to describe its symptoms in lurid detail, it is hardly to be wondered at that he asked the select audiences to which he read the *Confessions* 'to remember that one cannot take confession without exposing oneself to the inconveniences that are inseparable from this austere and sublime employ and that it was for their hearts to purify their ears'. He had all the more reason to do so as the assembled company, on one occasion men of letters, on another grandees and their ladies, also had to listen to a lengthy exposition of his infantile eroticism 'aroused by a childish chastisement received at the age of eight at the hands of a thirty-year-old woman', the parson's sister who was looking after him at the time. It was lengthy because to be interesting, to fit into the dramatic story of the 'unparalleled' life presented by the world-famous, nearly sexagenarian Jean-Jacques, the spanking of the young boy's bare bottom had, of course, to 'determine my tastes, my desires, my passions, my very self, for the rest of my existence'. And to win his listeners' compassion 'these strange tastes which persisted with a depraved and insane intensity' had, equally inevitably, to be a source of pitiful unhappiness; 'as I never dared to reveal my strange taste I have spent my days in silent longing in the presence of those I loved most.' The nearest he ever came to achieving the 'kind of pleasure I desire, to me the most delectable of pleasures', was 'to fall on my knees before a masterful mistress, obey her commands, beg her forgiveness'.

But if this picture of a sex-starved masochist, suffering a life-long martyrdom to timidity, drew a compassionate tear from his audience, he soon gave it cause to cheer up again when he proudly related an amorous exploit so fulfilling—apparently without any adventitious aids—that it nearly killed him. It was not a case of a delayed-action bomb exploding. Quite the contrary, for though he claims that, 'with sensuality burning in my blood almost from birth, I kept myself pure and unsullied . . . even after the age of puberty', his chastity had not been of the self-denying kind. He had long since learned 'that dangerous means of cheating nature which leads young men of my temperament to various kinds of excesses that eventually imperil their health, their strength and sometimes their lives'. Indeed, he became so addicted to masturbation that he claims to have risked his life with this type of erotic activity; 'seduced by the vice which shame and timidity find so convenient . . . I set about destroying my sturdy constitution.' (Perhaps it was an endeavour to make up for lost time since, judging by his faulty diagnosis of epilepsy at the age of sixteen, he appears to have discovered this means of cheating nature rather later than most.)

It was just as well, therefore, that at the age of twenty-one he was initiated into the mysteries of adult sex by 'Maman'. He had come to address her in this filial fashion partly because it was quite usual in his day for members of the household to honour its mistress with this name—Voltaire called his niece 'Maman' when she kept house for him—but also because for all of five years she had indeed been like a mother to him, giving him affection as well as board and lodging. She had taken him under her ample wing—ample because according to a friend and neighbour she had '*beaucoup, beaucoup d'embonpoint*'—when he was a sixteen-year-old vagrant freshly escaped from the harsh taskmaster to whom he had been apprenticed in Geneva. Whether it was out of the kindness of her heart, or because it was part of her function to catch Protestant souls for conversion to the true faith, or because she fancied him as a future lover, or because she had just grown fond of him—and most likely all these motives played their part—she kept him on and off for some ten years. It was generous indeed as, being a bit of a gambler fancying herself as a business-woman, she was far from rich and Jean-Jacques, unable or unwilling to hold down any of the jobs she found for him, made very little contribution to her household expenses. There came a time, however, when she decided he should make another kind of contribution. At any rate, that is what Jean-Jacques, never the most chivalrous of men and not always the most truthful, would have one believe. According to him, the only witness whose evidence is on record, she was prone to sleeping around; 'She conferred her favours lavishly; not,' he generously adds, 'not that she was a whore, she did not sell them.' She only did it 'to give pleasure to those she loved', and he saw nothing wrong in that; 'she could have slept with twenty men every day with a clear conscience.' Jean-Jacques 'knew her chaste heart and icy disposition too well to believe for a moment that the pleasure of the senses had any part in the surrender of herself.' And he knew it because when he 'clasped her rapturously in his arms' she remained 'tranquil . . . she neither received sexual pleasure nor knew the remorse that follows'; why, 'she could even interrupt her talk, if need be, for the act itself and then resume it with the same serenity as before'.

A less innocent or more modest lover observing these transports of tranquillity might have felt a twinge of anxiety, wondering whether perhaps his amatory techniques were at fault. And Jean-Jacques had all the more reason to do so as his temperament was so 'ardent and lascivious' as to render him all but sexually incontinent. Describing his experiences on the way to keeping amorous trysts with a lady he fancied when he was in his middle forties, he confessed that 'the mere idea of some slight favour awaiting me from the woman I loved, so heated my blood that I could not even make the short journey to her side with impunity'. But if the awful thought that he might have failed 'Maman' ever crossed his mind, there is no trace of it in his account of life with her. He never wondered why, if she were really so frigid, she should have invited him into her bed. It was all quite simple, he was 'perfectly certain' that she had done so only out of the goodness of her heart, because of her 'anxiety to preserve me entire for myself and my duties', because she 'saw that to save me from the dangers of my youth it was time to treat me like a man', and because she did not think it right 'that another woman should undertake the instruction of her pupil'.

It was *magnifique*. But of course, it was not *l'amour* as he had dreamt it.

For one thing she had gone about the whole business in a very unromantic manner, making her proposals in tones 'better calculated to instruct than seduce . . . laying down conditions [which, alas, he does not reveal] . . . and giving me eight days to consider them'. She had also made it clear that he would have to share her bed with the gardener-cum-man-of-affairs who was already installed there, which was 'very painful . . . really not worthy of either of us'. Finally and most awkward, though 'thirsting for a woman's love and burning with the desire to be a man', he did not really want to go to bed with his 'Maman'. Perhaps it was partly because she was so 'very, very obese' and, according to the same source, 'too busty', though she made up for these imperfections with her 'complexion of lilies and roses, her charming laugh, her vivacity and cultivated spirit'. But 'extremely seductive' as all these attributes made her, Jean-Jacques's withers, or rather his loins, remained unwrung. Not that he had not learnt to love her passionately: 'One day at table'—it was at the time when he had not yet been called up for amorous duty—'just as she had put some food in her mouth I cried out that I had seen a hair on it. She spat the morsel back on her plate whereupon I seized it greedily and swallowed it. In a word, there was but one difference between myself and the most passionate lover. But that difference was an essential one. My glances never went wandering indiscreetly beneath her blouse, though an ill-concealed plumpness in that region might well have attracted them. I felt neither emotion nor desire in her presence . . . By calling her Maman and treating her with the familiarity of a son I had grown to look upon myself as such, and I think that is the real cause of my lack of eagerness to possess her . . .'

What do do? He 'would have liked to have said: "No, Maman, it is not necessary, I can look after myself without that" ' (without her preserving him for his duties by taking him to bed). 'But I dared not because it was not the sort of thing one can say.' Naïve as he might be, he knew that hell hath no fury . . . But apart from the danger that 'Maman's' fury might lead to his dismissal from under her roof—had her 'conditions' perhaps taken the form of an ultimatum?—there was also another reason why he felt compelled to accept them. It would save a lot of trouble; 'without desiring to possess her I was glad to be robbed of the desire to possess other women.' And so, at the end of the eight days, 'which I could have wished centuries', the initiation at last took place. Needless to say, it was not an unmitigated success, though what took the bloom off the occasion were not those 'strange tastes' that were supposed to have ruined his sex life but about which we hear no more, not another word. By his own account it was a very natural sentiment that made him 'wet her bosom with my tears . . .; I felt as if I had committed incest'.

Even so, matters did not really turn out too badly. For one thing he soon learned the tricks of the gigolo-trade (a harsh word to use, too harsh if one gives him credit, as one most likely should, for mixed motives in accepting to assist the gardener in 'Maman's' bed.)* Wanting a 'mistress' but only having a 'tender mother and dear friend' to make love to, he solved the problem in the time-honoured manner of reluctant lovers: 'in my imagination I put a mistress in Maman's place endowing her with a thousand shapes', otherwise 'I should have had no physical pleasure'. As for the painful problem of having to share her with the gardener, this, too, found a solution. Contrary to what he might have feared, 'Maman' was not one for experiments *à trois*. In fact, he was not sure whether the gardener ever found out he had acquired a sleeping partner. And he was such a good fellow that, even if he had, it would not have mattered: 'he was so mature and so grave that he almost looked on us as two children who deserved indulgence and we both looked on him as a man worthy of respect whose esteem we must cultivate.' So a good time was had by all; 'how often Maman melted our hearts and caused us to embrace in tears telling us that we were both necessary to her life's happiness . . . Between the three of us was established a bond perhaps unique on this earth . . . Our habit of living together to the exclusion of the outer world, became so strong that if one of the three was missing from a meal or a fourth person joined us, everything was spoiled; and in spite of our private relationships even our tête-à-têtes were less delightful than our being all three together'. Moreover, even if any of Jean-Jacques's original distaste for sharing 'Maman's' favours remained, it was soon eliminated when the gardener moved to a less public resting place than 'Maman's' bed had become: his coffin.

*

Reading the pages describing his love-life with 'Maman' one is somehow reminded of that other immortal classic of unconscious humour, *The Young Visiters* by the nine-year-old Daisy Ashford. And it is the same when he tells of his experiments with the frail sisterhood. As he had

* However this may be, a letter he wrote to his father showed that at the age of twenty-three Jean-Jacques combined an eye for the main chance with a compulsive desire to wrap up its discoveries in thick layers of moral cottonwool. Asked how he proposed to make his living he replied that he was going to give 'Maman' proof of his gratitude for all she had done for him, by asking her to let him stay for life, 'showing how attached he had become'. That was 'not a frivolous manner of demonstrating my gratitude . . . and that solves all problems, I shall be set up for good in the happiest and most solid way, because apart from the advantages I will gain from it, the arrangement will be wholly based on goodness and virtue'.

'always had a horror of prostitutes' there were—or so he claims—only four such experiments in his life, the first two when he was thirty-one, in Venice, which 'is not the sort of town in which a man abstains from women'. As usual, it was somebody else's fault, his friends', that he lapsed from virtue; 'against my inclinations, my feelings, my reason and my will, I allowed them to drag me off' to visit a 'very good-looking' lady of the town. Even then his virtue would have survived unscathed had it not been for the lady's insistence and his own obliging nature. 'As her beauty was not of the kind that pleased me . . . I sent for sorbets, asked her to sing and, after half an hour, placed a ducat on the table preparing to leave.' But he had reckoned without her professional sense of honour; 'she was so strangely scrupulous that she would not accept money she had not earned and I was so strangely stupid as to give in to her scruple.'

The second encounter (whose tale he introduces with the tantalizing but mysterious promise that it 'plainly reveals my character, will give a complete knowledge of Jean-Jacques Rousseau') was even less rewarding, ending as badly as it had started. That was on board a warship where he and a diplomat-friend had been invited to dine and he had been 'sulking like a child' because the captain had not greeted their arrival with a gun-salute; 'I felt that I had earned some mark of consideration . . . and although the dinner was very good . . . I sat down in a bad humour, ate little and spoke even less.' However, things cheered up after dinner when a gondola came alongside disembarking 'a dazzling young person . . . more enticing than the houris of paradise'. She had no sooner set eyes upon him than 'she threw herself into my arms, put her lips to mine and squeezed me till I nearly choked to death . . . Passion overcame me so quickly, in spite of the spectators, that the lady herself had to restrain me'. So an assignation was made for the next day. But then things went badly wrong. On entering her room he had felt he was seeing 'the divinity in person'. And then suddenly, just as he was to 'pluck the fruit', his blood froze; 'my legs trembled, I sat down on the point of fainting and wept like a child.' A terrible question had struck him: How could it be that this divine person, who seemed 'perfect in mind as well as body, not only beautiful but also generous and good, was . . . a wretched street-walker on sale to the world?' There must be something wrong with her, 'a secret flaw that makes her repulsive to those who should be quarrelling for possession of her'.

It was these 'well-timed reflections' that had made him 'burst into tears'. However, ladies of the town have a way of coping with such tantrums; 'it was not difficult for her to dispel my melancholy.' And so, dry- and hungry-eyed again, he was on the point of 'sinking upon a breast that seemed about to suffer a man's lips and hand for the first time', when he suddenly discovered the secret flaw: 'I perceived that she had a malformed nipple,* I beat my brow, looked harder and made certain this nipple did not match the other.' Once having verified that his observations were scientifically correct, it was clearly the moment for some more well-timed reflections; 'I started wondering about the reason for this malformation . . . I was struck by the thought that it resulted from some remarkable imperfection of Nature, and after turning the idea over in my head I saw clear as daylight that I held in my arms some kind of monster rejected by Nature, man and love.' He made only one mistake: 'I carried my stupidity so far as to speak to her about the malformed nipple.' That had been a mistake because he was soon ready again to overlook the one Nature had made. But by then its victim had had enough. 'Leave the ladies alone and go and study mathematics,' she had said 'with cold scorn'. Nor did she keep the promise of another meeting he had nonetheless managed to extort from her. When 'conscious of my strange behaviour and regretting the ill-use I had made of those moments which could have been the sweetest of my life . . . I ran, I flew to her at the appointed hour', she had flown, too, and he was plunged into an 'insane regret' (he was never one for half measures when it came to feelings) 'that has never left me'.

The third experiment also came to nought. He and 'an inseparable friend' had decided to provide for their sex-life at an economic rate by 'an arrangement which is not rare in Venice', pooling resources to procure the services of a lady who would do for both. 'The problem was to find a safe one.' For he was mortally afraid—with good reason in those pre-penicillin days—of the pox, as venereal disease was then called. And he 'could not imagine that anyone could leave the embraces of a padoana (whore) unscathed'—which, it has been suggested, may have been the real subject of those 'well-timed reflections' that on the earlier occasion suddenly made the deathly cold flow through his veins. However, this problem was solved by his friend who made 'such thorough investigations that he unearthed a little girl of eleven or twelve whose wretched mother wanted to sell'. The arrangements they made for her future favours, including the provision of a spinet and singing lessons, 'cost us barely two sequins a month each, and saved us more in other expenses, but as we had to wait till she was mature we had to sow a great deal before we could reap'. However, they grew so fond of the little girl that 'however beautiful that poor child might have become, far from being the cor-rupters of her innocence we should surely have been its guardians'. At

---

* Had poor Zulietta perhaps suffered a bite from an over-ardent customer who had 'sunk upon her breast' before Jean-Jacques? Three years earlier, when Casanova had sampled her favours, he had found no flaw to report.

least, that is what he liked to think, for owing to his early departure from Venice he did not have 'time to play a part in this good work and I can only take credit in this matter for the inclination of my heart'.

It was not until the last time he tried his hand at commercial love, in Paris, that everything went more or less smoothly. He owed this happy consummation to a Lutheran parson who had 'furnished some rooms for a little girl that remained at everybody's disposal because he could not afford to keep her entirely on his own'. So one evening he invited Jean-Jacques and Grimm, then still the latter's 'intimate, inseparable' friend, to take turns with the girl, 'who did not know whether to laugh or to cry.' But if, for once, all went well, he paid for it with shame that overcame him to such a point that he had to have recourse to the classical remedy favoured by husbands (though not married he had already set up house with Thérèse) who polish up their tarnished self-esteem at the expense of their wives: 'I relieved my guilty conscience by a free and frank confession.'

*

If he had not been so desperately anxious to convince posterity of his addiction to virtue, one would almost think that in telling some of these tales, at any rate the first two, he allowed himself some irony, showed himself capable of laughing at himself. And, indeed, those of his biographers who call him 'utterly devoid of a sense of humour' are not wholly just. True, he was far better at laughing at others than at himself. It is typical that when he defends himself against the charge of 'having laughed only twice in his life' he instances an occasion when the laughter was at Thérèse's expense. Her howlers were his favourite stock-in-trade as a humourist; 'once I made a dictionary of her sayings to amuse Madame de Luxembourg and her blunders have become famous in the circles in which I have lived.' But there were nonetheless one or two occasions when he did indulge in a little gentle self-mockery, as when he relates how, at the age of twenty, he passed himself off as an orchestral composer. Although he could not 'score the simplest drinking-song' he found a credulous citizen to let him conduct his work at a concert in his house; 'never was there heard such a discordant row . . . the musicians were choking with laughter and the audience would gladly have stopped their ears.'

Practically the only other tale in the telling of which he takes himself less than wholly seriously—though its humour is only partly deliberate— is the one about his conquest by the forty-four-year-old lady whose 'complexion was spoilt by rouge'. He met her on a journey to go and see a doctor, at a time when he was 'visibly wasting away . . . so weak I could

hardly move . . . amazed to be still alive'. But no sooner had he set eyes
on the red-cheeked lady—or rather she on him for she 'undertook my
conquest . . . determined not to accept defeat'—than his illness, having
served its purpose of 'making me interesting,' was cured; 'I had forgotten
I was sick.' Not that he proved an easy conquest. The lady had an uphill
struggle to overcome his 'stupid bashfulness'. Fortunately she was 'an
intelligent woman who knew her way about the world and . . . made her
advances so cunningly that she would have seduced even an old hand at
the game'. And so when Jean-Jacques, 'not knowing what manner to
adopt or what to say . . . remained silent and looked sulky', she resorted
to the subtle tactics of 'putting her arm around my neck and pressing her
lips upon mine'. The result was all that she could have hoped for; 'I
became charming . . . Never have my eyes and my senses and my heart
and my mouth spoken so eloquently.' From the lady's point of view the
effort had been well worth it. For such an indefatigable lover did he show
himself that, had it not been for her unselfish concern for his health, he
might well have done himself an injury, just as when he was ruining his
constitution with his excessive recourse to do-it-yourself methods. 'During the short and delightful time I spent with her I had reason to believe,
from the restraint she imposed on me, that, although sensual and self-
indulgent, she preferred my health to her own pleasures . . . I was a
hundred times more successful than in my intercourse with Maman . . . I
was proud of my manhood . . . I shared the sensuality I aroused in her and
was sufficiently master of myself to look on my triumph with as much
pride as pleasure and thereby to derive the wherewithal to repeat it . . .'

*

As will have become clear, the love-life of the writer who, with his one
and only novel, is supposed to have done more than anyone to make
romantic as well as virtuous married love fashionable, in an age whose
trend-setting ladies had begun to tire of the games of amorous one-up-
man-ship, was singularly lacking in both these admirable qualities.
Mildly kinky in childhood, commonplace in adolescence, ignoble in early
manhood, squalid or absurd in its commercial phase, healthily robust only
in one brief episode, cruel and heartless—as will appear—in para-marital
form, it had been sex-life rather than love-life all along. What with his
resident 'Maman' being frigid, the itinerant mother of ten using too much
rouge ('I have only felt true love once in my life and that was not for her')
and the whores he abhorred lacking in sex appeal or perfect pectoral
symmetry, he never knew the kind of romantic love he idealized in his
novel until he reached the ripe middle age of forty-four. And when at last
it did come his way—which the virtuous variety he preached never did—

he handled the affair with a cunning that is more reminiscent of Iago than of Romeo.

It should be recalled, however, that in some ways the account to which the world owes its knowledge of his sex life, does him less than justice, in that it makes him out far more of a hypocrite, carrying his moral posturings to the point of absurdity, than he could conceivably have been in reality. The explanation of this distortion has already been given in an earlier chapter; the elderly St. Jean-Jacques he had become by the time he was writing the *Confessions* regularly takes off his halo to crown the young and far from saintly Rousseau with it. He does so only partly by design, to meet the minimum requirements of the public relations campaign. More often it was involuntary. Wishful thinking—in which he indulged freely ('everybody is naturally inclined to believe what he wants to believe')—had to fill the gap left by failing memory: 'I related the things I had forgotten as it seemed to me they should have been.' Or, as he put it somewhat more pretentiously but no less clearly elsewhere: 'abandoning myself both to the memory of the impression I had received and to what I feel now, I paint the state of my soul twice over, that is to say, as it was at the time the event occurred and as it is in the moment of writing about it.'

It is this habit of overprinting the feelings and thoughts of the past with those of the present that is responsible for the farcical passage explaining why he decided not to spend the winter with the vermilion-cheeked lady, as she had suggested, but instead to return to the arms of the potbellied one back at home. There were several reasons. First of all there was the danger that he might be found out, not by 'Maman' but by her new rival whom he had deceived in another way. For knowing that 'in polite society and with fashionable ladies the very word convert would ruin me', he had passed himself off as a respectable, native-born Catholic, claiming—though he had not a word of English—to be a Jacobite gentleman by the name of Dudding. His itinerant paramour and her travelling companions had swallowed it all. 'But it needed only one person in her home town who had been in England and knew English, to unmask me.' Then, even more worrying, there was the danger that he might lust after one of the lady's ten children, the sixteen-year-old daughter whose charms she had vaunted so much, boring him to tears with her 'maternal over-indulgence'. But was he to 'repay the mother's kindness by corrupting her daughter? The very idea horrified me. What a wretched state it would be to live with the mother, of whom I should be tired, and to be on fire for the daughter without declaring my feelings'. In fact, even apart from this additional complication, he was not really very keen to resume the affair; 'my attachment had certainly lost its early vigour'. Finally, there was his conscience about poor 'Maman'; 'already loaded with debt and incurring more by my wild spending, my generous Maman who was draining herself dry for me and whom I was deceiving most shamefully.'

Up to this point in his story he shows himself no better and no worse than the average young scallywag, taking pride, tinged with conventional remorse, in his escapades and enjoying himself in the humorous telling of them (including proud allusions to love-making in the lady's carriage and 'girls' whose favours he had enjoyed elsewhere on the journey). All the more absurdly incongruous is the ending of the tale, when St. Jean-Jacques creeps into the skin of young Rousseau. Having enumerated the mostly not particularly creditable reasons for refusing to keep his appointment with the lady whose 'main charms I had exhausted', he solemnly congratulates himself on the virtuous character of his decision: 'I had the inward satisfaction of being able to think well of myself, of knowing that I was capable of putting duty above pleasure.' And that he is not being ironical is clear from the way he goes on to relate how this moral victory led on to even greater triumphs: 'One advantage resulting from virtuous actions is that they elevate the mind and dispose it to attempt others more virtuous still . . . As soon as I had taken this resolution I became another man, or rather, I was once more the man I had formerly been . . . full of worthy sentiments and excellent resolutions . . . with no other thought but of guiding my conduct henceforth by the laws of virtue, devoting myself unreservedly to the service of the best of mothers . . . harkening to no other love but the love of duty.'*

But it is not till the end of this story that he fully earns his place in the front rank of comic writers, filling several pages of a work generally reckoned one of the great landmarks in literary history, with moral posturings as absurd as they are outrageous in their demands on the reader's credulity. For he goes on to relate how, back home with 'Maman', brim-full of virtuous intentions, his 'whole being was suddenly thrown into total disarray . . . I saw the happy future I had depicted for myself

---

* It would be less Pecksniffian if his hypocrisy were of the unconscious variety. But that it was not always honest self-deception, that he was not above presenting himself in a better light than he *knew* he deserved, is clear from a passage in the first draft of the *Confessions*. 'A hundred times,' he had written originally, referring to the servant-girl he had falsely accused of a theft committed by himself, 'I have imagined hearing her accuse me of being a scoundrel while claiming to be a honest man. How this has poisoned the praise I have received, how it has made public esteem a torment for me.' This recognition of the inexcusability of his conduct was struck out and replaced by the arguments already mentioned by which he seeks to persuade the reader that 'my crime amounted to no more than weakness' and that 'it must have been atoned for by all my misfortunes during forty years of honest and upright behaviour'.

vanish forever . . . It was a frightful moment . . . From that time, as a sensitive being, I was half dead'. Why? Because he learnt that 'Maman' had played tit for tat: 'I found my place filled by a tall, pale, silly youth . . . with a face as dull as his wits' who boasted endlessly of 'the marchionesses he had slept with' and, 'not content with possessing a most charming woman also kept, as an extra spice, an old, red-headed toothless chamber-maid whose disgusting services Maman had the patience to endure though it turned her stomach'. And what was even worse than finding his place in 'Maman's' bed occupied by such an unworthy successor to the gardener now in his grave, was that she did not seem in the least apolo-getic. Quite the contrary, she dared to suggest it was all his own fault. She, the most frigid of women, had the nerve to 'plead my frequent absences, as if she had been of a temperament that found it urgent to fill the void [sic]. "Ah Maman," I cried, my heart racked with grief, "have you the courage to tell me this? What a reward for such devotion as mine! . . . This will kill me but you will be sorry." '*

However, 'Maman' soon made it clear that she was perfectly happy to resume the old tripartite relationship; 'my rights remained unaltered.' This being perhaps rather more than he had bargained for, fresh from the delights of the real thing he had experienced in the arms of his far from frigid travel-companion, honour and duty had once more to come to the rescue. 'Never more powerfully swayed by the purity, the genuine-ness and the strength of my feelings for her and the sincerity and honesty of my soul, I threw myself at her feet, I embraced her knees and broke into floods of tears; "No Maman," I cried half distracted, "I love you too much to degrade you." ' Sharing her with another lover, which had been such a joy in the gardener's days, had now become unthinkable: ' "Posses-sion of you is too precious to be shared. The regrets I felt when first you gave yourself to me have grown with my love . . . You will always have my adoration. Be worthy of it always! . . . It is more necessary for me to respect than to possess you . . . It is to our heart's union that I sacrifice my pleasures. May I die a thousand times before I seek any that degrade the woman I love." ' Alas 'Maman' seemed unable to rise to his heights of self-denial. Though he had to admit that she made no overt passes at him, nor even 'insinuating suggestions and caresses', he could 'most clearly perceive that she secretly disapproved of my resolution'. There was no doubt in his mind that her 'growing coolness towards me' was due to the 'privation I had imposed on myself . . . which had no other motive

---

* The record shows that the 'tall, pale silly youth', had, in fact, already been installed there before Jean-Jacques went to Montpellier, that 'Maman' had been trying to get rid of him for some time past, that he had been plaguing her with money-begging letters and that he returned against her wishes.

than virtue, affection and esteem . . . but which is one of those things that women do not pardon'. And so he went 'to sigh and weep unobserved in the depths of the wood' until one day 'this life became absolutely unendurable' and he left, with a parting gift in the form of introductions provided by the hard-pressed lady who had kept him for nearly ten years but whom he was fortunately able to leave 'almost without feeling the slightest regret'.*

* The comment of a Rousseauphile scholar, writing in the early days of the century, affords a typical example of the lengths to which his idolatrous disciples will go. To him the fact that, after ten years, Jean-Jacques could leave his adored 'Maman' without batting, let alone moistening an eyelid, only adds to his glory: 'His stoic philosophy issues a tranquil challenge to weakness and human folly.'

CHAPTER NINE

The Sordid Romantic

'She could not take back her letters without returning mine. She told me she had burned them. I ventured to doubt it and I still do. But I am not afraid she has ever made ill use of them. I do not think her capable of that. Besides, I had taken precautions against it.'

EXCEPT for a quarrel with Diderot, which Madame d'Epinay with much tact and patience managed to patch up, the lull before the storm was peaceful enough. Not that life at the Hermitage was without its annoyances. There was the 'unavoidable servitude' to his hostess. Nor had dropping out delivered him from the droppers-in who had already made such a nuisance of themselves when he still lived in town; 'my distance from Paris [only six miles] did not prevent crowds of idle people . . . from coming every day to waste my time'. But worst of all was having Thérèse's mother on the premises. True, the septuagenarian lady had had her uses. The widow of a junior civil servant and considerably better educated than her semi-literate daughter, she had, in his Paris days, combined the functions of charlady and secretary. 'To spare the cost of a servant she came every morning to light my fire and attend to my minor wants. I meditated in bed with closed eyes and shaped and reshaped my sentences in my head with incredible labour. Then, when I was finally content with them, I committed them to memory till such time as I could put them on paper. But the break caused by getting up and dressing, made me lose everything and when I sat down before my paper, hardly a sentence came to me of all I had composed. So it occurred to me to take Madame Levasseur as my secretary. I dictated to her from my bed the work of the preceding night. And this method, which I have followed for a long while, has saved for me much that I might otherwise have forgotten.' So, but for the old lady's willingness and ability to help him forge the iron of his prose while it was hot, there might have been no prize-winning essay to put Jean-Jacques in orbit, no *Discourse on Inequality* and, who knows, no *Social Contract*.

But at the Hermitage she was more of a liability than an asset. For one thing she would bring all her greedy children and relations around. As they were 'so many bloodsuckers', Jean-Jacques had begged Thérèse 'not to let any of them come'. But the moment he lifted his heels to go to the Château, 'the Hermitage was full of people having a whale of a time'. And at least one of them, a brother of Thérèse's, was a very bad lot, having stolen all of Jean-Jacques's fine linen shirts of which he had 'forty-two' at the time. Even worse, however, was that Madame Levasseur 'tried to alienate her daughter from me'. As he had 'never felt the least glimmering of love for her . . . never desired to possess her . . . and as the sensual needs I satisfied with her were purely sexual and had nothing to do with her as an individual', it should not really have mattered all that much. But it did. For all this big, bold talk is flatly contradicted by other passages in the same book. It is one more example of that irresponsibility as a writer who throws on to paper whatever thought may pass through his head and whatever sentiment may for one fleeting moment be uppermost in his heart, and never mind if what he tells the reader at the bottom of the page makes nonsense of what he had just told him at the top.

In actual fact—if one can take anything he says for a fact—he had, certainly 'desired to possess' Thérèse when, in his early thirties, he first persuaded her into bed or, as he puts it, 'when the sympathy of our hearts and the agreement of our dispositions had the usual result'. For the twenty-three-year-old laundress, so backward that in spite of all his efforts 'to improve her mind . . . she never learnt to read properly . . . or even tell the time', had very little else than her body with which to attract his attentions. They were soon rewarded. There had been only one obstacle *en route* to the bedroom, a little misunderstanding about the causes of her initial reluctance. He had attributed it to concern for his health, fear she would give him 'the pox', whereas in fact she was only trying to stave off his discovery that she was no longer virgo intacta. Fortunately, that proved to be the least of his worries. He had given a 'shout of joy' when at last he understood the reason for her hesitation. He had cried: 'Ah, my Thérèse, I am only too delighted to possess you good and healthy and not to find something I was not looking for.' And so the 'intimacy which our common shyness seemed to preclude was very speedily formed'.

What is more, it lasted for life (or rather, cohabitation in the literal sense of the word did, for the time came when he returned to his old erotic self-service,. Though he had told Thérèse he 'would never marry her', he lived up to his promise that he would 'never abandon her either'. Ill-matched as they were, not so much Beauty and the Beast as the Maestro and the Moron, unpresentable as she was in the Great World Jean-Jacques was soon to conquer, he stuck to her to the end of his days. And, at least as meritorious, she stuck to him, in the triple role of intermittent concubine, sick nurse (with some very unpleasant duties such as passing catheters up his penis so as to help him to urinate) and cook-housekeeper who served but did not normally eat at table when there were guests, and who naturally stayed at home when the Maestro was with his grand friends at places like Chenonceaux. Even so, they did have many happy times together. She might be 'stupid' but 'with all her limitations the creature was a most excellent adviser . . . who had won universal esteem among ladies of the highest rank, among nobles and princes'. And so he lived 'as pleasantly with Thérèse as with the finest genius in the world . . . she had the heart of an angel, our affection grew with our intimacy, and we felt more strongly every day that we were made for one another'.

Of course, they had their ups and downs. There had been times when he felt that 'we always remained two separate people', that she 'left a void in his heart', that she did not provide him with all the 'intimate companionship of which I felt the need'. Partly due to her mother's machinations, 'Thérèse, dividing her loyalties, sometimes left me feeling I was alone . . . and the single idea that I was not everything to her caused her to be almost nothing to me'. It had become doubly painful when he had buried himself in the country, away from the friends with whom he used to seek compensation for the void in his heart and the boredom of living with the 'stupid creature'. Not unnaturally, after a decade together they had rather run out of conversation: 'We knew one another too well to have anything fresh to say.' And, of course, they had never had 'sufficient ideas in common to make any great store'. Yet another reason why time was beginning to hang heavy on his hands was that he was temporarily at a loss for something new to write about: 'I no longer had any scheme for the future with which to entertain my imagination, I could not conceive of anything more to wish, yet my heart was empty.' Clearly it was ready to be re-filled by a new occupant, all the more so as he had apparently proved no more successful sexually with Thérèse than with 'Maman': 'When I possessed her I felt that she still was not mine.' But then she, too, was disappointingly frigid; 'so cool are her passions that she has seldom felt the want of a man even when I ceased to be one for her'.*

So, what with one thing and another, he had arrived at the stage where, come the June-moon, a middle-aged man's fancy lightly turns to thoughts of bed. At first they had concentrated on 'all the persons I felt emotion for

---

* That enthusiastic practitioner of the *ars amatoria*, Boswell, formed rather a different impression of Thérèse. She congratulated him on his 'vigour' but complained of his 'lack of art' when he escorted her on her journey to join Jean-Jacques in England, in the course of which he claims to have acquitted himself on thirteen (presumably not consecutive) occasions.

in my youth', including the asymmetrical one 'whom my heart can never forget . . . my blood caught fire, my head turned despite its grey hairs'. But, as he knew that 'the time for love was past' and was 'too conscious of the ridicule heaped upon aged beaux' as well as 'too frightened of domestic storms . . . loving Thérèse too sincerely to expose her to grief', he gave himself over to day-dreaming, imagining 'societies of perfect creatures, celestial in their virtue and their beauty'. If one was an ordinary human being of flesh and blood it was more than one's life was worth to run into him on these occasions; such 'wretched mortals . . . got so rude a reception that it might almost be called brutal'. But apart from the fact that 'if people had been better able to read into my heart' they would only have found love there, he had an excuse; he was in the throes of artistic creation, conceiving the great love-story, *La Nouvelle Héloïse*, that would add immense new lustre to his name, especially among the ladies, and that came to be accepted by them as one of his most irrefutable credentials for canonization.

It was when 'the return of spring had redoubled my amorous delirium' that lightning struck in the shape of a celestial creature of flesh and blood, his landlady's sister-in-law, the Comtesse d'Houdetot. Admittedly she was celestial only in virtue: 'The Countess, who was getting on for thirty [she was in fact twenty-six], was not in the least beautiful, her face was marked by smallpox, her complexion was muddy, she was short-sighted and her eyes were rather too round.' According to contemporaries she was also 'exceedingly cross-eyed', but more than made up for these physical shortcomings by her 'angelic' nature as well as her talents which had enabled her, among other things, to write what Diderot called 'very pretty verse' including a 'Hymn to the Breasts sparkling with warmth and fire and voluptuous images'. Anyhow, as Jean-Jacques at the time was 'intoxicated with love lacking an object' and as she was not flat-chested like her sister-in-law, her plainness could not have mattered less. This was 'the first and only love of all my life'. That was clear from 'the delicious tremblings' he was seized with and which he had 'never experienced besides any other woman . . . the agitation, palpitation, convulsive movements, faintings of the heart'. He spares one no intimate details of these convulsions; the prospect of a kiss from the Countess 'so fired my blood that my head was dizzy, my eyes were dazzled and blind, my trembling knees could no longer support me, I had to stop and sit down'. These debilitating lapses used to occur when walking along the road to meet his goggle- and cross-eyed, pock-marked, muddy-faced love. What was worse, no sooner had he recovered from one such attack, than, in spite of his 'trying to think of something else', he would be in trouble all over again; 'before I had gone twenty yards the same thoughts, and everything that followed upon them, assailed me once more.' And so he always arrived at their trysting place 'weak, exhausted, worn out, scarcely able to hold myself up'. But there was still worse. Such, in spite of his forty-four years, was his sexual prowess that, as soon as he met the loved one face to face, 'everything was right* again, in her company I felt only the irksomeness of an inexhaustible and always useless vigour'. It was useless because the Countess not only had a Count for a husband—who did not matter any more than did Thérèse—but also a Marquis for a lover, who, unhappily, was a friend of Jean-Jacques's. For his sake—he was away at the wars—'she never forgot herself even when our intoxication was at its most dangerous height'. That was after weeks of meeting nearly every day and talking of nothing but love; 'we were both drunk with passion, she for her lover, I for her; our sighs and tears mingled.'

Came the evening when they enacted a love-scene worthy of one of the lusher women's magazines. Having 'supped together alone we went for a walk in the loveliest moonlight . . . Sitting with her on a grassy bank beneath an acacia in full flower I found a language really able to express the emotions in my heart . . . I was sublime . . . What intoxicating tears I shed at her knees! What tears I drew from her in spite of herself! Finally, in her involuntary excitement, she cried, "Never was there a man so tender, never a lover who loved like you. But your friend is listening to us and my heart could not love twice." I sighed and was silent. I embraced her. What an embrace! But that was all'. In short, nothing doing. What was worse, the Comtesse—so she confessed later in life—had spoilt the *moment suprême* (such as it was) with a fit of the giggles provoked by a rustic swearing at his horse on the other side of the garden wall just as Jean-Jacques was at his most sublime. It had been trying enough to drive even an ordinary lover to distraction. What it did to the athletic Jean-Jacques was much worse. It gave him a hernia: 'The continuance over three months of ceaseless stimulation and privation threw me into an exhaustion from which I did not recover for several years and finally brought on a rupture that I shall carry with me to the grave.' 'Such,' he concludes bitterly, 'was the sole, amorous gratification of a man whose temperament was at once the most inflammable and the most timid Nature can ever have created.'

In fact, he had done rather better than he gave himself credit for. There had not only been those exhausting anticipatory gratifications he had so often achieved single-handed on the way to meet his *inamorata*. There had also been, he recorded in a letter, 'that divine thrill, that swift and all-consuming fire quicker than lightning, that inexpressible moment' which he had experienced in her presence. Judging by what he goes on to say in

* 'Upright'? The original text reads: '*Tout était réparé.*'

this letter (which, on second thoughts, he decided to keep instead of despatching it) about his 'lassitude' and 'state of utter dejection which follows too great an indulgence in the most exquisite pleasures', he must have been consumed by this fire with much the same frequency as had already caused some concern for his health to the lady whose complexion had suffered from too much rouge. The difference with her muddy-faced successor was that, being his friend's mistress as well as 'adorned with every virtue, the idol of his heart', he could not bring himself to 'soil that divine image' by allowing her to participate in the joys of the 'inexpressible moment'. It was the Comtesse who had reason to complain of lack of amorous gratification—as, indeed, she seemed to do when she accused him of 'behaving with extreme refinements of cruelty'.

The reproach had led him 'to explain once and for all what you may expect; I may die of my passion but I will not soil your purity'. Unless, of course, she gave him half a chance: 'If I were to perceive any sign of weakness on your part I would immediately succumb . . . A hundred times I have willed the crime. If you, too, have willed it, I will consummate it and become at once the most perfidious and the happiest of men. But I cannot corrupt the woman I idolise.' What he could and did do, in and out of the moonlight, was to deliver her from temptation by endlessly talking about his mad love, pleading with her not to withdraw the favours to which he owed 'these ravishing ecstasies, these transports that were never made for mortal man.' 'Have I ever,' he asked in the letter he never sent but whose sentiments he never stopped impressing on the Comtesse, 'have I ever tasted your favours in such a way that I deserve to lose them? . . . Are my burning lips never again to lay my very soul on your heart along with my kisses? . . . My fatal passion is no secret to you, there was never a passion to equal mine, I never felt anything like it even in the bloom of my youth, it is strong enough to make me forget everything, even my duty . . . When I am with you virtue itself is not sacred enough to check my mad frenzy and make me respect the woman entrusted to me by a friend.'

But if he owed it to this friend to do no more than seduce the Comtesse with burning kisses and unshared ecstasies until she gave a sign that she was ready to participate in them, he also had a duty to his self-esteem. For he was beset by the suspicion that invariably gnaws at the middle-aged mind in these situations; was the young hussy perhaps leading him on so that she and her lover could have a good laugh at his expense? Somehow he had to ensure that she was not mocking him. And so, to cover himself against the long-term risk, he first of all saw to it that his letters would never fall into the wrong hands; though he did not believe her capable of 'making ill use of them', he had 'taken precautions against

it . . . a foolish but lively fear of ridicule had made me begin our correspondence on a note which secured my letters from being passed on'.
Regardless of her protests, which had 'only added to my fears', he had
insisted on addressing her with the familiar '*tu*', in those days used only
in bed (if there) even between husband and wife. 'If these letters ever
come to light,' he adds more truthfully than he knew, 'the world will
know how I have loved.'

He had also provided against the short-term risk that his love might
be leading him on 'in order to turn my head completely and then make
fun of me'. To guard against this danger he had demanded 'proof that
she was not fooling me . . . I became pressing, the position was delicate'.
So a 'bargain' had been struck: 'She refused me nothing that the tenderest
friendship could grant, she granted me nothing that would make her
unfaithful.' What she did grant was 'slight favours' incendiary enough to
afford its recipient the 'divine thrill' while leaving her reproachful of his
cruelty. Or so he says in the letter he filed. In his autobiography the
Comtesse finds no fault with his indulgence in solitary thrills. There she
appears immune to Don Juan Jacques who had the 'humiliation of seeing
that the fires her slight favours kindled in my senses did not convey the
tiniest spark to hers'.

*

If she had 'got off astonishingly lightly' when making her bargain with
him, so did he when the Marquis unexpectedly turned up and began to
show signs of suspicion. Once again his native prudence stood the
Citizen of Geneva in good stead. In order to provide the Comtesse with
proof of their innocence he sent her a letter couched in the most respectful
terms and full of harmless chitchat. Addressing her as 'Madame' instead
of 'Sophie', he expressed the hope to see her lover—'how eager I am to
embrace St. Lambert'—and recalled their 'delightful walks during which
we talked of everything that could be of interest to decent and sensitive
people'. But apparently the Marquis was not altogether reassured. For
when, shortly after, they all met at a dinner party, the atmosphere was so
strained, with the Marquis and the Comtesse looking 'extremely worried
and Rousseau hardly more cheerful', that the hostess, Madame d'Epinay,
who has reported the meeting, 'decided to leave them alone when the
meal was over, making the excuse that I needed a rest'. She missed a scene
that, as Jean-Jacques describes it, was worth staying for. Though the
Marquis was 'merciful' (which was not all that magnanimous since at the
time he had as yet no idea what Jean-Jacques had really been up to), he
'took unfair advantage in order to humiliate me'. He meted out the punishment most authors, foolhardy enough to inflict their writings on the ears

of their family or friends, sooner or later come to know only too well. But Jean-Jacques, who at home 'every evening read and reread the same two chapters' of his novel to Thérèse and her mother, had yet to learn his lesson. Just as Thérèse had regularly 'joined me in my tears', so her mother never stopped saying, 'That is very fine indeed, sir.' That was no doubt why it seemed an excellent idea to try and cheer up the embarrassed Comtesse and her sulky Marquis by reading them one of his latest efforts: 'After dinner I read a letter I had written to Voltaire.' But this time Nemesis did not tarry: the Marquis 'fell asleep as I read it and I, who was once so proud and now looked so stupid, dared not break off but continued reading as he continued to snore. Such was my humiliation and such was his vengeance'.

The situation became considerably tricker when, a few weeks later, the Comtesse told him that someone had talked out of turn. Though she did not know exactly how much the Marquis knew, he was clearly 'annoyed'. She herself was more than just annoyed, she panicked, made it clear that henceforward there would be no more 'slight favours'. As for Jean-Jacques, he felt pretty sheepish, 'ashamed', knowing that 'he was to blame in the eyes of a young woman . . . towards whom I should have acted as mentor'. What to do? Attack being the best form of defence he decided on a strategy so bold and so cunning as to seem almost incomprehensible in a man so feeble, so timid, so unshakeably convinced of his addiction to the truth. He composed a letter to the Marquis complaining of the Comtesse's changed attitude, blaming the Marquis for it, demanding an explanation and lecturing him on the impermissibility of adulterous liaisons like his. As he loved them both very dearly, so began this extra-ordinary epistle, he had a right to unburden himself of 'the wrongs he had suffered at their hands'. When the Comtesse had first 'begun to seek me out . . . I was lonely and sad . . . My heart wanted consolation . . . lonely and unhappy I grew attached to her . . . She promised me her friendship . . . Now all was changed, except for my heart . . . She receives me coldly, hardly speaks to me . . . finds a hundred excuses to avoid me, as if she were trying to get rid of me . . . I don't know what this sudden change means . . . But having responded to the advances made to me, having so to speak been forced to acquire a taste for her company which has now become necessary to me . . . I feel it is your humane duty to give me some explanation of her conduct . . . Do not all her feelings come from you? . . . Tell me, therefore, why has she grown so cold to me.'

He himself, so he went on, could think of only one explanation: had they, knowing his disapproval of illicit liaisons, perhaps been under the misapprehension that he had been trying to break up their affair? Of course, he did disapprove very strongly; 'I cannot help blaming your connection, you can hardly approve of it yourself.' His hope was that one day he might be able to make both of them see how much better it would be to 'forestall the inevitable end of illicit love by contenting yourselves with ties that are proof against the tooth of time and of which you can be proud in the face of the world'. But he loved them both so much, he felt so much 'respect for a union so tender, that I cannot bring myself to attempt to lead it to virtue'. Surely the Marquis must have realized that: 'Could you really have been afraid that I might have tried to prejudice her against you, that a misguided sense of virtue could have made me perfidious and deceitful? No, no! Jean-Jacques Rousseau's breast will never hold the heart of a traitor.'

It is all so outrageous, of such surpassing, farcical duplicity, out-tartuffing Tartuffe and out-pecksniffing Pecksniff, that only one explanation seems possible. And that is that he wrote it all in perfectly good faith, that his genius for wishful thinking plus the 'incredible rapidity' with which he continuously became 'another man', wholly oblivious of what he had been, done, said, thought, or felt, the moment before, enabled him to remain blissfully ignorant of having fallen somewhat short of his self-assessment as the most truthful and 'transparent' of men 'incapable of dissimulation'. It seems almost proved by the fact that some weeks later he saw fit to boast, to the Comtesse of all people, his accomplice in the deceit practised on her lover, of the 'frankness' of his letter to him.

However that may be, the letter, in the drafting of which the Comtesse appears to have collaborated, was a huge success. When, after an agonizing four weeks, the Marquis's reply at last arrived, he appeared to have accepted their story in every detail. He apologized for his 'stupid imaginings' and in addition made it clear that what he had so mistakenly feared was not, of course, that his friend had tried to corrupt his mistress's virtue but that he would persuade her to become altogether too virtuous for her lover's comfort. 'I was aware,' he wrote, 'of your austere principles, people had told me about them and she herself had spoken of them with respect.' That was why he had worried—which was very wrong of him; 'I am the only one to feel self-reproach, I am the only one to blame for her conduct . . . her heart has not changed at all, she loves you and honours you . . . and I myself had always dreamt of spending my life between you and her, if we could persuade you to come and live with us . . . I have made three people unhappy . . . Do forgive us and love us.'

Was the gallant soldier-poet, who some years previously had achieved the memorable feat of cuckolding Voltaire,* really so trusting as to be a

* The sage had found him on a sofa with Madame du Châtelet 'conversing together on matters that were neither poetry nor philosophy'.

dupe? Not necessarily. According to Madame d'Epinay's account—which, however, cannot be fully relied upon—his first reaction to Jean-Jacques's outrageous letter had been to say that 'the only possible response is a good thrashing'. If, instead of administering it, he grovelled, it may well have been to avoid scandal, because discretion was the better part of valour in dealing with a man as explosive as he was cunning, as impulsive one moment as he was devious the next. That was certainly the line the Marquis took when, six months later, he at last learnt the true facts. 'You need not worry,' the Comtesse wrote to the former beneficiary of her slight favours now finally dismissed. 'When he first learnt of your passion and what it had made you do, he ceased for a moment to believe in your virtue. Since then he pities your weakness more than he reproaches you for it, and neither of us would dream of joining those who would blacken you. We will always speak of you with esteem and not allow others to speak ill of you.'

This desire to avoid scandal was certainly one of the reasons why, until then, she had endured considerable provocation from her frustrated admirer, who continued to write to her for another six months after she had first told him there would be no further 'mingling of tears', let alone any other kind of mingling. His letters of the period make pitiful reading, as shaming as some of the worst pages of the *Confessions*, both in the absurd audacity of their moral pretensions and in the sheer nastiness when he climbs down off his high moral horse to abuse his lost love. Ostensibly turning over a new leaf, he declared that 'my desires which in my innermost imaginings dared to profane your charms . . . now have no other object than to render your soul perfect . . . Nearing death the ardour within me makes me feel I have been given a new lease of life in order to guide yours . . . I believe I am sent by Heaven to bring to perfection its noblest handiwork . . . I shall become better myself in trying to set you an example of the virtues with whose love I want to inspire you.' Though he had only just assured her lover for the second time that, in spite of his austere principles', he blessed their illicit union—'you both deserve to love one another till the grave'—he gave the Comtesse to understand that she should go back to her husband: 'The road to perfection is open to you. Your bear a famous name . . . Your husband is received at court, esteemed on the battlefield, good at business and owes his unvarying happiness to his marriage.' Once again, the apparent duplicity as also the plain non-sensicality of so many of Jean-Jacques's utterances—he knew perfectly well the marriage had been a disaster from the outset and admits it in the *Confessions*—leaves the reader speechless. It is the same when, recalling the days when he was still enjoying the Comtesse's slight favours, he takes comfort in the thought that 'the Eternal Eye had perhaps looked

kindly on the spectacle of two placid hearts encouraging one another in
virtue even though vile and corrupt spirits [the reference is to Grimm and
Madame d'Epinay] may have misinterpreted our relations in the baseness
of their hearts'. Or, better still, when he asks the Comtesse (to whose
refusal to accommodate his 'inexhaustible vigour' he owed his hernia) to
'imagine the universe peopled with an infinite number of spirits that
witnessed our most delightful encounters and murmured applause at the
spectacle of two tender honest friends offering sacrifices in the secret of
their hearts to virtue'.

Even for an eighteenth-century stomach, trained as it was to digest the
richest helpings of moral and sentimental bombast, all this must have
been hard to swallow. Quite likely, therefore, it came as a relief when
Jean-Jacques, interpreting the Comtesse's failure always to reply by
return of post as proof that she had joined his enemies, flew into one of his
furious tempers. 'You,' he raged, 'you, too, hate me?! You, who know my
heart, despise me?! Good God, I am supposed to be a scoundrel! . . . Ah,
if I am wicked, how vile is the whole human race. Show me a better man
than me . . . Adieu, cruel one! . . . I defy you to forget this heart of mine
which you hold in contempt but the like of which you will never find.'
For another five months he carried on in this style, his anger sometimes
suddenly giving way to pathetic contrition and then flaring up again,
venging itself in abuse of Madame d'Epinay, Diderot or Grimm and, last
not least, the Comtesse herself. Her 'shifty and ambiguous' letters were
typical of 'your sort of Society-people . . . Since you are ashamed instead
of proud of my friendship I withdraw it . . . What you really care for most
in this world is money . . . From now on I see only Madame la Comtesse
in you . . . You have sunk lower in my esteem than you imagine'.

Only towards the end of the sorry episode, or rather Jean-Jacques's
account of it, does he suddenly appear in a less unattractive light, recog-
nizable again as the human and even quite appealing character Hume and
others sometimes found him to be. It is when he describes a hilarious
luncheon party, with himself the butt of the laughter. By that time, some
five months after the Marquis had at last learned what the 'Eternal Eye'
had really seen, he had apparently come to look upon his unsuccessful
rival as a figure of fun. And so when he and the Comtesse, who for good
measure had also brought her husband along, found themselves at table
with Jean-Jacques, he was mercilessly teased. 'It may be guessed that
with the Comte d'Houdetot and Saint-Lambert present the laughter
generally went against me. Nor can a man embarrassed by the simplest
conversation be expected to have been very brilliant on an occasion like
that. I have never suffered so much nor cut a worse figure.'

*

As with the pages of the *Confessions* abusing Grimm, so one has to read every line of the hopelessly muddled and deceptive account of Jean-Jacques's *grande passion*, as well as every letter covering the period, in order to appreciate the towering heights of moral self-complacency to which he could rise, the grubby depths of duplicity, however unconscious, to which he could descend, the miracles of whitewashing self-deception he could perform. It is not a happy exercise, apt to leave one feeling pity for '*ce triste caractère*', as the Comtesse came to call him. But what makes one even sorrier for him is that his fame made him fall victim to the countless scholars employed by the Rousseau-industry. By their publications, painstaking researches and reconstructions of the past, they have preserved for the awed gaze of posterity every detail of a love-life so ignominious, so tawdry and squalid, as to warrant characterizing the pioneer of perhaps the most revolutionary movement in the history of literature as 'the Sordid Romantic'. All the more bewildering is it that such a man should have become venerated as a saint. That time was not yet. Indeed, in the days when he thought himself heaven-sent to complete the Comtesse's perfection, his reputation was reaching its nadir. 'I am obliged,' a friend wrote to him from Paris, 'to plead your cause every day. For heaven's sake come and defend yourself.' But at the very time when he fell from the high estate he had achieved six years earlier with his thirty-page pamphlet in praise of virtue, he was finishing the novel in praise of both sacred and profane love that would make him soar up again to reach still dizzier heights.

CHAPTER TEN

The End of the Affair

'My sadness, free from all bitterness, was the sadness of a too loving and tender heart which had been deceived by those whom it believed to be of its own kind.'

'GOOD but rarely comes from good advice.' Byron's dictum was certainly borne out by the experience of those who had tried to save Jean-Jacques from himself, warning him against indulging the corrosive suspiciousness and umbrageousness that sooner or later sapped the foundations of nearly every one of the friendships, so precious to a heart that craved 'to love and be loved'. Heaven knows, the man, who thought himself 'born for friendship', would have found it difficult enough to grapple his friends to his bosom with 'hoops of steel', even had he been the least distrustful of characters. The infantile quality of his egotism alone, once success had emboldened him to give it free rein, was such as to preclude lasting relationships with any but wholly selfless human beings, saints, or, at the very least, born mother- or father-figures. And so the efforts of old friends like Diderot and Madame d'Epinay, or new intimates like the Comtesse, were most probably doomed to failure anyhow.

They were not sparing with them. When in the early days of his stay at the Hermitage Jean-Jacques took violent offence at a phrase in a letter from Diderot, his hostess spent hours writing the most affectionate and tactful letters begging him 'not to let the seed of bitterness take root in your heart', and pointing out that 'before suspecting a friend of having failed one, one must have thirty incontrovertible proofs . . . For heaven's sake, calm yourself, do not fall out with perhaps the best friends you have, for a mere trifle'. Diderot himself, on another occasion when Jean-Jacques had flown into a rage at his meddling, asked him, 'What would become of our relationship if the harshness of your last letter decided me never again to interest myself in your affairs without being asked to do so . . . Am I not your friend? Have I not got the right to tell you everything I think to be mistaken and to let you know what I think is the right thing for you to do? Is that not my duty?' He, Diderot, was 'sick of this bickering, it is all so petty, I just cannot understand how such things can happen let alone continue, between people with a little sense, fortitude and broad-mindedness'.

But no one took more trouble to try and keep the forty-four-year-old sage from making a fool of himself than his long-suffering twenty-six-year-old lady-love. Her advice may not always have been very original— 'don't write letters on the spur of the moment, you must always sleep on them, otherwise you are likely to say things you will regret'—but it was unfailingly apposite. Like her sister-in-law she warned him against his congenital distrust of one and all, including his closest friends: 'Do remember how much one must hesitate to suspect of falseness and perfidy those one has thought worthy of one's esteem and one's friendship.' She warned him against his readiness to take offence: if Diderot had expressed himself with some heat, it was not, she told him, because he was 'tyrannical' but because he was worried that his friend would put himself in the wrong; 'one must excuse a forcefulness that is so tenderly motivated . . . you must not level accusations of tyranny against friends who love you too much not to worry when they think they see you making a mistake.' She warned him against wallowing in self-pity—'it seems your embittered heart takes pleasure in cultivating sentiments of affliction'— and against self-dramatization; 'your imagination and . . . your extremely hot temper make you . . . exaggerate your misfortunes.' She tried to show him the falsity of his theory that friendship was incompatible with gratitude for services received and should never oblige one to put oneself out; 'I will never regard services rendered by friends,' she wrote, 'as a yoke . . . They do not make me feel enslaved . . . I do not find it painful to sacrifice some of my liberty for their sake. What seems to you degrading slavery would to me be an act of gratitude I would accomplish with pleasure.'

Even her official lover, the Marquis, had things to say Jean-Jacques would have done well to heed. When the latter had motivated his refusal to accompany his ailing hostess on a journey to see a doctor in Geneva, with, among other things, his reluctance to 'appear in my native land . . . as her poverty-stricken valet,' the Marquis wrote: 'I would not have seen you in this light, I would have seen you as accompanying your sick friend or, at least, indulging the sweet sentiment of gratitude or, if you do not feel it, at the very least behaving with the manners that are appropriate in such a case.' Wise words, but they were all in vain. 'Manners indeed!' Jean-Jacques exclaimed indignantly to the Comtesse. 'Am I supposed to pretend to a gratitude I no longer feel, to be false so as to behave as a gentleman, to sacrifice sincerity to Good Form? No, Madame, no! I realise that in the great world manners have taken the place of sentiments but mine are such as they should be and have no need of disguise.'

*

The exodus from his life was led by Madame d'Epinay. The first cloud over their friendship had come with the arrival on the scene of the cross-eyed *femme fatale*. As already related, soon after her victim had won those slight favours which had yielded him so many inexpressible moments, she had reported that her official lover had begun to show signs of anxiety. Someone had talked. But who? And what exactly had the gallant Marquis been told? How much did he know? Only the answer to the last question seems to emerge with any clarity from the volumes devoted to scholarly investigation of this world-shaking problem: at the time he suspected Jean-Jacques only of lecturing the Comtesse about the immorality of her long-standing liaison. Whoever had alerted him had apparently given a very charitable interpretation of the goings-on under the moonlit acacia tree. But Jean-Jacques not unnaturally jumped to the panicky conclusion that the Marquis knew all there was to know. As for the identity of his informant, the obvious choice for Jean-Jacques, always ready to think the worst of his friends, was Madame d'Epinay, who was in regular correspondence with her lover Grimm, then away at the wars with the Marquis. And so, overnight, the late owner of the underpetticoat he had soaked with his tears and kisses became a traitress, accused in a letter he sent her of 'slander', 'trickery', 'sharp practice', and 'evil designs' to sow discord between 'two lovers dear to me, firmly united and worthy of each other's love'. He would 'hate' her to his 'dying day' if she really thought he could be so 'despicable' as to wish to endanger the Marquis's monopoly of the Comtesse's favours. All he wanted was 'to have an illicit love change into eternal friendship . . . I have never concealed from you nor from her how badly I think of certain relationships'.

At the time he deemed it more prudent not to reveal on what grounds he had selected his benefactress for the role of informer. But he made no secret of them to the Comtesse. 'Your sister-in-law,' he wrote to her, 'could not bear your making such inroads on her monopoly of me and my attentions . . . She had sworn to disunite of us. Indifferent to love, faith, honour and sacred friendship, she dared with her slander . . . to cast unworthy suspicions on two people to whom she owed the greatest esteem.' Nor was that all. She had also tried 'to sow discord in my little household whose peacefulness alone offers some compensation for its poverty'. Of course, all this was strictly confidential; even an 'extinguished friendship has its rights, which I shall always respect, determined to remain forever silent on Madame d'Epinay's odious conduct'. But forever is a long time. And so, when he came to write his memoirs, he explained even more fully how she had become a 'vile informer . . . who had seen nothing but evil in a blameworthy but involuntary emotion and who had not been able to believe or even imagine that true sincerity of heart that atoned for it'. She had sunk so low partly because she was jealous of her sister-in-law's conquest of her own private literary lion, the spectacle of which 'glutted her heart with rage and indignation'. But she was equally jealous of the Comtesse's hold on the Marquis whom she also wanted for herself; 'she had made innumerable attempts to detach him from her.' And she was aided and abetted by Grimm, her lover, who was jealous of Jean-Jacques; 'he had made several advances' to the Comtesse and could not stomach it 'that she preferred the older man to himself'.

As if all this were not enough to convict the accused of treachery, there was also the corroborative evidence supplied by Thérèse, who had behaved as befits the humble concubine of a great man by acting as his *postillon d'amour*. When her lord and master stayed at the château, as he often did, she not only saw to it that he received the letters the Comtesse sent to the Hermitage. She also frustrated the jealous châtelaine's attempts to intercept them, told her 'honourable and loyal lies', and resisted all attempts to 'rouse her jealousy'. No man could have wished for a sturdier ally in concealing his extra-curricular amours than Jean-Jacques claims to have had in his concubine. Such, he said, was Madame d'Epinay's furious determination to lay her hands on the Comtesse's letters that she 'carried her boldness so far as to frisk Thérèse' when she called at the château.

The treacherous lady herself tells a different and rather more plausible story in her memoirs. She makes no secret of having told Grimm of love-sick Jean-Jacques's apparent infatuation. And quite probably Grimm, the first to 'cool off', mentioned it to the Marquis. None of the actors in the melodrama was a saint, Thérèse, whom Jean-Jacques casts in such a selfless, heroic role, no more than the others. 'She assures me,' so reads one of the letters Madame d'Epinay claims to have written to Grimm, 'that the Comtesse visits the hermit nearly every day . . . She is jealous. I myself think she is either lying or that they have both lost their heads . . . Three days ago he sent me a message to say he could not come to see me because he was unwell. The same evening I sent to the Comtesse's house; he was installed there tête à tête and remained two days . . . This seems to me so odd and comical that I fancy I am dreaming . . . Thérèse has been several times to bring me her complaints but I have always made her hold her tongue . . . Really what foundation is there for . . . these tales . . . of a silly, jealous, chattering and lying woman who accused a woman we know to be giddy, trusting and certainly indiscreet but frank, honour-able, sincere and supremely good?'* So it was not altogether surprising that she resented her protégé's wild accusations. 'Although I feel pity for you,' she wrote to him, 'I have not been able to hold back the bitterness that filled my heart. I resort to tricks and cunning against you! I to be accused of the blackest infamy!' She had all the more reason to be angry as he had seen fit to end his letter with that breathtaking insolence he often displayed when in a tight corner. Admitting that his accusations might be ill-founded, he added: 'I shall perhaps have a great wrong to repair . . . But do you know how I shall atone for my errors? By frankly telling you what the world thinks of you and what breaches you have to repair in your reputation.'

It was taking a fearful risk. He had proffered, so he recognizes in his *Confessions*, 'the most open and atrocious insults' that could only too easily have provoked an answer 'so haughty, so disdainful and so con-temptuous . . . that I should have no choice but to leave her house on the spot'. And that would not only be exceedingly awkward—'I tremble at the mere idea of having to move,' he told the Comtesse—but would also set the scandal-hungry tongues wagging, something which she had begged him to avoid at all costs. However, his luck held: 'I got off with a fright'; Madame d'Epinay neither gave him notice nor demanded an explanation. Instead there was—or so he would have one believe—the customary ritual of mutual drenching; 'she threw her arms around my neck and burst into tears . . . I wept freely too.' But they were not tears of remorse. For he went no further than a conditional apology: 'I said I could not yet say anything about the basis of my suspicions and protested with real sincerity that if they proved ill-founded my whole life would be devoted to repairing my injustice.' Which, oddly, seemed to satisfy the lady who 'did not reveal the slightest curiosity as to the nature of these suspicions'. And so, thanks to Jean-Jacques's enviable capacity for instant oblivion, that was that; 'I soon forgot our quarrel.'

---

* A great deal of rather inconclusive research has been carried out by the Rousseau-industry, which thrives on unravelling these cobweb-covered mysteries, to try to establish which of the two memorialists, Jean-Jacques or Madame d'Epinay, took the greater liberties with the truth. But though it has been estab-lished that the latter's account has been edited, here and there, by Diderot and Grimm, there can surely be little doubt whose story of Thérèse's conduct carries most conviction. Moreover, if Madame d'Epinay was so concerned with her reputation as to indulge in the gross falsification of which she is accused by the Rousseauphiles, one wonders why she volunteered one bit of information that certainly did not help her image: to wit, that she infected her first lover, Franceuil, with a venereal disease she had caught from her husband who had caught it from one of his lady-friends.

The account fills one of those many pages in the *Confessions* so out-rageous in their incoherence and their implausibility that they pose a baffling problem. How could a professional writer who took great pride in his craft, making drafts even of most of his letters and composing his works very laboriously, have allowed such absurdly muddled passages as that about his reconciliation with Madame d'Epinay ever to reach the printer? His 'atrocious insults' had been 'inexcusable', and yet 'she threw her arms around his neck' and, though he maintained his 'suspicions' and she was 'cunning' as well as 'intriguing and implacable', he mingled his tears with hers, etc., etc. The confused nonsensicality of it all cannot easily be attributed to the mental derangement he suffered in his attacks of persecution-mania. At those times, describing the 'world of conspiracy' against him, he writes with such force as to be almost persuasive. It is only in telling his life-story that he often seems to prattle as heedlessly as a child, without any concern for order, consistency or verisimilitude. Capable of close and forceful reasoning when debating with his adver-saries, the attempt to reconcile the unedifying facts of his experience with the exigencies of the public relations campaign, as well as with his desperate need to persuade himself of his love of virtue and truth, proved too much for him. Add his addiction to wishful thinking, his failing memory and, last not least, that discontinuity of his consciousness that made him 'forget what he had been even an instant earlier . . . there is no link in our existence but only a succession of present moments . . .', and there one has a possible explanation for those passages that tax the readers' patience by their writer's apparent refusal even to try and make sense. In a letter dating from the time when he had left all but auto-biographical writing behind him, he made no secret of this abandonment of all intellectual self-discipline: 'Writing is a most painful duty to me. Nothing tires me more than thinking . . . It is no longer my business to reflect, compare . . . insist, do battle . . . I abandon myself to the impres-sion of the moment.'

*

If one can venture an explanation of how he came to write as incoherently as he did in his *Confessions*, there remains a further problem to which there seems to be no adequate answer. It is not how such a man as he showed himself to be, in his relations with nearly all the men and women who passed through his life, came to be hero-worshipped as the great moral leader of late eighteenth-century Europe. (Though that, too, is remarkable enough, it can be accounted for, if only by the fact that the overwhelming majority of his contemporaries never saw the depressing picture that emerges from the *Confessions*, which were not published until after his death. They knew and revered him as the author of *La Nouvelle Héloise* and *Emile* which, as will appear later, show the 'chameleon' at his most seductive, often unrecognizably different from the writer of the *Confessions*.) What is so baffling is that some in later generations, for whom the *Confessions* alone had really survived or, at any rate, become his masterpiece, could have found him irresistibly loveable—as many still do today. There is no more striking example than the famous literary critic of the last century, Sainte-Beuve. Though by no means of the school that is content to take Jean-Jacques at his own astronomical valuation, he nonetheless ends his profile with the statement that 'poetically speaking it will always be impossible not to love him'.

As may perhaps have transpired, the present writer has not found it, prosaically speaking, altogether beyond his powers. His difficulty is of a different nature: how to avoid forfeiting the interest or even the trust of the reader if, to present a faithful portrait, he must paint practically nothing but the most unsightly warts. If anything could be more boring and more suspect than hagiography it is surely its opposite, demonography. Fortunately, however, Burke exaggerated when, mistakenly holding Jean-Jacques responsible for the French Revolution, he denounced him as a 'man without a single virtue'. While there is undeniably very little in his private life to brighten up the portrait, at least some patches of light will appear in it when the public figure, Rousseau the author, has been painted in. And the sooner that can be done the better. That is why the reader will be spared such further illustrations of his '*triste caractère*' as are provided by the series of quarrels leading up to the final rupture with all his intimates of those days. Only this last act in the drama must still be briefly related.

*

The curtain went up on it two months after the touching scene in which, according to Jean-Jacques, his hostess, weeping copiously, had thrown her arms around her unrepentant accuser's neck. By her own account it had been rather the other way around; 'he threw himself at my feet with every sign of the most violent despair . . . admitted his offences, and swore that his life would not be long enough to atone for them.' And so she had promised 'oblivion', and that, again, was that. 'Let us hope,' wrote Grimm, 'that this will be the end of this ridiculous and extravagant affair'. Not altogether without reason—witness Jean-Jacques's early letter to his Swiss friend about his hopes of being able to steal quietly away—Grimm had felt for a long time that 'he had not been straightforward' with Madame d'Epinay; 'he allows others to speak disparagingly of you.' As matters turned out, his suspicions proved only too well-founded. That became clear when she decided to go and consult a famous doctor in Jean-Jacques's home town. Apparently she had been as good as her word about promising to forgive and forget. For she now suggested that Jean-Jacques might accompany her on the trip to Geneva. Whether she really wanted him to go or, as he maintains, was 'not speaking seriously', he was not in two minds about his answer. For a whole host of reasons, many of which he subsequently made clear in a letter to Grimm, he was definitely not in favour. One of them, which he inferred but had already made explicit on an earlier occasion, was that he did not suffer invalids gladly. At that time, urged to go and see an ailing friend who had asked for him, he had complied reluctantly indeed: 'We are three invalids here and I am not the one who requires least attention. I shall have to travel in the depths of winter . . . The roads are frightful . . . It is strange that a poor invalid, overwhelmed by his own ailments, should be the only one of more than two hundred friends Gauffecourt [the sick man] has in Paris, he wants to see.'* It was much the same when Madame d'Epinay fell ill. He was, he complained, at least as ill as she was, 'she had other friends, less ill, less poor, less keen on their liberty, less busy and at least as dear to her . . . why of all people would it be my duty and mine alone to accompany her . . . what has she ever done for me?' As he saw it they were quits; she had 'built him a little house', he had, 'out of pure friendship', given in to her ardent wish to install him there, she had 'moved heaven and earth and even intrigued to overcome my resistance . . . Often alone in the country she wanted me to keep her company, and having first made a sacrifice to friendship I now had to make one to gratitude'. Comparing his hostess's benefactions with his sacrifices, not just the 'sad indigestions' he had suffered at her too-opulent table but 'two years of slavery', there could surely be no doubt 'who was indebted to whom'.

As he soon realized himself, the letter in which he set out all these and many more reasons for his disinclination to accompany his hostess to Geneva, was not all that endearing. Written in 'the heat of indignation', he told his *confidante*, the Comtesse, 'it was full of things that my heart now disavows and of others that are striking truths emerging from my character and situation'. (As so often, he unwittingly hit the nail on the head with these last words, for the release, in the heat of the moment, of the meaner and pettier side of his nature was indeed very much part of his 'character'). For Grimm and Madame d'Epinay it was the last straw. 'Your monstrous ideas,' wrote the former, 'make me shudder with indignation . . . How dare you speak to me of slavery when I have seen

---

* It is revealing that in the *Confessions* this becomes: 'I hurried to poor Gauffecourt's . . . I never left his bedside until he was out of danger.'

daily all the tokens of the most tender and generous friendship you have received from this woman . . . I never want to see you again and I shall consider myself fortunate if I succeed in banning all memory of your behaviour from my mind.' His letter was soon followed by one from the châtelaine whom Jean-Jacques had meanwhile charged directly, in a letter addressed to her, with 'tyranny' and 'intrigue' to 'enslave' him. Not amused, she replied that his conduct made her afraid for him: 'It just is not natural to spend one's life suspecting and insulting one's friends . . . you abuse the patience my friendship for you has given me.' But another letter was required before he could be prevailed upon to free himself from the slavery he resented so much by the simple method of packing his bags. Though he was quite willing to admit that 'our friendship is dead' and that he 'ought to leave the Hermitage', he asked to be allowed to stay till the spring 'because my friends wish it'. He only decided to ignore his friends' wishes (in other words, the Comtesse, more anxious than ever to avoid anything that would set people talking) on receipt of an unmistakable notice to quit: 'After having shown you for years every possible evidence of friendship and sympathy,' it said, 'I have nothing left for you but pity . . . Since you wanted to leave the Hermitage and should have done so I am surprised that your friends prevented you. For my part I never consult mine over matters of duty and I have nothing more to say about yours.' But Jean-Jacques would not have been Jean-Jacques had he not made sure to have the last word. It took the form of a bread-and-butter letter of a decidedly original turn, such as might have been composed by an impecunious young man addressing a rich hostess whose weekend hospitality had cost him a fortune in tips: 'I thank you for the stay you persuaded me to make and my thanks would have been greater if I had not paid so dearly for it.'

*

Nothing but pity . . . There are moments when one shares Madame d'Epinay's sentiments. Not only because of that '*triste caractère*' with which a cruel fate had endowed poor Jean-Jacques, but also because of one feature of it: the duplicity that in the end 'disgusted' her, inspiring the 'profoundest contempt', was not even effective in the sense of being successful. For so hot was his temper that it regularly exposed his deviousness. There is no more striking example than his conduct when, shortly before the rupture with his hostess, he had received a letter from Diderot urging him to reconsider his refusal to accompany her on the journey to Geneva. It was a very friendly letter, pointing out the risk he ran of being thought ungrateful, admitting, however, that 'your health may be a stronger objection than I imagine', and ending with a plea to take it in the spirit in which it was written; 'I am writing this letter to fulfil an obligation towards you and towards myself. If it displeases you, throw it in the fire and pay no more attention to it than if it had never been written.' Fair enough, one would have thought. Not so Jean-Jacques who 'trembled with rage', dashed off a reply (including the *locus classicus* of self-pity already quoted: 'You care as little for my tears as about my life and health . . . if you could correct this fault in yourself . . . I would be a less pitiable person') and then rushed off to the château to read both Diderot's letter and his reply to Madame d'Epinay and Grimm. Not surprisingly they were 'flabbergasted'. For in his fury at his friend's well-intentioned meddling he gave away that he still harboured his old suspicions of his hostess. 'I was astounded,' she wrote to her sister-in-law, 'to learn from a letter he showed me in a moment of distraction that at the time when he asked me in tears to forgive him . . . he repeated to his friend Diderot the same old accusations . . . this duplicity revolted me.'

But was he really as treacherous as she thought? Or did he behave as he did only because of that 'incredible rapidity' with which he was continually becoming 'another man'? It could well be; two days after he had accused Madame d'Epinay of yet another crime, organizing a 'plot' against him, he was telling her that he was 'desperately worried' about her health, and if this was Machiavellianism it was hardly of the subtle quality the Maestro would have approved of. What is more, if Diderot's story is to be believed—and there is little reason not to believe the gist of it—he behaved with him in much the same reckless self-defeating manner as when he let himself be found out by Madame d'Epinay. According to this account the two friends met twice during the fateful year that had begun so auspiciously with the Comtesse's arrival on the scene and ended so disastrously with love-sick Jean-Jacques's ignominious expulsion from the Hermitage. At the first of these meetings he had declared himself tortured by the Marquis's suspicions which, he said, were wholly unjustified, aroused only by Madame d'Epinay's wicked trouble-making, since he himself had kept his guilty passion a secret from its object. Well, said Diderot, in that case why don't you write to the Marquis, admit your secret love and in so doing exonerate the Comtesse as well as yourself in his eyes? A good idea, said Jean-Jacques, and then, after his friend had left, sent the Marquis instead the lecture on the immorality of his adulterous relationship with the Comtesse already quoted. So unskilful a pupil of Machiavelli was he that he apparently completely forgot the old homily, 'oh, what a tangled web we weave'. For, as Diderot was a friend of the Marquis and friends are apt to talk about mutual friends, it should not have been beyond human foresight that he might soon discover Jean-Jacques's latest ploy. But what shows his ineptitude at sustained dissembling even more clearly is that, when Diderot did find out and asked for an explanation, Jean-Jacques obliged with exactly the same sort of give-away as had astonished Madame d'Epinay and Grimm. Here, he said, here are some of the Comtesse's letters, take any of them at random and you will read my justification. Whereupon it was Diderot's turn to be 'flabbergasted'. For the first letter he read confirmed that his old friend had played both him and the Marquis false when protesting he had never avowed his passion to the Comtesse nor attempted to win her away from the Marquis by moralizing about the sanctity of her marital vows. 'You must be mad,' Diderot had cried, 'to have exposed yourself to the risk of letting me read this, read it yourself, it is plain enough.'

Though he did not break with him then and there, it was the beginning of the end of their sixteen-year-old relationship. That is clear from the failure of Jean-Jacques's pitiful attempt, some two months later, to win back his closest friend. The letter he wrote to him at the time was again hardly of the type a prize-pupil of Machiavelli would have composed. It was very much a product of the pathetic, child-like chameleon whose nastiness and deviousness, normally coming to the surface only in times of stress, had subsided again. And nothing is more pathetic in it than his unawareness of the complexity of his own nature, so impulsive and impetuous as to render the stratagems imposed by his deviousness worse than ineffective. How could, he asked plaintively, how could so excitable a man as he was, really be perfidious? 'A knave is astute and cool-headed, a false man has self-control and does not fly into a temper; do you recognize these qualities in me?' But no answer came. Even the typical threat with which he concluded his appeal—'if I fall into despair and die cursing the ungrateful one whose misfortunes have made me shed so many tears . . . your nights may be haunted by the image of your dying friend. Diderot, think of it, I will not appeal to you again'—elicited no response.

The overt break came six months later when Jean-Jacques publicly accused Diderot of having betrayed the secret of his guilty passion to the Marquis. In so doing he turned out to be killing two birds with one stone, in the sense that it cost him the latter's friendship too. If anyone ought to know the truth of the matter, he, the Marquis, should. And it so happened that he had not only told Jean-Jacques a couple of months earlier that Diderot was innocent, but even seemed to have persuaded him of it. That is why he found the public denunciation of him as a traitor little to his taste. 'Sir,' he wrote to Jean-Jacques, 'our principles are too different for us ever to get along. Forget my existence . . . I promise you, Sir, to forget your person and to remember only your talents.' And so that, once more, was that, all his closest friends gone, Madame d'Epinay whose friendship had once been 'dearer than life', Grimm from whom he had been 'inseparable', Diderot from whom, in spite of everything, he still 'could not detach himself', as he wrote in his last desperate appeal, the Marquis and the Comtesse with whom he had once made a 'charming plan' for setting up a *ménage à trois*. All not only gone, all—though some mellowed as time passed—turned into enemies to whom he had become the 'moral dwarf on stilts' Madame d'Epinay called him, 'monstrous' in Grimm's eyes, 'odious', 'false as Satan' to Diderot, or at best, in the words of the Comtesse remembering him in old age, 'a pathetic figure'.

Only the hardest of hearts could remain unmoved at this cruel fate, however much Jean-Jacques—or rather the genes that had made him what he was—may have brought it upon himself. And yet, at times one's aversion becomes such as to leave no room for compassion. *Tout comprendre* may be *tout pardonner*. But *tout lire* in his case makes *tout comprendre* almost impossible. That feeling—which Madame d'Epinay expressed when she said his conduct was just not natural, so awful as to be 'incomprehensible'—never hits one more forcefully than when reading the account he gives in the *Confessions* of his refusal to accompany her to Geneva.

At the time, he explains, he had not been able to give the real reason without betraying secrets that were sacred to him. He had 'boldly, unreservedly, unswervingly' chosen to accept the 'ruin of his own reputation' by making the 'excuses' (contained in his letter to Grimm) that had enabled his enemies 'to rob me of public esteem'. And even now he would say no more than that he had been too well-informed 'to fall into the trap' Madame d'Epinay had set when she asked him to accompany her on the journey to see her doctor. Its 'hidden purpose' had been no secret to anyone in the château, he himself had it 'from Thérèse who had it from the majordomo who had it from the ladies' maid'. What this hidden purpose was would 'never escape from my mouth or my pen'. Had he not promised the châtelaine, when he had accused her of being a vile informer, that nonetheless 'your secrets shall always be respected, I shall never break my word'? He had indeed. So, even though she had long since become one of his most relentless enemies, 'who had added her efforts to those of the Grimm and the Holbach clique to sink me completely,' his lips would remain sealed.

In fact, there was no need to unseal them as he had already done so ten pages earlier on, where he had told of 'her affair with Grimm which was concealed from nobody, not even her husband, though she herself always stoutly denied it'. Once informed of this amour, it was not all that difficult for his readers to guess what he had heard from Thérèse (who had it from the majordomo who had it from the ladies' maid) about the hidden purpose of the journey to the famous Swiss doctor. What was less easy to divine was the nature of the 'trap' he claimed to have feared. Was it that Madame d'Epinay would try to unload the paternity of Grimm's child she was supposed to be carrying, but never gave birth to, on the virtuous Jean-Jacques? He does not say. He says no more about it than that 'Grimm was aware of the facts which I did not mention and which fully justified my conduct'.

There one has Jean-Jacques, not in the heat of the moment but ten years or more after the event, telling a tale so tall and crediting his former friends with designs on him both so vile and so absurd, that it seems an obvious fabrication even before one checks it with the known facts. The facts are, first that there is no record in Geneva of a birth of a foreign child at the time of her visit there; second, that Madame d'Epinay had already told Jean-Jacques of her intention to visit her doctor there seven months earlier so that the 'hidden purpose,' if she was pregnant by Grimm, could not have been an abortion; third, that she made no secret of her journey but in fact went with her husband, her son and his tutor—which she would hardly have done if she had a pregnancy to conceal from them. But what makes Jean-Jacques's retrospective insinuations even more suspect is that there is no trace of them in the letters he wrote at the time. He does not breathe a word of them even to his *confidante*. In so far as he reveals to her any reasons he had not mentioned in his letter to Grimm, they were, implicitly, that he did not want to be parted from her, and explicitly, that in spite of the tearful reconciliation scene with her sister-in-law, he still detested 'this woman whom I can neither love nor esteem and who wants to ruin me'. Again, there is not a line in his letter to Grimm that bears out his later claim to have let him see that 'I was not in the dark and that I found it strange the journey should be a duty for me whilst he was excused and his name not even mentioned'. What is more, when, seven months earlier, Madame d'Epinay, then 'still more precious than life' to him, had told him of her plan to go to Geneva and her reason for it, he had written to her doctor to say that he was 'very tempted to accompany her' and that 'both her heart and her body were much in need of it'.

So, what with one thing and another, it seems practically impossible to acquit him of deliberately inventing skeletons with which to fill his former friends' cupboards, partly in order to justify a conduct whose original explanation had done him no good and partly to revenge himself for their allegedly having revealed (which Grimm never did and Madame d'Epinay cannot be proved to have done) no less than five very real and redoubtable ones he had in his own cupboard: the children he had had by Thérèse and obliged her to leave to the tender care of the Foundling Home.

And yet, could he really have been quite so perfidious? The imagination recoils at the thought like a horse refusing an almost impossible jump. The villainy of it seems as much beyond one's powers of belief as the self-complacency and the egocentricity he never displayed more comically than when, at the very time he had become a moral outcast at the Hermitage, he exclaimed to the Comtesse: 'Oh, Sophie, I charge you with my glory, try to justify the tribute with which decent folk have honoured me, conduct yourself in such a manner that in seeing you and remembering me, people will say: Ah, how that man loved virtue!' It is this sort of statement that makes one ask a question akin to that which he had asked himself in his last letter to Diderot: can a fool—and who but a fool could have brought himself to write such lines—really be quite so false? Is it not much more likely that when he wrote his *Confessions*, Jean-Jacques, a genius at self-deception and by then seeing the world through paranoia-coloured glasses, had somehow persuaded himself the story he told about Madame d'Epinay's 'trap' was true? Whatever the answer, one can understand Grimm's exclamation: 'Good God, and such men the world calls philosophers!'

But so mighty is the power of the pen, and so busy was Jean-Jacques with it in these the most productive years of his life as a writer, that it was not long before the world of fashion would be calling him something even more honourable than a sage: a saint.

CHAPTER ELEVEN

Life at the Top

'The Duc de Villeroy, the Prince de Tigny, the Marquis d'Armentières, the Duchesse de Montmorency, the Duchesse de Boufflers, the Comtesse de Valentinois, the Comtesse de Boufflers and other people of that condition . . . consented to face a very tiring climb in making the pilgrimage . . . I owed all these visits to the kindness of M. and Mme de Luxembourg.'

THOUGH his sad experiences at the Hermitage had 'cured' Jean-Jacques of 'all vain dreams of friendship', he soon discovered the truth of the consoling old saw that there are better fish swimming than have ever been caught. Compared with the grand new friends he made when he moved to a small house he had rented in the neighbourhood, Madame d'Epinay and her lot were small fry indeed. The daughter of a mere baron, she had through marriage become a mere marquise, and as Voltaire had said, anyone with money could make that lowly grade in France (whose Roi Soleil had financed his wars selling titles by the gross and subsequently annulling them so he could sell them all over again). Like the châtelaine of Chenonceaux, in whose Paris house Jean-Jacques had had his first taste of high life, his hostess at the Hermitage really belonged to the world of finance. These ladies' menfolk, fathers or husbands, had made their money by contracting with the King for the collection of indirect taxes, an ungrateful task which, however, their corporation knew how to make profitable by employing a sort of private police force numbering over 20,000 men with extensive rights of search. And this tax-farmers' world, like that of bankers and merchant adventurers, had inter-married extensively with the old aristocracy. Far from forming a closed caste, many families with blood musty enough to have become truly blue recruited brides for their sons from among undistinguished but well-heeled young women who served them, in Montesquieu's picturesque phrase, 'as manure with which to improve their arid lands'.

There were no such malodorous flies on the Duke and Duchess of Montmorency-Luxembourg, who now showed an enthusiasm for Jean-

Jacques not even equalled by Madame d'Epinay when she had sent him her underpetticoat. No sooner had they learned of his arrival in the neighbourhood of their estates (on returning there, for their twice-yearly visit, when the Duke, a Marshal of France and a close friend of the King, could escape from Versailles) than they sent a servant to invite him to luncheon at the château, not once, but 'as often as I wished'. And so insistent were they, refusing to take no for an answer—for Jean-Jacques had 'trembled at the very idea of appearing before an assembly of courtiers'—that the Duke called on him in person. It was an anxious moment. For he came in state with a suite of half a dozen retainers, and the floor of the room in which Jean-Jacques had to receive them was so 'rotten' that he feared 'the weight of them all would make it collapse'. Whether it was because the Duke shared his fear of a collective tumble or, more likely, because he was by all accounts as kind and good-hearted a Grand Seigneur as ever was, he and his duchess pressed their new neighbour to move into a house on their estate known as '*le petit château*', while his own underwent the necessary repairs. It was all the more gratifying because, apart from being an 'enchanting abode', the offer of it proved that virtue need not always just be its own reward but sometimes pays off as well. 'I shall never forget,' Jean-Jacques wrote to his latest benefactor, 'that the Marshal, Duke of Luxembourg, when he honoured me with his visit and sat on a straw chair amidst my broken pots and pans, did so not because I had either name or fortune but because I had acquired some reputation for probity.'

Thus began a new friendship with the two grandest of the land who were soon gushing over him in the best manner of that gushing age. 'Your mind and even more your virtues,' the Duke wrote to his new friend, 'have filled me with esteem . . . I hope with all my heart that I may merit your friendship.' The Duchess went one better, expressing the 'infinite hope' that she might 'eventually merit a tiny part of your friendship'. At the same time she entered enthusiastically into the spirit of the tiresome act Jean-Jacques regularly put on and which was derived from his theory about the benefactor being beholden to the beneficiary. In reply to a letter of his designed to thank her without using the word—'I do not praise you nor thank you. But I live in your house. Everyone has his own language, I have said everything in mine'—she replied, 'It is not for you to thank us, it is the Marshal and I who are indebted to you and we would be even more grateful if you would have accepted a better set of rooms [in the petit château] than you have chosen.' She also assured him that he would not be bothered in any way: 'I cannot wait to get back to Montmorency, but have no fear, you will not be importuned, I know how you feel.'

He could hardly ask for more. But needless to say he did. He would only agree to satisfy his new hosts' longing to see him if they accepted his terms, the same as he had originally imposed on Madame d'Epinay. Typically, he did not hesitate to begin his letter to the Duke with a grouse about his hospitality: 'Sir, your house is charming . . . But staying there would be even more delicious for me if its magnificence and the care devoted to my comforts did not make me so aware of not being at home, on my own.' As for seeing them, there could be no question of it when they were surrounded by the 'multitude that is inseparable from your rank . . . I do not wish to satisfy their curiosity nor see, even for one moment, others than those that suit me . . . My nature cannot stand bother of any kind . . . Arrange things so I can see you alone, allow me to see you in no other way.' And for good measure he ended with another grouse, reflecting his concern with his image: 'While my stay here does not affect you in any way, it has extremely serious consequences for me. I know that even if I spent only one night here, the public, and perhaps posterity, would still call me to account for it.'

There is no record of the Duke having smiled, let alone gasped, at Jean-Jacques's certainty, even at this early stage in his career when he was still only in the foothills of the towering reputation he would achieve a few years later, that the public was keeping a close watch on his every move and posterity was preparing to do likewise. But it is unlikely he or his duchess were capable of such irreverence. For what is on record is that they both hastened to assure their guest of the complete freedom from bother he had demanded as the price for his willingness to accept their hospitality. 'You will only see Madame de Luxembourg and myself,' the Duke wrote, 'when you want to. As for guests we might have, you will see only those you wish to see and will not be importuned.' And once again the Duchess was even more respectful, apparently content to gaze at her new lion in speechless awe, so that he would not even be aware of her presence: 'Do not be alarmed, Sir, let me assure you that we shall in no way threaten your liberty, we want to see you often, in silence, you will not notice it.'

*

Their deferential attitude was all the more remarkable as, at the time Jean-Jacques came into their illustrious lives, he had not yet become the best-selling author of the love-story that took not only Paris but most of the capitals of Europe by storm. He was known only for some provocative essays, a few articles he had contributed to Diderot's *Encyclopédie* and one successful operetta. But what made his adulation by the Luxembourgs' and their set—which quickly followed suit—stranger still was that the meagre writings he had to his credit included the *Discourse on the Origin of Inequality*, in which he had fulminated against the rich and the grand in a style Lenin could hardly have bettered: 'I can prove that if we have a few rich and powerful men on the pinnacle of fortune and grandeur while the masses grovel in want and obscurity it is . . . because the former would cease to be happy the moment the people ceased to be wretched.' Had the Duke and his Duchess not read it? Or did they love its author all the better for it, grateful for the delicious *frisson* they derived from his thundering denunciations of their class? The intellectuals, later recalled a vicomtesse who had escaped the rather less agreeable shiver running down the spine of those of her class who rode in the tumbrils, 'had no more benevolent followers than the grands seigneurs. The horror of abuses, the contempt for hereditary distinctions, all those sentiments the lower orders have exploited in their own interest, owed their first burgeoning to the grand . . . With some of them the exaltation bordered on blind delusion'.

But one must turn again to the Comte de Ségur for the most illuminating description of how his class had felt in those years when the future still seemed shining bright with the promise of the new and better world dreamt by the intellectuals of the day. Some of his statements, particularly the references to what is nowadays called the generation-gap, strike a strangely contemporary note. 'Irritated by the tiresome etiquette of the old regime, estranged from our fathers who disliked our new fashion of simple egalitarian clothes [many of the young nobles of pre-revolutionary Paris adopted the bourgeois frock-coat] we felt inclined to fall in enthusiastically behind the bold writers. We were carried away by Voltaire, our hearts were touched by Rousseau. We took a secret pleasure in seeing them attack the old scaffolding that seemed ridiculously antiquated to us. And though it was our privileges that were being undermined, their little war pleased us . . . It was, after all, only a war fought with pen and paper which, we felt, could hardly do any real damage to the privileged way of life we enjoyed and which, because it had been ours for several centuries, we believed to be indestructible . . . We laughed at the alarm felt at Court and by the clergy . . . The idea of equality attracted us; it is agreeable to descend when you believe you can go back up any time you want to. Lacking foresight, we enjoyed at the same time the advantages of being aristocrats and the charms of the plebeian philosophy . . . We walked gaily across a carpet of flowers that concealed an abyss . . . Never was there a more terrible awakening preceded by a sweeter slumber and more seductive dreams.'

They were seductive not only to the young. Though the nobility of the countryside, mostly too impoverished to be able to spend much time in

Paris, remained largely unaffected by the new ideas, those who frequented the salons of the capital, so Walpole wrote to a friend, 'were all
devoutly employed in pulling down God and the King'. Atheism was the
reigning fashion. 'In social circles,' one of the King's minsters said around
the middle of the century, 'one dare not speak on behalf of the clergy.' Not
that high society had become a freemasonry of ardent unbelievers. 'You
must not think,' Walpole had continued, 'that the people of quality are
atheists, at least not the men . . . Poor souls, they are not capable of going
so far in their thinking. They assent to a great deal because they do not
know how to contradict.' And, he might have added, those who did know
did not dare to, since the fashion, decreed by the intellectuals, was to
revile Christianity. Their prestige was immense, especially with the ladies
who, a contemporary observed, 'have got the upper hand to such an
extent that men only feel and think as they do'. A certain Duc de Castries
proved himself a brave backwoodsman indeed when he remarked testily,
on hearing of Diderot's rupture with Rousseau: 'I hear nothing but talk
about these two. Can you imagine? People of no account, living on the
third floor!'

If high society was so ready to fall in line with the radicals of their time
it was partly because its members had some reason to feel they had little
to fear from them. And indeed, in so far as writers like Voltaire, Diderot
or Rousseau directed their shafts at the arbitrary, absolute power of the
monarch as well as at the intolerant despotism of the established Church,
there seemed to be an identity of interests between the men of letters and
the men of blue blood. Reduced to the status of servile courtiers, deprived
of any real power even in local government, left only with the enjoyment
of their fiscal and ceremonial privileges, absentee landlords obliged to
spend most of their time near the source of all honours, offices and
favours at Versailles, the aristocrats harboured a resentment against their
royal master that made them naturally receptive to the new ideas. Moreover, in their enforced idleness they had all the time in the world for the
spinners of words, the architects of a beautiful new dream-world, not only
to sit at their feet but to emulate them, adopt their profession, as did such
members of the nobility as Montesquieu, Buffon, Condorcet, Helvétius
and many others. Finally, and most important, the 'plebeian philosophy'
they so readily embraced did not aim at substituting the power of the
plebs for that of the King. Even Jean-Jacques, whose vast range of political
noises included the Leninesque as well as the Burkean variety, would have
had a fit at the thought. And so, as Tocqueville has pointed out, it never
occurred to the aristocracy that the intellectuals' criticism of the political
and constitutional *status quo* could be anything but beneficial to their own
interests, that it could awaken the lower orders as well as weaken the all-

highest. 'How could anyone,' so Ségur asked, 'fear that outburst of passions and crimes, at a time when all the writings, all the words and all the actions aimed only at the extirpation of vice, the propagation of virtue, the abolition of arbitrary rule . . . It was impossible for us not to embrace enthusiastically the hope men of genius brought us of a future in which reason, humanity, tolerance and liberty would rule.'

But it was not only because they felt they could afford to be progressive that the nobles echoed the intellectuals' protest against the injustice of the existing order (as did even the King who denounced the 'avidity of the rich as the cause of the general distress' and instanced the benefits they derived from the feudal '*corvées*' still exacted from the rural populace: 'almost all roads are made by the unpaid labour of the poorest who have but little interest in them, those who gain are the landowners, the privileged persons whose estates increase in value'). Especially the younger generation of aristocrats was moved by a wave of genuine idealism. The Comte de Ségur was by no means the only young noble who followed Lafayette across the Atlantic to risk his life in a war fought, not with pen and paper but with musket and cannon, for the 'plebeian philosophy' of his time.

*

If, to judge by some of Jean-Jacques's published statements, the Duke and his Duchess seemed to have clasped a revolutionary serpent to their bosom, there are many more to show that, owing to its timid, soft-centred nature, it was a very cuddlesome reptile whose hiss was meant only to attract attention. For every seismic slogan Jean-Jacques gave to a world soon ready to act upon them—'the fruits of the earth belong to us all, the earth itself to no one', 'man is born free, yet everywhere he is in chains', etc., etc.—there are a dozen exhortations to refrain from action. 'I would not,' he wrote to a correspondent who had told him of his desire to liberate the country from its chains, 'have anything to do with revolutionary conspiracies which can never be carried out without disorder, violence and sometimes bloodshed; in my opinion the liberty of the whole human race is not worth the blood of a single human being.' In the same essay in which he had sounded the trumpet of the class-war shrilly enough to please a Trotsky, he had warned against it in a manner that should have delighted the unfortunate Czar; 'people who make revolutions,' he had written prophetically, 'nearly always manage to hand themselves over to seducers who only make their chains heavier than before.' In dedicating this essay to his native republic of Geneva he had glorified its oligarchic constitution: 'The more I reflect on your civil and political condition the less I can conceive that the nature of human affairs could allow of a better one.' Commenting on a proposal (made by a fellow-intellectual of an earlier generation) for a certain democratisation of the French state, he recoiled in horror: 'Think of the danger of setting the masses in motion! Who could control the shock or foresee the effects it might have? What man of any sense would dare to abolish the old customs and give a different form to the State than that to which thirteen centuries have brought it?' When in the course of a quarrel with the Geneva establishment he let off some broadsides that enflamed his supporters to the point of planning subversive action, he begged them to desist: 'You are surely too decent . . . not to prefer peace to liberty', they should 'emigrate rather than rebel'. Much as he protested against injustice he took a very philosophical view of its ubiquity: 'It is in the nature of things . . . I suffer from it but it does not make me angry . . . If we were in the place of those who persecute us we would do the same.' Thus, had it not been for his 'fatal gift for epigrams', the stirring battle-cries with which he embellished his writings, he would have been fully justified in his complaint 'about people who insisted on seeing a trouble-maker in the most law-abiding man in the world with the greatest aversion to revolutions'. It was an aversion, incidentally, which extended to politics of any kind, hardly a mention of which is to be found in his thousands of published letters. Just as public disorder 'infuriated' him, so the public affairs of his time bored or annoyed him to the point where he could not bear hearing about them. 'Do not,' he wrote to one of his new lady-admirers, 'do not ever let me see a word in your letters about current affairs which I hate for a thousand reasons.'

So, even if his ducal benefactors were aware that on occasion he saw the members of their class as 'hungry wolves who, once having tasted human flesh, refuse any other nourishment', they could comfort themselves with the thought that their dear Jean-Jacques really meant no harm (ice-cold though his comfort proved to their grand-daughter whose 'pure face and maidenly timidity', much admired by Jean-Jacques, did not save her from being sent to the guillotine by the regime that invoked him as its patron saint). For just as he complained of those who took his revolutionary slogans at face value, so he remonstrated with disciples who echoed what they thought to be his advocacy of soaking the rich. 'You are too severe with the rich,' he wrote to one of them, 'you should remember that levelling down those who from childhood have developed a thousand wants unknown to the likes of us, is to make them more miserable than the poor; one must be just to everyone, even to those who are unjust to us.' Clearly, what he felt about the rich or, at any rate, said about them, depended on whether he happened to be wearing the demagogic hat he put on when 'firing a pistol in the street to collect a crowd', or that of the prudent, commonsensical, Swiss petit-bourgeois he so often showed himself in the commonplace homilies with which he usually ends up. His pronouncements in this latter role often sound as if they had been composed for a conservative party manifesto of Disraeli's time: 'It is not enough that the people should have bread so it can live within its estate. It must be able to live agreeably so that it will better fulfil the duties of its station, will worry less about escaping from it and allow public order to be more solidly established . . . The state only has firm foundations when all are content with their place in it.' He expresses no less impeccable sentiments about the sanctity of the right of property, 'the most sacred of all and . . . in certain respects more important even than liberty itself', the reason being that 'nothing is more fatal to morality and the republic than the continual shifting of rank and fortune among the citizens . . . Such changes are . . . the source of a thousand disorders and overturn and confound everything'.

The most dyed-in-the-wool conservative could not have asked for a more satisfactory statement of his case. But only eight pages later in the same essay this staunch defender of the social-economic *status quo* has suddenly become an out-and-out leveller, proposing to tax the rich so as to deprive them of all their 'superfluities' and no longer accepting the rich man's plea that 'what may be superfluous to a man of inferior status is necessary for him: this is false, a grandee has two legs just like a cowherd, and like him only one belly'. There then follows a page that could have been written for a socialist or even communist's electioneering campaign, all about the 'advantages of society being exclusively for the rich and the powerful . . . Even murders committed by the great are hushed up but if a great man himself is robbed or insulted, the whole police force immediately goes into action . . .'

If he veered so wildly from one extreme to another, now the true-blue Tory, now the rabid class-warrior, it was also simply a question of mood. Some of his letters, written in times of stress which always brought out the worst in him, like the one that proved too much for Grimm or the one in which he sneered at his beloved Comtesse's social status, are rank with a sour, vindictive self-pitying class-hatred. It was of a different kind from that of the great inventors of the class-war, men like Marx and Engels in whose motivation personal envy and rancour, born of inferiority complexes, played little or no part. In Jean-Jacques's case this sentiment was *fons et origo* of his fits of egalitarianism and humanitarianism. Though some of his more enthusiastic biographers credit him with 'immense pity' for his fellow men, and he himself claimed to feel an 'unquenchable hatred for the oppressions of the wretched people,' they figure surprisingly seldom in his writings. And such references as there are evidence at least as much dislike of the masses as pity. What had in fact made him rebel against the existing order was not the spectacle of their sufferings but the hurt this order had caused to his own class-conscious pride. It was, so he tells us in the *Confessions*, his humilating experiences as a lackey and subsequently as the ambassador's secretary in Venice, that had given him 'a very natural aversion for the apparent order of things' and 'left a seed of indignation against our absurd civil institutions which merely sanction the oppression of the weak and the iniquity of the strong'. And in one of those rare moments of modesty and true self-knowledge that make *Emile* by far his most attractive book, he admits that this aversion and this indignation were at bottom inspired by envy: 'The most difficult fault to overcome in me was a certain haughty misanthropy, a certain bitterness against the rich and successful, as if their wealth and happiness had been gained at my own expense and as if their supposed happiness had been unjustly taken from my own.' There is precious little evidence in his other writings or his letters that he ever did overcome this haughty misanthropy. His love of humanity was never of the kind of an Albert Schweitzer. 'It is because I love men,' he wrote to one of his foremost protectors (another whose head was to fall into the grisly basket), 'that I flee from them, I suffer less of their ills when I do not see them.' And towards the end of his life he did not even love men in this painless fashion. Not that he had come to hate them, for he was 'incapable of hatred', he felt himself 'too far above them to hate them'. But he could not deny that they inspired him with 'the contempt they deserve'. As a by no means unsympathetic biographer* has said, the only thing that seemed to matter to the man who devoted the last fifteen years of his life almost entirely to his public relations campaign, was that humanity should reform not its laws but its attitude towards Jean-Jacques Rousseau.

*

Considering the social climate of the time as well as the grandeur, the pomp and circumstance of the Duke's way of life, it was in no way surprising that even so republican a spirit as the 'Citizen of Geneva' (the appellation by which Jean-Jacques proudly distinguished himself from the servile subjects of the French King) should have stood in great awe of his new friends. Possibly, however, he carried his deference rather farther than most of his fellow-intellectuals. On one occasion when the Duke condescended to suggest going for a walk with a commoner of their mutual acquaintance, he was so overcome that he 'could not utter a word, I followed behind weeping like a child and longing to kiss the footprints

---

* Jean Starobinski.

1a. Denis Diderot.
From the portrait by
Van Loo in the Louvre

Photo: Giraudon

1b. Friedrich Melchior Grimm.
From an engraving
after Carmontelle

Photo: Mansell Collection

2a. Madame d'Epinay.
From the portrait by
Liotard in the Musée d'art
et d'histoire, Geneva

2b. Madame d'Houdetot

3a. Thérèse Levasseur as an old woman. From a pencil drawing by Naudet

Photo: Bulloz

3b. 'Maman', Madame de Warens. From an anonymous portrait in the Musée Rousseau, Geneva

4a. The Duchesse de Luxembourg

4b. David Hume.
From the portrait by Allan
Ramsay in the National
Gallery of Scotland

Photo: Annan

of the dear Marshal'. But there was nothing abject in his recognition that, much as the Marshal and he might love and esteem one another, the 'delicious intimacy' he demanded of friendship was too much to hope for. He had realized from the outset that the deference he could not root out from his heart presented an almost insoluble problem. In a dignified passage of a letter to the Duke he had explained his dilemma: 'How, Sir, am I to behave with you whom my heart honours and whose intimacy I should seek if I were your equal? Having always wanted to live only with friends I know only the language of friendship and familiarity. I am fully aware how much someone of my station must modify it with someone of your rank. But I am even more conscious of it that poverty, which debases itself, becomes contemptible; it has its own dignity . . . I am thus always afraid of failing you or failing myself, being familiar or fawning.'

For a while he had cherished the hope that, 'if we are both such as I like to think, we can give a rare and perhaps unique example of a relationship of esteem and friendship . . . between two men of such different stations that they did not seem capable of having any intercourse'. But three months later he had already found—or imagined—reason to despair of achieving the kind of contact he craved. And so he started one of those pretend-quarrels, writing one of those letters in which he seems to force the intimacy he wants through reproaches bordering on insults. 'How cruel your kindnesses are,' he wrote to the Duchess, 'Why did you come to trouble the peace of a solitary who had renounced the *douceurs* of life . . . I have never been able to resist caresses . . . It is all very well for you and the Marshal to speak of friendship. But I am mad to take you at your word. You make sport of me, I attach myself and the end of the game is that I am left with regrets. How I hate your titles and how I pity you for having to live with them. I know you have a loving heart . . . But with people of your rank and your way of life nothing makes a lasting impression, so many new things crowd in upon you all the time. You will forget me, Madame, after having made it impossible for me to follow your example. You will have done a great deal to make yourself inexcusable.'

Though much of it is Jean-Jacques at his worst, offensive, distrustful, demanding and self-pitying, he doubtless did have a point with his complaint about the impossibility of the kind of friendship he wanted with people who had other distractions and other duties than the 'unburdening of hearts' so dear to him. 'If only,' he sighed three years later when he performed a massive unburdening in four long letters to his friend and protector, the chief censor, 'if only Monsieur de Luxembourg were not a duke and a Marshal of France but a simple country-gentleman living in some old château . . . how happily we could have lived together.'

But if dukes and duchesses were not really to his taste, neither were the

rank and file of humanity. When in his twenties he had a short spell as a
clerk in a government office, he had found this 'most disagreeable employment' made even worse by the people he had to associate with, 'all those
clods, the majority of whom were extremely ill-kempt and unclean,
poisoning the atmosphere in the dreary office with their breath and their
sweat'. When some years later he was discussing terms for a job as tutor
he wrote: 'I am not much interested in money provided I am treated with
the consideration due to a gentleman who has fallen on evil times.' His
old-fashioned attitude to servants is well illustrated by the advice he gave
a princely admirer: 'Sack your servants on the spot the moment they fail
to obey your instructions.' Where his natural sympathies lay as between
the classes appears equally clearly from the account of his relations with a
bogus baron. He had taken to him, in his early fifties, because the
Baron 'had all the marks of a man of breeding which made me esteem him
too much not to love him'. So when a servant girl accused his new friend
of having got her with child he rushed to his defence, calling the girl 'an
abominable sow, dirty slut, the foulest, most stinking, hideous monster ...
I made every effort to get her arrested'. And even the discovery that the
Baron was an impostor and that the girl had spoken the truth could not
shake his conviction that 'he was a gentleman by birth'.

If it were not for the fact that revolutionaries of later ages have seized
upon the demagogic, revolutionary phrases Jean-Jacques has sprinkled
throughout his writings, so as to claim him for their cause, there would
have been no need to point out that he was no great egalitarian. None of
his fellow-intellectuals was. The 'progressives' of his day were far from
being radicals in their social-economic thinking (though Montesquieu
sounds surprisingly modern with his demand for a welfare state 'which
owes its citizens an assured subsistence including food, clothes, and a way
of life conductive to health'). By the standards of the age there was,
therefore, nothing particularly retrograde in statements of Jean-Jacques
that to our ears sound thoroughly reactionary. He held the common herd
to be quite incapable of cherishing 'the sublime notions of the God of
wise men; the laws of kindness and brotherhood which he imposes on us
will never be understood by the multitude [which] will always have gods
as stupid as itself'. In the same spirit he insisted that knowledge must
remain the monopoly of the intellectual élite, its vulgarization was much
to be deplored; 'what are we to think of the herd of textbook-authors ...
who have indiscreetly broken open the door of the sciences and introduced
into their sanctuary a populace unworthy to approach it.' He himself did
not write for the people: 'My books are not meant for them.' And when he
decided 'for once to conquer my distaste for addressing the people', he
in fact never came to write the piece he had in mind. Though on occasion

he makes a bow to the masses—'they constitute the human race, those who do not belong to them are so few that they are not worth bothering about'—he seems oblivious of their existence when fulminating against the corruption of 'society' by the arts and the sciences, to whose nefarious effects the eighteen million peasants and workers of the France of his day were hardly over-exposed. The community of his dreams which he describes in *La Nouvelle Héloise* is run by the lord of the manor in truly feudal style. Likewise, when he was asked to advise on a new constitution for Poland he insisted, in his far from radical proposals, on the necessity of making sure that 'the different ranks taking part in public festivals are carefully distinguished'. Evidently he still felt much the same at sixty as he had done at thirty when he had rhymed:

> Society would have no cause to give thanks
> If there were less inequality between its ranks.

His attitude towards the lower orders finds its most direct and un-equivocal expression in what he has to say about their women. After relating how disgusted he was by the advances of one of them, who 'thrust her dry snout into my face, all dirty with snuff, so I could hardly refrain from spitting into it', he goes on to explain that 'seamstresses, chamber-maids and shopgirls hardly ever tempted me, I needed young ladies'. He preferred them, he claims, not because of 'pride of rank', but because they had 'a better preserved complexion, lovelier hands, greater elegance in jewellery, an air of cleanliness and refinement . . . a finer and better gown, a neater pair of shoes . . . better done hair', as, no doubt, young ladies did have in an age when chambermaids and shopgirls were still far from earning the wherewithal for successful sartorial, cosmetic and capillary competition with duchesses, an age when bathrooms were few and the scent to mask the effects of their scarcity expensive. And just as one can, therefore, accept his disclaimer of 'pride of rank' as motivating his preference for ladies, so his warning, that 'it is difficult to find in the dregs of society a woman capable of making an *honnête homme* happy', need not necessarily convict him of class-prejudice. At a time when there was such a yawning gap between the educational status of the lower and the higher orders it was no more than an expression of that realistic good sense he displayed in so many other fields (all the more so as in eighteenth-century parlance *'honnête homme'* meant educated man as well as good man, gentleman).

*

This much having been said, the fact remains that he was certainly not the modern type of intellectual who, deriving a sense of guilt from his bourgeois origin, struggles to extirpate all vestiges of class-consciousness or, better still, cultivates the proletarian variety. Jean-Jacques remained throughout no less proud of his 'rank' than the Swiss burghers from among whom he stemmed and whom he once, in a letter to the Duchess, characterized as 'fuller of their birth than any bourgeois one has ever seen'. Nor did he make any secret of it: 'If there is a forgivable pride other than that which comes from personal merit it is pride of birth.' It was the ducal pair and their equally grand friends who almost seemed ashamed of their exalted status, so eagerly did they fall on their knees before the watchmaker's son from Geneva. The term is no exaggeration, witness a letter the Duchess wrote—when they had had one of their pretend-tiffs—and that started with: 'It is for me to throw myself at your feet;' and ended: 'I beg you on both my knees for a line to put my mind at rest.' No one, she said in another letter, 'could possibly be more distressed than I am by our separation, I would like to spend my entire life with you . . . I believe in your superiority, I respect it and love it'. If only he would condescend to come and stay with her at their mansion in Paris. But at least he could not stop her wishing he would: 'Fortunately you do not forbid me to hope and I would find it difficult to obey if you did . . . Adieu, Monsieur, there is no longer a moment in my life when I do not miss you, long for you, and love you.' The Duke was hardly less rapturous: 'How could you doubt,' he wrote from Versailles, 'that I think of you, even though I am at Court . . . I wish I could always be at Montmorency with you . . . In Paris as at Versailles the Duchess and I will be talking of you and our only dispute will be about who of us loves you most tenderly.' And Jean-Jacques, of course, replied in kind: 'Monsieur le Maréchal, there remains to me only one pleasure in life and that is to love you and to be loved by you. I feel that, if I were ever to forfeit it, I would have nothing left to lose.' The correspondence between the two men reached heights of cloying sentimentality that would have seemed almost suspect in any other age. When hard-pressed for time the Duke-Marshal, begged to do so by Jean-Jacques, would send a blank sheet to reassure his friend and protégé he was well and thinking of him, and Jean-Jacques would wax facetiously lyrical in his reply: 'I cannot, Monsieur le Maréchal, read your letter often enough, what abundance, what eloquence . . . Never did the Montesquieus, the Montaignes, the Pascals and the Tacituses of this world say so much in fewer words . . .'

It was all balm to the soul of poor, storm-tossed, soft-centred Jean-Jacques, just the kind of reassurance he needed after his fall from grace at the Hermitage. And it was all the more gratifying in that the Duchess, if not the somewhat simple-minded Duke, was renowned for her wit and discernment, as well as being exceedingly grand. 'Nothing,' the by no means over-indulgent Madame du Deffand had said of her, 'escapes the subtlety of her mind and the delicacy of her taste'. She was, so another contemporary of hers recalled in his memoirs, the recognised authority on good manners, the *arbiter elegantiarum*, the Emily Post of the Paris of Louis XV; 'Her empire over the young was absolute, in her house she kept the tradition alive of those noble and gentle manners which all Europe admired and vainly tried to imitate.'

No wonder, therefore, Jean-Jacques had at first been 'extremely afraid' of her. But it was no wonder either that, what with her 'intoxicating compliments', she had soon won him over. What is puzzling—or rather would be if it had not already been shown more than once that the author of the *Confessions* is an astonishingly careless writer—is that four pages after relating that he at 'at once became her slave' and that her conversation 'does not sparkle with wit', he informs the reader that he was 'never really comfortable with her' because he was 'in awe of her wit'. What he seems to mean is that his own slow-wittedness made him ill at ease with the gushing Duchess: 'I knew she was exacting in conversation . . . I knew that women and particularly great ladies absolutely demand to be kept amused and that it is better to offend them than to bore them.' And so he hit upon an idea to save himself 'the embarrassment of talking to her'. It was a bold scheme indeed; not every author would dare to risk the yawn, followed by the relapse into slumber, Jean-Jacques invited when, instead of trying to do his conversational duty by the Duchess with a cascade of merry quips, he sat by her fourposter bedside, at ten o'clock every morning, to read her his great novel. But it worked like a charm; 'the success of this stratagem exceeded my expectations.' The Duchess was absolutely bowled over; 'she talked of nothing but me, showed no other interest, paid me compliments all day long . . . insisted that I should always sit beside her at table and, when some nobleman wanted the seat, always said it was mine and made him sit elsewhere.'

It was in a sense the beginning of the end for Jean-Jacques. The acclaim he had enjoyed with his early writings had been perilous enough for someone so totally wrapped up in himself that he was congenitally incapable of seeing his own proportionate importance in the scheme of things. Lacking a self-deprecating sense of humour, he was singularly vulnerable to the dangers threatening all public figures in a period that was an Age of Flattery as well as of Reason and Sentiment. Its 'ridiculous habit of lavishing praises which had become practically obligatory' made Duclos wonder whether there was anybody 'who had not had his head turned when rising in the world'. There were moments when Jean-Jacques, glorified, sanctified and even deified by ever-increasing numbers, was aware of what the ridiculous habit was doing to him. 'The cloud of glory is intoxicating, I do not know whether it has gone to my head,' he wrote to a prince among his admirers who had done his utmost to make it do so, calling him 'the sacred image of virtue', erecting 'altars' to him in his heart, crediting him with 'the purest heart that ever existed'. And so, if the object of all this idolatry finally went mad with conceit, aggravated by the intolerable tension set up in his mind by the knowledge that the saint he was to his public had long since become a monster to most of those who knew him best, his hero-worshippers were at least partly responsible.

CHAPTER TWELVE

At the Feet of Julie

'I hate weakness in anyone . . . There is no virtue without fortitude and cowardice leads to vice.'

IRONICALLY, the man who is so often credited with having launched the Romantic Movement had to wait forty-four years before the Comtesse at last brought a few months of true if lopsided romance into his life. The lack of it until then had filled him with plaintive incomprehension: 'How could it be that, with such inflammable feelings, with a heart entirely moulded for love, I had not at least once burned with love for a definite object?' Of course, he had known calf-love, touchingly described in some of the best passages of the *Confessions*, as well as the bull-love the mother of ten had aroused with such cunning. But never the real thing, he had never 'tasted to the full . . . that intoxicating passion' for which his heart 'thirsted'.

It was partly just bad luck. But he was, perhaps, also rather less well-equipped for the earnest business of romantic love than he liked to think. The 'precautions' he took against being mocked or compromised, when at last he did meet his *femme fatale*, show a native prudence that is hardly a feature of the truly romantic temperament. Indeed, both in his letters and some of his books, he reveals a disabused, wordly-wise appreciation of the sadder facts of life that does not make for the careless raptures, let alone the durability of a *grande passion*. 'You have promised marriage?' he asked a love-lost acquaintance of his. 'How foolish you have been! . . . For Heaven's sake, remember that love is only an illusion, that one does not see things as they are when one loves.' It is the same spirit he evinces in *Emile*: 'Is not love a fancy, a falsehood, an illusion? We are far more in love with our own fancy than with the object of it. If we saw the object of our affections as it is, there would be no such thing as love . . . The joys of the senses are soon over, habit invariably destroys them . . . the imagination which adorns what we long for, deserts its possession.' Worse still, he adds in *La Nouvelle Héloise*, 'the distaste inspired by long possession is aggravated by advancing age and the fading of beauty.'

Fortunately there was one way of tasting the intoxicating passion without having to pay for it with the hangover of disillusionment, when the scales fall from the lover's eyes and the object of his passion loses the adornments with which his incandescent imagination has embellished reality. That was to settle for a mistress who had no adornments to lose because she had no reality, a woman who lived only in the imagination, not one of those imperfect products that come off the Creator's assembly-line but a 'celestial creature' made to order, custom-built by the customer himself. 'Seeing nothing that existed worthy of my exalted feelings', he invented the perfect woman and started to cover a ream of paper with sizzling love letters. It was the nearest he had ever come to employing his literary talents in the pursuit of love. For the one and only amorous letter on record dating from earlier days was hardly a mature effort: 'If I were to possess my adorable queen for only one minute, to be paid for by being hanged a quarter of an hour later, I would accept such a bargain with more joy than the throne of the universe.' As for the Comtesse, she only appeared on the scene after the bulk of the letters had already been composed. Originally written for his own satisfaction he later decided to make a book out of them.

It was a difficult decision to take for a writer who had made his name as a puritan moralist, denouncing the corrupting effects of the arts in general and of love stories in particular. His last published effort had been a vehement attack on their theatrical form. Yet here he was writing the very stuff he had utterly condemned. It was awkward indeed: 'After the austere rules I had so loudly preached, after so much stinging invective against effeminate books which breathe of love and languor, could anything more shocking be imagined than that I should suddenly enroll myself among the authors of the books I had so violently censured? I felt my inconsistency in all its force, I reproached myself for it, I blushed for it, I was angry with myself.' But there it was, it could not be helped, he simply had to get his 'voluptuous imaginings' off his chest; 'completely captivated I was forced to submit . . . and brave the world's opinion!' He would just have to rely on the 'love of virtue that had never left my heart' for, turning the 'erotic transports' in which he had composed the letters to 'purposes beneficial to morality', he would try to reconcile voluptuousness with virtue, not by running them in harness but by giving each a run for his money and eventually allowing virtue to win by a short head.

Opinions differ, and always have differed, as to whether these praiseworthy purposes were achieved, whether *La Nouvelle Héloise*, a love story in letter-form like Richardson's *Clarissa* which Jean-Jacques had taken as his model, was a moral or a licentious tale. Voltaire, whose scornful enmity Jean-Jacques had recently incurred with his denunciation of the theatre, so dear to the Grand Old Man then managing one of his own at his château near Geneva, called the book a 'mixture of debauchery and moral commonplaces . . . One of the infamies of this century is to have applauded this monstrous work'. His friend Madame du Deffand found it 'false, exaggerated and disgusting . . . I have seen nothing more contrary to good morals'. Madame Necker, whose husband was to try and save the Ancien Régime from financial collapse, held that 'nothing is less moral than an edifice of virtue built on the débris of vice. Rousseau put morality in his book but it is not a moral work'. The Archbishop of Paris denounced it as 'insinuating the poison of voluptuousness while seeming to proscribe it'. And in his Preface the author himself warned (with his usual modesty) that 'any girl who dares to read even one page is lost'. However, as 'chaste girls never read love stories' and as he had made it clear in his subtitle, 'Letters of Two Lovers', what his book was all about, they only had themselves to blame for their inevitable ruination should they be so abandoned as to open it. Moreover, while he could perfectly well understand people might object to its first part (where voluptuousness makes all the running), he could not possibly esteem 'anyone who thought ill of it after having read it from cover to cover; such a person would be no better than a hypocrite and a liar'.

The reason why the first part was fatal to girls was that in it his dream-woman, a teenage girl called Julie, goes a good deal further down the primrose path than just reading love stories. In fact, she continues right to the end of it, unable to resist the advances of a young man out of a lower social drawer, called St. Preux, whom her baronial parents had invited to act as her tutor. Though living in the same house, he deluges her with passionate letters. By eighteenth-century standards they were so outspoken that some of them were deemed worthy of the place of honour in an erotic anthology published some fifteen years later. By ours they seem comical rather than exciting. Thus when Julie forgets 'the modesty and virtue dear to me' so far as to give him a kiss, she gets but poor thanks: 'Keep your kisses; I cannot bear them, they are too acrid, too penetrating, they pierce, they burn right into the marrow . . . It was poison I gathered from your lips . . . it is killing me.' When at a later stage in their affair he is waiting for her in her room, where they are to have their one and only night of love, he passes the time by dashing off another letter. Penning away in breathless excitement: ('What good fortune to have found ink and paper! I am expressing my feelings in order to temper their excess') he grows lyrical about her corset, left lying about, presumably to save him the tricky business of unlacing or unhooking it: 'This corset, so slender, which touches and embraces you, what an enchanting form, in front two gentle curves, oh voluptuous sight! the whalebone has yielded to the force of the impression!... delicious imprint, let me kiss you a thousand times.'

It is a pity that again there is no record of how the Duchess and her Duke (who attended the bedside readings) reacted to such titbits which shocked Voltaire as well as filling him with derision. All one knows is that they found the work as a whole 'the most beautiful book in the world'. 'Only a soul like yours,' the Duchess wrote to its author, 'could have written it'. And they were far from being alone in this view. Overnight it became a runaway bestseller, with piratical publishers cashing in on it in London, Hamburg and many cities of France, while booksellers were renting out copies by the hour to eager readers unable to buy. 'What a book,' the Marquise de Polignac wrote to another lady of the same rank, 'and what a soul he must have to have written it . . . a heart so sensitive, delicate and virtuous that the whole of humanity is honoured by it. My first reaction was to have the horses harnessed and go to Montmorency to see him at all costs, to tell him how superior his tenderness seemed to make him to all other men.' A lady-in-waiting of the Duchess of Orleans declared that 'she could not imagine there could be any sensitive woman who would not seek him out to devote her life to him'. A princess in Paris was so enthralled when she started the book, before going to a ball at the Opera, that she could not tear herself away and was still reading, at four in the morning, missing the party. And it was not only the ladies who were moved to floods of tears. A general wrote to say that when he had reached the last of the hero's letters he 'no longer wept but howled like an animal'. An English bishop held it to be 'the most exquisite work ever' because written by 'a man of virtue'. Perhaps thinking of the poet Thomas Grey who had spoken slightingly of its 'absurdity and insipidity', he warned critics 'not to speak ill of it to me; I could never esteem such a person'.

A young man who became a leading publisher was only one of many admirers who raised Jean-Jacques to godlike status; 'Long since given over to the deceptive illusions of an impetuous youth,' he wrote, 'a powerful god was needed to pull me up from this abyss. You, Sir, are the god who has worked this miracle. After the happy reading [of *La Nouvelle Héloise*] I burn with the love of virtue . . . All those who will have the happiness of reading your works will find a guide in you who will lead them to perfection.' Young Necker, at odds with his wife on this point, exclaimed about the 'thousand sublime passages' he had found in the book. And even among the intelligentsia with whom it found little favour —Grimm criticized 'the absurdity of the story, the lack of plan, the poverty of its execution, the bombast of its style'—there were some who joined the reading public in singing its praises. The 'right-wing' essayist and journalist Fréron, though not blind to the 'prolixity of the style' and the 'defective characterisation', nonetheless felt compelled to admit that 'one cannot read the book without becoming better or at any rate wanting to become better'. The mathematician and physicist d'Alembert called it 'one of the best books I have read'. And another of Diderot's collaborators on the *Encyclopédie* went so far as to tell Jean-Jacques that he and his mistress both felt he was 'a divine man'.

*

If for the great majority of readers he had been wholly successful in achieving 'purposes beneficial to morality', it was because Julie's fall in the early part of the book was soon shown to be only a *reculer pour mieux sauter* towards spotless virtue. Obedient to her father she renounces her lover, marries an elderly gentleman of her own class and becomes a model wife and mother (though sorely tried by her husband who had the singular idea of inviting her ex-lover to come and live with them). Thus sacred love, left standing at the starting gate when the story opens, soon catches up with profane love and—with a little help in the form of Julie's death at an opportune moment—wins comfortably. It is once again the old technique of loosing off provocatively to draw an audience and then treating it to an old-fashioned sermon, this time on the sanctity of marriage. The author himself makes no bones about that: 'To be useful in what one wants to say,' he explained in the Preface, 'one must first make sure people will listen.' And to make them receptive to one's sermons, one must enable them to identify with the examples of virtue presented to them. That is what Richardson, (whose Clarissa, resisting all onslaughts on her virtue, was too good to be true) had failed to do. And that was why Jean-Jacques had made Julie succumb: 'If she had always been good she would have been much less effective; whom could she then have served as a model?'

It is all fair enough. But, of course, this technique had its dangers. As Julie was his dream-woman, painted in the rosiest of colours and credited with every possible virtue, he inevitably invited the accusation that he condoned if not applauded her early conduct, which by the standards of the age was strictly immoral. For though the intellectuals, with their rejection of Original Sin and their divinisation of Nature, were in theory all for the emancipation of man's passions, they were not so bold or so logical as to preach free love, certainly not for young girls. The sexual revolution had to wait for the pill. For Voltaire Julie was no better than a 'whore'. And if the foremost enemy of the Church so fully endorsed its teachings on the subject of the chastity demanded of unmarried women, one can imagine how the general public felt about it. Indeed, so unpermissive was the climate of the age that Jean-Jacques risked no ridicule

when he let his Julie wail about 'the abyss of shame' into which she had
been plunged by . . . a kiss. And so far did the law go in protecting young
women that domestics or other men living under the same roof with
them faced, in theory though no longer in practice, the death penalty for
taking them to bed. Decent, old-fashioned adultery was in general
accepted as in the nature of things, at any rate by the Paris *haut monde* of
the time. Once safely married off, usually by parents taking little notice
of the bride's preferences, young ladies could afford, though only with
considerable circumspection, the joys of illicit love. Before marriage they
were wholly taboo.

But Jean-Jacques had not only affronted this sacred convention when
he allowed the heroine of his sermon to lose her virginity in a rip-roaring
affair (though, what with the acrobatics being limited to a single night, it
was really more of a paper passion). What made him all the more vulnerable to the charge of having written a book that would deprave and
corrupt was its genesis. Having started it by writing love-letters to an
imaginary mistress, so as to satisfy his hunger for the intoxicating passion
he had never tasted in real life, the hero of the book he subsequently made
out of them was really Jean-Jacques himself: 'I identified myself with
him as far as I could,' he wrote in the *Confessions*, 'endowing him with the
virtues and the faults I felt in myself.' That, of course, is why St. Preux
soon ceases to be the 'vile seducer' Julie initially calls him. He is exoner-
ated, first in a footnote in which the Jean-Jacques of flesh and blood
points out that his paper twin is excused by his 'extreme youth' and 'his
sincere love of virtue'. Next he is exculpated all over again by Julie who
takes all the blame upon herself: 'He is not guilty, only I am . . . He was
never capable of being false to his vows. His virtuous heart does not know
the abject art of injuring the one he loves . . . He knows how to conquer
his passions.' And on her deathbed she goes so far as to make out that she
seduced him instead of *vice versa*: 'I threw myself at his head, he respected
me.' Apparently Jean-Jacques, forgetful and careless as always, over-
looked that in the earlier part of the story he had made his hero use all the
arts of seduction including the blackmail of thrice-repeated threats of
suicide.

Thus the guardians of the official morality could hardly be blamed for
accusing him of making seduction respectable, and not only the seducer
but the seducee as well. For, being Jean-Jacques's dream-woman, Julie
could not really be sinful either. And so, while she moans a great deal
about her 'shame', she is comforted by a great friend who asks her why
'true love should be degrading', and by her lover who assures her that 'it
is the first law we must obey . . . the purest law of nature'. And as if this
were not enough both parties are constantly told by their doting friends

that they are above the rules governing ordinary men and women: 'Your two souls are so extraordinary that they cannot be judged by common rules. For you happiness is neither to be attained by the same manner nor is it of the same kind as that of other men . . . your hearts are out of the ordinary.'

No wonder the Archbishop found fault with it. And no wonder either that hostile biographers, writing in Victorian times, seized on the 'permissive' passages to make their case. What might seem surprising, however, is that even highly respectable historians, like the scholarly and penetrating Ernest Seillière, go to surprising lengths in quoting out of context and thus make Jean-Jacques appear an enemy of the traditional morality. It is a measure of the intensity of feeling aroused by the man, of whom it has been said more than once that you either adore or detest him. And it certainly justifies his complaint about 'that odious manner of judging a work by shreds picked out here and there'.

Of course, it can be argued that he has only himself to blame for the misrepresentation of his thought, that his incoherence and the irresponsibility with which he scatters contradictory ideas and values all over his books, makes it practically impossible to know what he stands for. In the very sentence in which he voices his complaint about selective quotation he almost admits that he hardly knows himself what he really believes, speaks of his mind as 'overwhelmed by many ideas, diverted from one by the other, wellnigh incapable of assembling them'. It is as if his inability to tolerate any restraints on his freedom to do as he pleases, went so far as to make him fear even to commit himself to ideas or values.

But the book among all his writings which is least vulnerable to the charge of equivocation is exactly the one here at issue. However true it may be that, as a contemporary critic said, he gave illicit love 'the tone and the airs of virtue', in the end, indeed, long before the end, he comes heavily down on the side of angels of unquestionable respectability. He was at heart far too much of a conservative to be able to do otherwise. In so far as he echoes the intellectually fashionable insistence on the rights of Nature, it was, so a modern historian of the period has said, 'but a feeble abortive rebellion against conventional morality'. Certainly the letters he received from admirers shows that the public read his book as an exhortation to sacrifice romantic passion to old-fashioned virtue. And that is why the work that some thought no better than a sermon in praise of fornication, did more than anything he had written before to raise him in the public estimation to the level of sainthood. Not that it had the merit of novelty. Richardson, widely read in France, as well as French writers like Prévost, had already castigated 'love with the light touch', as one could call the attitudes then in vogue, when matrimonial bliss was a

subject for mockery by the playwrights of the day. With his call for a
return to earnestness and buckets of sentiment, Jean-Jacques was swimming with rather than against the stream.

*

That the Duchess thought so highly of his book as to want to embrace
its author ten times a day should hardly be a matter for surprise. The
more 'depraved' society is, he had sourly said in his Preface, 'the more
people love moral lectures. It enables them, at no greater cost than a few
idle hours of reading, to satisfy such little taste for virtue as they may
have left, sparing them the need to practise it'. And the Duchess had been
depraved indeed before, like Julie, she had reformed as the dutiful wife
of the good Marshal. Whereas Jean-Jacques's dream woman had had only
one lover, the Duchess (according to a jingle composed by a courtier who
got slapped for his impertinence) had had dozens:

> When first she appeared at court
> She seemed with love to burn.
> Using flattery of every sort
> Everyone had her in turn.

The recipients of her favours, so one of her contemporaries noted, had
included not only 'actors and even more obscure persons' but even her
brother. Indeed, if one is to believe the famous historian Jules Michelet,
she had been so diabolical a trollop as to have corrupted a woman-friend
to the point where the latter died of sheer shame; 'having won the tender
friendship of the Duke's first wife she dragged the couple off to priapic
bacchanalia where the poor creature, degraded before her husband's eyes
as the instrument of everyone's pleasure, became an object of contempt
and perished', thus leaving the way clear for her successor in the Duke's
affections. But as there is reputed to be more rejoicing in Heaven over
one sinner repentant than over ninety-nine shirts stuffed with virtue; as
she was, in Madame du Deffand's words, 'loyal to her friends, sincere,
discreet, helpful and generous'; as, in Jean-Jacques's eyes, she still bore
the vestiges of her 'early and radiant beauty'; as the Duke was such a dear
and, most important, as both these exalted personages were all over him,
it was only natural that the stern moralist was prepared to let bygones be
bygones and never even breathed a word about or raised an eyebrow at
her lurid past.

What might seem less easy to understand is that so sophisticated a lady,
in common with so many of her contemporaries, should have revelled in
a book whose qualities were perhaps most fairly summed up by Madame
du Deffand when she said that it 'had some very good bits drowned in an

ocean of eloquent verbiage'. But there are a number of explanations for its huge success. One was that it seemed to offer the best of both worlds. With only a little wishful reading those, like the Duchess, who had tasted the pleasures of both sacred and profane love, could find in it a justification, not to say a glorification, of their purple past as well as their snow-white present. And those who had made do without, could find comforting reassurance that in plumping for virtue they had backed a winner. But even more important was that both derived a great boost to their pride of womanhood from Jean-Jacques's tale. After so many romances, whose heroines were far from heroic, mere playthings of licentious lady-killers or at best willing partners in their amorous jollifications, here was a woman made into a veritable cult-object. And here was a woman's life described in the round, not just its brief moments of romance but in all its preoccupation with matrimony, maternity and domesticity. More gratifying still, the heroine was a formidable character towering morally and intellectually above her lover.

It was odd, inasmuch as Jean-Jacques was anything but a feminist. In his attitude to women, as in so many other things, he was normally a true, hide-bound Swiss, a firm believer in the doctrine that women should stick to '*Kinder, Küche, Kirche*'. And not only was their place in the home but even there they should limit their activities and their interests strictly to the feminine sphere. 'The search for abstract and speculative truths . . . is beyond a woman's grasp . . . In general women like and appreciate no art . . . Their writings are as cold and pretty as they themselves and contain as much wit as you like but never a soul.' Why, the poor things were not even capable of man's noblest passion; 'they do not know how to describe or to feel the sentiment of love.' Nor had they any moral sense: 'Consult the women's opinion on bodily matters, in all that concerns the senses. Consult men in matters of morality and all that concerns the understanding . . .' Women's vocation was to be man's delectation; 'Woman is specially made for the delight of man . . . To be pleasing in his eyes . . . to win his respect and love . . . to make his life pleasant and happy, these are the duties of woman for all time . . . Formed to obey a creature so imperfect as man . . . she should learn easily to submit to injustice and to suffer the wrongs inflicted on her by the husband without complaint.'

And yet, in his one and only novel, it is very much the heroine who lays down the law, in every way her lover's moral superior. It is all the more curious as St. Preux, by the author's own admission, is but a carbon copy of himself. And himself at his most unattractive, peddling his wonderful heart: 'Ah, Julie, you will look in vain for another heart akin to yours, a thousand will adore you, mine alone knew how to love you;'

boasting of the greatness of his soul: 'Without you, you fatal beauty, I
should never have felt this unbearable contrast between the grandeur of
my soul and the meanness of my fortune;' whining with self-pity: 'I have
done everything to please you and you renounce me, you were entrusted
with my happiness and you destroyed me;' always finding excuses for his
transgressions which are never really his fault, never intentional: 'My
inexperienced heart recognized the danger only when there was no longer
time to escape . . . mine was an involuntary crime.' Like Jean-Jacques he
is voluptuously lachrymose: 'I shed copious tears and this state was not
without some pleasure, I wept hard and long and was comforted.' Like
him he is appallingly egocentric; having lost his Julie he wishes she were
dead: 'I should be less unhappy . . . Her happiness is my torment.
After having torn her from me Heaven has deprived me even of the
pleasure of regretting her loss. She lives but not for me. She lives for my
despair.'

It is the Jean-Jacques one has come to know so well from his autobiographical writings and his letters, the Jean-Jacques one has so often
longed to seize by the shoulder to shake some fortitude and honesty into
him, make him face the sophistry of his excuses, open his eyes to his
boundless selfishness. All the greater the surprise when one finds that
the heroine he has put into his novel, his dream-woman, does precisely
that. When his twin St. Preux, in his first letter, begins by expressing the
hope that 'I will never forget myself to the point of saying things which
are not proper for you to hear' and then, of course, lets himself go, she
points out that he is trying to have his moral cake and eat it: 'A virtuous
heart would subdue its feelings or keep silent.' When, forced by his threat
to kill himself, she avows that she reciprocates his passion—'the danger
to your life tears the secret from me'—she leaves him no illusions about
his responsibility: 'Led imperceptibly into the snares of a vile seducer I
see . . . the horrible precipice to which I am running . . . You see the
disorder in my heart, you take advantage of it in order to ruin me . . . You
have made me despicable . . . If you are not the lowest of men, if some
spark of virtue still shines in your soul, could you be vile enough to abuse
the fatal confession which my delirium tears from me? . . . For your own
sake at least, take pity on me . . . You will be virtuous or scorned, I shall
be respected or cured of my passion.' When, assured that he 'would
shudder to lay a hand upon your chaste form', she recovers her peace of
mind and he complains of her blooming in the glow of guiltless love—'how
I hate the robust health you have regained at my expense, how much I
would prefer to see you still ill rather than see this contented air'—she
scores a bull's-eye with the disdainful remark that 'to complain of my
health is a curious sign of affection'.

When he, again typically, advances all sorts of specious excuses for his decision to bed her as soon as he gets a chance—'I am resolved not to refuse any opportunities that may come my way . . . I have undertaken a charge above my powers . . . I have given a rash pledge, I am amazed that I have kept it so long . . . One deserves to fail when one imposes such perilous trials upon oneself . . . I am tired of suffering uselessly . . . without being given credit for it . . . You are too ungrateful . . . I have conquered my passion for two months, you owe me the reward for two centuries of suffering . . .'—she does not spare him her scorn: 'So you would like to have the pleasure of vice together with the honour of virtue? Is that your morality? Ah, my good friend, you grow tired of being honourable quite quickly.' When she sends him some money he needs to go on a journey and he returns it with the pompous message that he had allowed her to become the 'mistress of my fate' but not 'the arbiter of my honour', she gives him a spirited ticking off such as many of Jean-Jacques's friends must often have longed but rarely dared to administer: 'Your letter is pitiable . . . How contemptible you are! . . . Since when has it been vile to receive things from those one loves . . . I like neither people affecting excessive punctiliousness nor false points of honour.' When her father puts the first spoke in the wheel of their plans for marital bliss and her lover, in transports of self-pity, starts accusing her of having led him up the garden path—'cruel one, did you deceive me only to make my sorrow finally more intense and my humiliation more profound?'—she is hardly less severe in her strictures on his egocentricity and his unmanliness than Jean-Jacques's most merciless biographers: 'How can you feel only your own griefs, how is it you do not feel your friend's too? Consider the different position of my sex and yours in our common misfortune . . . It is for me to be weak and miserable . . . My fault is irreparable . . . But you whom shame does not degrade . . . how dare you lower yourself to the points of sighing and sobbing like a woman and flying into a rage like a madman? . . . Learn to bear misfortune and be a man!'

Nor does she show any patience with the moral whitewashing to which her lover, again exactly like his inventor, invariably resorts when confessing his transgressions. Many a biographer has censured him for it, shown how he gives himself absolution for his sins and even prides himself on them because of the virtuous repentance they inspire. But few have pointed out that he himself, speaking through Julie, was the first to condemn these attitudes: 'I am afraid,' he makes her say to St. Preux, 'that by dint of remorse and excuses you might in the end make a merit of a fault so fully atoned for.' There is many a passage, in the novel as well as in his life story, in which the twin St. Preux—Jean-Jacques does exactly that, proclaims his belief in virtue on the cheap, sins without tears or, rather and even better, sin *with* the delicious tears of proud repentance. But when St. Preux invites Julie, meanwhile dutifully married, to such a feast—'we shall be guilty but not at all wicked, we shall still love virtue, far from excusing our transgressions we will sigh over them, we will weep together'—she will have none of it: 'I tremble to think that people who have adultery in their heart dare to talk of virtue.' She no longer has any illusions either about having had the angels on her side when engaged in their 'criminal affair . . . our frenzied passion had deceived us, disguised our transports as a sacred exaltation so as to make them still more precious and deceptive'.

On this point, too, even some of Jean-Jacques's fairest biographers have not always done him justice. It is true that at times he makes a virtue of being in love while, as one of these biographers has said, the mutual devotion of lovers, however self-sacrificing, is in fact no more than an *égoïsme à deux*. Whereas the Age of Chivalry had seen love as the reward and the encouragement of virtues beneficial to others, such as courage, self-control or generosity, Jean-Jacques, it is said, makes it out to be a virtue in itself. But does he really? The answer as so often is yes and no. Speaking with the voice of St. Preux, he does. Speaking with that of Julie, he recognizes that lovers 'always see only themselves, never think of anything but themselves'.

No one, finally, has taken Jean-Jacques more forcefully to task for his compulsive self-justification than his own Julie does when she upbraids his alter ego for the account he gave her of his fall from grace in a Paris brothel. His letter starts with the type of breast-beating so familiar from the *Confessions* ('I am vile, base, contemptible'), followed by the usual enumeration of enough mitigating circumstances to warrant an acquittal. As with Jean-Jacques in Venice, so with St. Preux in Paris, it is, of course, the fault of others that he had been led astray: 'Some officers contemptuous of the simplicity of my old Swiss morals and resolved to make me change my attitude.' When he discovered, from 'the gaudy dress' of the ladies with whom they had taken him to dine, and from these ladies' inability to 'keep up a rational conversation', that he had fallen among whores, it 'was too late for me to back out'. So he decided 'to devote the evening to my function as an observer', making the most of 'the only opportunity I might ever get for studying this type of woman'. However, as they were 'so avaricious . . . that they never spoke from the heart' (as well as distracting his attention from his studies by 'disordering their dress to excite his desires'), he drew 'but little profit' from them. But much worse was that when he discovered he had been 'tricked' into drinking too much (the water with which he had throughout diluted his wine turning out to be wine also), it was 'too late; the evil was done'. He passed out, it seems, and did not come to until he 'woke up in the arms of one of these creatures'.

It is the Jean-Jacques of the *Confessions* in every word. But whereas there, and in all the rest of his autobiographical writings, he leaves the reader exasperated, not to say revolted by the falsity of it all, here he himself, with Julie as his mouth-piece, gives voice to these very feelings: 'Your excuses are pitiable! It was too late to back out! As if there were some kind of decorum to be observed in such places! . . . Or as if it were ever too late to stop oneself from doing evil! . . . You talk of devoting the evening to your function of observer. The idea! What a function! . . . Your excuses make me blush . . . If you must be contemptible at least be so without pretexts and do not add lying to debauchery . . . As for converting your comrades to your principles . . . you ought not to meddle with reforming others until you have nothing left to reform in yourself.'

*

What *is* one to make of this Rousseauphobe Jean-Jacques who appears on the scene in the guise of Julie? It is tempting to ascribe the latitude he allows her—and which gives his novel the character of an essay in self-criticism—to his masochism. Did he not claim to find 'the most delicate of pleasures' in 'falling on my knees before a masterful mistress, to obey her commands and to have to beg for her forgiveness'? But though most of the verbal flagellation is indeed carried out by his dream-woman, a male character in the story lends a helping hand. It is left to him, an English lord (who tries to help the two lovers by offering to set them up in one of his estates and making over half his fortune to him), to administer a much merited drubbing of the kind the Marquis de St. Lambert must have longed to give Jean-Jacques when he was making life difficult for the Comtesse: 'You speak highly of the manner in which Julie fulfils her duties as a wife and a mother, but when will you follow her example and fulfil your duties as a man and a friend? A woman has triumphed over herself and a philosopher does not succeed in conquering his passions! Do you wish then always to be a mere prater . . . and limit yourself to the writing of good books instead of doing good deeds? Take care . . . I hate weakness in anyone and I do not like to find it in a friend. There is no virtue without fortitude and cowardice leads to vice . . . Wretch! If Julie were weak you would succumb tomorrow and would be only a vile adulterer! . . . Be ashamed of yourself!'

There could not be a more striking contrast with the wriggling and the whining of the sanctimonious Jean-Jacques who persuaded himself that he was hardly to blame in the affair with the Comtesse: 'They alone had done the mischief and it was I who had suffered . . .' It is one more example of the complexity of a heart cherishing both old-fashioned, self-denying honour and new-fangled, self-indulgent sensibility, capable of chivalrous impulses as well as the basest cunning, aspiring to honesty and addicted to sophistry, valuing courage and fortitude and lamed by cowardice and feebleness. And therein lies one more reason for compassion, for reminding oneself, even when the story of his rise to sainthood seems most comical, that his was, in fact, a tragi-comedy.

CHAPTER THIRTEEN

The Awkward Idol

'I want my friends to rely on my sentiments rather than on their eyes and ears, and, when they should see me being rude, not to believe it.'

'I have that in my heart which dispenses me from being polite.'

REVENGE may be the 'poor delight of little minds' that Juvenal called it, but to Jean-Jacques it was not the least of the joys provided by success. His pride had suffered badly from the indifference of the world—and particularly its ladies—when he had not yet made his mark on it. Those had been the days when 'the pretty women of France had the effrontery of treating me as a nobody, even to the point of dining with me in the insulting familiarity of a tête-à-tête and kissing me in front of everybody in the most disdainful manner, as if I were their nanny's grandfather'. But now, with the huge success of his love story, the boot was on the other foot: 'The women,' he tells us in the *Confessions*, 'were wild about the book and its author. Such was their infatuation that there were few of them, even of the highest rank, whose conquest I could not have made had I attempted it. I have proofs of this which I do not care to write down, proofs which did not require putting to the test.'

He does not divulge why he never savoured any of these conquests. What he does reveal is that, already a few years before he had made his surprising re-entry on the literary scene thinly disguised as the Great Lover that was St. Preux, he had in fact ceased to operate as such even with Thérèse. Having got her with child five times—and without child by making her send them to the Foundling Hospital—he had preferred to condemn himself to 'abstinence' and make do with the 'compensatory vice' which had the additional advantage of being less 'deleterious' to his health. It was hard luck on all those grand ladies who started queuing up for his favours, once he had bowled them off their feet with his scorching love-letters to Julie. And that, as he saw it, was why they eventually nearly all 'cooled off', just as 'Maman' had done and as Thérèse did, too. (He 'noticed' that in her case this process, not altogether surprisingly, 'coincided' with his decision to exchange the cooperative rough and tumble of the conjugal couch for the solitary hurly-burly of the chaise-longue.) 'Knowing only the physical side of love,' he wrote in the *Dialogues*, the ladies had credited the author of *La Nouvelle Héloise* with 'a very strong sensuality which alone, they believed, could have inspired such tender sentiments . . . It was not difficult to imagine the price he was made to pay by those whose curiosity in this respect he failed to satisfy'.

The Duchess was only one of many whom he had offended by not responding more adequately to the endearments she had lavished upon him. 'I felt myself losing ground with Madame de Luxembourg . . . I hardly saw her any more except at table, even the place I had at her side was no longer reserved for me . . . As I had not a great deal to say to her, I was just as glad . . . Everything I might say or do seemed to displease her.' At first, so he told a correspondent, he had attributed it to 'a quite natural boredom with my conversation and my gaucherie in company; but there was more to it, I had too many indications of her secret hatred . . . caused by certain blunders on my part of the kind that women never forgive.' The same type of 'blunder' had alienated her sister-in-law, the Comtesse de Boufflers, as beautiful but much younger and, being the mistress of a prince of the blood, at least as well-connected. 'The marks of friendship with which she honoured me, affected me perhaps more than they should have. She noticed this . . . But as I felt it was hardly for Jean-Jacques to compete with the mighty of the land I withdrew.' That was one of the reasons why since then 'she hates me the way a woman does'. And, of course, it had been no different with Madame d'Epinay. When her heart had first 'been glutted with rage and indignation' because of his interest in the Comtesse, 'she almost made me advances while overwhelming her sister-in-law with rudenesses'. As for the latter, her *amant-en-titre* did not know how lucky he was that his friend had not made more of a play for her: 'She was after all a woman, he was away, temptations were great and frequent; it would have been very difficult for her always to defend herself with equal success against a more persistent lover.' As it was she had only escaped by dint of her extraordinary loyalty: 'Ah,' he had said to her, 'how proud St. Lambert would be of your fidelity if he knew what it had to contend with.'

Considering his modest record in bed, both quantitatively and qualitatively, it may seem odd that he should have come to fancy himself as Don Juan Jacques. But apart from the fact that a kindly Providence has equipped Man with an in-built tendency to seek comfort in such wishful thinking at the age when he is ill-advised to put these fancies to the test, Jean-Jacques had more encouragement than most to indulge in them. It was not so much that he was deceiving himself as that he benefited from a case of mistaken identity. 'What won me the women's favour,' he explained, 'was their belief that I myself was the hero of my novel.' The dour moralist they had seen in him until then seemed to have revealed himself as a mystery-man with an extravagantly romantic past and, who knew, an equally agreeable potentiality for the future. 'They were all convinced that it was impossible to depict the raptures of love unless one had felt them.' And he had been careful not to disabuse them: 'I refused either to confirm or deny an error that was to my advantage.' Hence his reputation for irresistibility. 'A sensitive woman,' declared a countess, who had never met him, 'could refuse nothing to the passion of Jean-Jacques unless she were of quite extraordinary virtue.' His own special Comtesse had only just managed this feat, and she was quite willing to agree, when looking back in old age, that he 'turned all women's heads except mine'.

So he had ample excuse for believing himself a *'tombeur d'âmes'*, as the French call the male counterpart of the *femme fatale*. Moreover, as a contemporary noted, it was very much the fashion in those days to treat literary lions to displays of emotion 'closely resembling that of the most passionate love'. To the Duchess Jean-Jacques had been 'the most lovable and most loved of men', and his novel so superb that she felt she would defile it by reading it in the corrupt atmosphere of Versailles: 'The court is not worthy of it.' Her sister-in-law had told him that he deserved 'statues and the praise of all humanity'. Another lady, the Marquise de Verdelin, explained humbly that 'my attachment to you has nothing to do with your sublime genius. I cannot rise to such heights. The goodness of your soul . . . the love of virtue for its own sake, these are the things that make me wish you happiness, for the honour of humanity as much as for the happiness of those who know you'. And there was also something else that was bound to make him see himself as a bit of a lady-killer; these great ladies seemed willing to put up with any amount of boorishness on the part of their hero. Nor were they put off by demonstrations of pomposity and touchiness comical in their naïveté, as on the occasion when he rounded on the Duchess because she had dared to give Thérèse a dress: 'You pretend you are only giving my housekeeper a present . . . Is this worthy of you? Have you such contempt for me that you think you can get around me this way?'

It was as unjust to the Duchess as it was hard on Thérèse, for Madame la Maréchale had in no way disregarded his wishes. 'Are you not unjust?' she asked plaintively, 'Had you not given me permission to make Mlle Levasseur a present of a dress provided only it was very ugly? And have I not done exactly as you told me?' However, nothing could stop her from loving him. 'You threaten not to love me anymore . . . But in spite of your menaces I love you from the bottom of my heart and I assure you I shall never change.'

It was much the same when the Marquise who could not rise to his sublime genius but venerated him for his love of virtue, had presumed to send him some delicacies for his table. He had already had to give her a severe reprimand for another offence earlier the same year. At that time she had incurred the charge of thinking him just a little egocentric (as she well might, for he had told her: 'You only give yourself migraines to make me miserable'). How, he had asked indignantly, how could she have misinterpreted his words in a sense 'so unworthy of me'? If she wished to remain his friend she had better realize once and for all that he was congenitally incapable of less than commendable feelings: 'I want my friends to rely on my sentiments rather than on their eyes and ears, and, when they should see me being rude, not to believe it.' As she had evidently fallen short of this total faith she would find it extremely difficult working her passage back into his esteem: 'Oh, how long it will take you to re-establish yourself in the good opinion I had of you.'

All the greater her foolhardiness in risking his displeasure with the presents she sent him later that year. True, like the Duchess she was not really guilty of the charge laid against her. 'You told me,' she wrote pathetically, 'that M. Coindet was coming to lunch with you and it was only pride in our local gâteaux and in the wine from my father's vineyard that made me want to send him what you call a present but for which you surely should not have to thank me as I did not take the liberty of offering it to you. What with my usual stupidity, I doubtless failed to explain this clearly. I offer you a thousand excuses.' Far from placating Jean-Jacques, her explanations and apologies only earned her an even harsher rebuke than the first. 'You only offer me excuses so as to try and make me feel I owe them to you . . . I have made no difficulties over your first presents or gifts or whatever you like to call them . . . When they became more frequent and embarrassing I have told you so. Then you started using Mlle Levasseur and M. Coindet as pretexts; as if what is sent here could fail to appear on my table! I am tired of these games and I will not put up with them any longer.'

It took as great a *grande dame* as the Duchess to get away, if not with the ugliest of dresses for Thérèse, at any rate with pots of butter for Jean-Jacques. When he objected that she had sent him more than the quantity authorized and that he could not touch it as that would make him feel as if he were 'eating his own condemnation',* she rebelled: 'To punish you

* When he had eaten two of four chickens sent to him by yet another admiring Marquise, he had suffered a severe attack of moral indigestion; 'now that I have eaten them,' he told her 'the best thing I can do is to forget all about it.'

I am sending you these twelve pots.' But the bravest of the brave was Madame de Boufflers. When he told her he could not continue to accept the occasional gift of a brace of pheasants shot by her lover, the Prince de Conti, she warned him that such 'affectations' might in the end 'obscure the lustre of your virtue'. It was not a warning he was prepared to take to heart. But he would make an exception for the Prince: 'To refuse presents of game from a prince of blood,' he admitted in the *Confessions*, 'is more like the behaviour of an ignorant and presumptuous boor than of a proud man . . . anxious to preserve his independence.' History does not record whether the Prince appreciated this preferential treatment at its true value, as did the Scottish Earl whom Jean-Jacques honoured by consenting to accept a pension from him, and who told him: 'I cannot tell you how flattered I am.' Meanwhile it is worth noting that he felt no compunction about accepting the continued use of the 'enchanting abode' the Duke and Duchess had put at his disposal at the time when his own rented house was being repaired. It was no more than his duty, he wrote to a friend, to retain the use of it: 'I owe it to all the kindnesses they have shown me not to give it back, at any rate not so soon. So now the man who in the winter of 1757 did not have a stone on which to rest his head has the two prettiest apartments he knows.'

*

Were it not for their occasional rebellions against Jean-Jacques's harsh rule, one would be tempted to conclude that the Luxembourgs and their set, who so long put up with him, must have been the most fatuous intellectual snobs. But there is another and less arrogant explanation for his having won their hearts and having kept them, for quite a time, overflowing with affection; to wit, that he was not in fact as insufferable as would seem from the letters quoted here. As the Duchess and her sister-in-law were ladies of considerable discernment there must have been more charm to him, or even just more common humanity, than meets the historian's eye. The wholly impossible Rousseau, rude, tiresome, pompous, umbrageous, selfish, churlish and all the rest, must have made way for the shy, affectionate, soft-centred Jean-Jacques more often than one can see from the available evidence.

It is a recognition that makes the biographer painfully aware of the limitations of his craft. Drawing not from life but from a haphazard collection of surviving documents, forced to select from among the unmanageable mass, unable to gauge their relative value as evidence of the characteristic they reveal, and most of all, lifting them out of the stream of time, his portrait cannot but over-emphasise certain features at the expense of others. Even if he succeeds in subduing the feelings of like or

dislike a sitter like Jean-Jacques inevitably inspires, even if his picture is
wholly objective, it will still be far from realistic. For while it may, with
luck, truly render the proportion between black and white in his character,
the two will scarcely fade into one another to form all those shades of grey
that one mostly finds in real life. And even if the picture should be built
up, like a pointilliste painting, out of all the colours of the rainbow, with
the thousands of little touches provided by the documents, they will still
not fuse to render the colour of living reality because, unlike those applied
by the brush of a Seurat, they are not seen simultaneously but only in
succession.

*

This much having been said, the fact remains that Jean-Jacques was not
the most rewarding of idols to worship. No one learnt this more painfully
than a youngish demi-bourgeoise—only one of her parents had modest
quarterings—who, unlike the duchesses and marchionesses who nearly all
despaired of him in the end, remained passionately devoted through thick
and thin. But then, in a way she had asked for the mostly very thin time
she got. For she was one of that army of admirers of whose importunities
he had good reason to complain: 'I am overwhelmed with unsolicited
memoirs, verses, dissertations, praises, criticisms, and everyone wants an
answer, to deal with it I would need ten secretaries.'

    At first she had been diffident enough, really asked little more than an
autograph, promising not to write again if only he would indulge her
'passionate desire to have one letter from you'. But within three weeks she
was already bullying him: 'So you won't write to me? So you are not what
I thought you were from your novel, the cult I made of you was not better
than idolatry?' For hers was neither a blind nor a deferential devotion. As
in the course of many years' correspondence she gradually came to know
her hero, she made no secret of the disillusionments she suffered, spared
him no criticism. Thus, when he claimed the right to be impolite, because
'I find that in my heart which dispenses me from being polite', she gave
him a little lecture that was completely on target: 'Well, Sir, I have that
in my heart which—though I do not pride myself on it—makes it no
effort for me to be polite . . . The desire to contribute to the satisfaction
of all those approaching me, the fear of being disobliging, makes my
manners affectionate; and that is true politeness.' Complaining of his
failure to write she did not hesitate to reproach him with 'being just like
all other men, always ready for a moment's amusement but incapable of
staying the course . . . St. Preux, St. Preux', (she had cast herself in the
role of his Julie) 'how little you resemble your author . . . I am afraid
that, indifferent to what people think of you, you do not try hard enough

to merit their good opinion . . . I should have known better than to think you perfect.'

It was acting the part of the scolding Julie in altogether too life-like a manner to please Jean-Jacques. In a letter ending with a contemptuous taunt at her class—'you are much more typical of your milieu than I had thought'—he told her he was not interested in 'reproaches and abuse' and that he could 'manage very well without the esteem' she had threatened to withdraw. However, whether because of her persistence or because her spirited reprimands—in conjunction with the confession that she had dreamed of him 'all night'—got the better of the self-confessed masochist in him, the time came when she won her battle: 'my heart cannot resist you any longer.' It was the beginning of a paper-honeymoon in the course of which their relationship warmed to the point where he started calling her Marianne, felt free to ask her how old she was, requested a description of her appearance, asked for and received a picture and even found the piece of land in the neighbourhood she had asked for so as to be able to come and live near him. 'Oh my friend,' she wrote to him in those days, 'if only I had got to know you earlier . . .'

But already the honeymoon was over and she had cause to complain of neglect. It earned her only the same sort of harsh reply she had received when, still an importunate stranger, she had as yet no claim to his indulgence. After having pleaded ill-health and work as excuses for his failure to write, he once more poured scorn on her for belonging to the idle rich, whose members 'having nothing to do but write letters, think that the same holds for their friends . . . Your friendship is precious to me. But my tranquillity is even more so. And since I can apparently have only a stormy correspondence with you, I would rather have none at all'. As she was as determined to idolize him as to scold when she thought he needed it, his wish to be left in peace remained unfulfilled. Within a few weeks he had again become 'My dear, adorable Jean-Jacques, never will anyone love you as I do . . . you merit that people should erect statues to you . . . You should govern the universe'. But at the same time she once again usurped the real Julie's privilege of telling him some painful home-truths. Not only did she criticize him for his self-pity, his 'feebleness in adversity'. When he took offence at this and began to sulk, she made matters worse by urging him not to be so touchy and asking whether he could really be 'so vindictive as to sacrifice the most sacred ties to the frivolous interests of vanity . . . Must I believe that you would disavow so many assurances of friendship because I have allegedly stopped flattering you? . . . Am I to think that for you to be loved is to be applauded . . . that all your virtues are only those of the mind, that below the attractive surface there is a faulty nature, that your writings are a mask with which you have gained the esteem of the public and the almost divine cult I have made of you?' Of course, for her to ask such questions was to answer them: 'No, my friend, I cannot believe it.' But when he, ignoring subsequent apologies, refused to abandon his huff, another outburst released some further and equally apposite questions: 'What! You whom I thought perpetually busy doing good, you take pleasure in causing me pain . . . What use are your lessons to me if you deny them by your example? What virtue can I still believe in if yours is but a mirage?'

It was only when he learnt that she had suffered the loss of a dearly loved sister that he relented. But subsequent events showed she had not really been forgiven. For when, after five years' correspondence, their paths could at last have crossed, in Paris, he did not let her know he had arrived there. And when she found out and wrote to him, reproachfully but as always swearing eternal love, he replied that he could not see her: 'I would get into trouble with my old friends if I were to accord preference to new ones.' When she finally did manage to see him it was only by calling at his house and sending up a pitiful message: 'For heaven's sake do not be angry with me.' And five years later it was the same unhappy story all over again. Once more finding himself in Paris, Jean-Jacques did not alert the faithful if often tiresome Marianne who three years earlier had bravely gone into print to defend his preposterous conduct in a quarrel with Hume, and only five months earlier had once again assured him that 'my feelings for you are akin to the love that the devout feel for God'. And such indeed they were, triumphing over all the bitter disillusionments she had suffered, just as the faith of the believer in the deity's all-goodness remains unshaken by the presence of evil in his creation. What, she exclaimed when she learned that for the past month he had been living practically around the corner, 'what could I have done to merit such crushing coldness? Love is subject to such revolutions. But friendship! . . . I just do not understand.' But no explanation was forthcoming. An icy little note of eight lines explaining that it was not convenient to meet and closing with the heart-chilling formula, '*Agréez, Madame, je vous supplie, mes salutations et mon respect*', was all she got for her pains. It caused her to ask one more of those questions that were far too near the mark not to have hurt: 'How can someone, rejecting with such unbending hardness the efforts of a friend who has never faltered in her attachment to you, claim to be the most loving of men?' But even his reply, including her among the ever-growing number of friends that had allegedly joined the 'plot' against him, could only momentarily shake her devotion. Three months after she had indignantly protested against his 'odious suspicions', she was again assuring him she would humbly await 'the return of your confidence'. Within the year she was offering to check the pirated edition of his work for the falsification he complained of and, despite his refusal, set to work on it. In the last letter she ever wrote him, two years before his death, she told him her friendship for him did not require the return of his: 'Have I not got your works . . . have I not the memory and the proofs of the tender affection with which you once honoured me? . . . I don't know whether it is possible to stop loving you.'

*

If the book that won Jean-Jacques the indestructible devotion of poor Marianne proved so exceptionally popular with the ladies it was by no means only because it was a love story. It was at least as much because its heroine, once she recovers from romantic love, shows herself as down to earth as the members of the weaker sex—as it then still was—are biologically bound to be. Marital law and order was what they required to fulfil themselves. Love in the sense of *amour-passion* was only a bonus they could well do without. In Jean-Jacques's view marriage was all the better for its absence. 'What perhaps still misleads you,' Julie tells St. Preux, 'is the thought that love is necessary to form a happy marriage. My friend, that is an error . . . A certain conformity, not so much of stations and ages as of characters and temperaments, is enough . . . Love is accompanied by continual unease . . . little suited to marriage.' That was why she would no longer marry her lover even if she were free to do so: 'If I had my own choice of a husband I swear by God it is not you I would choose'. Love being but a passing fancy, they would probably 'get thoroughly sick of each other . . . I have only known you in love, how do I know what you would be like once you had fallen out of love? . . . I am sure you would have remained virtuous . . . But how many virtuous men are no less insufferable husbands for all that!' It was hard on poor St. Preux, as indestructibly romantic as only a man can be, but certainly bound to please the author's commonsensical woman-readers.

Another reason why his publisher struck gold with the book lay in the fact that there was a great deal in it appealing to much larger numbers, men as well as women, than the small section represented by the Duchess. To the rising middle class it offered gratifying denunciations of the nobility. 'The odds were always twenty to one that a gentleman was descended from a scoundrel . . . What has the nobility done for the glory of the fatherland or the happiness of the human race? Mortal enemy of the laws and of liberty, what has it ever produced but tyranny and oppression?' The salons of Paris were a sink of iniquity: 'Adultery is considered perfectly proper . . . Even affairs have become as degraded as marriage . . . the lovers seeing one another for the sake of amusement or out of necessity or by force of habit . . . The heart does not come into it . . . As for the physical side, anyone will do . . . Why should one be more faithful to a lover than to a husband? . . . With most of the women the lover is treated as one of the servants, if he does not do his duty he is dismissed and one takes another, if he tires of the job or finds a better one he quits . . . Some women go so far as to take the butler as their lover.' Admittedly the members of this wicked world talked brilliantly and conducted their conversations with exquisite courtesy. But their art only served 'to give currency to the lie . . . to question the dictates of virtue . . . and to make error fashionable.' Behind their politeness there was only insincerity; 'their sentiments do not come from their heart, their speech does not represent their thought.'

It was, of course, but a replay of the denunciation of Paris society with which Jean-Jacques had first achieved fame and notoriety ten years earlier. But there is a difference. Perhaps partly to take the wind out of the sails of the critics but more likely because he had mellowed with success or rather because, vastly successful, he could afford to be as incoherent as he liked and so remain uncommitted, keep all his intellectual options open, he no sooner utters a condemnation than he takes it back, or at any rate casts doubt on its validity. 'Who am I to pass judgment?' St. Preux asks after having berated Paris society; 'I see only the surface of things.' Once again using Julie as the mouth-piece for his self-criticism he gives himself a severe dressing-down for generalizing, moralizing and attitudinizing: 'Like an ill-tempered child you criticise without due consideration . . . before knowing whether it is slander or observation . . . I would rather you were deceived by appearances than that you moralised at your hosts' expense . . . I suspect all observers who pride themselves on their wit, I always fear that unwittingly they sacrifice truth and justice to the pleasure of showing off and turning a phrase.'

There is no more striking example of this continued equivocation than his long description of the ladies of Paris. It distressed one of them to such a point that, though he was a 'sublime genius . . . one of the greatest men of all centuries', she did not intend to 'erect altars' to him; instead she would limit herself to 'burning incense on altars that others, less tolerant, would have destroyed with pleasure'. It would have been very generous had she not been so unjust, a typical case of that affliction all writers suffer from: readers who cannot read. For St. Preux's report to Julie, who had asked him to tell her something about 'these elegant and celebrated women . . . the most seductive creatures in the universe', renders him far from guilty of having 'inhumanly blasted them . . . covering them with ignominy'.

True, he has them in and out of bed, even with majordomos, at disconcerting speed. But, he adds, 'this picture is doubtless exaggerated, I don't know anything about it at first hand, and I may not have understood clearly what I have been told'. True, they are not a bit like the matchless Julie. But, he tells her, 'I represent them to you, perhaps not as they are, but as I see them'. True, they are 'skinny', their eyes 'show more fire of anger than of love', they consider 'the *pudeur* that distinguished and embellished your sex as vile and middle-class . . . No decent man would not lower his eyes the way they look at one . . . They have a soldierly bearing and speak in the tones of a termagant . . . or, if they are pretty, their manners are simpering . . . Their coquetry is disgusting and their manners immodest . . . They are incapable of either inspiring or feeling love'. Quite an indictment. But followed by an equally strong acquittal. They are so 'charitable to the poor and the oppressed' that he was 'deeply moved'. They are more 'enlightened, talk more sense, show more judgment than anywhere in the world . . . They are most helpful friends. Though they may pride themselves on their wickedness they are good in spite of themselves . . . They are the refuge of the unhappy . . . They listen to them, console them, serve them . . . the frivolous life they lead does not stop them from interrupting their pleasures to help the needy . . . They alone are responsible for such little humanity as one still finds in Paris . . . Underneath the fashionable vices one must parade in its society, lies a basic good sense, reason, humanity and natural goodness'. Enough lovable qualities, one would have thought, to make them capable of inspiring and feeling love after all.

*

Though the Paris scene Jean-Jacques presented to his readers had its redeeming features, it was still hell compared with the rural paradise where his Julie lives out her days in a state of pristine virtue. Curiously, life there, portrayed by the writer who was to inspire generations of egalitarians with his revolutionary slogans, was so idyllic largely because she and her husband had solved the servant problem. More than half the forty odd pages eulogizing their ways are devoted to a description of how skilfully they manage their staff of 'eight house servants, not counting M. Wolmar's personal valet', and an unspecified number working in the vineyards of his estate. They are all as happy as can be because their masters are Lord and Lady Bountiful personified. So good is Julie to them that 'within twenty-four hours they have become her children . . . they fly at her least wish . . . one never sees them idle or making mischief but always engaged on some useful task'. Nor do they ever abuse the amiability of their employers—Julie even dances with them at their harvest festivals—by forgetting their place: 'The masters' affability in no way leads to insubordination, they can lower themselves to the servants' level and treat them as equals without the latter being tempted to behave as if they really were.' And even if one of them should ever 'forget himself' that poses no problem; 'instead of spoiling the atmosphere of the party by reprimanding him he is just dismissed, without hope of appeal, the next morning.' No wonder, therefore, the workers are so devoted to 'the sacred interest of the master' that they let it prevail over any feelings of solidarity or friendship with their colleagues, informing against them whenever duty calls; their employers have achieved the 'sublime' feat of 'transforming the vile trade of informer into a function of devotion, integrity, and courage'. Class-warriors would find them wholly unresponsive; 'if some strange valet were to come and tell them that master and servants are in a state of war with one another and that for the latter to do their worst by him is only to carry out just reprisals . . . no one would understand'. As the estate is almost wholly self-sufficient, isolated from the outside world, and as they, therefore, 'never hear that other masters are unlike theirs . . . they, in their simplicity, praise God for having created the rich for the happiness of those serving them'.

Such is the ideal society dreamt of in his more relaxed moments by the writer who, when his blood is up, rings the changes on the theme that 'the fruits of the earth belong to all, the land itself to none'. It is a society run along mediaeval lines and governed in a feudal spirit of such perfection as never dwelt in the bosom of even the most parfit gentil knight. But Julie's success with her staff is not only due to her moral qualities. It also owes a good deal to a diplomacy that does not shrink from the deception essential to the successful practice of this art: 'As servants can only be made to behave properly by constraint the whole art of the master is to conceal it . . . so as to make them think they want to do what they are made to do.' One must begin by 'catching them young in order to get them the way one wants'. No less important is to make sure the sexes are kept separate as much as possible; it only makes for trouble in the house 'if the butler seduces the chambermaid'. Not that 'undue familiarity between the sexes should be avoided by laying down laws which they would only violate in secret'. What one should do is to see to it—without seeming to do so—'that they have neither the opportunity nor the desire to see one another', and this one must achieve by 'giving them different occupations, habits, tastes and pleasures . . . and by keeping them busy all the time'.

The great problem is to keep them out of the inn on Sunday, 'which one cannot forbid them to visit and where talk with comrades and the frequentation of debauched women are apt to make them incapable of service in a thousand ways and unworthy of liberty'. But Julie has solved this problem, too, by providing fun and games for them on the estate:

'who can run fastest, throw a stone farthest' and that sort of thing, with prizes for the winner. Though these involve some expense, Julie's husband has worked out that he 'gets the money back several times over', in terms of the good service obtained from the servants, 'grateful to their master for their pleasures . . . and all the stronger in their work for the vigorous exercise they get from them'. Of course, anyone who prefers to go to the inn is perfectly free to do so. He only gets the sack; 'we regard such a taste for license as suspect and promptly get rid of anyone displaying it.' As for those many who are 'eager to send their children to the towns to study . . . they are never helped'. Instead they are 'shown the error of their ways', warned that for 'one who makes his fortune there are hundreds who perish', told to be content with the state unto which it has pleased God to call them.

Though it is doubtless perfectly true that the drift to the towns hardly promoted the greatest happiness for the greatest number, it might seem strange that Jean-Jacques, himself once a servant who had considerably bettered himself by study and subsequently seeking his fortune in the metropolis, should have disapproved so strongly of this ambition in others. He even went so far as to declare that 'the poor man has no need of education'. But as already pointed out earlier, though he liked to call himself a 'man of the people', he did not identify with them, and least of all with the servant class. The humiliations of the *déclassé*, which the young man of bourgeois origin had felt when a lackey among lackeys, as well as the knowledge he had gained of their far from irreproachable ways, had only intensified his distaste for the members of this class. Nor were his experiences when he came to know them from the other side of the social fence, as a guest in the châteaux of the grand, such as to warm his heart to them. Both his letters and his autobiographical writings are full of bitter and wholly understandable complaints. 'Any other man who visits a country house is waited on by his own valet . . . Being without one, I was at the mercy of the house-servants . . . And being treated as their master's equal I had to treat them accordingly and even better than anyone else would, since I had more need of their service . . . Although I limited my small gratuities to the places where I stayed frequently, they were nevertheless ruinous to me.' Even dining out in Paris could run one into a lot of expense; 'instead of allowing me to send for a fiacre the lady of the house would order the horses to be put on to the carriage and have me taken home. She was delighted to be sparing me twenty-four sous for a cab. But she did not think of the crown I had to give to her footman and coachman.' What made it even worse was that these servants were invariably 'very sly and very grasping . . . scoundrels who knew how to manage things so that I should need them all, one after the other'. But worst of all was the scorn with which he was often treated by them, witness the account of his plight when staying in the château of a princely protector. 'Honoured by the master of this house I certainly did not imagine that I would be exposed to the disdain of the servants . . . They had expected the protégé of the Prince . . . to be a man with grand airs, lace, ribbon, plume, at the very least a sword. Imagine what my appearance did to them. They thought the Prince, trying to bamboozle them, had sent a scoundrel to spy on them.'

It is all these unhappy experiences that account for the old-fashioned paternalistic character of the society of his dreams, with the lower orders kept in their place by a benevolent autocrat. Not surprisingly this solution for the problem of the governance of men is poles apart from that advocated for the society of his theorizing thought. The former, ruled by Julie and her husband, is made up of individuals, as real to his imagination as the men and women he had known in real life, admittedly idealized versions of social reality but living reminders of its intractability for all that. The latter, the society of his *Social Contract*, consists only of 'the people', a huge, ghostly abstraction that can be moulded into any shape one fancies, wholly divorced from visible and tangible reality and thus providing no disintoxicant to the mind inebriated with logic, containing no ballast to arrest the flight of the imagination.

But there is one thing the ideal society of his novel had in common with that of his political treatise. That is the reliance on the 'art of concealment' which the 'Lawgiver' or 'Guide' of the *Social Contract* practises no less than Julie to make the 'sovereign people' think they have and live by a will of their own. And as a penetrating student* of Jean-Jacques's thought has pointed out, the need for this art is so much one of his pet themes as to entitle him to a place among the pioneers of that manipulation, the 'human conditioning', carried to perfection by the Big Brothers of our century.

*

There is one other thing to be said about the ideal society pictured in Jean-Jacques's novel; it has many of the hallmarks of the hippie's conception of the good life. And this, too, may well have had something to do with the astonishing popularity of the book. The success of the essay, that had first put him on the road to glory ten years earlier, had already shown how receptive the reading public was to denunciations of the artificialities of a highly sophisticated civilization (or, as its defenders would say, how grateful was that part of the public that was incapable of meeting its challenge or rebelled against its demands). He had been bent

* L. G. Crocker.

on exposing the evils of a world for which he felt much the same distaste as contemporary 'affluent' society arouses in the devotees of the 'counter culture' of today. Now, in his picture of Julie's domain, he painted the delights of the 'alternative society', a community whose spirit if not its structure was in some way remarkably like that of a modern commune; 'a small number of sweet, peaceful people united by reciprocal needs and goodwill, working together for a common purpose . . . No one is jealous, no one thinks he can do better for himself except by adding to the common weal.' It is economically self-sufficient and in so far as it must trade with the outside world it does so by barter, 'avoiding the use of money as much as possible'. Its members have 'only useful possessions' and desire nothing else. For the more gadgets a man invents, Jean-Jacques says elsewhere, striking a modern note indeed, the more dissatisfied he becomes; 'with use these conveniences lose almost all their power to please, they come to be seen as necessities till the want of them becomes far more disagreeable than their possession was a source of pleasure . . . It is very imprudent unnecessarily to multiply one's needs.' And again like the moderns, he was hostile not only to the spirit of the 'consumer society', especially in its urban form—'man is not made to live in anthills'—he was an enemy also of technocracy then still in its infancy. Resenting the high human cost of industrialization and its counterpart, division of labour, detesting 'those stupid trades in which the workmen mechanically perform the same action without pause and almost without mental effort', a Luddite wanting 'to forbid the use of any machine or invention which would shorten the time taken by work, decrease the number of men working or produce the same effect with less trouble', he, too was not so much a rebel without a cause as a rebel without a hope, a *laudator temporis acti.*

CHAPTER FOURTEEN

The Maestro and the Moron

'I decided to improve her mind. I was wasting my time . . . She has never been able to read properly . . . Her blunders have become famous in the circles in which I have lived . . . It did not suit me to enter into an eternally binding commitment . . . I had declared in advance I would never abandon her nor ever marry her.

Necessity and the honour of the woman who was dear to me, prevented me from fulfilling the most sacred duties.'

THE luckless Marianne was far from being the only one whom Jean-Jacques, the author, had filled with feelings so 'akin to the love the devout feel for God, 'as to be proof against acquaintance with Jean-Jacques the man. Nor was it only women who prostrated themselves at his feet, only too visibly made of clay. Some of his male devotees went so far as to proclaim themselves unworthy of him because of venial sins, such as impatience, ill-temper and rudeness, of which he himself had and indeed acknowledged his full share. Had he been capable of laughing at his own moral pretensions he would have derived a wry amusement from the eagerness with which some of these admirers gave him, not so much the benefit of the doubt as the benefit of divinity, exempting him, on the principle *quod licet Jovi non licet bovi*, from the standards applying to ordinary mortals. A delightful example is the letter from a young fellow-intellectual who had known him for years and more than once found himself on the receiving end of his idol's self-confessed 'roughness'. Writing at a time Jean-Jacques was composing an offensive and ill-tempered letter to Marianne, sneering at her 'idle-rich' mentality, he sighed, 'I wish I could be a hermit like you so as to become better. Since I have a wife and a child and servants I am more impatient than ever, I lose my temper, I swear, I quarrel . . . That is why I have delayed writing to you. I did not feel worthy of it. I needed a few days of peace in the home and calm in my heart before I dared to approach you.' He was filled with a veneration and a love so deep that when he had last said goodbye to Jean-Jacques, he had 'wept all the way from Montmorency to Paris'. 'What need,' he asked in another letter, 'does God, that unknown being I adore and love in you, have of angels to reveal his will?'

There were quite a few among God's servants who fully agreed. Even before Jean-Jacques had publicly parted ideological company with such atheists as d'Holbach, Helvétius and the hardly more respectable Diderot —which he did when he made his dream-woman Julie a believer—a Swiss parson had already put him on a par with Christ: 'I shall try to follow in Jesus's and your footsteps.' Though two years later the good cleric was a little put out that the 'advocate of suffering humanity, the apostle of virtue, the comforter of the poor, the worthy emulator of St. Peter,' had found it necessary to paint 'those inflaming pictures' of Julie in love, he nonetheless waxed so rapturous as to allow his pen passages of an improbable purple: 'My heart is stirred by the mere mention of your name . . . It flies out over the hills of Montmorency, trembling at the sight of your roof. There, it says, there he lives. Quivering it enters, it hears your voice, a sweet trepidation takes hold of it, it rushes to your bedside and soaks your hands with tears. Oh, Rousseau, how many hearts have I here described!' And when in the writings of his later years the worthy emulator of St. Peter came to the defence of beleaguered Christianity in more explicit form, the chorus of adoration rose to a blasphemous crescendo: 'Divine man!' 'Man whom I dare compare with the divinity!' 'Unique being on an earth little deserving of your stay!' In fact, it came to be too much of a good thing even for its beneficiary. 'Do not,' he said to a friend who wanted to introduce one of these fanatical admirers to him, 'do not bring him along, he frightens me, he has written me a letter in which he puts me above Christ.'

However, as Mirabeau's father said, 'not everybody was capable of appreciating the sublimity of his soul'. Many of those who had got to know him best had proved singularly incapable of it, quite unable to agree that Jean-Jacques 'was perhaps the most virtuous man that ever lived'. It was a thought that could not but cast a cloud on the new happiness and reassurance he had found, first in the warm embrace of the ducal set and subsequently in the adulation of the new worlds he conquered with his rapidly multiplying writings and whose inhabitants ranged all the way from simple parsons to mighty princes. The company he now kept might be far grander than that from which he had been expelled, but the enemies he had made in the latter 'moved freely in the fashionable world', while he himself, 'a foreigner, isolated, without family or backing . . . fearlessly following the paths of uprightness . . . was in solitary retirement . . . though only twelve miles from Paris thoroughly cut off from the capital'. What was worse, these relentless enemies, the 'Holbach clique', led by Grimm and determined 'utterly to destroy my reputation', had the key to the cupboard with his five baby-skeletons. They knew that the writer who had sung the praises of virtuous matrimonial and family-life so eloquently that he had inspired many to mend the error of their ways, was not himself the most exemplary of family-men.

It has faced his hagiographers with a problem for which none of them has ever found a satisfactory solution. To acquit him of being a heartless parent, by claiming as some have done, that he never had any offspring to send to the Foundling Hospital, was to leave the idol still a fearful liar. For had he not asserted in the most unequivocal manner, both in his autobiographical writings and his letters, that Thérèse bore him no less than five children? And had he not also confessed to occasional attacks of tearful remorse at their abandonment? Nor was it easy to make white lies of these assertions. The motive which, according to this theory, had driven him to lie his head off, the desire to conceal his impotence, was hardly such as to add greatly to his moral stature. The only way to do that was to make out—as others have—that he had taken Thérèse's sins upon himself, that the children were not his, that she wanted to get rid of them and that he claimed parenthood and accepted the odium of being an unnatural father only to protect his concubine's reputation. But the reader will probably agree that fair comment on this suggestion would be: '*C'est magnifique mais ce n'est pas Jean-Jacques.*'

The less fanatical among his admirers have, therefore, sought to mitigate rather than to explain away the offence by placing it in the context of his time, as indeed one should. They have pointed out that in his day babies were left on people's doorsteps in their thousands, as if they were milk-bottles. According to Jean-Jacques himself, the figure for the year 1758 was 5,082 for Paris alone. Seen in this light it was perhaps only natural that he should have felt no qualms about following suit, especially as at the time he first contracted the habit he had not yet discovered his vocation as an example to mankind. They were the days when he frequented a luncheon-club where the talk was 'risky but never vulgar . . . and the man who best helped to stock the Foundling Hospital was always the most applauded'. Moreover, if the young rakes he met there saw nothing wrong in this activity, neither did the highbrow friends he regularly lunched with at Baron d'Holbach's table and who were fully in the picture—'I told everyone who knew of our relationship'. At least, there is nothing on the record to show they disapproved, relations with Grimm and Diderot were never warmer than in those happy days when he was 'inseparable' from the former and went 'at least every other day to spend the afternoon' with the latter, then in prison.

One cannot help but wonder, however, whether he had told them of the price in tears he had to exact from Thérèse every time he got her with child. Her sufferings form a part of the familiar story that has received strangely little attention, even from his hostile biographers. The critical emphasis is nearly always on his dereliction of duty as a father, almost to the exclusion of any reference to the heartlessness of his attitude towards his mistress who had to pay for her lover's refusal to accept responsibility for his offspring. We have his own word for it that she was no unnatural mother; he had 'the greatest difficulty in the world' in persuading her to leave the fruit of their amours to the tender mercies of the over-stocked hospital. And no wonder; in those days sixty-five out of a hundred of its inmates died in their first year and only five survived into maturity, nearly all to become beggars and vagabonds. No wonder either, therefore, that Thérèse never learned to resign herself to the 'good and sensible arrangement' as he called it in the *Confessions*; 'when the same inconvenience was removed by the same expedient there was no greater willingness on the mother's side, she obeyed with a sigh.'

More likely it was a fearful scene, rather than a sigh. If only because the arguments he used, presumably those he puts forward in the *Confessions* as well as in a letter written at the time, only added insult to injury, to say nothing of the unfeeling levity with which he approached the whole painful matter. 'When I was growing plump at Chenonceaux,' so he introduces the theme in his *Confessions*, 'my poor Thérèse was doing the same in Paris, though in another way, and when I returned I found the work I had set under way further advanced than I had expected.' If this was the spirit in which he came home from his luncheon-club to tell Thérèse of the 'good and sensible arrangement' favoured by his cronies and which he was 'cheerfully resolved to adopt without the least scruple', one need be no expert in the female psyche to imagine her reaction. And if, meeting resistance, he really used the extraordinary argument he claims to have put forward, one can only hope, for his sake, that it left her speechless. For it was none other than that depriving her of the bastards he had fathered was 'the sole means of saving her honour'. There could be no question of achieving this worthy end by the more orthodox procedure of making an honest woman of her. He simply was not the marrying type: 'It did not suit me to enter into an eternally binding commitment and no one will ever convince me that it was my duty to do so.' Thérèse had no claim on him; 'I had declared in advance I would never abandon her nor ever marry her.' In this sense he had done better than his friend Diderot who 'had a Nanette as I had a Thérèse. Though she was 'a foul-mouthed shrew', Diderot had married her, because he had promised to do so; 'but I made no promises and was in no hurry to imitate him.' Anyhow, saving Thérèse's honour by legitimizing her children would not solve his problem. On the contrary, it would be the ruin of him, both as a man of letters and a man of principle. He would have to lower himself to writing for money and as he could hardly hope to make enough, with squealing brats all over the place, he would have to start pulling strings to land himself some sinecure. 'How could I feed a family?' he said in a letter to a lady who had apparently taken Thérèse's side. 'If I were to resort to the writer's craft, how would I achieve the tranquillity of mind necessary for lucrative work, my garret filled with domestic cares and the disturbance of children? . . . It would be necessary to indulge in intrigue and manoeuvring, to seek some base employment and to eke it out by the usual means . . . in short, to stoop to all those infamous acts which inspire me with so justifiable a horror.'

As for any anxieties Thérèse might feel about what would become of her little ones, there was nothing to worry about. They would be in excellent hands, he told his correspondent, 'all the better for not being delicately reared since it makes them more robust . . . Thanks to their rustic upbringing they will be happier than their father'. Why, he positively envied them; 'I could have wished and I still do wish,' he said in his autobiography, 'that I had been brought up and nurtured as they have been.' Which must have seemed odd to Thérèse, As Jean-Jacques was not reluctant to talk about himself, she had presumably heard all about his privileged childhood; how 'no royal child could have been more scrupulously cared for'. But if he really took the line with her he indicates in the *Confessions*, she is likely to have thrown the kitchen stove at him long before he came to the bit about envying the fate of her children. And if she had not, she must surely have done so when she heard his 'weightiest' reason for getting rid of her babes. It lay in his anxiety to keep them from being defiled by contact with his mother-in-law. However useful she might be as a charlady-cum-secretary, as a grandmother she would be a disastrous influence. And not only that; 'her other children and grandchildren, too, were so many bloodsuckers . . . I trembled at the thought of entrusting mine to that badly brought up family.' Nor, at a later time, would he hear of accepting Madame d'Epinay's and the Duchess's offers to help; the children 'would have been led to hate their parents and perhaps betray their parents, it is a hundred times better they have never known them'.

While there is nothing in the record to throw any light on Madame d'Epinay's offer, the role played by the Duchess appears from two letters. Written at a time when he believed himself to be at death's door, Jean-Jacques had asked her to look after Thérèse and told her about the 'five children that have all been sent to the Foundling Hospital'. While he did not even have a record of the dates of their birth, the swaddling clothes of the eldest had borne an identification mark. 'If it should be possible to find this child [which according to the *Confessions* the Duchess had offered to adopt] that would make its tender mother's happiness.'

It is the only time he shows any concern for her feelings, any awareness of the sufferings he had caused her. On all other occasions when he speaks of 'remorse' it is always at his failure as a father . . . and always followed by the self-exculpating 'but', witness the following examples. 'I was wrong but I have often blessed Heaven for having safeguarded the children from their father's fate.' 'I neglected my duties but the desire to do harm never entered my head and a father's feelings cannot speak very loudly for children he has never even seen.' 'My fault was doubtless grave, impardonable, but it is the only one and I have fully atoned for it.' 'I am accused of being an unnatural father but the fact is that I took this step to save my children from a fate that would almost inevitably have been a thousand times worse.' 'I sent my children to the Foundling Hospital and, if the occasion arose, I would do the same again, with even less hesitation. I know full well no father is more tender than I would have been.'

As for the concern he showed for Thérèse's happiness when writing to the Duchess about the only one of her children it might be possible to retrieve, it proved of short duration. For when she set searches in motion he asked her to desist; 'the success of your efforts could no longer give me undiluted satisfaction . . . You have given me the most touching and precious proof of your friendship, that makes up for everything, my heart is too full of you to feel the lack of what I am missing.' On second thoughts he feared that, far from making Thérèse happy, the return of her first-born 'already formed for better or for worse' (he would have been about sixteen) might prove a disastrous present to someone so 'easily dominated'.

What Thérèse really felt about it all is as unknown as what she thought on those five occasions when she had her child taken away from her as soon as she had laboured to give it birth. The only thing on record are those six words about her lover having had 'the greatest difficulty in the world' in persuading her. But they speak volumes. And as there is no indication that she was anything but a perfectly normal woman they entitle one to think that sorrow must have made way for indignation as she listened to his arguments, indignation for anger, anger for contempt and—if he ended up speaking to her in the same tones with which he finally exculpates himself in the *Confessions*—contempt for pity. For that is the sentiment one is left with when one sees how he stills the small voice of conscience with a deafening blast on the trumpet of his self-conceit. Could it be, he asked himself, could it be that the cheerful lack of scruple, with which he had resolved on the good and sensible arrangement, showed him to be just a little heartless? It could indeed . . . if he were not Jean-Jacques, 'if I were one of those low-born men in whose breast no real feeling of justice and humanity ever arose . . . But my warm-heartedness, my acute sensibility . . . my innate goodwill towards my fellow men, my burning love for the great and true, the beautiful and the just, my horror of evil in every form, my inability to hate, to hurt or even to wish to, that softening, that sweet and tender emotion I feel at the sight of all that is virtuous, generous and lovable; is it possible that all these can ever dwell in the same soul along with depravity which quite unscrupulously tramples the dearest of obligations under foot? No, I feel and boldly declare—it is impossible. Never for a moment could Jean-Jacques have been a man without feeling or compassion'.

*

While ignorance of the kind of compassion he lavished on his mistress may partially account for the apparent unconcern of his friends, it is not the only explanation nor perhaps the most plausible. For it is not easy to reconcile with the fact that all who knew Thérèse agreed she was not the most reticent of women. Moreover, as Diderot's daughter has related, she and her mother often came to him for money, saying they were 'dying of hunger'. So he must have had a pretty clear picture of his friend's home-life. And if that did not lessen his esteem for him, it must have been at least partly because the wives of intellectuals, to say nothing of concubines, were expected to tolerate much more than it would be advisable to inflict on them in our day and age. Thus, literary lions who married beneath them, as both Jean-Jacques and Diderot had done, could relegate their life-partners to the kitchen while they enjoyed themselves in the salons and châteaux of their aristocratic admirers, without raising any eyebrows. It was agreed that, if the ladies were not 'sortable'—and certainly semi-literate Thérèse was not; though 'good and very lovable', Jean-Jacques once explained in rejecting an invitation on her behalf, 'she is not at all made to appear in grand company'—they had better stay at home. Their lowly status as well as the exalted one of their master is nicely illustrated by the attitude of the memorialist who, recalling that Jean-Jacques was once seen to help Thérèse with lacing her corset, exclaimed: 'Such traits show what a virtuous soul had Jean-Jacques.' What the ladies themselves thought of their treatment is not on record. Nor do we know how Thérèse felt about being banished from her own table—as she habitually was when Jean-Jacques had guests (whom he occasionally entertained with funny stories of her stupidity just as he had amused the Duchess of Luxembourg with his dictionary of her howlers). This did apparently shock some of his blue-blooded friends a little: 'I was astonished,' recalled a count who took a good many meals with him at one time, 'that never, in spite of my invitations, would he allow her to join us at table;' she only appeared from time to time to bring in the food when Jean-Jacques 'made merry at her expense'. But there is no evidence that his fellow-intellectuals thought any of this rather hard on her. Indeed, according to a contemporary who quotes d'Holbach, they had so little sympathy for her, or at any rate found her so unworthy of their friend, that they entered into a 'friendly conspiracy to break up the bizarre and ridiculous combination'.

Yet there came a time when even one of these conspirators, Diderot, felt that Thérèse was not getting a fair deal. That was when she was made to pay a far heavier price for Jean-Jacques's pride and principles than just forfeiting the present of a dress. On this occasion it was a royal pension he refused. It was offered to him by the King in recognition of his merits as the author and composer of the operetta he had enjoyed so much. From Thérèse's point of view the offer could not have come at a better time. Until then her lord and master had been able to include poverty among the compelling reasons for regular visits to the Foundling Hospital. It is impossible to say whether, at the time the King deprived him of this argument, she was once again with child and whether Diderot had this in mind when he urged him to accept the King's offer. Jean-Jacques tells one no more about it than that his friend 'regarded my indifference towards the pension as a crime. I might be disinterested on my own account, he told me, but I had no right to be so on behalf of Madame Levasseur and her daughter. I owed it to her, he said, to neglect no possible honest means of providing for their subsistence . . . I could not appreciate his principles and we had a very lively argument on this point'.

As so often the quarrel between the two friends had started with Diderot 'laying down what he considered I ought to do', which earned him among Jean-Jacques's partisans the reputation of a bullying, interfering busybody. But if ever he could invoke the rights and, as he saw it, the duties of friendship, he was entitled to do so on this occasion. Altogether apart from the fact that, though no richer than his friend, he regularly subsidized his dependants (as did Grimm and d'Holbach), no one had a better right to reject the old plea that the sacred cause of art and literature exempts its practitioners from the responsibilities and duties incumbent on ordinary mortals. For he himself had originally undertaken his back-breaking labours on the *Encyclopédie*, not for the love of the Cause, the light it would spread, but for the sake of the money he needed to acquit himself of these family responsibilities. He had wanted to devote his talents to the drama. But he had sacrificed his ambition to his duties: 'If I had not had a wife and children to think of,' he once said wistfully, 'I would not have renounced my natural vocation.' And so one can imagine that his argument with Jean-Jacques, who could not see his point, was indeed lively.

Doubtless the latter's argument with Thérèse was even stormier. Much as she might sympathize with the reasons he invoked for his reluctance to face the monarch, the embarrassment he might suffer owing to his 'frequent need to retire' and his 'confounded shyness' hardly seemed to justify foregoing the King's lifelong bounty.

Admittedly these disabilities did present a problem. For he would need all his wits to circumvent another problem and one of his own making: how to thank the King, who would be rewarding him for his contribution to the arts, 'without abandoning the severe air and tone' he had adopted in his violent denunciation of them barely two years earlier. It was a real poser. And even if he managed to solve it and think up 'some great and useful truth in the form of a choice eulogy', it was bound to have gone right out of his head at the crucial moment. That was a prospect which, together with the possibility he might not be able to contain himself, 'terrified' him.

He had perhaps a stronger case—though for Diderot he did not—when arguing that he owed a greater duty to the cause of truth than to his dependants: 'If I took the pension I should have to flatter or be silent . . . Farewell, truth, liberty and courage!' It sounded admirable. But it would have sounded even better had he not followed it up with a superbly practical afterthought: 'Besides, what assurance had I that it would really be paid?' It is one of those many occasions where one would almost think he was laughing at his own moral pretensions, aiming at comic effect by their sudden deflation. But it would be more charitable to see such admissions of mixed motives, the exalted and the expedient that so often work in harness in the human heart, as proofs of fearless honesty. Which indeed they would be, if only the honourable motive were not always presented as the one that swayed every action, if only he would not regularly whip out his halo to crown himself the best of men.

*

Unlike many great men whose reputations have not benefited from the literary proclivities of those who knew them best, whether wives or maîtresses-en-titre, Jean-Jacques was fortunate in that his life-partner had little inclination to take to the pen. She left no memoirs and only one of her letters seemed to have survived, showing an orthography of such originality that one should perhaps be grateful there are no others to decipher. Writing after his precipitate flight from France, she assured him of her anxiety to join him in exile: *'Ceu n'atan que leu moman pour vous reu goindre e vous sanbracés du fon deu mon quer'*, meaning: *'Je n'attends que le moment de vous rejoindre et de vous embrasser du fond de mon coeur;*' and continuing, 'you know that wherever you may be I would want to join you, even if there were seas and precipices to cross'. It is certainly a letter full of love and devotion. But one loving letter hardly disproves the fact that she suffered many a winter of discontent in their thirty-five years together. In fact, there is evidence, in a pitiful letter written by Jean-Jacques seven years later, that she had more than once wanted to leave him: 'I know one must not attach too much weight to what is said in the heat of a quarrel. But you have reverted to the idea too often not to take it seriously . . . Adieu, dear friend of my heart . . . if we do not see one another again always remember the only true friend you ever had and ever will have.'

It was the kind of letter that might only too easily have proved the last straw. For it started with the breathtaking claim that he was in no way to blame. 'For the twenty-five years that our union has lasted I have sought my happiness only in yours . . . I have omitted nothing that I thought could contribute to your felicity. I simply would not know how to do more for it, however ardently I wished to do so.' In short, he had been the ideal husband. But the fact of the matter is that he had never been and never became her husband at all. What he referred to when, in the same letter, he prided himself on having only recently shown that 'your honour is as dear to me as your happiness', was the mock marriage he entered into after a quarter of a century of living in sin* (though during the last thirteen years it was replaced by the 'compensatory vice') and after an engagement of less than 120 seconds: Thérèse, he told a friend later, 'had no idea of what I wanted to do two minutes before'. The idea had apparently come to him out of the blue, which, however, raised no problems as its execution required no formalities of any kind. Acting as his own priest, parson or registrar, he solemnly declared he took Thérèse for his wife while the few friends he had invited to witness this do-it-yourself wedding acted as witnesses. According to one of them the bridegroom, who even took on the role of best man by making a speech, 'employed a language so sublime that we could not follow him until noticing this, he gradually came back to earth' and, among other things, congratulated them on their good luck in knowing him: 'One day people will erect statues to me . . . It will then be no empty honour to have been a friend of Jean-Jacques.'

A year later the 'marriage' appeared to be on the rocks, owing to Thérèse's no longer reciprocating his own unchanging feelings of

---

* A trial period he recommended for general adoption. 'If all marriages started with such an attachment of twenty-five years,' he wrote to a friend, 'don't you think they would mostly prove more harmonious?'

'tenderness and attachment'. Apparently she simply could not bear him
any more; 'not only do you no longer take pleasure in my company, you
have to make a big effort even to spend a few moments with me just to
be obliging.' But as things turned out she did not desert him, perhaps
partly because of his heartrending pleas: 'You know my fate, it is such as
one would not dare to describe since no one would believe it. The only
consolation left to me was to unburden my heart in yours, when I talked
of my sorrows to you they were relieved, when you pitied me I no longer
pitied myself . . . It is certain that if I must live without you, absolutely
alone, I am a dead man.' What is more, the first words she spoke after
Jean-Jacques's death are supposed to have been: 'If my husband is not a
saint, who is?' But as no man is a hero to his valet let alone a saint to his
wife, the encomium was doubtless pronounced in the spirit of *de mortuis
nil nisi bonum*. There is every reason to think that she spoke rather more
from the heart ten years later when she horrified an interviewer with
her sacrilegious remarks about the then duly canonized Jean-Jacques:
'Who would believe that this woman does not love him? But there it is.
She speaks ill of him. She said he had many faults and told me a thousand
other enormities.'

Considering what life with Jean-Jacques must have been like, it would
not seem all that surprising. But if he had treated her badly, posterity was
to do much worse. No sooner had Jean-Jacques immortalized her in his
memoirs than his disciples decided that the lady was for burning and
began to immolate her on his altar. Renowned writers like Madame de
Staël not only made 'the atrocious urgings of that unnatural mother'
responsible for the fate of Jean-Jacques's children but blamed her even
for his death; he had killed himself (in fact he died in his bed) 'because
he had discovered her vile inclinations for a man belonging to the lowest
of the lower orders'.* Even among serious scholars there are many who
feel compelled to try and rub off some of his moral stains onto Thérèse.
Thus such leaders in the field of Rousseau-studies as the editors of the
Pléiade edition of his works do not hesitate to call her his 'accomplice' in
the abandonment of his children, even though he himself made it perfectly
clear she was his victim. Stranger still, not a few of his biographers seem
to have known her better than he did himself, making her out a far worse
character than one would gather from his own descripton. 'Stupid' is the
only pejorative term Jean-Jacques uses. Apart from that she was 'a simple

---

* The unspeakable fellow whom she did indeed marry a year after Jean-
Jacques's death—thereby putting another nail in the coffin of her reputation—was
the English valet of the Marquis on whose estate they had lived for the last two
months of Jean-Jacques's life, and who was much disgusted with 'her malice in
robbing me of a useful servant'.

girl without coquetry', 'tender and virtuous', 'a successor to Maman', 'an excellent adviser in difficult circumstances'. She had 'the heart of an angel', when he confessed he had gone whoring he received nothing but 'touching and tender reproaches without a trace of anger', when he had been carrying on with the Comtesse she had been 'honourable, loyal and generous'. She was 'timorous and easily dominated', he had 'always loved her because of her good heart, sincere affection, exemplary disinterestedness, impeccable fidelity'. Though 'she was not without faults, she had a beautiful soul', 'she has rare virtues, an excellent heart, good morals, she serves me with the attachment of a daughter for her father rather than a servant for her master', she was 'my sister, my only true friend, the sweetest consolation of my life'.

Needless to say she was not nearly as much of an angel as he would have one believe. He painted her in such glowing colours, partly out of loyalty and partly vanity, hurt by the way his former friends of d'Holbach's luncheon table had laughed at him for his choice of life-partner. Her fidelity in bed was not proof against his desertion of it.* And some of those who came to know her found her less than perfect in other ways too. Madame d'Epinay called her a 'gossip', 'jealous' (which she had plenty of reason to be at the Hermitage) and 'mendacious'. Jean-Jacques's host in England thought her a 'poison tongue' and as such a baneful influence on someone whose native distrust needed no encouragement. A neighbour of the Duchess, who also saw something of Thérèse,

---

* But then, Jean-Jacques had a curious way of dealing with those who made attempts on Thérèse's virtue. Witness the incident on a journey from Paris to Geneva during which their travel companion, a close friend of his, set out to corrupt her. 'A gouty old man of over sixty, impotent and worn out by his pleasures and dissipations', he had gone about it in 'the most shameful way . . . offered her his purse and tried to excite her by reading her a filthy book and showing her obscene pictures'. Perhaps because at that time Jean-Jacques, then forty-two, had not yet discovered that the compensatory vice was better for his health, Thérèse behaved irreproachably: 'in her indignation she threw the beastly book out of the window', got out of the carriage where the impotent but apparently far from harmless satyr had been propositioning her, and told her lord and master all about it. It was a bitter blow to him: 'I sustained a shock to my confiding nature . . . For the first time in my life I found myself compelled to . . . withdraw confidence and respect from a man whom I loved and who, I believed, loved me.' But of this the dirty old man, bumping along in the carriage, as indignant Thérèse and wrathful Jean-Jacques strode on by its side, remained blissfully ignorant; 'I found myself compelled not to reveal my scorn and to hide in the depths of my heart those feelings that he was not to know.' One wonders why. His own explanation that he never let on, 'so as not to betray Thérèse', is so puzzling that one cannot but ask whether it might have had anything to do with the fact that the treacherous friend, who had behaved like a 'he-goat', was someone of considerable standing in Geneva where his services might come in useful.

thought the Englishman's strictures 'perhaps too severe' but did suspect her of 'aggravating her master's anxieties instead of calming them'. But Hume, though assured by some that 'she was the cause of my quarrel with Rousseau', thought her 'a good girl, less coarse than I was led to believe'. And while there is no doubt that she caused Jean-Jacques much trouble by her inability to get on with the servants in the grand houses where they spent so much of their time, there is not nearly enough evidence to justify the treatment she has received at the hands of those who did not shrink from making their hero a liar, or at best a dupe, in order to make him into a saint. Disregarding Jean-Jacques's account of the happy six years they had spent together in Paris—one of the most attractive as well as most convincing passages of the *Confessions*—a leading nineteenth-century biographer* asked how 'the creature he deigned to call his companion, with her contemptible character, her native coarseness, her stupid gossiping, her cupidity and malignity' could have made a proper home for him; 'she had made him distrustful, misanthropic, mad, she was his evil genius, this villainous Thérèse . . . surly, money-grabbing, brutish, scandal-mongering, boozing, licentious.'

Though not all Jean-Jacques's admirers went quite so far, the vilification of the lady of his choice became such common form in the last century that even those who had no need of sacrificial flesh to burn on his altar, neutral or hostile biographers, mostly joined in. To one of the former, 'stupid, tyrannical, treacherous Thérèse was responsible for all the serious transgressions of Rousseau'. For one of the latter, not afraid to hit the nail on the head with his statement that 'unvarying egoism was the key to Jean-Jacques's character', she was 'that slattern, that strumpet, that dull and so commonplace gossip . . . cunning . . . and hypocritical'. As already indicated, dispassionate scholarship has long since accepted that there is no basis in known historical fact for the ill-repute in which Thérèse was held (and to which mere class-prejudice, contempt for her 'vile blood', had made no small contribution). But just as nothing succeeds like success, nothing sticks like mud. And that Jean-Jacques's reputation still profits from the former law just as Thérèse's still suffers from the latter, was never shown more clearly than when, 150 years after his death, a Rousseauiste biographer† set about rewriting the Maestro's account of their relationship, so as to show how noble his role had been. 'At no time,' he wrote 'does one see him indifferent to Thérèse, he looks after her with touching care.' Far from having bedded Thérèse for his 'amusement', as Jean-Jacques tells us himself, 'it was through the breach of pity that this girl had entered his heart'. And far from having momentarily recoiled from doing so because, as he says, he was misled into thinking

* M. G. Streckeisen-Moultou.   † C. Ferval.

she had 'the pox', it was because he 'thought she was a virgin' and he had 'scruples'.

Even Jean-Jacques, so insistent that posterity should give him his due, could hardly ask for more striking proof of its willingness to give him considerably more than that.

CHAPTER FIFTEEN

At His Worst and at His Best

'Show me a better man than me!'

'In continuous ecstasy I composed the fifth book of *Emile* . . . Ill-humour had prevailed in everything I had written in Paris but with the first thing I wrote in the country it had gone.'

WHILE home-life with Jean-Jacques was clearly no picnic it had its consolations, and never more so than during the two years when he was writing the book that was to win him the martyr's crown and thus hoist him to the summit of his fame: *Emile*. It was not that during such periods of hard work he was particularly companionable. According to a fellow-writer who at one time was an intimate of his ménage, Jean-Jacques, when in labour, would not speak to Thérèse 'for weeks on end'. But better a happy mute around the house than an unhappy chatterbox. And happy he certainly was at this time, indeed, he was working 'in continuous ecstasy'. It was mostly, no doubt, because it is no small joy for a man of ideas—and few men had a larger assortment—to let himself go, knowing he can pour them out as the fancy takes him without any risk of the world's publishers failing to queue up for the resulting hotchpotch. Nor was the ecstasy of this intellectual orgasm in any way diminished by concern for its consequences. For as he recognized no more responsibility for his brain-children than for those of his loins, he could father them in careless rapture, without a moment's worry about how to support them all, wildly contradictory as so many of them might be.

There were other things, too, that helped to make this period perhaps the best of his life. What with his two residences, the little town house he had rented and the 'enchanting abode' lent to him by the Duke and used 'as if it were my country-house', he was most comfortably installed. On the domestic front all was peace and quiet, now that, having deserted Thérèse's bed, he no longer had to save her honour at distressingly frequent intervals. And what made life more peaceful still was that he had at last got rid of the chief bloodsucker, his mother-in-law. Though he had 'never ceased to treat her with respect and to show her . . . the attention and consideration of a son', he could no longer look at her 'without contempt', as she was always 'scolding her daughter for being too fond of me . . . while she owed her subsistence to me'. And so, regardless of Thérèse's pleading—'she tried to shake my will but I was inflexible'—he had finally told her to go, promising 'to provide for her keep as long as I could'. Like her daughter the old lady was to pay a heavy price for the immortality he bestowed on her. For few of those in whose accounts she figures seem to have allowed for the fact that sons-in-law are not usually the most objective character-witnesses. Apart from the valuable—by his own account invaluable—services she had rendered him at a crucial point in his career, the fact that Diderot, Grimm and Madame d'Epinay are all on record showing concern for her welfare (the latter two giving it the concrete form of a pension when Jean-Jacques sent her packing) would seem to indicate that she was perhaps not quite so much of a 'snake in his bosom' as he made her out to be.

However this may be, home-life with her departure had become much less of a strain. And social life too had become markedly more peaceful since he had left the Hermitage, with all its drama and its agonizing reappraisals. As Grimm reported to his subscribers four years later: 'Jean-Jacques had probably been as happy at Montmorency as a man with so much bile and vanity could ever hope to be.' The only intellectual fish in the ducal pond, 'he relished the incense wafted at him by the grandest and most distinguished of the realm, not to mention the masses of charming women swarming about him'. Not that he found all of them to his taste. There was one marquise in particular so 'antipathetic' that only his discovery of her talent for delicious tear-shedding made him unbend at last: 'She had her troubles as I had mine. Mutual confidences made our meetings interesting. Nothing draws hearts together so much as the pleasure of weeping together.' For, of course, even these happy days were not all milk and honey. During the whole of the four-year period, so he maintains, he did not enjoy 'a single day's good health'. It is one of those statements, like the one about the 'total sleeplessness' he suffered ever since he had reached the age of twenty-six, that may be taken with a ton of salt.* But there is no reason to doubt his account of the crisis he lived through when the end of the catheter he often needed to help him urinate broke off in the neck of his bladder and he had to go through a painful probing operation before he could be assured he was not going to die.

---

* A contemporary who accompanied him on a botanizing excursion and who heard him snoring his head off all night, has reported how, asked whether he had slept well, he replied: 'I never sleep.' The correspondence shows him telling a friend 'my health is in a state of collapse you can easily imagine', five days after he was reported by another acquaintance to have 'recovered' and to be 'gay and contented'.

Meanwhile the price of fame had more than kept pace with its extent. The idolatrous ladies made as much of an 'unbearable nuisance' of themselves with their 'endless little messages and little presents' as the small fry of the literary profession bothering him with requests for advice or criticism, and costing him a great deal in postage (in those days often payable by the addressee). 'All the little writers in Paris,' he complained, 'send me their wretched brochures.' In fact, it came to the point where he felt obliged to put an advertisement in the *Mercure de France* 'begging all authors no longer to send me their works and all *Beaux Espirits* no longer to write me congratulatory letters, even postage paid'.

But worst of all was that fame brought requests for help in deserving causes such as Voltaire often embraced. Just about the time the latter began to exert himself so strenuously on behalf of the unfortunate Protestant Jean Calas who was tortured and broken on the rack, a victim of '*L'Infâme*', Jean-Jacques (long since officially returned to the faith of his Calvinist forefathers) received a plea from a young man in the south-west of France begging him to come to the rescue of a Protestant Minister and ten co-religionaries who had been attacked and thrown into prison. 'Is it possible,' the witness of their sufferings exclaimed, 'that thinking human beings are capable of such inhumanity and barbarism? Famous author of the divine *Julie*, deign to take an interest in these poor unhappy mortals, innocent of any crime. A letter from you to our provincial governor would carry great weight.' Perhaps he was unwise in concluding his letter with a eulogy that was rather too oecumenical in scope to be wholly tactful: 'I read your works with infinite pleasure, also those of M. de Voltaire.' For all he got for his pains was a whole list of reasons why Jean-Jacques, 'though indignant at the fearful sufferings of our unhappy brethren,' could and would do nothing for them. First of all he found it difficult to believe that they had not given the authorities some cause for their treatment of them, like violating the ban on Protestant assemblies; 'the word of God is implicit on the duty of obeying the law.' Secondly his intervention would do more harm than good, 'for the friends of the truth are not popular with the powers that be'. Thirdly it was not his business; 'everyone has his vocation on earth, mine is to tell the public hard but useful truths . . . I have made it a rule to leave it at that, never to condemn . . . a man or an action but only vice'. He had always preached 'humanity, gentleness and tolerance and it was not his fault that people had not listened to him'. As for Voltaire (whom his correspondent had also approached), 'he would certainly be listened to if he spoke up on behalf of our brethren . . . But, my dear Sir, I doubt if he will put much heart into his recommendation, he has not got the will, I have not got the power, and so the just suffer'. In fact, Voltaire did write to the Governor. Jean-

Jacques never lifted a finger even when assured that if only he would write a petition 'in your beautiful style', it would be used in such a way that 'you would not risk anything . . . I assure you, Sir, that if you wish it, no one will ever know you wrote it'.

But by the time he received this new plea he had a better excuse; the broken catheter that had laid him low six weeks earlier. Thinking himself at death's door, he had more urgent things to do than try and save his co-religionaries. He had to put at least the outline of his public relations campaign on paper, which he managed to do in four long letters setting out 'the true motives of my conduct, my tastes, my character and everything that happens in my heart . . . With this hasty sketch I tried somehow to make up for the Memoirs I had planned to write'. By the time his health had recovered sufficiently to allow him to reconsider his original refusal to do anything for the martyred brethren, their leader had been hanged and three others had been decapitated. All their young champion's desperate efforts to save them had been in vain. But the experience does not seem to have left him feeling even slightly disillusioned. In the eyes of the humble the great can rarely do wrong. His letters remained as loving and deferential as ever. 'I had only hoped for a single page', he said in one of them, 'but it is not to be thought of any more, you are too ill.'

*

Ill-health and importunate admirers were not the only things that made the ecstasy in which Jean-Jacques worked on his new book a good deal less than continuous. On top of all this he had a lot of trouble with his publishers. The long-suffering Rey, in Amsterdam, had annoyed him so much that at one stage he would no longer do business with him except on a cash and carry basis. For old times' sake he would allow him to publish *The Social Contract* (which he also prepared for press during these years of intense productivity); 'but I will not let it out of my hands without money.' And if Rey had behaved badly his new Paris publisher was even worse, driving him to distraction with the delays in getting *Emile* into print. The 'impudent scoundrel' had been found by the Duchess who felt that her protégé was not doing as well as he should out of his writings; 'she was always reproaching me for letting my publishers trick me and promised to get me a better deal.' It was yet another sign of her unshakeable devotion. For she was by no means as enthusiastic about the new book as about the love story he had read to her.

When they had mingled their tears over its last page, and Jean-Jacques was again faced with the old problem of keeping the great lady amused, he had resorted to the same expedient as before. 'As a means of keeping in with Madame de Luxembourg', he started reading her his latest: 'But that was not so successful, perhaps because the subject (education, religion and a host of things) was less to her taste or perhaps she finally got tired of so much reading.' Clearly, however, it was not only the book but also its author she found a little tiring at times. However gratifying it might be to be told that 'the only consolation left to me in life is to feel my heart melt in thinking of you', his insistence on equally effusive replies by return of post came to be something of a strain. When he complained to the Duke that he found 'the silence of the Maréchale terrifying, I fear I have been too trusting, the less I understand of this frightening mystery the more it appalls me', she exploded: 'Will you never learn how I feel about you? Must I tell you for the hundredth time that I love you with all my heart?' Even so, she took it upon herself not only to organize a Paris edition of the new book but also to have its publication sanctioned by the King's literary watchdog, the chief censor Malesherbes.

*

It was to this benevolent, liberal-minded figure, the embodiment of understanding patience with 'the touchy self-love of men of letters' (which Jean-Jacques had the endearing nerve to deprecate in his rivals) that he addressed the four long letters intended to make do as an *apologia pro sua vita* if he did not live to write his Memoirs. They were composed at a time when he had cause to be apologetic. Enraged by the delays in getting his new book into print he had been wildly lashing out at his Paris publishers, accusing them of being in league with the Jesuits to suppress or falsify it. As he imagined himself to be dying at the time, the panic inflaming his native mistrust to the point where he saw Jesuits under every bed was surely not as inexcusable as he himself, in a sudden fit of self-abasement, made it out to be: 'I shudder to think how contemptible I have become.' But, of course, the thought was no sooner uttered than it was made to perish. Jean-Jacques contemptible? 'No, the man who for fifty years carried the heart in his bosom I now feel again within me, has nothing to do with the one who could forget himself the way I have done.' He was in no way responsible for the actions of the wicked stranger who somehow had wriggled himself into his skin and whom he dismissed, as an irrelevancy, with an ease that Dr. Jekyll must greatly have envied when he had his own problem with Mr. Hyde: 'I take not the slightest interest in him who has just been usurping and dishonouring my name.' He remained 'strongly persuaded that of all the men I have known no one was better than me'.

It was a comforting persuasion that had helped him a great deal when struggling to rise out of the slough of despond into which events at the Hermitage had cast him. Though 'guilty beyond measure', he was not really so: 'If I was partly to blame for all that has happened it was to a very slight extent. Was it I who had sought out his mistress? Was it not she who had come to me? Could I avoid seeing her? What could I do? They alone had done the mischief and it was I who had suffered from it.' Seeing himself as 'on the whole the best of men', with a heart 'that needs only to be known to be loved', the hostility he had aroused was no cause for worry; 'I look into my heart,' he wrote to a friend, 'and remain calm, determined to break with all those whose hearts are not worthy of mine.' Only the wicked hated him: 'How often have I had occasion to con-gratulate myself on seeing rage in the eyes of rogues and only benevolence in those of virtuous people.' His enemies could only hate him 'because of the harm they have done me . . . in their hearts of hearts they honour me'. And just as he was in no way to blame for the loss of his old friends, so the sins to which he confessed, and which anyhow were not really his fault,* did not worry him overmuch.

He had two ways of preventing them from doing so. One was to enter his sufferings as well as his good deeds on the credit-side of his moral balance sheet. If he had 'little fear of carrying the sin [of having borne false witness]† on my conscience at death', it was because 'the crime must have been atoned for by all the misfortunes that have crowded the end of my life and by forty years of honest and upright behaviour'.‡ This type of double-entry book-keeping had already assured him of a credit balance in the days when he had only his suffering to offset his sins: 'The misfortunes that have long since befallen me,' he wrote to his father at the age of eighteen, 'atone only too fully for the crimes of which I feel guilty.'

The second moral pain-killer he used was closely related to the first. Looking into his heart—'than which there was never a better one, more tender, more just; wickedness and hatred never approached it'—he found it simply incapable of evil of any kind. And even when Mr. Hyde usurped it, wrong-doing to such a heart was so painful, so severe a punishment,

* Even when in his late sixties he prepared to meet his Maker, he was ready with the old formula: 'I shall bring the Almighty, if not the offering of good works other men have stopped me from doing, at least the tribute of a host of good but frustrated intentions.'

† When a lackey, he had accused a fellow servant of a trifling theft he had com-mitted himself.

‡ Better still, 'criminal', 'diabolical' and 'infernal' as his behaviour had been, it was once more not really his fault. If only the master of the household, where the incident occurred, had known how to appeal to his better nature he would have confessed then and there. If he 'had taken me aside and said "do not ruin that poor girl, if you are guilty tell me so", I should immediately have thrown myself at his feet. But all they did was to frighten me when I needed encourage-ment. My age should also be taken into account . . . really, my crime amounted to no more than weakness'.

that the slate was wiped clean straightaway. 'I am punished sufficiently in the very act of committing a crime.' Already as a young man, reprimanded for some juvenile prank, he had declared solemnly that, because of this self-purifying quality of his heart, 'no man was ever more worthy of forgiveness'. Far from inducing humility, the avowal of his sins seemed to him proof of his fundamental goodness, filled him with pride in the innocence of his heart. The principle by which he lived was not the one he loudly proclaimed, *'vitam impendere vero'* (I dedicate my life to the truth), but rather *'peccavi ergo probus sum'* (I have sinned, therefore I am righteous).

It was this unshakeable belief in his fundamental goodness that filled him with such happy anticipations of eternal life, not only in heaven but also on earth, in the heart of that 'posterity which will honour me and bless my memory . . . because that is my due'. If only his contemporaries were not so wicked and so blind he would have received the honour due to him already. Indeed, he felt obliged to warn them that if they persisted in denying him his due it would be at their own risk and peril. 'Woe unto you,' he wrote in one of his religious treatises, 'if your heart does not bless a hundredfold the virtuous and steadfast man who thus dared to teach humanity.' He also had a word for their rulers: 'I say it without fear, if there were a single enlightened government in Europe it would have erected statues to me.' Fortunately, posterity could be relied upon to correct their omission (which indeed it did) for 'posterity is always just'. So, of course, was the deity which guaranteed him an equal reward in the next world. It was inconceivable that a man 'who had suffered all the ills of this life . . . should not have compensation to look forward to'. Though, being only human, he had sinned he was not worried about his destination in the hereafter; 'while my faults frighten me my heart reassures me, I would leave this life with apprehension if I knew a better man than me. But I have seen them all . . .'

Pending celestial compensation for his sufferings here on earth—which was 'guaranteed by Nature itself'—he had one friend of flesh and blood always ready to console him for the loss of all those who had abandoned him. And this one man, in whose company he felt happy and at peace was, of course, Jean-Jacques himself. This was the friend he referred to when he told the Comtesse, after his expulsion from the Hermitage, that he had 'only one friend left, I never really had another, he alone remains loyal to me in adversity . . . all the rest have vanished'. Deserted by all his former friends, he was 'renewing the acquaintance with an old friend whom the others have made me neglect and who is surely worth more than the whole lot of them'. 'In thinking of the prize my heart has merited,' he wrote elsewhere, 'I forget my misfortunes, my persecutors and my disgrace . . . In spite of all the unhappiness that should have embittered it, there had never yet been a human heart so far removed from wickedness . . . In the fifteen years in which I have exercised the sad profession of letters, it did not contract any of its vices; jealousy, envy, intrigue, charlatanerie never approached it'. His sadness, 'free from all bitterness, was only the sadness of a too loving heart which had been deceived by those whom it had believed to be of its kind, until it had been forced to withdraw within itself'. But it was richly rewarded for doing so. 'There is no greater delight,' he told a lady admirer, 'than that which one takes in oneself when one's heart is content with one.' Telling friends about his doings he repeatedly uses the untranslatable phrase, '*je jouis de moi-même*'. When a young woman asked him a recipe for the happiness she had not found with her fellow-creatures, he told her to follow his example and withdraw within herself. 'After finding oneself so dissatisfied with others, what a pleasure it is to return to one's own house . . . There is no sweeter sentiment than self-esteem and no more agreeable occupation than to heighten it . . . the source of all my consolation lies in my self-esteem.'*

*

Was it perhaps only whistling in the dark, these breath-taking assertions about the honour due to him in heaven and on earth? There is good reason to think so. For they were never more outrageous than when he was, or imagined himself to be, under attack. It is no accident that cry of supreme moral megalomania, 'Show me a better man than me, if I am a scoundrel how vile is the whole human race!', had escaped him in a moment of the despair he felt at the thought that even his beloved Comtesse was turning against him. It is no accident either that the demand for statues dates from a time when he had fallen foul of both the great Churches, Protestant as well as Catholic, nor that his autobiographical writings, mostly composed when he had come to see himself as the victim of a worldwide conspiracy, should contain by far the largest proportion of his claims to a seat at the celestial High Table.

But perhaps the best proof, that blowing himself up into a gigantic moral frog was only his peculiar method of self-defence, lies in the fact that the book he wrote when he felt most secure, cosseted by the Duke and his Duchess, is strikingly free from any such exhibitions. Though it is in part a development of his *idée fixe* about the corrupting effect of life in society upon man born good, its tone and spirit as well as the values it

---

* The young woman's reply was not such as to endear her to Jean-Jacques who never wrote again. His recipe for happiness seemed to her no better than self-complacency, 'being immune to remorse, being pleased with everything about oneself, applauding oneself'.

inculcates, are so different from those of his other writings that this time he really does seem to have 'become another man'. He himself recognized that it was at least partly due to the euphoria he knew, first during the honeymoon period of his stay at the Hermitage (whose literary product, *La Nouvelle Héloïse*, already shows the new Jean-Jacques in Julie's strictures on St. Preux) and subsequently with the Duke and Duchess. 'Ill-humour,' he wrote in the *Confessions*, 'prevailed in everything I had written in Paris, but with the first thing I wrote in the country it had gone.' And in the last thing he wrote there, *Emile*, the conceit and arrogance this ill-humour induced had largely gone with it. A Jean-Jacques shows himself who no longer poses the baffling question how he could ever have made any friends, how Thérèse could have put up with him for some thirty-five years, how Hume and others could ever have thought him modest and charming and good company. If he sometimes talked as he wrote in *Emile*, the mystery is solved.

The contrast with the insufferable Jean-Jacques he had so often exhibited in his earlier writings and was again to show, once the idyll with the Duke and Duchess came to an abrupt end, hits one in the eye with the very first page of the new book. It is marked by a simple and genuine modesty that is as notably absent from the essays with which he first bludgeoned his way into the salons, as from the insanely conceited auto-biographical writings. 'This collection of scattered thoughts and observations,' so he introduces a work that is indeed a very mixed bag, 'has little order or continuity . . . For a long time I hesitated whether to publish it . . . It is one thing to publish a few pamphlets and quite another to write a book. After vain attempts to improve it I have decided that it is my duty to publish it as it stands . . . Even if my own ideas are mistaken my time will not have been wasted if I stimulate others to form correct ones.' The most he would say for his book was that it might not be found 'entirely useless'. In much the same humble spirit he repeatedly begs the reader's indulgence for his digressions and exaggerations. 'I know I have said too much but I sometimes let myself be carried away by my arguments . . . My digressions are too frequent to be borne with patience.' Better still, he not only shows a genuine modesty of which one had thought him wholly incapable, he goes out of his way to condemn the vices in which he had seemed steeped beyond hope of redemption: pride, vanity and ego-centricity. 'The illusions of pride are the source of our greatest ills . . . this is the fault we have most to fear for it is the most difficult to eradicate . . . Great men . . . are modest . . . Man can be cured of any folly but vanity . . . Those who are always occupied with their own concerns are too keenly affected to judge wisely of things, they consider everything as it affects themselves . . . Anything which upsets their own advantage ever so little seems an upheaval of the universe . . . The wicked man centres all things around himself.'

Reading such passages, as surprising and refreshing as those in which he used his dream-woman Julie to pass the most severe strictures on his alter ego's feebleness, touchiness, self-pity, self-deception and self-complacency, one is confronted with a new riddle. How could a man be so critical of the faults of character he exhibited on so heroic a scale? How could he be so to the point in his condemnation of egocentricity—which he had already qualified earlier as 'that contemptible activity of the ego . . . that constitutes the life and being of little minds'—and yet almost invariably give his condolence-letters the form of: 'I am grieved to hear of your loss, but wait till you hear what's happened to me.' How could he be so conscious of the folly of vanity and yet make such an immortal fool of himself with his staggering displays of it? One possible explanation, already suggested in an earlier chapter, is that he was as much a tragic as a comic figure, that he was aware of his hopeless inability to measure up to his own standards, that he knew himself as well as he claimed to do when he said in one of his letters to Malesherbes: 'No one in the world knows me as I do myself . . . I recognise my great faults, I feel my vices painfully.' But only ten lines further down he shows himself to be wholly unaware of the greatest of them all when he makes that appalling claim, so often repeated in his letters as well as his autobiographical writings, about never having known anyone better than himself.

*

If the Jean-Jacques who shows himself in *Emile* is such an appealing figure compared to that which looks out at one from nearly all his other major works, it is not only because for once he felt sufficiently secure to relax, make do without the hectoring tone of the Angry Middle-aged Man struggling to arrive, or the compulsive bragging that was his conditioned reflex when under attack. It was also because his picture of the ideal man, product of the ideal education he outlines in this work, is worlds apart from the self-portrait of the *Confessions* and the pastiche he made of it when painting St. Preux. Just as his dream-woman, the forceful Julie, had precious little in common with her feeble-hearted lover, so his dream-man Emile is as different from Jean-Jacques as the young gentleman mass-produced by Dr. Arnold's Rugby was from the modern hippie. In many ways Emile is a forerunner of that breed of men brought up in what has been disparagingly referred to as 'muscular Christianity'. He has been physically toughened up from childhood by being taught the habit of 'ice-cold baths, summer and winter'. His tutor has kept him chaste and wholesome by tiring him out in the hunting field; 'the languors of love

are born of soft repose and tender feelings are stifled by violent exercise.'
In telling him the facts of life—at a time when he is so exhausted by a
hard day across the sticks that 'he may listen calmly'—marriage is
extolled as 'the sweetest form of society' and 'the most sacred and
inviolable of contracts', and he is given 'a true but terrible picture of the
horrors of debauch'. His moral code is summed up in the traditional
precept 'love your neighbour as yourself, that is the whole law'. He is no
intellectual but a man of character and judgment; 'no one will praise his
intellect but everyone will be ready to make him the judge between men
of intellect and his judgment is sane.' He is thoroughly conservative, 'he
never runs after new ideas' having been taught that 'all wholesome ideas
. . . were among the earliest known and at all times formed the bonds of
true society'. He knows better than to 'seek distinction by means of
[new] ideas that are injurious and fatal to mankind'. But he is no cold-
hearted reactionary, he is 'imbued with a tender love of mankind . . .
softened by the sight of human misery . . . He shares the sufferings of his
fellow-creatures' and knows that 'man is the same in every station of life'.
Though of good family he manages to appear classless, 'acts in such a
way that he is not a member of any class but takes his place in all alike'.
He is practical, 'a man of common sense who has no desire to be anything
more'. He wants to distinguish himself as a sportsman instead of as a wit
or a thinker; 'he will want to be the swiftest runner, the strongest wrestler
. . . the readiest in games of skill.' He is not interested in being thought
'wittier than another, a better speaker or more learned'. He is self-
confident enough to be at home in the world, 'indifferent whether people
esteem him . . . neither shy nor conceited.' His courtesy is not that of the
fop but 'dictated by humanity; he will not give up his place to another for
mere external politeness but will willingly yield it to him out of kindness,
if he sees the other is being neglected and this neglect hurts him'. He is
no great talker; 'he says little for he is anxious not to attract attention.'
For the same reason he abides by the rules of the social game; 'he con-
forms . . . not so as to affect the airs of the man of fashion . . . but to pass
unnoticed.' His manners are impeccable: 'easy not haughty . . . never
pompous or affected.' He shows due respect to his elders; 'he will not
have the effrontery of the young fop who . . . interrupts the old in order
to amuse the company.'* He is 'never careless of his clothes' though
never showing off 'by a display of wealth'. He is apt to be tongue-tied in

---

* Deference to the young was apparently as much the fashion in Rousseau's
time as it is in ours, witness the reply he quotes of an old gentleman who was
asked by Louis XV whether he liked the present century better than the last:
'Sire, I spent my youth in reverence towards the old, I find myself compelled to
spend my old age in reverence to the young.'

the presence of women, 'shy and timid'. He is 'modest and respectful to married women . . . eager and tender towards young girls.' In short, every inch one of nature's gentlemen.

Such being Jean-Jacques's ideal man, one can understand the final boost his appearance gave to the already towering esteem in which his creator was held by those unaware that in nearly every way he was Emile's complete antithesis. But there are many other reasons why the book, which he himself called 'his best and most useful one', endeared him more to his readers than anything else he had written. One of them is that it contains several passages which are indeed delightful, especially after all the bombast, the rhetoric and the cloying sentimentality of his earlier writings, irresistible in the simplicity and the freshness both of the language and of the values extolled in these digressions giving Jean-Jacques's idea of the good life.

Take those pages in which one only has to substitute the word motor-car for post-chaise, to make them wholly apposite to our own age. How to be deplored are those, he says, who sit 'dozing in a post-chaise with closed windows, travelling yet seeing nothing, observing nothing, making the time between start and arrival a mere blank and losing in the speed of their journey the time they meant to save . . . Those who ride in nice, well-padded carriages are always wrapped in thought, gloomy, fault-finding or sick while those who go on foot are always merry, light-hearted and delighted with everything . . . You start in your own time, you stop where you will, you do as much or as little as you choose. You see the country, you turn off to the right or the left . . . Do I see a stream, I wander by its banks, a leafy wood, I seek its shade, a cave, I enter it, a quarry, I study its geology. If I like a place I stop there. As soon as I am weary of it I go on. I am independent of horses and postillions. I need not stick to regular routes or roads. I go anywhere a man can go. I see all that a man can see. And I am quite independent of everybody. I enjoy all the freedom a man can enjoy . . . How cheerful we are when we get near our lodging for the night. How savoury is the coarse food. How we linger at table enjoying our rest. How soundly we sleep in our hard bed. If you only want to get to a place, you may ride in a post-chaise. If you want to travel you must go on foot'.

Or again, take almost any passage in the ten pages he devotes to a description of what he would do if he were rich: '. . . On some pleasant shady hillside I would have a little cottage, a white house with green shutters . . . I would have a poultry yard and instead of stables a cowshed for the sake of the milk I love. My garden should be a kitchen garden and my park an orchard . . . I would gather around me a band of friends who know what pleasure is and how to enjoy it, women who can leave their armchairs and betake themselves to outdoor sports, who can exchange the shuttle or the cards for the fishing line or the bird-trap . . . All the pretentions of the town will be forgotten . . . Exercise and an active life will improve our digestion . . . Every meal will be a feast where plenty will be more pleasing than any delicacies . . . We shall make our dining-room in the garden, on a boat, beneath a tree, sometimes at a distance from the house, on the banks of a running stream on the fresh green grass, among the clumps of willow and hazel. A long procession of guests will carry the material for the feast with laughter and singing. The turf will be our chairs and table, the banks of the stream our sideboard and our dessert is hanging on the trees . . . No tedious flunkeys to listen to our words, to whisper criticism of our behaviour, to count every mouthful with greedy eyes, to amuse themselves by keeping us waiting for our wine'.

To the jaded literary palate of the age, surfeited with the elegance, the wit and the glitter that had long been *de rigueur*, as formal and stylized as the intricacies of the minuet, such passages seemed to bring a breath of fresh country air into the salons heavy with scent. No one expressed their effect more graphically than the Marquise, once a leading literary hostess but now retired, who wrote to Jean-Jacques: 'The best possible augury for your book is that it has done terrible things to my nerves. When I read something and my nose does not twitch it means it's all cold and flat. But if I can no longer move either feet or hands, my eyes blink and, above all, the tip of my nose crinkles, it is proof of a superior style. And that is the state in which I find myself.' In singling out the style of the book as a guarantee of its success, she hit the nail squarely on the head. For it was not as if the ideas he developed were strikingly novel. Just as he had not shown himself an original thinker with his critique of intellectualism, the exaltation of sensibility and the glorification of the simple life, so his thinking about education, as a process that must keep pace with the development of the child's mind and makes it learn from experience rather than from books, largely followed the lines already adumbrated by Montaigne and made more explicit by Locke and others. As a leading Rousseauiste scholar* of our days has said: 'No one sees him any longer as an innovator . . . his prodigious success was due, not to the originality of his views but, on the contrary, to their already being so widely diffused.' Swimming with the current, it was by his manner of doing so, whether wildly splashing about as in his early writings or frolicking as in *Emile*, that he attracted attention. It was to this he mostly owed his proclamation by the great educational reformers of the nineteenth century, like Pestalozzi or Froebel, as their foremost source of inspiration. Even Madame de Staël who thought the world of him—'the

* A. Schinz.

most astonishing genius, the purest heart, the strongest soul . . . the most sublime faculties a man has ever been gifted with'—did not go so far as to credit him with an original mind; 'he has invented nothing but he has infused everything with fire.' And her contemporary, the mathematician, philosopher and radical, the Marquis de Condorcet, felt no different; 'among the modern intellectuals he is one of those who has said the fewest novel truths but has had the most influence because he knew how to win the soul of his readers.'

What won it for him when he wrote about a subject like education, dry indeed compared with that dealt with in his love story, was partly the chirpiness with which he handled it, skipping merrily from one wholly irrelevant digression to another. As, for instance, on what sort of woman to marry: though 'great beauty is to be shunned', great ugliness is even worse; 'repulsion increases rather than diminishes and turns to hatred, such a union is hell on earth, better death than such a marriage.' Or on the danger of corsets, 'cutting a woman in two like a wasp', which, 'carried to an incredible degree of folly in England, must sooner or later lead to the degeneration of the race'. Or on the bitchiness of women when among themselves; 'their manner is so constrained, their attentions so chilly, they find each other so wearisome that they take little pains to conceal it and thus seem sincere even in their falsehood.' Or on the futility and worse of the medical profession, about which he has things to say many in our day and age would and do say about its psychiatric branch; 'medicine is all the fashion these days . . . the amusement of the idle who do not know what to do with their time and so spend it in taking care of themselves.' Add to all this the fact that, when he returns to the point and resumes the exposition of his ideas on education, he does so not in the form of a treatise but that of a novel, the story of an ideal tutor bringing up a child to become the ideal man—and the readability of the book will need no further demonstration.

Such was the success it owed to this quality that something which had been urged in vain by the great Buffon as well as by all the hygienists of the age, to wit, that mothers should suckle their own children, only found favour with society when Jean-Jacques backed it up in *Emile*. True, the new fashion (whose most enthusiastic adepts were led to unbutton themselves even *en plein comité*) never won the wholehearted approval of the highest in the land. 'Some of our young women,' the King wrote eight years later to his grandson, the Duke of Parma, 'have taken to it. Personally I cannot recommend it nor advise against it. But it is not something husbands should favour . . . as it leaves their wives' bosoms—surely a very agreeable part when it is pretty, as, I am sure, is the case with your wife—much the worse.'

But it was not the deleterious effect of Jean-Jacques's teaching on this agreeable part nor his animadversions against encasing it in corsets, that caused the authorities publicly to burn his new book and to issue a warrant for his arrest within a fortnight of its appearance. He had to flee because there were ingredients in the hotchpotch that gave offence to even nobler causes than the King cherished in his concern with the female anatomy. It was '*l'Infâme*' he had provoked to strike him down. Only, by placing a crown of thorns on his head instead of the rope around his neck, as it had done six months earlier with the offenders he had then been too busy to help, it raised him to a pedestal so high that to many, including at moments Jean-Jacques himself, it seemed difficult to distinguish from the structure to which a man had been nailed at Golgotha.

CHAPTER SIXTEEN

The Wretched Advocate of God

'If my soul were not immortal God would be unjust.'

IF EVER Jean-Jacques had good reason to indulge his habitual inclination
to feel sorry for himself, it was at two a.m. on the fateful June night, all
but three weeks before his fiftieth birthday, when he learnt from his
ducal friends—who had sent their steward to wake him and bring him to
the château—that there was a warrant out for his arrest and that he would
be well advised to leave the country without delay. It could not be more
unfair; here were all the most prominent writers of the age, from Voltaire
downwards, busily pouring contempt on the Christian religion, and yet
the authorities picked on him, the odd man out, as the target for their
wrath. But then, in a way he had only himself to thank for it. For he had
violated the first article of the unwritten concordat between the intellectuals and their betters, the lords spiritual and temporal. Strictly observed
by all those who were spreading the news that God was dead, it laid down
that such obituaries—and for that matter, dissent in general—should
remain unsigned or published under a pseudonym. To defy this tacit
convention was to ask for trouble at a time when God was still very much
alive in the minds of his servants who, numbering over a hundred thousand and occupying the place of the 'first estate' in the body politic,
formed the spiritual strong arm of the all-powerful monarch.

Though the law exacting the death-penalty from writers guilty of
'attacking religion' remained a dead letter, there were enough cases of
ordinary people executed for professing the wrong religion, to make those
without any feel that discretion was the better part of valour. The four
Protestants whom Voltaire had tried but failed to save, were followed into
the grave only two years later by forty who had violated the ban on
attending predications of their faith in the open air. An eighteen-year-old
nobleman who had stuck out his tongue at an effigy of the Virgin Mary
carried in a procession, was only saved from having the offending member
torn out, prior to the whole of him being roasted, by the conversion of this
sentence into death by hanging.

With such ferocious goings-on still the order of the day—in the provinces if not so much in Paris where, a memorialist of the period reports, 'a priest could hardly show himself in the street without being hooted at'—it was small wonder the indignation of the intellectuals was matched by their caution in expressing it and their readiness to recant. When Diderot was jailed for a piece of atheistic writing, he promised on his 'honour' that he would never again allow such 'intellectual excesses' to escape from his pen. And even Buffon, an aristocrat of considerable public standing in his province, meekly submitted to the demand that his great natural history should toe the line of Genesis. Faced with the vastly superior power possessed by the defenders of the old faith, the partisans of the new one had little choice but to wage their fight with the methods the weak have always used against the strong, planting their intellectual time-bombs under the cover of darkness or smuggling them in from across the border. It was thus they had infiltrated and finally conquered the world of the salons, to the point where both secular and spiritual authority (many of the latter's leaders having themselves become decidedly shaky in the faith) eventually abandoned serious attempts to regain the lost ground. Provided the outward appearance of respect for religion was kept up and its enemies remained in decent if transparent obscurity, they could permit themselves to denounce Christianity as 'the inexhaustible source of murders and atrocities', 'the grave of reason', 'a heap of manure', 'the work of a few ignorant and crafty men who, like the founders of all religions, have exploited the credulity of the people to plunge them into the most shameful superstition'. They could even employ more deadly weapons than abuse, the mockery at which Voltaire (who called Christ 'an enthusiast of good faith with a weakness for publicity') showed himself a past-master, witness the occasion when he was moved to reverence by the splendour of a sunrise and cried out, 'Oh, Mighty God, I believe in thee,' only to add, 'as for Monsieur le Fils and Madame la Mère, that is another matter'.

*

Though in *Emile* Jean-Jacques, too, had deviated from the line regarding these two, he had never allowed himself any such levities, let alone abuse. And he had all the more reason to feel hard done by when he was singled out for punishment, because he had not only refused to add his influential voice to the chorus of unbelievers but had even gone out of his way to upbraid them as vigorously as they themselves attacked '*L'Infâme*' and all it stood for. It had been a bitter disappointment to them, a breaking of the ranks their cause could ill afford: 'What will become of our little group,' d'Alembert asked anxiously, 'if it does not remain united?' In the days when Jean-Jacques attended those interminable luncheons over which the atheist Baron d'Holbach presided, they had thought he had become one of them. That had been the time when, as Diderot put it with the atheist's supreme contempt for belief, 'Jean-Jacques had taken off his blindfold'.

He had done so only after he had tried both creeds, that of Geneva as well as Rome. Brought up in the faith of Calvin he had abandoned it when at the age of sixteen he had crossed the border into Catholic Savoy and there took the 'self-interested scoundrelly' step of abjuring it. Needless to say, however, it had not really been his fault, the priest who had first taken the young vagrant under his wing 'should have saved me from ruin and sent me back to my family . . . instead of encouraging my follies'. As he had that 'aversion to Catholicism which is peculiar to our city . . . I never thought for a moment of changing my faith . . . All I wanted was not to upset people who were kind to me'. It was only in the moment of solemn abjuration that 'young though I was, I knew that . . . I was going to sell my religion . . . and should therefore deserve the contempt of mankind'. But, of course, to back out at this late stage, 'to break all the promises I had made and deceive the hopes I had encouraged . . . required a courage that was impossible at my age'.

There followed a brief period in which the humiliations he suffered as a flunkey in Turin filled him with such 'bitterness and spite' that he came to see all religion as 'but a mask for selfishness and its holy services as a screen for hypocrisy'. But once happily installed with 'Maman', a fellow-convert who had as light a touch in matters religious as amorous, his 'native aversion' to Catholicism evaporated to the point where he grew 'sincerely attached' to it. Only during the early years in Paris, associating with Diderot and his like instead of the clergy that used to frequent 'Maman's' house, and again embittered by failure and frustration, did he relapse into the disenchantment he had known in Turin. Clearly, however, it was no wholehearted conversion to the cause of the unbelievers: 'He swung back and forth', Diderot recalled, 'between atheism and superstition.' As always determined to keep all his options open, refusing to surrender any part of his freedom by committing himself to one side or the other in the great argument, he took up his lonely position in the no-man's-land between believers and unbelievers.

The first public indication that he was going to train his guns on the high priests of Reason as well as those of Faith had come in the prize-winning essay with its exaltation of the heart as the path-finder to virtue. It was a reaction against the intellectualism of the age which he soon carried so far as to declare that 'reflection is contrary to nature and the man who meditates is a depraved animal'. Of course, as always, he can be shown to have exalted the reasoning faculty as much—'reason alone teaches us to know good and evil'—as he decried it when he called it 'the foundation of evil'. But he found its exercise little to his taste: 'I have sometimes thought quite deeply, but rarely with pleasure, nearly always against my will. Rêverie I find relaxing and amusing, reflection tires and saddens me. To me thinking was always a painful and charmless occupation.' His natural habitat was not so much the ivory tower of the mind as the wide open spaces of the heart where he could go *à la recherche du moi perdu*, the naturally good self, lost among the ravages wrought by life in society, corrupted in the sense of having become 'Other-directed' instead of 'authentic', as the jargon of our day would have it. Inside the nimble dialectician, the sophist and the logic-chopper he showed himself to be in some of his writings, there was a hippie struggling and often managing to get out. It is not only anti-intellectualism and its counterpart, a vague religiosity, he had in common with the exponents of the 'counter-culture' of today. He also had their yearning for complete, wholly spontaneous human relationships, communication so facile, total and direct that it has no need even of language, indeed, rejects it as a barrier: 'To people with sensitive hearts,' he wrote, 'it seems that what they feel should be clear and penetrate into the heart of the other without needing the chilly medium of words.'

*

When at the age of forty-two Jean-Jacques completed the spiritual circuit that had started in Geneva and had led him, via the Pope's Rome and Diderot's Paris, back to the Church of Calvin, it was not a question of *on revient toujours à son premier amour*. His return was no more inspired by a reawakening love for Geneva's teaching than his desertion, twenty-six years earlier, had been motivated by infatuation with its Roman competitor. He had abjured his ancestral faith from hunger, he was converted back to it because he wanted to regain the proud title of 'Citoyen de Genève' with which he had been signing his essays but which he had in fact forfeited on becoming a Catholic. 'Fêted and made much of by all classes,' so runs his account of a visit to his native town when in the first flush of fame, 'I felt ashamed of being excluded from my rights as a citizen . . . So I decided publicly to return to Protestantism.' It is as frank an admission of religious opportunism as that about his 'selling' his faith when a teenager. But those who accuse him of having sold it twice over do him less than justice. For on this second occasion he no longer really had a faith to sell. Under the influence of Diderot and his circle—to say nothing of his native aversion to any kind of restraint, intellectual as well as social—he had emancipated himself from all religious dogma. He had only parted company with his atheist and deist friends in that he still called himself a Christian, instead of reviling the creed as they did. But as his faith did not go much beyond belief in the existence of a benevolent deity, the immortality of the soul and the reward awaiting the just in the other world, he was a Christian, not in the manner of Calvin, Aquinas or any other theologian, but *à la manière de Jean-Jacques*. And as religious dogma, the source of so much strife, was in his view both meaningless and irrelevant to the code of conduct laid down in the Gospel, and he was, on the other hand, a firm believer in law and order as a precondition for such conduct, he had no difficulty in accepting the principle *cuius regio eius et religio*: 'The Gospel being in my opinion the same for all Christians . . . it seemed to me to rest with the sovereign in each country to settle the form of worship and the unintelligible dogma as well. It was, I thought, the citizens' duty to accept the dogma and follow the cult of their country as prescribed by law . . . Since I wanted to be a citizen I had, therefore, to become a Protestant.'

Though it was thus hardly in the spirit of the Prodigal Son that he returned to Geneva, its ecclesiastical authorities leant over backwards to facilitate his readmission to the citizenship he coveted. They did so no doubt partly because of his fame (slender as was its base in those early days when he had still only his prize-winning essay and his operetta to his credit). For just as there is one law for the rich and one for the poor, so there is one law for the famous and one for the obscure. But if they were so co-operative it was also because the Geneva clergy, infected with the critical spirit of the age (and following in the footsteps of a famous preacher who, already half a century earlier, had begun to stress that a Christian way of life mattered more than adherence to 'sterile and abstract dogma'), were themselves far removed from the fierce dogmatism that had animated the founding fathers of their church. And so they had no great problem of conscience to overcome when relaxing the rules on behalf of the local boy who had made good. Had they applied them in all their rigour Jean-Jacques would have had to expiate his youthful apostasy with a few days in prison as well as submit to the humiliating ritual of begging the consistory's forgiveness on bended knee. And had he not been such a big fish in the parsons' net it is doubtful whether they would have been quite so willing to overlook the little matter of his relations with Thérèse. As it was, he was able to persuade them that, though he shared a room with her, his physical condition was such as to make him quite incapable of conduct that would disqualify him for the required certificate declaring his morals to be 'pure and irreproachable'.

*

As he made no bones about it that his return to the Protestant branch of the church was politically motivated, it did not provoke any rupture with his Parisian friends for whom ecclesiastical authority in any form was an abomination. In those days he still called himself a 'Philosophe', hailed Voltaire as 'our leader' and warmly applauded an article of Diderot's glorifying reason, philosophy, sciences and the arts. It was not until the publication of *Emile*, seven years later, that he really put his religious cards on the table, and this time in a manner that could not fail to provoke both parties. In *La Nouvelle Héloise* he had tried to reconcile them, show that one could be a believer, as Julie became, without being a fool or a hypocrite, just as one could be an atheist, as her husband was, without being immoral. He had used his position in no-man's-land to plead with both sides, ask for mutual understanding and tolerance. In the chapter of *Emile* he devoted to his 'Profession of Faith', he fired off powerful salvoes in both directions. The atheist and deist intellectuals were 'all alike, proud, assertive, dogmatic, professing even in their so-called scepticism to know everything, proving nothing, scoffing at one another . . . They overthrow, destroy and trample underfoot all that men revere, they rob the afflicted of their consolation in their misery, they deprive the rich and the powerful of the sole bridle of their passions . . . Braggarts in attack they are weaklings in defence . . . They are agreed only in arguing with each other . . . Every one of them knows that his own system is based on no surer foundations than the rest, but he maintains it because it is his own. There is not one of them who . . . would not prefer his own lie to the truth which another had discovered. Where is the philosopher who would not deceive the whole world for his glory? If he can rise above the crowd, if he can excel his rivals, what more does he want?'

It was strong stuff, which accounted in no small measure for the book's success with 'the crowd', those many who were not won over to the cause of what was, after all, but a small coterie of not over-modest intellectuals with their following in the Paris salons. But the latter's enemies, the churchmen, hardly fared better when Jean-Jacques turned his guns around and let go at them, questioning the foremost articles of their creed, not only the miracles the Gospel attributed to Christ and the prophecies of the old Testament, but the authority of Revelation itself, indeed, the very concept of Faith invulnerable to Reason. 'Your God is not ours . . . The God whom I adore . . . has not given me understanding in order to forbid me to use it . . . To tell me to submit my reason is to insult the giver of reason . . . There is nothing so incontestable as the principles of Reason . . . I do not see how any man can convince another by preaching a doctrine contrary to reason . . . I must have reasons for submitting my reason . . . The gospel is full of incredible things repugnant to Reason . . . As regards Revelation, I find objections against it which I cannot overcome.'

No wonder Diderot found his former friend as 'confused' as in the old days, when he seemed to have done away with his 'blindfold' and yet clung to it; 'his ideas have no stability, he is a man of excesses who is tossed from atheism to piety.' And indeed, parts of the *Profession of Faith* might have been written by Voltaire, who, in fact, praised its author for having 'attacked the Christian religion with much eloquence and wisdom', just as Grimm wrote that 'Rousseau proves . . . the absurdity of Christianity and Revelation with a good sense and a lucidity to which there is no answer'. Yet, while exalting Reason with the best of the out-and-out rationalists, he reviled them because they did not share his belief in the 'holiness' of the Gospels, the 'Godlike' nature of the life and death of Christ, the 'immortality of the soul' and the dispensing of divine justice on Judgment Day by a loving God to whom he cries out: 'The best use I can make of my reason is to resign it before thee.' The explanation of this ambivalence, this trying to have the best of both worlds, Faith and Reason, which made him write such 'confused balderdash' (Diderot's term), could once again be found in that refusal of his to accept any form of restraint. Just as he rebelled against the demands Faith made on him for the submission of his Reason, so he rebelled against the demand of Reason that he should surrender the comfort Faith had to offer.

He has been singularly frank about the fact that it was above all this comfort, the *quid pro quo* the Christian obtains for his willingness to submit his reason, that made him break with the unbelievers, whether atheists and materialists like Diderot, Helvétius and d'Holbach or deists like Voltaire for whom the supreme intelligence he saw at work in the universe was not that of a loving Father and Judge of Man but an engineer running an immense mechanism of which Man formed but a tiny cog. Though for Jean-Jacques the immortality promised by the Christian religion was 'perhaps an illusion', he was not prepared to discard it, because 'there was none more consoling . . . it diminishes the horrors of the grave, detaches us from a life we must lose'. That was why 'nothing in the world would ever make him doubt' that 'the soul was immortal and that there is a benevolent Providence; I feel it, I believe it, *I want it** . . . I have suffered too much in this life not to expect another one'. Far from virtue being its own reward its practice made sense only as long as one could be sure of being recompensed in the hereafter; 'if you take away eternal justice and the immortality of my soul, I can only see folly in virtue.'

One could hardly have a clearer admission that his faith had its roots

* Author's italics.

in wishful thinking (as indeed he readily admitted; 'everyone is inclined to believe what he hopes'). Unlike most of us, however, Jean-Jacques managed to prove to himself that his hopes were certain of fulfilment. It was a matter of elementary logic: 'If my soul were not immortal,' he wrote to a Swiss parson, 'God would be unjust.' Which was, of course, absurd. It is one of those statements, so breathtaking in their colossal naïve egocentricity, that at first sight one hardly takes in their full import. But it is clear enough; there had to be a hereafter, not only because Jean-Jacques was entitled to compensation for the terrible time he had had on earth but also because he had earned the reward of the just, worked his passage to the pearly gates. That the immortality of man's soul he had thus demonstrated could prove worse than a mixed blessing, that St. Peter might be less accommodating than the Geneva clergy had been, and send him to the nether regions, never seemed to occur to him. Not that he believed the Elysian fields to be open to all and sundry, without their counterpart where the wicked fry. Quite the contrary, the latter's very prosperity here below was another proof, like his own undeserved sufferings, that there was another life to come where they, too, would receive divine justice: 'If I had no other proof of the immortality of the soul than the triumph of the wicked . . . in this world, that alone would be enough to stop me from doubting it.'* The thought of the punishment they would receive and the anticipatory terror they would suffer on their deathbed was one of the many things that made the belief in life beyond the grave so consoling; 'it makes us bear the vexations and the atrocities we suffer at the hands of the great . . . I am not ferocious by nature but when I see there is no justice in this world for those monsters, I like to think there is a hell awaiting them . . . Having lived as scoundrels it is good to think they will die in despair.'†

*

It might seem ironical indeed that the writer who, by common consent, did more than any other to set in motion a religious revival at a time when Christianity was very much out of intellectual fashion, should have been vigorously persecuted by the Churches of both Rome and Geneva. But it

* He was not sure, however, that he would be able to maintain his faith in divine justice if it were put to too great a test. 'If Hume should not be unmasked,' he said at a time when he had come to regard the Scotsman as a traitor, 'I will find it difficult to go on believing in Providence.'

† P. M. Masson, the scholarly and far from Rousseauphobe author of the three-volume study of Rousseau's religious thought, who quotes this passage from Madame d'Epinay's Memoirs, sees no reason to doubt its veracity. Needless to say, however, Jean-Jacques can also be quoted rejecting the idea of eternal punishment as 'not in harmony with man's weakness and God's justice'.

is by no means incomprehensible. Because he offered his readers the best of both worlds, the pride of Reason as well as the comfort of Faith, his rejection of the fundamentals of the Christian creed was far more dangerous to its hold on the public than the uncompromising rationalism of those like Helvétius who left Man face to face with a purely material universe presided over by Death, or, at best, with a deity wholly indifferent to man's fate and holding out no more hope of survival to him than to a fly on the wall or a worm in the ground. Compared with the atheists' and deists' 'desolating doctrines', as Jean-Jacques called them, his *Profession of Faith* was a siren song, as seductive in its manner as in its content. How appealing was its intellectual modesty in an Age whose writers too often claimed to have all the answers: 'we are surrounded by impenetrable mysteries . . . I only make up my mind trembling and I submit to you my doubts rather than my convictions.' What a relief to readers, surfeited with rival philosophical systems explaining the universe, weary of the battle about Christian dogma that had been raging for so long, to find a book dismissing all the argument as irrelevant to the only thing that really mattered: Christian conduct. What refreshing, good, middle-brow sense Jean-Jacques seemed to talk: 'Has this world always existed or has it been created? Is there one source of all things? Are there two or many? What is their nature? I know not. And what concern is it of mine? . . . I abjure these idle speculations which . . . cannot affect my conduct nor be comprehended by my reason . . . I give no heed to dogmas about which so many men torment themselves. To love God and to love our neighbour as ourself, that is the whole law.' And how reassuring it was to be told that, though we are all 'God's children' and 'there is another life to come in which He will reward the just', one need not swallow all the 'repugnant', 'incredible' things in the Gospel, accept it as His word. How gratifying that one could thus have Heaven and proud Reason too.

How liberating, finally, to learn that one should 'yield nothing to the authority of parents and pastors . . . that there was no better interpreter of God's will than one's own conscience . . . divine instinct, immortal voice from Heaven . . . infallible judge of good and evil making men into God'. What a boost to one's pride could be derived from these words. And what limitless scope there was for inventing one's own moral code if one took Jean-Jacques's word for it that 'conscience never deceives us . . . what I feel to be right is right, what I feel to be wrong is wrong'. What intoxicating perspectives of freedom from all external restraint, all authority, all tradition, all the world's accumulated experience and wisdom in fashioning the Christian ethic. On top of all this, how eminently practical and convenient was his advice to enjoy these freedoms to one's heart's content but avoid trouble with the religious Establishment by paying lip-service to its creed and abiding by its rules and rites: 'Let us respect public order. In every country let us respect the laws, let us not disturb the form of worship prescribed by the laws. Let us not lead the citizens into disobedience.'

Thus, once again, he ends a forceful challenge by taking the steam out of it. As with the denunciation of the arts and sciences and the discourse on inequality, he cries havoc only to adjure his followers: for heaven's sake do not let loose the dogs of war. It is scarcely surprising, however, that this perfunctory bow to established authority did no more succeed in appeasing it than the postscript, in the form of a footnote, in which, for good measure, he exalts bigotry, religious fanaticism, as in some way 'less harmful' than the humanism of his fellow-intellectuals. That, too, is typically Jean-Jacques, yet another example of that inability of his to commit himself to any value, not even the tolerance he had preached throughout his *Profession of Faith* and whose opposite he had called, only four pages earlier, so 'contrary to good morals' that 'the duty of following the religion of our country does not go so far as to require us to accept doctrines . . . such as intolerance'.

It is only fair to admit, however, that this maddening irresolution is, up to a point, a *défaut des ses qualités*, that it is the reverse side of his open-mindedness, his ability to see every side of every question. For if he finds virtues in religious bigotry and faults in the atheists' humanism it is only partly because he cannot resist taking another swipe at his enemies. It is also because he sees that 'fanaticism, though cruel and bloodthirsty, is still a great and powerful passion which stirs the heart of man teaching him to despise death and giving him enormous motive power which needs only to be guided rightly to produce the noblest virtues, while irreligion and the argumentative philosophic spirit . . . enfeeble life'. It is not the only time he has furnished a profitable theme to fanatics of our century who, not 'guided rightly', faced their contemporaries with a choice between murderously invigorating nationalism or communism and 'enfeebling' humanism, a choice which the best of them were, to their eternal honour, not open-minded enough to leave unresolved.

*

As the *Profession of Faith*, apart from echoing the atheists' and deists' ridicule of Christian dogma, was essentially, in its rejection of all intermediaries between God and Man, a profession of extreme Protestantism, it is no cause for wonder the authorities of a country, where orthodox Protestants risked death by coming out in the open, should have reacted forcefully. But those manning the trenches on the other side of the no-

man's-land in which Jean-Jacques wandered about, switching his fire
from right to left and back again, had perhaps even more reason to worry
about his effect on their battle for the people's soul. Much as he might
deride the beliefs held by the men of God, his *Profession of Faith* remained in its overall effect a most seductive and superficially persuasive
plea for a return to religion, a resurrection of God. What caught the
public attention was not Jean-Jacques's rationalist arguments against
faith. That was very old-fashioned stuff, hawked about in countless
atheist and deist pamphlets for thirty years past. It was his appeal to
sentiment, of a vaguely religious nature, that found response with a
generation exhorted, even by men of thought like Diderot, to cultivate
sensibility, regard the heart as at least the equal of the head in its capacity
for seeing the light. 'I have lived for several years in dreadful scepticism,'
wrote a young man in Bordeaux, 'the *Profession of Faith*, that divine
work so apt to make true Christians, has dissipated all my doubts. Thanks
to you, Sir, I am as happy as a mortal man can be. How much I owe to
you!' It was, Masson adds, the avowal of a whole generation whom
Rousseau enabled to believe again. 'Voltaire,' wrote a young Swiss parson
of Jean-Jacques's day, 'destroyed the faith of those who still doubted . . .
Rousseau has made doubters again of those who long since ceased to
believe.'

*

So, in a sense, the man whom Madame d'Epinay found out to be 'a moral
dwarf on stilts' had earned his halo after all? If, judging by the effects of
his preaching, he has indeed done more than any other man of his time
to shore up the Christian ethic with a foundation of religious sentiment,
it would seem difficult to dispute the claim widely put forward on his
behalf. But one should be under no illusion as to the nature of this sentiment. It was hardly truly religious in the original sense of the word as
'binding' man to his God. Such constraint was the last thing Jean-Jacques
could or would accept. He believed, not because he felt he could not help
it, was bound, but because, as he said, he *wanted* to believe. And he
wanted to, not because he felt that what he believed was true, but because
it was so comforting, happy-making. With many others of his time, like
the scientist Maupertuis who changed sides in the battle between unbelievers and believers because in the long run the former's doctrines were
too 'desolating', Jean-Jacques held that whatever made you happy must
be true. 'When I try to understand the nature of God,' Maupertuis had
said, 'my reason is confounded . . . and all the sects leave me equally in
the dark. If, therefore, in this profound night I find the system which
alone can satisfy my desire for happiness, am I not bound in this to find
the guarantee of its truthfulness?'

In other and cruder words, you embraced Christianity for what you could get out of it. In this sense Jean-Jacques's religion was a purely utilitarian one, whose many benefits were set out in a book by one of his most prominent disciples, Louis XVI's unsuccessful finance minister Necker. They included not only a ticket to the hereafter issued by a God described as 'the first inventor of happiness and the only guarantor of ours,' but also 'the maintenance of public order . . . an extra bulwark around the possessions of the rich' and, of course, plenty of what Marx was to call opium for the people: 'the more taxation keeps the people in misery the more necessary it is to give them a religious education, for it is the unhappy who above all need a powerful chain and a daily consolation.'

But there is something else as well that makes Jean-Jacques a religious revivalist of an unusual character. In the Christianity he preached there was little left of its fundamental articles of faith, which to him were not much better than divisive and unintelligible dogma. Far from really having shored up the Christian ethic with a foundation of religious belief, he had joined hands with his fellow-intellectuals in sapping faith as, at best, irrelevant and unnecessary to Christian conduct. He effected a religious revival only by providing those whose hearts yearned for religion and its comforts but whose intellectual scruples barred the way, with a church that, as Masson puts it, was hardly more than an 'evangelical atmosphere in which they could fraternise, in the freedom of God's children, with all other hearts in love with Jesus'. But however much the latter might thank him for making them, as he claimed, 'true Christians', their teacher was in fact incapable of the humility that marks the Christian spirit and that Burke called 'the deep and firm foundation of all real virtue'. If they thought him a Christian saint they were buying not a pig in a poke but a frog in a dog-collar self-inflated to the point where he more than once seemed to identify himself with Christ. Take for instance the following passage about the Redeemer which even the Rousseauphile Masson* admits to be suspiciously reminiscent of his autobiographical writings: 'His vile and cowardly compatriots instead of listening to him began to hate him just because his genius and virtue which made them aware of their own indignity . . . What made him fail . . . was not only the baseness of his people incapable of all virtue but the too great gentleness of his character.' He does not, in fact, hesitate to mention himself in the same breath with Christ. 'Jesus whom this century has disowned because

---

* He manages to describe the man who spent the last fifteen years of his life reviling his enemies and whose last book opens with a reference to 'the refinement of hatred with which they have sought out the most cruel torments for a sensitive heart', as 'inexhaustibly charitable, calm, resigned, forgetting his enemies and incapable of hating them'.

it was not worthy of understanding him, Jesus who died after having wanted to make an illustrious and virtuous people of his fellow-country men, the sublime Jesus did not wholly die on the Cross. And I who am but a wretched man full of weaknesses but who feels a heart within me which no guilty sentiment ever approached, am therefore certain I shall live.'

Though these assimilations with Christ are but implicit—and, indeed, he sometimes reprimanded those of his admirers who made them explicit —he was not afraid to claim a place among the Prophets and the Saints, declaring that 'Providence which brought me into this world among men, had made me of another kind than they' and that 'my heart feels worthy of the same price as the martyrs who suffered for the truth'. And there is more. Next to passages such as these, which led Masson to characterize Jean-Jacques's religion as a 'Christianity in which he shares the honours with Christ', there are others in which he claims to share them with the divinity itself, aspiring to become 'free and good and happy like Him'.

The 'humility' he preaches when writing his *Lettres Morales* at the end of his relationship with the long-suffering Comtesse, does not stop him from claiming a place next to God, on account of the elevated sentiments of which man is capable. Taking yet another swipe at his rationalist fellow-intellectuals, with their 'puerile' pretentions to fathom the mysteries of creation, he exclaims: 'Let us be humble about our species so that we can be proud of ourselves as individuals', proud of 'our love of celestial virtue, of those sublime elevations of spirit which take us out of ourselves and raise us into the Empyrean by the side of God'. And there are still other passages so suggestive of his ego's desire to extend itself over the whole of the universe, absorb it within himself, that there seems to be no room left in it even for the divinity. 'In his paradise,' so Masson concludes, 'God himself would discreetly retire so as to make room for Jean-Jacques.'

No wonder, therefore, the guardians of the faith which demands moral as well as intellectual humility, hardly found his teaching such as to make true Christians of his followers. In their view there was not likely to be much rejoicing in Heaven over the repentance of a sinner who even in ripe old age would still always qualify his *peccavi*: 'I am a man and so I have sinned . . . But never did crime approach my heart, I feel I am as just, good and virtuous as any man on earth.' As Mauriac has said, 'Nothing could be further removed from the Christian spirit than the ridiculous pharisaical exordium to his autobiography: "Eternal Being", let the numberless legions of my fellow men gather *round me** and hear my Confessions . . . Let each of them reveal his heart at the foot of thy Throne

* Author's italics.

with equal sincerity and may any man who dares, say: "I was a better man than he." ' 'No crime that he avows,' Mauriac comments, 'can inspire greater horror.' Yet he admits that 'this soul swept by self-love', as his fellow-Catholic Maritain called Jean-Jacques, 'remains nonetheless, in the century of Voltaire, the wretched advocate of God'. And wretched though his self-deifying religion may have been—which those who only knew his *Profession of Faith* could hardly have guessed—there seems to be no denying that the religious revival that started in his day and was to spread wide and far in the next century, was at least partly his handiwork.

Which, however, still leaves open two questions. The first is whether his religion without tears, his faith without humility, his do-it-yourself salvation, seduced more people away from the 'desolating doctrines' of the unbelievers than from the demanding creed, according to which the hope and comfort Jean-Jacques offered free has to be paid for with the submission of proud Reason as well as the humble acknowledgement of man's innate sinfulness. The second is whether, by making the individual conscience the sole and sovereign arbiter of right and wrong, he really served the cause dearest to his heart, Christian conduct, or sowed the seeds of moral anarchy. Whatever the answer, it would be difficult as well as uncharitable to deny him the one great and redeeming merit with which Masson credits him at the end of his long study. To wit, that he reawakened the love and respect for Christ that were in danger of being swept away by the rejection of the Christian faith in the France of his day.

CHAPTER SEVENTEEN

Persecuted and Unfrocked

'How grandly you hold forth, you men secure in your power . . . You proudly crush the weak . . . You sweep us before you like dust . . . without right or reason, without contempt, even without anger, simply because you find it convenient.'

'I never exposed nor allowed to be exposed any children at the door of any hospital.'

UNTIL the dramatic turn of events of that June night when Jean-Jacques's ducal friends bundled their protégé into one of their carriages and out of the country, the comic element in the tragi-comedy of his life seems the dominant one. It is provided not only by the absurdities to which he was reduced by the incompatibility of the two tasks he set himself in his memoirs: to win friends and influence people, and to treat the world to a history-making, trend-setting essay in the art—or, as some, like Voltaire, would say, bastard art—of total self-revelation. His correspondence, too, is full of the insane conceit, the breath-taking egocentricity, the transparent moral posturings and affectations, the childish cunning and the solemnity masking the intellectual chameleon's essential frivolity, that all go to make him such a comic figure.

It is only fair to recall, however, that he has been well served in this role by the no less solemn determination of so many supporting players to take him at his own sky-high valuation. If the first act of the drama, that opened with the hero's sudden entrance on to the Paris stage in the character of Savonarola, provided so much comedy it is not so much because of his own unsuitability for the part as because of its rapturous reception in the salons, High Society's eager adoption of one of those intellectual fashions that suddenly raise an unsuspecting author, guilty only of a *boutade* like Jean-Jacques's, to vertiginous and unassailable heights of fame.

Prominent among those who dared to defy the fashion and mock its beneficiary was Horace Walpole, unlike most of Jean-Jacques's critics hardly a rival. 'No amount of talent,' he said, 'will stop me from laughing at a man if he is a charlatan' (which was what he considered him to be:

'I have a profound contempt for Rousseau'). At the time when the cult first swept the salons the Englishman's accusation—which was, in fact, not uttered until some fifteen years later—might well have been at least partly justified. As suggested earlier, one need be no Rousseauphobe to suspect that in those days there was indeed a good deal of the publicity-seeking show-off in Jean-Jacques. Nor is it easy to take him seriously as the tragic figure he made himself out to be at the time of his expulsion from Madame d'Epinay's Hermitage. Tragedy presupposes a capacity for deep feeling, intensive because prolonged suffering. And it will long since have become clear that it is doubtful indeed whether the man who claimed an all-time record for sensibility but who forgot with 'incredible rapidity' what he had been like a moment earlier and who, in addition, was a self-confessed wishful thinker with a genius for escapism into beatific self-complacency, was capable of any but the most ephemeral sentiments. That is why his moaning and wailing, right up to the day when the Duke's horses were harnessed to speed him to safety across the Swiss border, carry so little conviction, arouse so little compassion and thus leave one free to enjoy the comedy he so richly though unwittingly provides.

*

But from this point onward the spectacle begins to sadden rather than amuse. It is not that he suffered the material hardships that are the lot of the ordinary refugee. The famous more often thrive on persecution. Become a martyr at the hands of unloved Authority—and a martyr in a very popular cause, the religious ideas he had so seductively put across in *Emile*—his star shone brighter than ever. The Marquise back home who assured him that no amount of persecution could diminish 'the veneration the universe has for you', may have indulged in the over-statement that was the fashion of the age. But the Comtesse who wrote, 'All Europe has its eyes fixed on you'—she referred, of course, to the only Europe that had any existence for her, its tiny social and intellectual élite—hardly exaggerated. Leading lights in both spheres, kings as well as philosophers, went out of their way to comfort the illustrious heretic. Frederick the Great offered to build him a house, thus fulfilling the prediction of another admirer, d'Alembert (one of the few members of the old d'Holbach set he had not yet alienated, though he had attacked him bitterly enough). 'The King,' d'Alembert had written, 'will doubtless receive a man of your reputation as he should . . . realising how rare are men like you and how much glory is to be obtained by harbouring . . . persecuted virtue . . . While the imbeciles chase you, men of letters . . . place you at their head . . . giving you a foretaste of the respect with

which posterity will pronounce your name.' From the other end of
Europe came an offer of hospitality issued by Catherine the Great's
famous lover, Count Orloff. From across the Channel came assurances of
profound respect, indeed of 'reverence', extended by Hume who had
been particularly impressed with Jean-Jacques's rejection of the Prussian
monarch's offer. It was not in fact as unique a 'phenomenon in the republic of letters' as the Scotsman called it. D'Alembert had also turned a
deaf ear to Frederick's blandishments, telling Madame du Deffand: 'I
will eat bread and nuts, I will die poor, but I shall live free.' What was
doubtless unique was the phrasing of Jean-Jacques's refusal, very much
in the grand literary manner and of a boldness, not to say an insolence,
one cannot help but admire in one temperamentally so timid and, moreover, at the mercy of the Prussian monarch on whose territory he lived
at the time. 'You want to give me bread,' he wrote. 'Are none of your
subjects in need of it? Remove from my sight that sword that blinds and
wounds my eyes. It has done its work only too well . . . If I could see
Frederick the Just and the Feared make his people happy at last . . .
Jean-Jacques Rousseau, the enemy of kings, would go and die of joy
on the steps of his throne.'

He had couched his letter in these tones, so he relates in the *Confessions*, 'in order to bring to his ears the sacred voice of truth which so
few kings are born to hear.' But when the King made no reply he had
second thoughts: 'Perhaps I failed to strike the right note', it could well
be that the 'frankness of my enthusiasm was at bottom no better than
clumsy pedantry'. It is one of those unexpected admissions that suddenly
make one see the insufferably pompous and self-complacent Jean-Jacques
as the attractive figure so many of his friends had found him at times,
endearing, or at any rate pardonable for his absurd presumptions, because
of his childlike inability ever to be really serious. That was certainly the
spirit in which the warrior-king took his blustering letter, witness the
sentiments he expressed to his governor in Neufchâtel (and which will
doubtless find an echo in the hearts of all men of action, statesmen or
politicians, subjected to criticism by men of letters): 'The poor fellow
does not know the difficulties . . . If he knew the crafty men I have to deal
with he would discover them to be rather more of a handful than the
"philosophes" with whom he has fallen out.'

In addition to the flattering invitations that reached the pampered
martyr in those days from all over Europe, he was besieged by ever-
growing hordes of importunate admirers, many of them no better than
vulgar sightseers 'who had not even read my works but who nevertheless,
so they told me, had travelled hundreds of miles in order to see and admire
the illustrious man, the celebrated man etc., flinging in my face the

coarsest and most impudent flatteries'. It sounds as if he had at last
become immune to them, as if he had recovered from the fearful inflammation of his ego, aggravated if not caused by more than ten years'
exposure to idolatry. But that was far from being the case. Some of his
most preposterous statements date from this period. For, as already
indicated, he never blew his own trumpet more deafeningly than when
under attack. He did it not only in public, to encourage himself in battle
with his official persecutors, as when he said they would erect statues to
him if only they had enough sense to realize how infinitely much humanity
owed to his teaching. He treated his private correspondents to much the
same braggadocio (so well characterized by Thomas Adams who 150
years earlier had said: 'You shall easily know a vainglorious man; his
own commendation rumbles within him till he hath bulked it out, and
the air of it is unsavoury'). Jean-Jacques kept on bulking it out in letter
after letter: 'Let the fools and the knaves,' he wrote to his Amsterdam
publisher, 'burn my books as much as they want . . . they will nonetheless
make posterity bless the only author who has ever written for the true
good of society and the true happiness of men.' The nose of the Marquise
that had twitched so appreciatively on reading *Emile* received an even
stronger dose of unsavoury air: 'It would have been a very great
honour for your Government,' he wrote to her, 'if J.J.R. could have
lived and died there quietly, but the narrow-mindedness of your
little parliamentarians* has disabled them from seeking the nation's
glory.'

There is much else in the correspondence of these years showing him
still so much the same old horror-comic that it requires a considerable
effort of understanding for the afflictions besetting him, to see him as a
tragic as well as a comic figure. Thus, when he learned from the Duke's
steward that the man he loved so much had died, he found it a suitable
occasion to pour out his self-pity, dismissing the Duchess's loss as nothing
compared to his. 'She does not lack consolations,' he wrote to the
steward, 'but I, abandoned by the whole world, remain alone on earth,
crushed by troubles, without friends, without resources, without consolations.' There was only one thing he was thankful for, and that was
that the steward had not forgotten him: 'If I had learnt the news through
public channels it would have been too cruel a proof that I no longer
count for anything in that illustrious house . . . at which I was once so
fêted.' As for his letter of condolence to the widow herself, he saw fit to
end it with the suggestion that she should really have written one to him:
'How much more I am to be pitied than you.' He also managed to explain

* He meant the judges on the Tribunal known as the 'Parlement' which had
condemned *Emile* to be burnt and ordered its author's arrest.

that it was really her fault he was so miserable. She had alienated the Duke's affection for him; 'following your example he had stopped taking an interest in my miseries . . . he had forgotten me . . . Till the last moment you enjoyed his tenderest affection. Only death could take him away from you. But I have lost both of you while you were still full of life.' That is why he was so much more to be pitied.*

Even if, as Condorcet and Madame de Staël have said, he was anything but an original thinker, in the genre of condolence letters he proved himself a true innovator, witness these further examples. When the faithful though by no means uncritical Marianne suffered the loss of a dearly loved sister, he wrote to her: 'Your tears will dry but my miseries will end only with my life; may this make you respect them henceforward.' When, not long after his expulsion from the Hermitage, another lady-admirer told him of the death of a friend of hers, he replied, 'I grieve for you but I know people who are unhappier than you. Really, Madame, it is much more cruel to suffer the loss of a living friend.' When the Duke's sister died he again could not resist a reference to what he himself had suffered from those 'hardly worthy of survival', explaining that 'the more I am moved by my friends' sorrows the more bitterly I feel my own'. When informing a Swiss woman-friend of the death of one of her relations he offered her the consolation that he himself remained among the living; 'when my hour strikes you will lose a real friend while in him [the dead man] you have lost nothing of the sort, far from it.' And when in his autobiography he tells of the death of 'Maman' he congratulates her on her good luck in no longer having to witness his sufferings. Instructing her to reserve him a place in Heaven next to her—'Go, taste the fruits of your own good deeds and prepare for your pupil the place he hopes one day to occupy'—he exclaims: 'You are indeed fortunate, amidst all your misfortunes, that by putting an end to them Heaven has spared you the cruel spectacle of mine.'†

*

* One marvels at the forbearance these grand ladies habitually showed their idol. Far from rebelling, the Duchess uttered only the mildest reproof and took great pains to tell Jean-Jacques how much she and the Duke loved him, why the latter had not been able to write, that he had been too ill, etc., etc.

† The exception that confirmed the rule was a letter to d'Holbach, written at a time when the two had already fallen out, but in which Jean-Jacques condoled with him at the loss of his wife. 'It was so touching', d'Holbach is quoted as having said at the time, 'that I imagined my sorrows had reawakened his friendship.' In this connection the reader should once again be reminded of the limitations, not to say the deceptive nature, of the biographer's craft. Jean-Jacques was by no means always as absurdly self-centred, egotistical, vain and conceited, as would appear from so many utterances quoted in these pages. Among his roughly

If in the third act of the tragi-comedy, which can be said to open with Jean-Jacques's flight to Switzerland, the tragic element prevails over the comic, it is only partly because these last fifteen years of his life came to be marked by periods when he suffered pitiful paranoid brainstorms. For one already begins to feel sorry for him, however much aversion his conduct and the character it reflects may continue to inspire, when at the age of fifty he fell victim to the religious persecution that played a considerable part in the genesis of the disease. The first blow, struck at him by the highest judicial authority in Louis's France, under the law forbidding attacks on religion, was by no means the most painful one. He could at any rate console himself with the thought that he had asked for it, as indeed he had when he put his name to a book containing challenges to the official creed that had long been commonplace among intellectuals but were rarely if ever proffered openly. The Court's decree left no doubt about it that this was why it had dealt so severely with him. 'Considering,' said the preamble, 'that the author of this book has not hesitated to name himself, it is important to make an example of him, as well as of all those who have co-operated with him in the printing or the distribution of it.' Though a couple of years later he spoke scornfully of the 'cowardice' of writers who hid behind pseudonyms or anonymity, it was not so much defiance or principle that had made him stick his neck out, as faith in his 'excellent backing', his powerful protectors.* They numbered not only the Duke and Malesherbes, the chief censor, who had given him his sanction and even assisted in correcting proofs of *Emile*, but also a new and even more highly placed admirer, a cousin of the King, the Prince de Conti. And he had no fear that they 'would leave him in the lurch', as it was they, in particular the Duchess, anxious to get him the best possible financial terms, who had persuaded him to have the book published in Paris as well as in Amsterdam. He, himself, had not liked the idea, as the authorities were considerably less tolerant of works printed at home than brought in from abroad. But in the end he had agreed, pocketing his money and also resigning himself to the usual deception practised by his Paris publisher, who, to minimize his risk, had put a Dutch imprint on the book. Of course, he found it 'repugnant to see the work of a friend of the truth begins with a lie', all the more so as the publisher (who should

eight thousand published letters there are many in which he appears a perfectly ordinary human being, no different, no better and no worse, than the rest of us, but, as such, no more interesting either. Which is, of course, why these moments are apt to receive insufficient attention for a truly balanced picture.

* Seven years earlier he had told an admirer who was worried he might get into trouble with his writings that she need have no fears: 'Never . . . will any of my works appear without official sanction . . . One must obey the Prince and submit to the law.'

have used Dutch type, among other things necessary to 'mislead the public') had made it a 'wholly fruitless lie'. However, he told him, 'Do as you think fit.'

It was the Prince who, on that June night when the curtain went up on the last act, had rushed a special messenger to the Duke and Duchess with a letter warning that 'nothing can avert the blow . . . At seven o'clock tomorrow morning the warrant will go out and they will send immediately to arrest him. I have obtained an assurance that if he makes his escape he will not be pursued. But if he persists in courting trouble he will be arrested'. To flee or not to flee, that was the question that now faced Jean-Jacques and that was feverishly debated at the Duchess's bedside whither he had been summoned in the small hours of the morning. According to his account of the meeting she was 'very agitated'—as she well might be since she could be charged with having aided and abetted him. So—in a manner that is less than clear—he 'nobly' sacrificed himself for her sake by consenting to flee. The letters of the period, however, lead one to think he played a rather less heroic role. They make one suspect that he was as anxious to get away—not unnaturally, considering his was, on the paper of the law, a capital offence—as his protectors were to see him beyond the reach of the public prosecutor who might well ask some—for them—awkward questions. 'They [the Court] would have made me suffer the most cruel tortures,' Jean-Jacques wrote to a Swiss friend a few days after his escape, 'they would have burnt me alive.' At the same time he thanked the Prince de Conti for having spared him this fate: 'I owe your Highness my life.' But he told Thérèse, who had remained behind, that 'the true motive' for his flight had not been fear for his own safety at all: 'If no one had been in danger of being compromised I would certainly never have gone.' And in the *Confessions* he makes out that, if it had not been for his fear of compromising the Duchess, nothing would have induced him 'to renounce the opportunity of facing the music so as to be able to defend my reputation'. In fact, he nearly refused to do so. When the Duchess said 'not a word to show she was grateful . . . for my sacrifice . . . I was so shocked that I even considered changing my mind'. He decided against it, only because of the timely arrival of the Duke and the Prince's mistress who paid him the homage he wanted: 'They did what Madame de Luxembourg should have done, I allowed myself to be flattered.' That clinched it.

*

Though the country to which he fled proved a haven where, thanks to the hospitality of friends and admirers, he suffered no hardships, the three and a half years he spent there were embittered by a running battle with its Protestant authorities, temporal as well as spiritual, that filled him with a sense of grievous injustice. It had been hard enough that his attempt to bring religion back into fashion had been so little appreciated by its official champions in Catholic France, the secular power that had the book containing his *Profession of Faith* publicly burnt, the theological faculty of the Sorbonne that had condemned it four days earlier, and the Archbishop of Paris who, two and a half months later, made it the subject of an episcopal letter in which Jean-Jacques was accused of trying 'to establish the sway of irreligion'. As if he were one of the 'd'Holbach clique' of atheists or deists! As if he had not incurred their virulent hostility by his denunciations of their 'desolating doctrines'! As if he had not pleaded the cause of God and Jesus! And as if he had not done it so persuasively that he had many a letter to prove his readers had responded to his call!

It was unjust indeed. And not only that, it was insulting. For the Archbishop had not been content to denounce his philosophical views, his belief in the natural goodness of man, his rejection of original sin and of miracles, his doubts about Revelation, all the things in which he showed himself only a child of his time, at one with the great majority of the intellectuals. That great Prince of the Church, 'Christophe de Beaumont, Duke of St. Cloud, Peer of France, Commander of the Order of the Holy Ghost', etc., etc., had stooped to calling him names: 'blasphemous, impious, slanderous, swollen with pride and self-love, devoted to voluptuousness rather than God . . . setting himself up as the teacher of mankind but aiming only to deceive it.' It inspired Jean-Jacques to compose an answer many of whose passages must have made the Archbishop feel very uncomfortable. 'Fair enough,' he wrote, 'that you should wish to preserve your flock from the poison of my book. But why all the personal remarks about its author? I wonder what effect you expect from such unchristian conduct.' He felt he had deserved them all the less as he had certainly not put his heretical views across in an aggressive spirit. Though there were a few pages in his *Profession of Faith* that mocked the belief in miracles and seemed to exalt Reason in the manner of Voltaire, its overall effect was not only that of a plea for a return to religion but also, due to that inability of his to commit himself or stick to any strongly held opinion, far from assertive. With good reason he could ask his opponent whether, 'even if I were in the wrong . . . my book did not merit some indulgence . . . a book whose author shows himself so little affirmative, so little decisive, and who warns his readers so often to mistrust his ideas . . . a book that breathes only peace, gentleness, patience, love of order, obedience to the laws, even in religious matters'. As his had indeed been a plea for tolerance he could legitimately claim that, if his *Profession of*

Faith had been the religion of France, 'rivers of blood would not so often have inundated its fields . . . this gentle and gay people would not have amazed others by its cruelty in so many massacres and persecutions . . . the innocent Calas would not have been tortured and broken on the rack'. He had surely only shown good sense when he had urged less emphasis on divisive dogma and more on the conduct prescribed by the Gospel; 'we spend our lives arguing, tormenting, persecuting and fighting one another about things we least understand and which it is not necessary to understand . . . That is so convenient; it costs so little to adhere to dogma and so much to practise morality.'

There is much in his reply to the Archbishop that is so to the point, reading it one feels so strongly he was in good faith when claiming to be a champion of 'the cause of God' and a bridge-builder between the men of letters and the men of God, that his bitter resentment at being reviled by both, as an enemy of their respective camps, seems wholly understandable. One even begins to understand how the injustice of it provoked him into bulking out that blast of unsavoury vainglory about deserving statues that disfigures a document which, however, ends on a note of such dignity as one had not thought to be within his register: 'How grandly you hold forth, you men secure in your power. Recognising no rights but your own nor laws other than those you impose, far from making it your duty to be just you do not even feel obliged to be human. You proudly crush the weak without having to answer for your iniquities to any-one . . . You sweep us before you like dust . . . without right or reason, without contempt, even without anger, simply because you find it convenient . . . Monseigneur, you have publicly insulted me, I have proved that you have libelled me. If you were a private person like myself I could force you to appear before an equitable Tribunal . . . But you hold a rank which dispenses you from being just, and I am nothing. Nonetheless, you who preach the Gospel, you, prelate, delegated to teach men their duty, you know what yours should be. As for me, I have performed mine. I have nothing more to say to you and I hold my peace.'

*

Outrageous as had been the misfortune he had suffered at the hands of the Catholic establishment in Paris, it was as nothing compared to the bitterness of finding himself equally persecuted, once more misunderstood and misrepresented, by its Protestant counterpart in his native Geneva. Papists, after all, would be Papists. But that the rulers of Calvin's *Civitas Dei*, which had played such a glorious role in the struggle against the heavy hand of Popery, that they should join in the clamour against his timely call for a return to God, that really was too much. In fact, they had done worse. Within five days of his crossing the Swiss border into the canton of Berne, the Genevese authorities had copied their opposite numbers in Paris, burning his book and ordering his arrest should he ever set foot on to their territory. As if that were not enough the government of Berne three weeks later followed suit by informing him that he had out-stayed his welcome. It was only thanks to the protection of Frederick the Great that three years were to pass, spent on his territory—as it then was —of Neufchâtel, before he was forced to move once again and, finally, after yet another expulsion from Berne, sought and found asylum in England.

It all seemed the more grievously unjust as he felt himself on even stronger ground in his conflict with his fellow-countrymen in Geneva and their co-religionaries in the other territories, than when he had been condemned by the spokesmen and the henchmen of the Church of Rome. It was one thing for a Catholic to declare him an enemy of the cause of God, because he elected to serve Him in his own way, interpret the Scriptures as he saw fit, preach a faith that recognized no higher authority than his own conscience enlightened by his own reason. The adherents of a religion rooted in the belief in man's innate sinfulness and his conse-quent need of guidance by the Vicar of Christ in order to live in its founder's spirit, could do no other than oppose those who asserted man's natural goodness and rejected all intermediaries and all external authority in the interpretation of God's word. Their respective starting points alone were such poles apart that a bridging of the gulf was no more possible than that a compromise can be struck between humility and pride. For the Archbishop and his like, Jean-Jacques, however sincere and ardent his adoration of Jesus, however plausible his plea for concentrating more on Christian conduct than on dogma, however helpful in discrediting the fashionable enemies of Christianity and in preaching obedience to the religious laws of the land, could not be the defender of the cause of God. To them he was, not because of his personal character known only to a very few, but because of that philosophical starting-point of his, with all the attitudes that flowed from it, the embodiment of *superbia*, pride, the foremost of the capital sins. Though sharing it with most of the intel-lectuals of the Age, wedded as they, too, were to the belief in man's natural innocence, he was more dangerous because, unlike them, such an eminently persuasive advocate of the comforting cause of Jesus.

But if the hostility he had aroused in the Catholic camp was, therefore, only to be expected, it was, so he argued, quite another thing for the progeny of the great Reformers to burn his book, order his arrest, chase him from pillar to post because he refused to toe the Protestant party-line, claimed the right to be his own master in God's house, reject such parts of his Word as he could not bring himself to believe were really His. Was not this claim the essence of the Reformation? 'When the Reformers detached themselves from the Roman Church,' he recalled during the battle of the tracts he waged with his persecutors, 'they were asked by whose authority they deviated from the accepted doctrine. They said: by our own, by the light of our reason, they said that the sense of the Bible was intelligible and clear to all men . . . who could interpret it each in his own fashion.' What right, then, had any Protestant, magistrate or parson, to demand he should submit to their authority? 'Let anyone prove to me that in matters of faith I must abide by someone else's judgment and I become a Catholic tomorrow.' Having been persecuted, the Reformers themselves had become persecutors; 'through disputing with the Catholic clergy their own spirit became captious and argumentative . . . Calvin was doubtless a great man . . . But he was only a man and a theologian at that. Moreover he had the pride of genius, aware of its superiority and intolerant of challenges to it . . . That was the spirit of the Reformers. But it was not the spirit of the Reformation.'

Though historically quite untrue—the free-thinking with no scriptural holds barred that Jean-Jacques stood for was far from having been the essence of the Reformation—it was a telling point in his battle with the Protestant clergy, many of whose members had long since become nearly as 'advanced' in the faith as he himself. That had made their desertion of his cause, when after some hesitation most of them sided with the secular authorities, so doubly painful. 'The Church of Geneva,' so the ever lonelier occupant of no-man's-land wrote bitterly, 'seemed for a time to have come closer to the true spirit of Christianity than any other', which was why, 'deceived by appearances', he had originally (in the dedication of the *Discourse on Inequality* to the Republic of Geneva) sung its praises. And now these men who 'don't know what they believe, who dare not answer when you ask them whether Jesus Christ is God or what mysteries they admit', had turned against him. 'They would rather abandon their own cause than support mine . . . these same parsons, once so helpful, suddenly become so strict . . . Their only way of proving their faith is to attack that of others . . . They want to prove by their ingratitude that they have no need of my help and think they show themselves sufficiently orthodox in showing themselves persecutors.'

It was not, of course, the best way to win them to his side. And he only made matters worse by abusing them for their 'ridiculous arrogance' and adding one of those absurd passages about how his readers should 'bless a hundred times the virtuous and steadfast man who had dared thus to teach humanity'. It is all the sadder he spoilt his case in this way as it was quite a good one. Though some of the Geneva parsons may have abandoned him because he had gone too far even for their advanced thinking and others may have realized how close his religion really came to making a foursome out of the Trinity, with Jean-Jacques at its head, there is no doubt that expediency also played a considerable part in their desertion. They cannot but have found the case he made against them difficult to answer. If only because there were few things he was better at than arguing a brief. He had the lawyer's ability to put up a very plausible, even if specious argument, for almost any cause the mood of the moment induced him to defend. And he could not only chop logic with the best of antiquity's sophists, he could also pull out a surprising number of registers ranging all the way from the bombastic to the sardonic. In short, had it not been for those unfortunate derailments when his vainglory rumbled within him, one would be tempted to say that he was at his best when he replaced the moralist's halo, the educationalist's mortar-board, or the demagogue's Phrygian cap with the barrister's wig.

*

Alas, he had been imprudent enough to take on an enemy who did not hesitate to hit way below the belt. The timing of the blow, moreover, was such as to make it cruel indeed. It landed during a period when its recipient was busy defending himself (against the charge of being the anti-Christ in person) with the argument that Christian conduct, not dogma, was what mattered and that his conduct was such as to validate his claim to be a true Christian, indeed, a better one than those who were steadfast only in the faith. 'I am a Christian,' he had said in his reply to the Archbishop, 'not as a disciple of the priests but as a disciple of Jesus Christ . . . They live as people who are convinced that we only need to believe in this or that article of faith in order to go to Paradise. I on the other hand hold that practising what Jesus preached is what matters in religion, that one must be an honest man, merciful, humane, charitable, and that whoever is really such, believes enough to be saved.' True Christians, he said when battling with his Protestant adversaries, 'try to observe what Christ demands of us . . . we are Christians in that we live by his word, you by believing in him.'

It seemed a very persuasive argument, one up for Jean-Jacques. But if ever pride came before a fall it was now. Perhaps the disastrous tumble might still have been avoided if he had not provoked the most ruthless among those to whom his moral conceit offered such a tempting target, the Grand Old Man of letters, capable of behaving in less than the grand manner when his blood was up. Their relationship had started amicably enough with Jean-Jacques showing proper deference and Voltaire, though unable to resist making gentle fun of his early efforts, assuring him that 'in spite of my poor jokes no one esteems you more and is more disposed to love you tenderly'. As at the time he expressed these sentiments the new boy had already acquired considerable repute and as Voltaire did not suffer rivals gladly—'he seems to want to bury them all alive,' Buffon said of him—his esteem was doubtless largely of the kind the famous habitually show their newly arrived brethren in celebrity, the greatness that sets them jointly apart from *hoi polloi.* There was certainly nothing in the character and manner of Jean-Jacques, and very little in his writing, to make it at all possible for Voltaire to love him dearly. The two men—of whom it is not known with certainty whether they ever met—were doomed to detest one another, not only because of professional jealousy but also because the ability to turn very nasty was about the only thing they had in common.

It was Jean-Jacques who took the initiative in the battle of the giants, a literary rank which, in the eyes of many, he had come to share with Voltaire by this time. He did so with a letter, written when he was still with the Duke and Duchess, the gist of which he summed up in a statement that certainly had the merit of being unequivocal; 'I do not like you, Sir . . . In fact, I hate you.' Of course, he was in no way to blame for harbouring such unchristian sentiments; 'it is not my fault . . . I hate you as a man better fitted to love you had you so willed it.' But Voltaire, who six years earlier had set himself up as a grand seigneur in Jean Jacques's homeland, had willed the opposite. With his campaign against *'L'Infâme'*, his ridicule of the belief in a benevolent Providence, and the wicked theatre productions he put on at his château which was much frequented by Geneva's ruling class unable to share Jean-Jacques's disapproval of the Thespian art, he had 'ruined the city'. Worse, he had ruined Jean-Jacques: 'You have alienated my fellow-citizens from me. It is you who have made life in my native land unbearable to me. It is you who will cause me to die on foreign soil, deprived of all a dying man's consolations and so little honoured as to be thrown into the gutter whilst all the honours a man can expect will follow you to your grave in my country.'

There was no answer. But Voltaire who had already shown the quality of his esteem in a pamphlet ridiculing *La Nouvelle Héloise*, made no secret of his feelings to his friends. Jean-Jacques was 'a despicable wretch', 'a little man bursting with vanity, who wants his country to talk of him alone', 'the most detestable madman', 'an insolent rascal', compliments returned by their beneficiary who called Voltaire a 'buffoon, mountebank, tiger thirsting for my blood'. He only reverted to open hostilities, however, when—understandably incensed that the 'champion braggart of impiety' should be smiled, indeed, fawned upon by Geneva's patriciate while he, the defender of the cause of God, was outlawed—he revealed Voltaire's authorship of a particularly virulent pamphlet denouncing the Bible as a tissue of absurdities, frauds and contradictions. Whether or not Voltaire in his château really had much to fear from this 'criminal, cowardly act . . . of a stool-pigeon', as he called it in a letter to Jean-Jacques's private duchess, his fury was such as to inspire a revenge marking as low a point in the history of literature as some of the worst pages of the *Confessions*. It was not so much that, in the pamphlet he wrote for this occasion, he opened the cupboard containing Jean-Jacques's five baby-skeletons. Though he has been widely and severely censured for doing so, it is difficult to see what obligation, except that of professional solidarity, he had to help Jean-Jacques keep his guilty secret. One could even argue that it was his public duty to unmask the man who had so successfully put himself across as a paragon of Christian virtue. It was not as if Voltaire owed his knowledge of the reality behind the moral façade to once having been on intimate terms with him, as had Grimm who, incidentally, set an example to the journalistic profession by his refusal to scoop the world by breaking the sensational story. All he ever said about it in his reportage, four years after he had come to see Jean-Jacques as a 'monster', was that 'his private life was interesting but written only in the memory of two or three old friends who feel they owe it to themselves never to describe it'.

As Voltaire had not been one of them Grimm perhaps found his pamphlet 'disgusting', not because it unmasked an impostor but for three other and very good reasons. The first was that it libelled Jean-Jacques as a syphilitic which he was not, and as the murderer of his mother-in-law, which he doubtless often wanted to be but never became. The second reason for finding that Voltaire's latest anonymous effort did him no credit, was the disguise he had seen fit to don; of all things he adopted the style and expressed the sentiments of a Geneva parson shocked by Jean-Jacques's refusal to believe in miracles. The third reason was that he, the enemy of '*L'Infâme*' and the champion of tolerance, now incited to the most extreme forms of persecution: 'One feels pity for a madman. But when madness turns into rage . . . tolerance becomes a vice . . . He must be taught that if an impious novelist can be lightly punished a vile trouble-maker merits capital punishment.'

The only comfort for partisans of Voltaire is that his enemy's response was almost on a par. He showed himself once again the 'friend of truth' by publishing a statement that he had 'never exposed nor allowed to be exposed any child at the door of any hospital', which satisfied the lawyer in him as he and Thérèse had not left their five babies on the doorstep, as Voltaire had written, but had stood on it knocking at the door to hand them over.

Only the farcical elements in the shaming spectacle of these two famous men of letters dragging one another down into the depths of scurrility and mendacity affords some relief. One was provided by a princely admirer of Jean-Jacques who wrote to tell him that 'the horrible calumnies with which an infamous pen has tried in vain to blacken you are only another proof of your virtue'. But the best we owe to Jean-Jacques himself; when he sent Voltaire's pamphlet and his own denial to a friend, he found this a suitable occasion for the exclamation: 'Oh, when the veils are torn away and posterity will love and cherish me!'

CHAPTER EIGHTEEN

Jean Jacques's Chamber of Horrors

'As soon as a child opens its eyes it must only see the fatherland till death . . . live for nothing else.'

'Make man one and you will make him happy . . . Give him all to the State or all to himself.'

'If government, based on the rule of law, is not possible—and I candidly avow I do not think it is—we must go to the other extreme . . . and establish the most arbitrary despotism conceivable.'

OF ALL the different types of headgear worn by man, none, it seems, is more difficult to dislodge than the halo. Voltaire's attempt to destroy the aureole around the head of '*le bon Jean-Jacques*' was quite unsuccessful. The great majority of the faithful remained unshaken in their determination to hear no evil, see no evil, speak no evil. Even when assailed by agonizing doubts they reacted in the spirit poor Marianne showed when, forced to wonder whether her hero had 'fraudulently gained the public's esteem', she exclaimed: 'No, my friend, I will never believe it . . . whoever would accuse you of so many horrors would in my eyes only be an infamous calumniator.'

That Voltaire's attempt to show up his hated rival proved such a signal failure is all the more striking evidence of the near-indestructibility of established reputations since Jean-Jacques himself had lent a helping hand. Apparently persuaded that the contents of the scandalous but only partly libellous pamphlet circulating in Geneva would soon be the talk of Paris, he instructed his French publisher to reprint it, together with his denial of all its accusations, true as well as false. It was daring indeed. For there were, after all, quite a few, like Grimm and Diderot and Madame d'Epinay, who knew what value to attach to these denials and who could only marvel at the breathtaking audacity of his last word on the subject: 'I would rather have done that of which I am accused than to have written such a pamphlet.' But it paid off. Both the admiring letters and the offers of hospitality that continued to pour in from the four corners of Europe showed that, in the public eye, he was far from having been defrocked. The only satisfaction Voltaire tasted was to see his rival so wholly taken in by the disguise he had adopted, that he publicly accused a prominent Geneva parson of having written the infamous pamphlet. It gave rise to an exchange of letters with the indignant cleric* in which he once again displayed the talents of the shiftier type of lawyer but which he described in the *Confessions* as showing more clearly than ever 'the uprightness and the generosity of my soul'.

Looking back on these troubled times—or, rather, projecting himself forward into the good books of posterity—he claims having felt that the hour had come when he could afford to retire from the literary battle-field. 'The noble enthusiasm that had dictated my writings . . . offered such eloquent testimony to the quality of my soul, just as my entire conduct did as regards my character, that I needed no other defence against my calumniators.' Much as his enemies might try to blacken him, he was sure that those who refused to be deceived would always find that 'with all his faults and weaknesses', he was 'a just man, good, without bitterness, without hatred, without jealousy, quick to recognise his own faults, quicker yet to forget those of others, seeking all his happiness in loving . . . and carrying sincerity in all things to the point of imprudence and the most incredible disinterestedness'.

In actual fact he had been filled with a fierce desire for revenge. It was directed not so much against Voltaire as against his informant, in which role he cast Madame d'Epinay. Without betraying her confidences, he wrote to a friend, he would get his own back on her, he 'knew enough about her to show her up for what she is . . . she does not realise how well-informed I am'. But she would discover it when she read his *Confessions* on which he had now begun to work. Another one-time friend, too, found himself the recipient of rather less elevated sentiments than those with which Jean-Jacques credited himself in retrospect. When Diderot, through an intermediary, made overtures for re-establishing relations, he was totally rejected: 'I never rekindle friendships that have been extinguished, this is my most inviolable principle'. And meanwhile a newcomer in his life,

* There had been a time when he had been cast, as were so many of Jean-Jacques's acquaintances at one time or another, in the arduous role of the only friend he had left: 'Apart from God, the fatherland and the human race,' Jean-Jacques had written to him, 'there remains no feeling of attachment in my heart except for you.' However, he had added in his inimitable manner, 'I have had so many sad experiences of man that I would not be surprised if you, too, were to deceive me.' In this sense the good cleric, suddenly accused of villainy, had been forewarned. But he could hardly have been prepared for the kind of argument his one-time friend used when refusing to substantiate or withdraw his accusation: 'I need not tell you why I will not withdraw, no one knows it better than you . . . Your letters have persuaded me that you are the author [of the pamphlet]. That is why I will not publicly withdraw, as you ask of me, for I do not want to be a liar. All I could say . . . is that it may be possible you are not the author.'

a rich admirer called Dupeyrou, was learning that Jean-Jacques was not
the easiest of men to get along with. If you did not satisfy his insatiable
hunger for pity, so he discovered, you were likely to be told off sharply:
'In my present horrible condition of body and soul I expected a word of
consolation from you.' And if you were so ill-advised as to explain you
had not written because, not having had any answer to many earlier
letters, you were afraid you might have 'offended' or 'given sorrow', you
were warned that unless you accepted an epistolary one-way traffic the
whole relationship was at an end: 'Don't ever count my letters or else
let us break.'

*

Though the literary giant's attempt to expose the moral giant as a dwarf
on stilts had badly misfired with those who mattered, it did have some
effect with those who did not, the small fry of peasants and artisans
among whom Jean-Jacques lived in the territory of Neufchâtel and with
whom he finally became so unpopular that he felt forced to flee from their
wrath. The experience filled him with indignant astonishment: 'The
people of the district should have loved me as did those of every other
place where I have ever lived.' Instead they gradually became 'incensed
against me, publicly insulting me in broad daylight . . . I was preached
against from the pulpit, called the anti-Christ and chased in the country
as if I were the werewolf'. It was partly due to Voltaire's pamphlet. He
had 'proof that it had been applauded as much by the women here as it
has caused indignation in Geneva and Paris . . . their poison-tongues
distilled more venom than the serpents of Africa'. But he was also reviled
—and from the pulpit at that!—on account of his own writings. No
wonder he was indignant. He, Jean-Jacques, defamed as an enemy of
Jesus!

   And yet, in a way those who adopted this attitude could make out a
case for it. It was not so much because of the reserves about Jesus's
divinity and his supernatural powers which he had formulated in the
Profession of Faith. He had given even greater offence by what he had
said in another book published at just about the same time, the famous
Social Contract. There he had treated the teaching of Christ almost
contemptuously, as fit only for slaves. It might be 'holy and sublime', but
it preached only 'servitude and dependence . . . True Christians are made
to be slaves and they know it and do not mind . . . Imagine your Christian
Republic face to face with Sparta or Rome; the pious Christians will be
beaten, crushed and destroyed before they know where they are, or they
will owe their safety only to the contempt the enemy will have for them'.
Moreover Christianity, which wanted 'all men to recognise one another

as brothers', in a spirit of 'meekness', was fatal not only to the state's independence but also to its cohesion, law and order within its borders. Did not its Catholic form give men two different masters to serve, King and Pope? 'That was so clearly bad that it was a waste of time to prove it, all institutions that set men in contradiction to themselves are worthless.' In short, Christianity made bad citizens; 'far from binding the hearts of the citizens to the state, it has the effect of diverting them from all earthy things. I know of nothing more contrary to the social spirit.'

To be a good citizen, Jean-Jacques argued, you must make patriotism your religion. The cosmopolitanism of his contemporaries who 'mocked' it, filled him with contempt; 'today there are no more Frenchmen, Germans, Spaniards, or even English, there are only Europeans', a deplorable state of affairs. You should do everything in your power, he told Polish leaders who had asked him to advise on a new constitution, 'to give your people a natural aversion from mixing with foreigners'.* So as to make thorough-going nationalists of them they should 'invent all sorts of national games and festivals and solemnities'. They should model themselves on the legislators of antiquity, of Sparta and Rome, and like them organize 'spectacles which by showing the people the history of their ancestors, their misfortunes, their virtues and their victories, inflame them . . . and attach them strongly to the fatherland which they were never allowed to forget'. Jean-Jacques went even further than those of his modern pupils who invented the Nuremberg rallies and harnessed sport to the service of the nation with such institutions as *Kraft durch Freude*. He advised his Polish clients they should 'abolish all ordinary entertainments . . . like theatres, comedies and operas that distract people . . . and make them forget their country and their duty'.

Still more important: if you wanted to make good citizens, virtuous in the sense of living only for the fatherland, loving its laws and the duties they imposed on one, you had to drill them from the cradle to the grave. 'As soon as a child opens its eyes,' Jean-Jacques wrote, 'it must see the

---

* 'Everything, he said elsewhere, 'that facilitates communication between the nations carries to each not the virtues but the vices of the other . . . No foreigner had ever entered Geneva without doing it more harm than good.' Needless to say he was no more consistent in this attitude than in any other. The 'hatred of foreigners', which he calls 'inevitable' and 'a defect of little importance' in the opening pages of *Emile*, has become, towards the end of the book, a 'prejudice' against which he recommends the use of a foreign correspondent as 'an excellent antidote against the sway of patriotic prejudice to which we are all liable'. What is more, he had moments when he was all for what is nowadays called 'making Europe'; 'If ever a European Republic were achieved, one day would be enough to make it last forever, so great would be the advantages everyone would derive from it.'

fatherland and it must see only the fatherland till death . . . live for nothing else . . .' Indulging his habit of going out on the most extreme logical limbs, he leaves the inventors of organizations like the Hitler Jugend or the Komsomol far behind; 'children must not be allowed to play separately as the fancy takes them but always together and in public so that they always have a common aim.'

But it takes more than even this type of education to keep the sovereign people of Jean-Jacques's dreamland so replete with civic virtue that they will think of nothing but the common weal. Since they form a 'blind multitude . . . that rarely knows what is good for it' there is need for a 'Lawgiver' whose task is to frame the laws as well as to condition the people in such a way that they will give his laws the assent without which they would not feel they were free. By means of 'censorship' which 'regulates' men's 'judgment of what is good' the mysterious Father-figure (Jean-Jacques does not tell us where he is to come from or by whom he is to be appointed, though presumably not by the blind multitude) 'secretly' fashions 'public opinion', prevents it 'from being corrupted' and sometimes 'fixes it'. As a recent biographer* has pointed out, this idea of the need for thought-control, manipulation or brainwashing as it would nowadays be called, turns up in many of Jean-Jacques's writings. 'The greatest talent a ruler can possess,' he wrote in an article for the *Encyclopédie*, 'is to disguise his power so as to make it less odious . . . The most absolute authority is that which penetrates into a man's innermost being and concerns itself with his will.' Likewise Julie's husband, as was noted in an earlier chapter, is praised for his skill in the 'master's art' of making his servants feel free by 'concealing restraint', so that 'they think they want everything they are made to do'. And the technique is recommended even more explicitly in *Emile* whose readers are told that in educating their children they must always 'let the child think that he is the master . . . There is no subjection so complete as that which keeps the appearance of freedom; that is the way to capture the will itself'.

The 'Lawgiver', however, has such a difficult task that he must employ a stratagem parents can manage without. Faced with the 'common herd', which is incapable of responding to 'appeals to reason', he must have recourse to arguments of 'a different order', pretend to be the voice of 'divine authority' so as to '*constrain*'† the people and make them '*obey freely*† and *bear with docility the yoke of public happiness*'.† Jean-Jacques does not specify the identity of the divinity whose invocation works this miracle of enabling people to do freely what they are constrained to do. But it is certainly not the God of that Christianity which preaches only 'meekness', as fatal to the survival of the state as its 'exclusive preoccupa-

* L. G. Crocker.   † Author's italics.

tion with heavenly things' is incompatible with civic virtue, good citizenship, law and order, public happiness. The 'religion which the citizens
should have' must be one that makes them 'love their duty', not as
brothers in Christ but as fellow-countrymen, patriots.

It is a purely 'civil profession of faith with a few simple dogmas', and
the God its adherents must worship is the State, the collective self. For
the central dogma they must recognize (on pain of being banished and
on pain of death if, having recognized the dogma, they 'behave as if they
do not believe it') is the 'holiness of the social contract and the laws'. The
other one, which posits the existence of an 'all-mighty, intelligent and
beneficent divinity', dispensing justice in 'the life to come', only serves
to provide the citizens with the carrot and the stick without which, in spite
of all conditioning by the Lawgiver, they cannot be relied upon to be so
virtuous as to live only for the common weal. For, as he had put it elsewhere, 'the sublime notion of the God of wise men ... will never be understood by the multitude which will always be given Gods as stupid as
itself'.

*

It is yet another example of Jean-Jacques's carelessness as a writer and
lack of seriousness as a thinker, that he should allow these views to go
before the public almost simultaneously with the ardent plea for a return
to Christianity in his *Profession of Faith* (which, among other things,
described 'all religions as so many salutary institutions'). Quite possibly
he was not even aware of the flagrant contradiction, had not bothered to
re-read or revise the chapter on religion in *The Social Contract* which he
had written ten years earlier, when he was still very much under the
influence of the atheist Diderot and a regular guest of d'Holbach. For all
one knows he had simply fished the yellowed manuscript, originally
meant to be but a fragment of a much larger work on 'Political Institutions', out of an old trunk and sent it to his publishers.*

However this may be, the doctrine that the Christian religion was not
one a self-respecting and freedom-loving community could afford, was

---

* *The Social Contract* itself shows even more clearly how little trouble he took
with his writing. Firing off his pistol in the street with its famous opening passage,
'man is born free, and everywhere he is in chains' (Jean-Jacques at his sloganeering best, for both assertions are, of course, as gratuitous as their juxtaposition
proved incendiary), he follows it up with a profession of ignorance about the cause
of man's enslavement. 'How has this change come about? I do not know.' This
from the author who had devoted a whole essay, the one on the *Origin of Inequality*, to prove that it had been brought about by the 'rich' who had 'conceived the profoundest plan that ever entered the mind of man', imposing their
'fetters' on the poor in the name of law so that 'all ran headlong to their chains in
hopes of securing liberty'.

hardly calculated to endear him to those who took their Christianity seriously. And hence, too, the warnings from the pulpit which, among other things such as Thérèse's unpopularity with the locals, helped to arouse such hostility among the 'rabble', that one night stones were thrown at his house, 'one nearly hitting me in the stomach'. Seeing the 'frenzied fury of the populace' he decamped, leaving Thérèse to cope with the luggage and, presumably, with the frenzy. 'Thank heaven,' he wrote three days later, 'I am safe, away from Motiers. Unfortunately my house-keeper is still there. But I hope the government will restrain those desperadoes.'

Declining offers of hospitality from 'Lord Walpole', the Duchess of Saxe-Gotha and Frederick the Great, he settled for a house on a small island in one of the Swiss lakes where, thanks to his childlike capacity for instant forgetfulness of the tears he had shed a moment earlier, he had 'the happiest time of his life', enjoying himself so much, botanizing, going for walks, letting his rowboat drift on the still water and, especially, 'being out of reach of the wicked', that he would happily have been imprisoned there for good; 'I came to wish with extraordinary fervour that, instead of only tolerating my residence upon the island, the Bernese would make it my prison for life.' Indeed, when he was informed that the authorities were no keener to have him as their guest than three years earlier, he asked them to keep him as their prisoner instead, 'in one of your châteaux'. But even though he promised to pay his own expenses and never to put pen to paper again, they refused to oblige.

Though, as he said himself, he still had 'powerful, illustrious friends who, I am sure, love me from the bottom of their hearts' (even those who had long since 'cooled off', like his old love and her marquis, came to the rescue, offering refuge), it would be uncharitable to dismiss the wailing about his 'unprecedented misfortunes' that fills his letters of those days as mere ritual unworthy of compassion. He may have suffered from an *embarras du choix* as regards comfortable havens, but he did experience some real hardship, inasmuch as travel in winter was no great joy in those days, especially if you were in poor health. Whether it was as bad as he made it out to be when he wrote to a friend 'you can easily imagine the wretched state of my health' is another matter; only five days earlier someone had described him as 'having recovered, he is gay and con-tented'. However that might be, he felt he could not travel alone; 'I would love to come and stay with you,' he told his Amsterdam publisher Rey who had invited him, 'but I cannot travel by myself, I would need a companion.' But when Rey sent him an emissary, the hapless man was despatched straight back charged with a reprimand for his employer. Though Jean-Jacques was touched by his friend's devotion, he was annoyed by his 'stupidity'. He should have realized that 'one does not dispose of a grown-up man without consulting him'; he no longer wanted to go to Amsterdam, it was too cold. So the expense of the courier's journey was just so much money down the drain. He himself certainly could not contribute to it, all the less so as 'all my friends seem determined to ruin me by saddling me with huge expense for the postage I have to pay on receiving their letters'.

Not that he had real money troubles at the time. 'I have got enough to live on for a long time,' he wrote to his Paris publisher. For one thing he had made a deal with Dupeyrou whereby the latter had bought the rights to all his existing and future works. For another he had got himself a second annuity, this time pressed upon him by the Jacobite Scottish laird who acted as the Prussian King's Governor of Neufchâtel and with whom Jean-Jacques had become very friendly until the Scotsman, too, eventually cooled off. The correspondence of this period, moreover, is full of letters of admirers telling him he could draw on them at any time, which he was occasionally happy to do. 'I shan't think of refusing the thousand francs, I accept them with great pleasure,' he wrote to a marquise who had also helped to get him a passport enabling him to pass through France on his way to England where Hume had long since urged him to seek asylum. By way of reward he told the lady that he was 'absolutely decided to see no one in Paris except you'. But he made it clear to his publisher that he would not in fact even see her: 'I want to see absolutely no one. So please do not announce my arrival and don't mention it to anyone.'

Was it because he craved the solitude in Paris he had enjoyed so much on his island? Or did he only intone the theme 'I want to be alone' the more to be sought after? That has been suggested by someone who saw him often in Switzerland and who was by no means unsympathetic to him.* Whatever the truth of the matter, his return to France was far from remaining unnoticed. 'The house where I am staying,' he wrote from Strasbourg, 'is full of people from morning to night . . . I receive untold signs of good will, all the prominent people in this town seem determined to shower favours on me.' In fact, it became too much of a good thing; 'the many dinner-parties and the frequent visits from young women and fashionable people . . . became such a bother and so detrimental to my health that I have had to break with it all.' In Paris, where he was lodged in a house belonging to the Prince de Conti, his resolution to see absolutely no one proved even more ineffective. So great was the press of people who wanted to gaze at the great man that he had to receive them even while changing from his nightshirt into his day-clothes. 'I have callers . . . from the moment I get up till the moment I go to bed and

* Comte d'Escherny.

I am forced to dress in public.' 'The number of visits M. Rousseau receives,' so reported the representative of Geneva in Paris, 'is quite incredible . . . In a superb library . . . he gives a kind of audience, from nine to twelve and from six to nine. One of Madame de Boufflers' lackeys does the introductions. He has a writing desk by his side for there is a constant stream of notes and messages from beautiful ladies inquiring after his health.' If he really hated it as he claimed to do—'I have never suffered so much'—he had at least the consolation that this triumphant return to the capital must have been exceedingly galling to that 'buffoon' in his Swiss château, Voltaire.

*

More than one of the great ladies and gentlemen who, like Malesherbes, came to pay court to him, would one day have some excuse for cursing his memory rather than bestowing the blessings on it which he himself so confidently anticipated. Rattling across the cobblestones in the wooden carts that took them on their last journey, they might well have felt with the King* that it was all the fault of the man they had hero-worshipped in the good old days. Though modern scholarship hardly subscribes to this view and holds rather that the Terror was inherent in the revolutionary situation itself, it can be argued that Jean-Jacques's prescription for 'public happiness' was not without its effect on the men who sought to promote it by chopping off the heads of all those accused of congenital inability to bear its 'yoke' with the required 'docility'.

At the time of its publication, however, and for nearly three decades thereafter, *The Social Contract* attracted but little attention; while its import into France—it had been printed in Holland—was forbidden, the book was not burned. Only in Geneva did it suffer the same fate as *Emile*. Not surprisingly perhaps. For the patrician oligarchy that had usurped power in a republic whose constitution recognized its citizens as sovereign, had more reason to be on the alert against republican doctrines than the ruler of a nation where the divine right of kings was still widely respected and autocracy, provided only it was enlightened by reason rather than sanctified by faith, was not as yet seriously challenged even by the leading intellectuals of the day. In Geneva both books were declared 'bold, scandalous, impious', as 'tending to destroy' not only the Christian religion but also 'all governments'. It was perhaps the bitterest blow of all. And Jean-Jacques reacted to it as might be expected. To prove a

---

* According to an author of the period the prisoner King Louis had 'sorrowfully recognised that Jean-Jacques, with the complicity of Voltaire, had ruined France'. Likewise, Madame de Staël quotes Napoleon as having said that Jean-Jacques 'had caused the Revolution'.

prophet without honour in his own country was too much even for his ardent nationalism. When his half-hearted attempt to incite the citizenry to force a withdrawal of the insult offered him by their rulers—his one and only excursion into practical politics—failed to meet with sufficient response, he washed his hands of his native land; 'seeing myself deserted by my fellow-citizens I decided to renounce my ungrateful country ... by which, as a reward for the honour I had tried to bestow on it, I found myself so disgracefully treated.' And so he wrote a letter to the authorities formally abdicating his citizenship; he broke with his national family just as he had already broken with so many of his friends.

That the book which has kept his name alive more than any other did so poorly in France at the time it appeared, in 1762, can be accounted for in a number of different ways. For one thing there was nothing very novel about his contention that authority, to be legitimate, should derive from a covenant with the people. Grotius, Locke and many others had written along these lines.* (Jean-Jacques himself was the first to admit it. 'Locke, Montesquieu and l'Abbé de Saint Pierre,' he said when complaining of Geneva's treatment of his book, 'have dealt with the same matters, often as freely . . . And they have all been left in peace.') Another reason was that, unlike nearly all Jean-Jacques's other works, *The Social Contract* was not exactly bedside reading, an essay in logic-chopping at times so obscure that he himself said of it towards the end of his life: 'Those who boast of understanding all of it are cleverer than me, it is a book that should be rewritten but I no longer have either the time or the energy.'

Another reason was that, again unlike *Emile* in which he had developed quite a few ideas on education of practical value to his age, his abstract theorizing about the ideal society was in no way relevant to the problems preoccupying those who longed for a new order. While it was doubtless true that, 'when the citizens love their duty, . . . every difficulty vanishes and government becomes easy', this statement was an eye-opener only to those needing a blinding flash of the obvious. And as the architect of the dream-world, outlined in *The Social Contract*, had pointed out in an earlier article on the same theme, that its proper functioning presupposed no less than 'sublime virtue' on the part of its inhabitants, its blueprint was hardly of much use to ordinary mortals. Nor was its design such as to appeal to the generation that was to forge the declaration of the Rights of Man. For in Jean-Jacques's ideal society there would be precious few

* What was novel, Professor Cranston says in his illuminating introduction to the Penguin edition of the book, is that, in Rousseau's view, sovereignty not only emanates from the people (who can transfer it to a ruler of their choice) but should stay there, be exercised by the people.

of these; the individual would have to 'alienate himself totally, with all his rights, to the whole of the community'. Taught to live for the state only and conditioned by the Lawgiver, brandishing the heavenly carrot and the stick, so as to make men think such self-immolation on the altar of the community was what they wanted, they would practically cease to exist as individuals with their own opinions and desires; 'each individual will no longer believe himself to be one, but part of the unity and recognisable only in the whole.' It is a thought that Hitler, Lenin, Stalin, and Mao have very much made their own. 'Only by acting in and through the community,' the late East German party-boss Grotewohl echoed Jean-Jacques, 'can the individual find himself.'

There are some, however, who hold that the contradiction is more apparent than real, that to debit Jean-Jacques with a passing fancy—few if any of his pronouncements convey more than that—for wholesale collectivism, is to do him a grave injustice. According to one of the shrewdest students* of *The Social Contract* he never meant to say that it demanded the renunciation of all civil liberties. 'What Rousseau is saying is that instead of surrendering their liberty by the Social Contract they [the people] *convert* their liberty from independence into political and moral freedom, and this is part of their transformation from creatures living brutishly according to impulse, into men living humanly according to reason and conscience.' It may well be so. But if that is all he meant, what a pity he did not say so. How regrettable that he enabled the enemies of freedom to invoke his great name for their cause. How justified seems the condemnation of his political writings, already quoted here, as 'irresponsible'. How odd they should nonetheless have formed the object of such a 'colossal' amount of 'minutely detailed research and penetrating analysis', as a prominent participant† in this labour of love has called it. How sad, finally—but how understandable, indeed inevitable, considering Jean-Jacques's self-confessed difficulty in thinking straight and expressing his thought clearly—that all this effort has been in vain, that, as the same labourer in his overgrown, jungle-like vineyard has said, 'the sharpest conflict of interpretations remains'!

*

Considering Jean-Jacques's inability to suffer any restraints, his conception of happiness as never having anything to do he did not feel like doing, it is strange indeed that his dream-world seems infused with the spirit—though not, of course, equipped with the machinery—of the nightmare world of Big Brother. And it becomes all the stranger that he should at

---

* Maurice Cranston.   † E. Cassirer.

times have preached a collectivism so extreme as to demand the dissolution of the individual into the community, when one recalls his insistence on the uniqueness of the self, the supreme joys to be found in withdrawing into it, the sovereignty of the individual conscience. Originally inspired by the humiliations he had suffered as a lackey in Turin and a secretary in Venice, the ideas he developed in *The Social Contract* form his contribution to the discussion of the age-old problem of how to reconcile liberty with law and order, self with society, nature with culture, or, as he put it, 'private happiness' with 'public happiness'. In his eyes the obvious solution of this commonplace conundrum—a compromise leaving the individual with as much liberty as is compatible with the law and order necessary to enjoy it—was no solution at all just because it was a compromise. To have rights as an individual as well as duties as a member of society, to be neither wholly free to indulge one's fancy nor so exclusively devoted to the community as not to have any such fancies, was to have one's heart 'torn into two'. And that, for a man like Jean-Jacques, to whom the idea of the most trifling social duty was abhorrent and who knew himself incapable of the moral effort required to do something he did not feel like doing, was strictly unbearable. To avoid being torn, to be happy, one had to be either all out for self, or all out for the community; 'make man one and you will make him as happy as he can be, give him all to the State or all to himself.'

Both recipes for happiness are, of course, demonstrably absurd. To seek it in total individual freedom, at the cost of anarchy, is as self-defeating as to seek it in total devotion to the community at the cost of abdicating all individuality. The reconciliation of liberty and law Jean-Jacques offers in *The Social Contract*, and which he claims to be reconciliation without tears, without sacrifices of either private or public happiness, is somewhat in the nature of a semantic confidence trick. All men needed to do, to have the best of both worlds, freedom from constraint and yet the protection offered by law, so he argued, was to make the laws themselves. For once you have imposed the laws on yourself, however onerous, you can no longer feel you are being put upon, made to do things you do not want to do: 'You remain as free as before.' What is more, having wanted the laws you cannot but love the duties they impose —which, as already noted, 'makes all difficulties vanish'. Thus you enjoy the private happiness of feeling free as well as the public happiness of law and order—provided, of course, all have wanted the laws, that everyone feels them to be just and fair. But, happily, this they are bound to be since 'the general will is always righteous, tends to public advantage' and 'the people making laws for itself cannot be unjust'.

So far, so good, the word-game is brought to the desired conclusion. A

slight hitch arises only when Jean-Jacques descends from the stratosphere
of abstractions to the untidy reality here below. Even with the help of the
all-wise and all-good Lawgiver, the 'blind multitude', he admits, 'will
not always know what is good for it,' what makes for public happiness.
To be able to do so its members would have to be 'illuminated' by
'sublime virtue', never think of themselves and their private interests,
love their fellow-countrymen as themselves (not their neighbours for
'every patriot hates a foreigner'), live only for the fatherland, which is
why the Lawgiver must be capable of 'changing human nature'. Pending
that happy consummation his proposals will not always receive unanimous
assent, there may be dissenters unable to appreciate that they are for the
public good. But no matter, the dissenting minority will still not feel
constrained by the majority, unfree and therefore unhappy. Or rather, it
should not feel any of these disagreeable sentiments. Why not? Because
of the small print Jean-Jacques has slipped into *The Social Contract* when
he added that 'apart from the primitive contract the vote of the majority
always binds the rest'. Very sensible, of course, and enabling the lawyer
in Jean-Jacques to argue that the promise of freedom and happiness for
all contained in his prospectus would always be fully met; having freely
signed the contract providing for majority rule no signatory could ever
claim laws were being imposed on him. If, for instance, the majority
should deprive him of the private happiness he derives from visiting the
theatre Jean-Jacques disapproved of so much, he should still feel as free
and, therefore, as happy as ever.

As for those dissenters, who cannot rouse themselves to this degree of
euphoria, they are to be dealt with in much the same manner as those who
are shown the error of their ways in what the communist world calls
'struggle sessions', where the majority wrestles with the souls of recal-
citrant party-members. Even when persuasion fails, when the dissenters
become party-splitters and as such have to be punished, they are, in
Jean-Jacques's immortal double-talk, only 'forced to be free'. It is the
kind of freedom from which so many millions in our century have fled,
the kind of 'public happiness' whose 'yoke' so many found so heavy that
in Berlin a wall had to be built so as to make those remaining behind 'bear
it with docility'. Jean-Jacques had no illusion about this, was not really
taken in by his own semantic gamesmanship, witness his characterization
of the liberty his dream-world would have to offer: 'Proud and holy
liberty! If . . . people could know you, if they realised how your laws are
more austere than the harshness of the tyrant's yoke, they would fly from
you with fright as from a burden that would crush them.' And so, he
himself fled from one nightmare-world to another. He feared, he said in
a letter to Mirabeau's father, that one would have to go to 'the other

extreme' to find a solution for the problem of the governance of men, 'establish the most arbitrary despotism conceivable'.

*

So was he really at heart the antithesis of a democrat? Many have maintained it. But as many have denied it. As already indicated, together the two parties have expended an immense amount of energy and ingenuity on the interpretation of his scriptures, weighing every word, seeking to penetrate the meaning he attached to it, giving due consideration to every qualifying clause,* attempting to 'unify his thought'. One sometimes wonders why. What is it that has made so many erudite scholars take so frivolous or so slapdash a writer so seriously? It may partly be due to the common confusion of obscurity with profundity. For the cumulative effect of Jean-Jacques's inability to commit himself, the 'chaos' of his ideas Diderot complained of, his highlighting of every side of every question, is that of a gathering darkness. But it is surely as much because of that self-perpetuating and self-expanding nature of a reputation for greatness already touched upon in another chapter.

That his political writings should have been analysed with such infinite painstaking care is all the more curious as he himself has made every effort not to be taken too seriously. He not only repeatedly emphasized his aversion to intellectual effort and his lack of talent for it: 'I have extreme difficulty in writing . . . Not only do I find ideas difficult to express, I find them equally difficult to take in.' He also specifically warned the readers of some of those writings against making too much of them, as on the occasion when he put some ideas on paper for a constitution for Corsica whose leaders, having thrown off Genoese rule, asked him to draft one. He had put these ideas forward very tentatively, he said, 'as it is very possible I am wrong and I would hate to have you adopt them to your detriment'. It sounds surprisingly modest. But then, as a constitutional draftsman he had plenty to be modest about. For they were peculiar ideas indeed, such as that all who were still bachelors at forty should be deprived of citizenship, which should also be the fate of men marrying women twenty years younger or older. Nor is the most famous of his political essays, *The Social Contract*, without the sort of passages that tax one's patience with a writer who takes so little trouble to maintain the barest minimum of consistency, who is so addicted to childish exaggeration—'the moment a people allows itself to be represented, it is no

---

* Such as, for instance, his observation that the 'total surrender' of the citizen's right to 'liberty' is not so total as to include liberties the community feels he need not give up.

longer free, it ceases to exist',*—who indulges so freely in the kind of specious reasoning Madame du Deffand called 'false and wearisome'.

What sense does it make to say of the *'censorship'*† that 'so far from being the arbiter of public opinion it only *declares'*† it, or that it 'upholds morality by *preventing*† public opinion from growing corrupt' and some-times even *'fixes'*† it but that this *'regulated'*† public opinion is nonetheless *'not subject to any restraint'*.† Why bother to try, with the help of what the Germans call *Hineininterpretieren*, to make sense of a writer who so clearly shares Humpty Dumpty's determination that words shall mean what one wants them to mean? 'If you want us to get on,' he said to Madame d'Epinay when she objected to his boorish remark about not being for sale, 'I advise you to learn my dictionary; believe me, my words rarely have the ordinary meaning.' In fact, so obscure are they that even renowned political scientists, like the late G. D. H. Cole, have felt bound to admit that 'the General Will, the most fundamental of all Rousseau's political concepts', is well-nigh incomprehensible; 'no critic of *The Social Contract* has found it easy to say either what precisely its author meant by it or what is its final value for political philosophy.'

One passage will suffice to show Jean-Jacques's thought on the matter to be so confused that it may well not have any value at all. The General Will, so it starts, is 'the constant will of all members of the State' and the constant will, it is clear from the context, is the will to abide by majority decisions, to enthrone the rule of law democratically arrived at. So far so good, and, indeed, he still makes sense when he goes on to say that by virtue of such agreement to differ men are 'citizens and free'. But who can make head or tail of what follows? 'When a law is proposed in the popular assembly what the people is asked is not exactly whether it approves or rejects it but whether it is in conformity with the general will.' In other words, faced with a proposal to ban the theatre or disenfranchise over-age bachelors, the citizenry must decide whether it violates their constitu-tional obligation to respect majority rule, which seems about as sensible as consulting the Ten Commandments to decide whether or not to have ham and eggs for breakfast. But if one assumes that the General Will must, therefore, be less limited in scope than Jean-Jacques has just given one to understand, his further observations throw an even eerier light on the workings of his mind. Those who are out-voted, he tells us, are thereby shown to have been mistaken about what was the general will: 'When the

---

* It will no longer surprise that in an article dating from much the same period the people appear to be capable of survival under representative government. Taxes on necessities, one reads there, must have the consent 'of the people or its representatives'.

† Author's italics.

opinion that is contrary to my own prevails, this proves neither more nor less than that I was mistaken and that what I thought to be the general will was not so.' In his dream-world—which, it is only fair to say, he himself knew to be just that and nothing more—minorities only vote the way they do because they do not realize they really want the same as everybody else; only in the moment of proving a minority do its members make this comforting discovery. And so, far from regretting their defeat, they are much relieved. For, odder still, victory would have been fatal to the achievement of their real wishes; had the vote gone the other way it would not have been an expression of the general will. 'If,' so Jean-Jacques puts it, 'my particular opinion had carried the day I should have achieved the opposite of what was my will and I should not, therefore, have been free.'

With all respect for the countless scholars who have laboured so mightily to fathom his meaning, it is difficult to resist the temptation to go even further in disrespect for the oracle than Lord Morley who dismissed *The Social Contract* as mere 'logic-chopping'. For logic, let alone sense, seems so far to seek in passages like those quoted here, as to leave one no choice but to qualify them as nonsensical. And yet, still, year in year out, the most scholarly studies of his social and political thought continue to come off the press. Nor is the endless stream likely to dry up because the author* of one of the very latest, an admirably close-reasoned and dispassionate analysis, comes to the conclusion that Jean-Jacques's sociological theorizing was not only 'incoherent' but downright 'absurd'.

There is only one thing that might perhaps be thought even stranger than the indefatigability of the Rousseau industry. And that is that those like the present writer who marvel at it, should nonetheless feel impelled to join its ranks.

* J. Charvet.

CHAPTER NINETEEN

Oh, What a Fall Was There!

'I came here universally esteemed and respected . . . Why have I been robbed of it all? . . . What have I done to merit such cruel treatment?'

WHERE Voltaire, trying to topple Jean-Jacques from his pedestal, had signally failed, he himself finally succeeded. Within a year from his triumphant stay in Paris as the guest of the King's cousin, besieged from dawn to dusk by an army of admirers, he had managed to alienate nearly all of them including even such long-standing devotees and leaders of opinion as the Duchess. 'He has not a friend left,' wrote a fellow-countryman . . . 'Without exception people speak of him only as a wicked rogue. Never has a man been sunk more rapidly and thoroughly.' It was an exaggeration, by a former friend who now bore him nothing but ill-will. There still were some of the old faithful left: 'I would deny the evidence of my own eyes,' wrote Marianne, 'if they were to be struck by appearances disadvantageous to your character.' But she could not deny that the likes of her, those whose 'stamp is such as to resist the contagion' were in a 'minority'. In the world of Paris salons, where alone reputations were made and unmade, his name had become, if not mud, the next best thing to it.

Considering the heights to which he had been raised Mark Antony's lamentation inevitably comes to mind. David Hume had been at a loss for words to describe Jean-Jacques's glory in those few days he spent in Paris whence the Scotsman, then secretary to the British ambassador, would soon take him to England. 'It is impossible to express the enthusiasm of this nation . . . All the world, especially the great ladies tease me to be introduced to him . . . No nation was ever so fond of genius as this and no person ever so much engaged their attention as Rousseau. Voltaire and everybody else are quite eclipsed by him.' He himself fully shared in the general enthusiasm. Already at the time of the flight to Switzerland, three and a half years earlier, he had written to say that 'of all the men of letters in Europe . . . you are the one I most revere'. He had also offered to make use of his 'connections with men of rank in London' to try and secure him a royal pension. Moreover, he would be happy, he said a year later, to have him as his guest, though he feared that, what with his house being 'in the midst of the city', his offer might not 'prove agreeable'.

In actual fact his reverence for his famous Swiss colleague was not quite so unreserved nor so wholly disinterested as it sounded. He admired, so he told their mutual friend, the Comtesse de Boufflers, 'the lofty spirit of the man' as well as his eloquence; 'he gives to the French tongue an energy which it seems scarce to have reached in any other.' But he had to agree with Jean-Jacques's critics that there was always an element of showing off in his writing, 'some degree of extravagance' which made one suspect 'he chooses his topics less from persuasion than from the pleasure of showing his invention, surprising the reader by his paradoxes'. As for his motives in offering Jean-Jacques hospitality and his services, though professional solidarity with a fellow-intellectual victimized by religious intolerance doubtless played a large part, it was not unmixed with other sentiments. 'It would be a singular victory over the French,' he wrote to a Scottish friend, 'to protect and encourage a man they had persecuted.' And this would, of course, add not only to the nation's renown but also to his own; 'I am sensible that my connections with him add to my own importance.' Not that he really needed to bask in his colleague's glory. For those were the days of *Anglomanie*, when visitors from across the Channel were very much in fashion and few more so than intellectuals like Hume or Walpole. Hume's presence in Paris, so reported a contemporary, 'was regarded as one of the most beautiful fruits of the peace . . . The great and pretty ladies play up to him for all they are worth'. 'They run after me,' said Walpole, 'as if I were an African prince or a trained canary.'

No wonder, therefore, '*le bon David*', as Hume was often called, and '*le bon Jean-Jacques*', as he remained to the great majority of his readers, freely indulged in that *commerce d'encens*, that exchange of huge bouquets with which the Great in the world of letters almost invariably opened relations. Just as Jean-Jacques and Voltaire, knowing one another only from their writings, had started with the ritual professions of 'tender love', so did Jean-Jacques and David. Replying to the Scotsman's expression of 'reverence', the Citizen of Geneva went into raptures about the 'talents and virtues' of his new acquaintance. They inspired him with 'the most tender friendship for you . . your genius would elevate you too far above men if your heart did not bring you close to them again . . . What transports of joy would not I feel in setting foot on the happy land where David Hume was born.' But that was not to be until three years later when at last he decided to take the good David up on his pressing invitation;* 'in five days I shall throw myself into your arms . . . delighted to be greatly indebted to the most illustrious of my contemporaries whose goodness surpasses even his glory.'

Not altogether surprisingly, the two celebrities who had been so happy adoring one another from a safe distance, found it rather more difficult to keep up the temperature of their elevated sentiments once they met face to face. For a short while all went well enough. Mollified by the warmth of the reception Paris had given him, Jean-Jacques seems to have been at his soft-centred best. His new friend and protector found him 'mild, gentle, modest and good-humoured . . . His modesty seems not to be good manners but ignorance of his excellence . . . I do not know any man more lovable or more virtuous'. The only fault he could find with him was a 'tendency to harbour unjust suspicions', at least, that is what his quarrels with his old friends made one think. But personally he felt that 'I could spend my life with him without the slightest cloud ever coming between us'. For a few weeks circumstances continued to be such as to bring out the best in his illustrious refugee, honoured as he was even by royalty, to say nothing of his acclaim by the press. 'It is incredible,' Hume reported 'the enthusiasm for him in Paris and the curiosity in London.' In his honour Garrick put on a special performance at Drury Lane which the King and Queen attended and where, according to Mrs. Garrick, who shared a box with Jean-Jacques, 'he was so anxious to display himself and hung so far forward over the front of the box that I was obliged to hold him by the skirt of his coat that he might not fall over into the pit'. They were the days of the honeymoon in the relationship of the two writers. Jean-Jacques, who had 'kissed' David and 'covered his face with tears' on landing at Dover, was still telling a friend back in Paris that 'this worthy man merits forever all the benedictions of my heart', just as David was enthusing to their mutual friend, Madame de Boufflers, about his 'pupil' being 'very charming, always polite, often gay, perfectly sociable'.

*

But it was not long before irritation began to cloud the sky on Hume's side and distrust to darken it on Jean-Jacques's. Before their first month in England was over, a friend of Hume reported him to be 'confoundedly weary of his pupil, so full of oddities and absurdities'. In fact, even before their arrival, on the crossing to Dover, the Scotsman had already had occasion to learn something of these affectations, in particular the fuss

* He had resisted it until then, partly because he had no natural liking for England 'whose inhabitants call themselves good-natured though nobody else would think of doing so'.

Jean-Jacques habitually made about his health; 'he imagines himself very infirm, he is one of the most robust men I have ever known, he passed ten hours in the night-time above deck during the most severe weather when all the seamen seemed nearly frozen to death.' And he was soon to have a touching demonstration of the oddities of which his pupil was capable. That was some two months later, on the eve of Jean-Jacques's departure from London to install himself and Thérèse in the stately mansion in Derbyshire a rich admirer, called Davenport, had put at their disposal at the nominal rent his guest insisted on paying him.

Alas, this last evening with David had not proved a success. Jean-Jacques had waxed indignant when he found out that, to save him the expense of the journey, his new landlord had pretended that he had an empty carriage going back north, a well-intentioned deceit in which Hume had aided and abetted. It made its beneficiary so angry that even after having blown off a great deal of steam, so Hume told Madame de Boufflers, he sulked for an hour, resisting all his friend's attempts 'to revive the conversation', until at last he got up from his seat by the fire-side, 'walked about the room a little . . . and then suddenly sat on my knee, threw his arms around my neck, kissed me with the greatest ardour and bedewed my face with tears . . . "Oh, my dear friend," he exclaimed, "is it possible you can ever forgive my folly? This ill-humour is the return I make for all the instances of your kindness towards me." ' And that appeared to be that. Though when he wrote to David a few days later he felt obliged to read him another little lecture on his part in the matter, it had by then become a 'trifling fault' which had apparently left no mark on his feelings: 'If I live in this agreeable asylum as happily as I hope to do, one of the greatest pleasures of my life will be to reflect that I owe it to you.' And a week later Hume was still his 'dear patron' whom he 'embraced with all his heart'. No wonder either. For the *patron* had made the handsomest of apologies: 'I ask you a thousand pardons for the slight deceit practised in your favour . . . Mr. Davenport regrets it, too, and, on my advice, has resolved never again to entertain such schemes.' Even if he had his tongue in his cheek, solemn Jean-Jacques certainly did not seem to notice it.

So all might have been well had he not shared the bitter fate lying in wait for all celebrities who prove a nine days' wonder. Within ten days of his arrival an article had appeared in a London paper which, after much praise, allowed itself some mild irony at his 'mistaking novelty of opinion for justness of thinking'. In vain did loyal old friends back in France, like the Marquise de Verdelin, urge him to 'treat the papers with the contempt they deserve; it is those people's job to write for a living, they have spoken well of you until their readers got bored, so they now have to speak ill of you, since everybody only wants novelty'. The change of tone in the press, which seemed to him 'so sudden and thorough that . . . none has ever been more astonishing,' was more than he could bear with equanimity. It was bad enough that there were some notable figures in London who had given him a very chilly welcome from the start, men like Samuel Johnson and Edmund Burke, the first of whom had called him 'the worst of men, a rascal who ought to be hunted out of society. Three or four nations have expelled him and it is a shame that he is protected in this country . . . I would sooner sign a sentence for his transportation than for any felon who has gone from the old Bailey these many years'.

But even worse were the jokes these English, 'noted for their cruelty' caused by 'their predilection for beef', indulged in at his expense. There was one, in particular, so much on target that it was cruel indeed, a letter concocted by Walpole but published under the name of Frederick the Great. 'You have made yourself sufficiently talked of for singularities little becoming to a great man . . . My dominions afford you a peaceful retreat . . . If you persist in perplexing your brains to find new misfortunes, choose such as you like best. I am a king and can make you as miserable as you wish.' It was followed a few days later by an article describing him as a 'charlatan . . . whose only and ardent ambition is to be talked about . . . and who finds his greatest pleasure in the publicity accompanying his expulsion from one city after another'. And as if his English hosts did not prove disrespectful enough, his old enemy Voltaire chimed in with an open letter—though he denied authorship and cannot be proved to have written it—making fun of his wild contradictions as well as his outbursts of colossal conceit. 'How is it you can say quite blandly that an enlightened state would erect statues to you? You are like a child that, having blown soap bubbles or made little circles in the water of a well by spitting into it, considers itself very important . . . The newspapers in England will talk of you as the great Jean-Jacques, as they talk of the King's elephant or the Queen's zebra. For the English are amused by rare specimens of all species though they do not usually esteem them.' Wholly unable to laugh off such mockeries (as Walpole advised him to do; 'you have been an idol, you are such no longer . . . I counsel you to make fun of me as I have of you'), he appealed to a neighbouring earl for protection: 'Where would I be more likely to find a protector worthy of my confidence than among that illustrious nobility which it pleased me to honour, little realising that one day I would need its help to defend my own? . . . I came here universally esteemed and respected even by my enemies. Why have I been robbed of it all in your country? What have I done to merit such cruel treatment . . . The countries where I am known will not judge me as does your ill-informed public. The whole of Europe will continue to do me the justice

England refuses me. The brilliant reception I recently enjoyed in Paris proves that, wherever my conduct is known, it earns me the honour that is my due.'

It was very much in character; Jean-Jacques, whose modesty in fair weather Hume had mistaken for the real thing, reacting to head-winds by shouting his self-praise from the house-tops. And he was equally true to form when he picked on his benefactor, of all people, as the party responsible for the decline in his popularity. Just as nine years earlier he had declared his friend and hostess at the Hermitage guilty of the blackest treachery, so he now accused Hume of it. Just as he had then been wilfully deaf to those who had tried to save him from himself, so they now got little thanks for their efforts to make him see reason. 'You reproach me for giving in to odious suspicions,' he wrote to Madame de Boufflers; 'perhaps you would have done better to apply your lectures to yourself, not be so ready to think ill of me.' 'I am tired,' he told Dupeyrou, 'of being reprimanded by my friends when I deserve their applause.' And just as he had at first not indicated how he really felt about Madame d'Epinay so he now left Hume in blissful ignorance of suspicions that quickly ripened into an unshakeable conviction.

The good David's guilt had been proved beyond a reasonable doubt on that memorable evening when he had jumped on his knee, and (according to Jean-Jacques's account) David's only reaction to having his face bathed in kisses and tears had been to make soothing noises like tut-tut and come, come, and there, there: 'Tapping me on the back, he repeated several times, "Quoi, mon cher Monsieur, eh, mon cher Monsieur, quoi donc, mon cher Monsieur." He said nothing more and I felt my heart chilled.' By the standards of the age it was indeed a far from satisfactory response to such an emotional outburst. Even so, it would hardly seem to justify turning his great friend and benefactor then and there into the personification of Perfidious Albion. It was not as if, having seen so much of his dear patron for the past three months, he had lacked opportunity to discover that his Scottish friend no more had the gift of the gush than his English host Davenport, 'who,' so he complained, 'shows me much affection in the services he renders me but never says anything and never responds when I pour out my heart, I never saw a man so reserved'. If only he had not fallen out with Madame d'Epinay! She could have warned him not to expect too much from '*le bon David*'; she had learned that not even the most alluring temptresses could drag a tender sentiment from his lips. At a party, whose hostess went in for charades, so she relates, 'the celebrated historian had been cast for the part of a sultan sitting between slaves and employing all his eloquence to win their love. He was placed on a sofa between two of the prettiest women in Paris; he stared at

them, smote the pit of his stomach and his knees several times and could
find nothing to say to them but; "well, young ladies, there you are, then?
Well, there you are! There you are!" He kept on saying this for a quarter
of an hour. At last one of the young ladies got up and said impatiently:
"Ah, I expected as much, this man is good for nothing except to eat veal!"
Since then he has been banished to the role of spectator.'

However, as Jean-Jacques explained to friends he took into his confidence a couple of weeks later, it was not really David's failure to respond
with a few kisses and tears of his own instead of fobbing him off with taps
on the back, that had proved his guilt. It was the context in which he had
administered them. For what Jean-Jacques, in a moment of remorse at his
suspicions, had exclaimed between kisses and sobs was surely challenging
and provocative enough to draw more than a 'polite embrace' from even
the most tight-lipped Scot. 'No, no,' he had cried, 'David Hume is not a
traitor.' That was why the soothing taps and 'there theres' were so
incriminating as to 'destroy any return of confidence'. Would an innocent
man, so he asked in the nineteen-page indictment he drew up with rather
less than his usual lawyer's skill, would such a man allow a friend, and a
protégé at that, to voice suspicions of treachery without at least asking
what the devil he meant by it all?

It was a good question. But not a question David would find it difficult
to answer when at last he was presented with the charge-sheet. That was
nearly four months after the 'heart-chilling' night on which his protégé's
suspicions had been finally, fully and irrevocably confirmed. During that
period both parties had been busy, though in rather different ways. David
had been pursuing his efforts to complete the arrangements for the royal
pension which Jean-Jacques had graciously consented to accept. He had
found it all the more acceptable as the King wished his munificence to
remain secret. That suited the monarch because he did not want to give
offence to those members of the clergy who disapproved of Jean-Jacques's
religious notions. And it suited Jean-Jacques because, as he explained in
a letter to a friend, 'being kept secret it was an unmistakable expression
of the King's esteem, whereas a public award was open to the suspicion
of being made out of vanity, an affectation of royal concern for men of
letters'. However, when David brought him the good news that all the
formalities had now been completed he discovered that his revered colleague was hard to please. Leaving the letter unanswered he wrote to the
King's minister instead, to say that he now found the secrecy 'awkward',
as preventing him from 'feeling honoured in the eyes of the public'. What
was more, he was so beset by 'unexpected and cruel afflictions' that his
mind was 'too troubled' to enable him to decide whether he could really
accept the pension after all.

Not unnaturally both Hume and the minister were put out, placed in a most embarrassing position *vis-à-vis* the King. 'Your letter to the Minister,' Hume wrote, 'has caused us a lot of trouble . . . But what pains me even more is to hear of your great sorrow', at whose nature he could only guess. Was the cruel hoax Walpole had perpetrated perhaps at the bottom of it? If so Jean-Jacques should know that 'Walpole is very annoyed he should have caused you such offence and that his bit of nonsense was never intended for publication'. Little did '*le bon David*'— who was not so '*bon*', so besotted with his literary lion as never to have enjoyed a laugh at his expense—little did he know that his own alleged treachery was the true cause of Jean-Jacques's afflictions and that for the past six weeks he had been telling his friends including his father-confessor Malesherbes all about it. What a 'false friend' '*le bon David*' had turned out to be. How 'sinister' were his intentions. How he was 'secretly but unceasingly working to dishonour me with astonishing success; in the last six weeks all the papers which at first only honoured me have changed their tune and now only show contempt'. How unhappy Thérèse and he had been staying in his lodgings: 'What hatred and disdain the servants showed me and how infamous was their treatment of Mlle. Levasseur.' How the 'people closest to Hume most clearly showed their contempt'. How the man 'with whom I had never had a quarrel . . . opened his arms to me in my distress, only to strangle me when I threw myself into them'. How he had abused Jean-Jacques's trust in allowing him to pay the postage on his mail, which he himself found too costly, by spying on him, tampering with his correspondence; 'the letters I write do not arrive, those I receive have been opened.'

These were the thoughts which had apparently passed through his head that last night in London when he sat by the fireside in David's lodgings and found his host's 'eyes fastened on me . . . with a dry, ardent, mocking, searching gaze . . . I tried to return his gaze. But meeting his eyes I felt myself shudder . . . Unless relief came I felt I should suffocate'. He was only saved from this fate by the sudden fit of 'violent remorse' and the 'transport of affection' that landed him on David's knee but evoked only that heart-chilling because so damning response of 'come, come', and 'there, there'. What with such uncontrovertible proof that his friend was hand in glove with his enemies in Paris, there could, of course, no longer be any question of accepting a royal pension arranged through his good offices. And so, when the false friend told him he had managed to get the King's agreement to make his munificence public, he replied that he would not touch the pension with a bargepole. 'You have brought me to England,' he wrote to him, 'allegedly to procure me an asylum but in fact to dishonour me, and you have devoted yourself to this noble task with a zeal worthy of your heart and an art worthy of your talents . . . I owe it to myself to have nothing more to do with you and to accept nothing, how-ever advantageous to me, in which you have been the mediator . . . This is the last letter you will receive from me.'

*

If it had indeed proved his last word, the scandal this exceedingly dusty answer was bound to cause, might not have taken on quite such damaging proportions. The London coffee houses and the Paris salons, where the falling out of the two fashionable celebrities soon became the talk of the day—'a declaration of war between two great European powers,' reported Grimm, 'could hardly have made more noise than this quarrel'—would have had little choice but to dismiss it as wholly incomprehensible, the product of a disordered mind meriting only compassion. Or better still from Jean-Jacques's point of view, some of the mud he had thrown at '*le bon David*' might even have stuck, not only because *aliquid semper haeret* but also because, as already indicated, the latter's original reverence for the writer had not wholly survived closer acquaintance with the man. His sense of humour had not allowed him to protest against the leg-pulls of the cult-debunking Walpole. His genuine desire to get his protégé a pension had not stopped him from making discreet enquiries into Jean-Jacques's financial situation, so as to make sure he really needed it. 'He is a bit inclined,' he had written to a friend when still unaware he had been promoted to chief enemy, 'to make himself interesting by complain-ing of his poverty and his ill health. But I have discovered . . . that he has certain resources, admittedly very small, which he has concealed from us.'

But if, therefore, '*le bon David*' had not proved capable of that blind devotion Jean-Jacques, though singularly incapable of it himself, de-manded of his friends, he was certainly far from meriting the treatment his protégé saw fit to mete out to him. 'Monstrous ingratitude,' he called it in a letter to Davenport. His challenge to his pupil to substantiate his 'scandalous lies' provoked the nineteen-page letter. Though Walpole was hardly unprejudiced, his characterization of the document as 'a wretched collection of puerilities, petty suspicions, lies, vanity, nastiness, insults and much else of the same order' is difficult to fault. It showed the shifty Jean-Jacques of that other great crisis, when he had accused Madame d'Epinay of treachery, all over again. Just as in the letter that had then disgusted Grimm to the point where he broke off all relations, so he began his indictment of Hume with the usual appeal for pity: 'I am ill and little disposed to write.' Again, as on the earlier occasion, he rebutted the charge of ingratitude with the argument that he had nothing to be grateful for. To be sure, Hume had at first been very kind and very helpful; but 'as for

the real good done me, these services are more apparent than weighty . . .
I did not come as a beggar to England asking for my daily bread. I brought
that with me . . . I was not so absolutely unknown that, had I arrived alone,
I should have gone without help or counsel . . . A multitude of country
houses were offered to me . . . If Mr. Davenport had been good enough
to give me this dwelling it was not to oblige Mr. Hume . . . All the good
that has befallen me here would have befallen me in much the same way.
But the evil that has befallen me would not have happened'. The 'sudden
change of tone in the press, in a country where my fame was most securely
established' and where Hume 'had so much influence with men of letters
and publishers', was clearly his doing. So was Walpole's cruel hoax, the
rudeness of Hume's landladies, and indeed, every one of the sufferings
and indignities he had reported to his friends and now recapitulated in the
indictment. As for proof, he naturally did not have any of the kind Hume
demanded since 'the first precaution taken by people who carry on a
secret plot is to hide their proceedings so well that . . . no case can be
established against them'. But he had plenty of circumstantial evidence,
'proofs that bring inward conviction to an honest man' such as the fact
that Hume was friendly not only with the press but also 'has all my
enemies for friends'. There was also the fact that, though Hume knew his
friend had been 'mortally afflicted' by Walpole's hoax, 'he did not write
me a word . . . did not care if my happiness were ruined'. And finally, the
most damning piece of evidence, there were 'those little taps on the back
and the "Mon cher Monsieur" of the man who thus answered the
suspicion that he might be a traitor'.

Such was the case for the prosecution. It would hardly have been a very
strong one even if the defence had not put in a document casting grave
doubt on this last bit of evidence, the only one perhaps worthy of an
answer and, indeed, the only one Hume bothered to answer. He produced
the letter he had written to Madame de Boufflers two weeks after the
emotional scene on the eve of Jean-Jacques's departure from London
during which, according to this account, there had been no question of
any accusations of treachery. Moreover, he asked, if Jean-Jacques's
version of the scene were correct and his worst suspicions had been confirmed by David's back-tapping and soothing words, why had he sent him
a gushing letter four days later saying how grateful he was for his 'sincere
friendship' and again, a week after that, had ended yet another with, 'I
embrace and love you with all my heart'. But what, of course, proved
even more damaging to the prosecution was Jean-Jacques's failure to
produce an even half-plausible motive for the crime imputed to the man
in the dock. At the time he had been preparing his case, outlining it to
friends, they had all urged him to drop it, pointing out that one's secret

enemies do not usually move heaven and earth with ministers and at Court to get one a royal pension. But while Jean-Jacques admitted that the traitor's activities on his behalf presented a baffling problem—'they were not natural'—he stuck to his guns, offering an explanation so tortuous that, as even his faithful Marquise de Verdelin had to admit, 'no one here believes Hume wanted to damage you'. Nor was he able to think of any more original explanation for the Scotsman's alleged enmity than the one which had already done service for all the other fellow-writers with whom he had fallen out: jealousy. When Jean-Jacques had been a guest of the King's cousin in Paris, David 'had perhaps seen more,' so the indictment insinuates, 'than he liked to see of the favour and the warm welcome I received there from so great a Prince'. 'All his attentions were for me,' he added in his letter to Malesherbes, 'Hume somehow was forgotten'—which his 'jealous heart' had not enjoyed.

*

Considering the disenchantment Jean-Jacques's treatment of Hume caused those who had so long been taking him at his own valuation, their reaction was remarkably indulgent. Among his enemies there were, of course, some who exulted, like Voltaire who wrote a long letter to Hume that is perhaps not among his greatest contributions to literature, witness the following passage: 'If he should need it, one could throw him a hunk of bread on the dunghill where he lies gnashing his teeth at the human race. But it was necessary to show him up for what he is so as to enable those who might feed him to guard against his bites.' But those who had most reason to feel vindictive, those whose cult of an idol, now revealed to consist of uncommonly common clay, made them feel distinctly sheepish, showed themselves merciful indeed. In vain did Voltaire attempt to enlist the highest ranking among them, Frederick the Great. 'You ask me,' wrote the King, 'what I think of him? I think he is unhappy and to be pitied . . . Only depraved souls kick a man when he is down.' Madame de Boufflers, who only four years earlier had told Hume that 'there was no sweeter, kinder, more compassionate man . . . his virtue seems so pure, so constant, so all-embracing' and who now had to admit that his conduct was 'atrocious' and 'inexcusable', that he had forgotten 'all decency', that in his 'crazy . . . criminal pride' he had allowed himself 'to believe what he never should have believed', nonetheless urged his victim to forgive and forget or at any rate to ignore the libellous insult, keep quiet about it.

Not unnaturally the Scotsman's own initial reaction, when, out of the blue, had come his protégé's brief letter making him out a false friend, had been rather less magnanimous. Rousseau, he wrote, 'is surely the blackest and most atrocious villain . . . I am heartily ashamed of everything I ever wrote in his favour'. And perhaps to forestall inevitable smug reminders from those like d'Holbach who had warned him that he had taken 'a serpent' to his bosom, he wrote to him: 'You were quite right, Rousseau is a monster.' However, all those who knew about the quarrel at first counselled him against taking his accuser to the court of public opinion. 'Dear friend,' wrote the great economist Adam Smith who was then in Paris, 'I am thoroughly convinced that Rousseau is as great a rascal as you and every man here believe him to be. Yet let me beg of you not to think of publishing anything to the world.' That would only 'make people speak ill of men of letters', d'Alembert warned. And Walpole, in his usual superior manner, ridiculed all the fuss: 'Your set of literary friends are what literary men are apt to be; exceedingly absurd, your friends talk loftily as of a challenge between Charles the Fifth and Francis the First . . . Many a country squire quarrels with his neighbour about game and yet they never print their quarrels.'

But it was not so much the advice of his friends as the action of the one who had overnight become his enemy which made Hume hesitate. Once Jean-Jacques had made his case in the nineteen-page indictment, he felt 'relieved . . . it is a perfect frenzy and consequently puts my mind quite to rest'. One does not know, he told Davenport, 'whether to be angry or to pity him'. To publish, he admitted to Madame de Boufflers, would be 'utterly to ruin the unhappy man . . . a piece of cruelty I cannot resolve to commit even against a man who has for too long deceived too great a part of mankind'. If he finally decided to publish nonetheless, with most of his friends now supporting him, it was partly because of the challenge contained in a letter Jean-Jacques had written to his Paris publisher who had circulated it widely, and partly because he knew his accuser was working on his public relations campaign. 'It is extremely dangerous for me,' he told Madame de Boufflers, 'to remain entirely silent as he is at present composing a book in which it is very likely he may fall on me with an atrocious lie.' And so he published his 'Concise account' of the controversy which, Grimm reported, 'monopolised all conversation in Paris for eight days, though not in London where there are more important actors to hiss . . . The English were foolish enough to take much less interest in this affair than in the formation of the new Ministry'.

Though Grimm knew better than anyone what Jean-Jacques was capable of, he did not wholly approve of Hume's action. Like Madame de Boufflers, who was sure her former idol could only have composed his indictment in a fit of rage, 'out of his mind with fury', he felt one should be 'tolerant of madness'. (Neither of them knew that, far from having

dashed off the letter on the spur of an angry moment, it was a rehash of
the letters its author had been writing to trusted friends for the past three
and a half months, nor did they know that it contained long passages
which he had simply copied from the one to Malesherbes*). Both were
ready, as were many others, if not to condone at least to explain his
conduct as that of a man of unsound mind—a charitable attitude that
reason itself imposed since the sudden and ferocious turning on a friend
seemed inexplicable in any other way. Even the injured party felt bound
to admit that the 'frenzy' of one whose 'brain has received a sensible
shock' was a more plausible explanation than the one he had entertained
earlier and according to which Jean-Jacques had 'wanted to bring on the
pension merely that he might have the ostentation of refusing it and that
he sought by a pretended quarrel to cancel all his obligations to me'.

Subsequent actions as well as writings would seem to prove the
charitable interpretation of his conduct fully justified. And indeed, the indictment itself already contained passages only too indicative of the
pitiable condition in which it had been composed. Had he been in his
right mind exercising his lawyer's skill, even an advocate so inclined to
throw in every argument he could think of, however unlikely to impress
the jury, would hardly have offered the 'dry, ardent, mocking, searching
gaze' of the defendant's eyes in evidence. Nor would he have used a
mysterious exclamation, overheard when the two were still devoted
friends. 'It was the first night after our departure from Paris,' so one of
the counts in the indictment began, 'we slept in the same chamber. I
heard him several times cry with great vehemence, "I have got hold of
Jean-Jacques Rousseau." ' At the time he had not seen anything sinister
in these words. On the contrary, accustomed as he was to being regarded
as the social catch of the century, they had seemed perfectly natural: 'I
could not but take the words in a favourable sense.' It was not until later
that he had 'comprehended their full force' and that, like the 'long and
fatal looks he so frequently cast on me', they filled him with a 'kind of
shuddering horror'.

*

They are not the accents of a man of sound mind. Clearly his brain had
already been attacked by the illness that was to make him fill most of the
three hundred pages of the *Dialogues* and many of the one hundred and
sixty of his last work, the *Rêveries du Promeneur Solitaire* with the paranoid

* Is it one more illustration of his laziness as a writer and his lack of seriousness,
even in so grave a matter, that he did not bother to transpose these passages
(which naturally spoke of Hume in the third person) so as to fit them into a
letter to him? His own convoluted explanation carries little conviction.

ravings that also recur throughout the second half of the *Confessions*. To give but one example out of hundreds, this is how he described what the organizers of the 'most baleful, terrifying plot' had done to him: 'They have erected impenetrable walls around me burying me alive among the living. It is perhaps the most astounding enterprise ever conceived, its total success shows the genius of those behind it, and what is no less astounding is the zeal with which the entire public lends itself to it . . .' Fortunately, as he himself has acknowledged and as has been confirmed by someone who knew him at this time of his life, 'these dark moods overcame him only at intervals and in sudden fits'. And there is another reason why his type of madness does not easily arouse as much compassion as perhaps it should. 'For an author to grow dizzy with self-love,' so Chateaubriand has put it, 'to be always so busy with himself that vanity finally inflicts an irreparable injury on his brain, that, of all the causes of madness, is the one I understand least and with which I find it most difficult to sympathise.' It is a diagnosis of the origins and the nature of Jean-Jacques's paranoia that seems difficult to fault. What had brought on the attack during his stay in England, inflamed his congenital suspiciousness to the point of seeing conspirators under every bed, was after all, by his own admission, nothing but hurt pride, resentment at the decline in his popularity. And twha had made him feel that 'the whole English nation' was backing his detractors was nothing but that raging inflammation of the ego which made him see himself as the centre of the universe. As was said by Burke who claims to have had 'good opportunities of knowing his proceedings almost from day to day . . . vanity was the vice he possessed to a degree little short of madness'.

But what makes it even more difficult to sympathize with the sufferings it caused him, is that he never showed his other and equally unendearing traits of character more clearly than when in the grips of this vice: the willingness to believe the worst of people whom he suspected of thinking him less than the best of men; the duplicity that he had shown as much in his treatment of Hume as in his quarrel with Madame d'Epinay; the self-pity that had made him accuse one of his most loyal friends and protectors, the Prussian king's Governor of Neufchâtel, of being a fair-weather friend, just as he had done with the Duke and Duchess—'you find me too unhappy to go on loving me.' Finally, the almost comical insolence that enabled him when he left Davenport's mansion at Wootton (where the staff had made life unbearable; 'I would rather put myself at the mercy of all the devils of hell than at those of English servants') to improve even on the highly original bread-and-butter letter with which he had taken leave from his hostess at the Hermitage. 'The master of the house,' he now saw fit to tell his English host, 'should know what goes on there, especially when he has foreigners to stay. If you don't know you are at fault. If you do know and allow it, you are even more at fault. But worst of all is your quietly staying at Davenport without worrying whether the man you had promised to come and see here, is comfortable or not. That is more than enough for me to know what to do. Tomorrow, Sir, I leave your house.'

One might think that, in turn, this would have been enough for his host who a few weeks earlier had told him that 'if you dislike Wootton' he could offer him another house 'three times as large'. But not at all. 'Wootton is and always will be at your service,' he wrote after Jean-Jacques had graciously signified his willingness to return, 'knowing you are too honourable a man to allow continuance of the annoyances that had forced me to leave.' Even when he was toppled from his pedestal, the sweet smell of the success that had raised him there apparently still clung to him so powerfully as to win him an indulgence no ordinary mortal could have hoped for. Torn to shreds and bespattered with mud, the emperor's clothes still impressed, winning him plaudits. There is no more striking proof than that even Hume—who to his eternal credit successfully completed his efforts to get Jean-Jacques his pension* as well as urging influential French friends to protect him should he return to France—claimed to see 'strong traces of his wonted genius and eloquence' in the pitiful, shaming document that was the indictment and which its author himself called 'a prodigious example of fortitude'. Indeed, Hume went so far as to attach the label 'remarkably sublime' to a peroration that, had he but known, was Jean-Jacques at his worst, pretending to a humility and a moral gallantry of which he was wholly incapable and had no intention of even trying to practise. 'If you are guilty,' so it ran, 'I am the most unfortunate of mankind, if you are innocent I am the most culpable. You even make me desire to be that contemptible object . . . prostrate at your feet, crying out for mercy . . . publishing aloud my own unworthiness and paying the most explicit homage to your virtues . . . If you are innocent justify yourself. I know my duty; I love it and shall always love it, however difficult and severe.'

This from the man who had already made it clear in the opening page of his indictment that no argument could shake the 'innate conviction of his heart' and whose most inviolable maxim 'was never to rekindle a friendship'. The man who had told one of his trusted friends six weeks earlier that, much as he longed to be in the wrong and 'with tears of joy to show the whole world all his [Hume's] virtue and all my own indignity', this could never be: 'No, till my last hour my heart will be broken by the deadly conviction that the best of men has transformed himself for me

* He accepted it, only to renounce it again a year later.

alone in the blackest.' The man, finally, who, in a letter to one of his few remaining friends, invoked his 'remarkably sublime' peroration to rebut the charge that he lacked the moral courage to admit himself in the wrong, only to go on to say that there was 'no point in any further exhortations', since 'a reconciliation between David Hume and Jean-Jacques Rousseau is so entirely impossible that not even God could bring it about'.

CHAPTER TWENTY

Death and Resurrection

'Among those who distinguished themselves in the career of letters and philosophy, there was one man who, through the loftiness of his soul and the grandeur of his character, showed himself worthy of the role of teacher of mankind . . .'—Robespierre

'Divine man! I have seen you in your last days. And this memory is to me a source of proud joy. I have contemplated your august traits. I have understood all the sorrows of a noble life devoted to the pursuit of truth'—Robespierre

FEW who lived to see Jean-Jacques's fall can have imagined that, long before the century was out, he would be back on a pedestal twice as high. But such is the power of myth hallowed by fashion. Voltaire turned out to have rejoiced prematurely at his rival's exposure as the charlatan, the madman, the monster of ingratitude and falsity Diderot, Grimm, Hume, Walpole, Adam Smith and so many others had come to see in him. He had little reckoned that the idol, who was such no more even in the eyes of his most devoted admirers like Madame de Boufflers—'all your friends,' she wrote to him, 'are dismayed and reduced to silence . . . Madame la Maréchale de Luxembourg and myself impatiently await your explanation of this incomprehensible conduct'—would soon be revered again as he had never been revered before, declared worthy, by the whole French nation assembled in homage, of the statue he had long claimed his due, his tomb even before then a place of royal pilgrimage, its contents subsequently transferred to that mausoleum of the Great, the Pantheon, where Voltaire himself was laid to rest. And how dizzily the Grand Old Man must have spun, his teeth rattling in his skull, as he found himself compelled to spend eternity under the same vaulted roof with, of all people, the detested Jean-Jacques.*

The latter did not, in fact, have to wait for posterity to fish him out of

---

* As things turned out their cohabitation lasted only a few years at the end of which persons unknown, who held timid peace-loving Jean-Jacques responsible for the sanguinary excesses of the Revolution, broke open his tomb and scattered its contents to the winds.

the sea of mud he had thrown at Hume and in which he himself was supposed to have sunk without trace. In an age so in love with sentiment that it was inclined to take lachrymose effusions of sensibility and rhapsodizing about the beauties of virtue, which was Jean-Jacques's strong suit, as proof of a noble soul, *'une belle âme'*, there were many who, like his faithful Marianne, refused to be disillusioned. 'I have read Hume's documents to several of my fellow-countrymen,' wrote an English squire, 'and they are all agreed that, even if you were at fault, it would be the fault only of a great and noble soul, ill-fitted to associate with that cold, unfeeling heart.' Another country-gentleman, Malthus's father, who was so moved by Jean-Jacques's writings that the 'moment I pick up one of your works my heart is so torn that I have to put it down again', begged him for a word of reassurance that 'you are not ill nor unhappy and that you know I love you'. Nor had he run out of illustrious admirers in France, anxious to have him as their guest. The Marquis de Mirabeau, father of the great orator, filled several pages with a description of the six properties he was happy to put at his disposal. Though the letter was not unlike the brochures issued by the shadier operators in the travel business, in that some of the properties on the Marquis's list were hardly habitable, the one Jean-Jacques chose proved satisfactory enough for him to express his gratitude in his usual, inimitable manner: 'One must enjoy your kindnesses and not thank you for anything more.'

But then, he had some reason to harbour a grudge against his new host, right from the beginning. For though the Marquis credited him with 'a heart without falsity, malice, baseness or cupidity', this had not stopped him from telling his hero a number of home-truths and offering him some very pertinent advice. Jean-Jacques had been 'mad' to expect Hume, a very good fellow if tactless and rude, to gush over him. The machinations of which he accused him were simply 'ridiculous'. As no one was perfect, he should look 'for the best in his fellow men'. He was far too keen on being popular and talked about. His enemies were figments of his imagination. And when Jean-Jacques, not deigning—or finding it inexpedient—to react to such irreverence, put in his customary claim to pity—'take into account that I have neither rank nor fortune, am infirm, ageing, abandoned, persecuted, detested . . . I want to be forgotten . . . If the example of an innocent and simple life is useful to men, that is the only thing I can still do for them . . . I am determined to live only for myself and a very few friends, and even them I do not really need'—he found his host far from sympathetic. How dared he call himself abandoned when 'there are so many like me who want to serve you'! What right did he have to call himself persecuted? He had only himself to blame for the condemnation of his book. The best remedy for self-pity was to say to oneself, as the Marquis did every time he was tempted to think himself unhappy: 'If I am suffering it must be indigestion.' As for Jean-Jacques's flight from society, it was only his 'touchiness' that made him dislike it, his criticism was very 'superficial', he saw only its 'ridiculous' outward appearance, his inability 'to put up with the annoyances of every day life was only the rebellious impatience of a child that is not allowed to go and play'. He had 'indulged', and indeed, 'abused' his sensibility to the point where 'reason, strength, justice, charity and many other faculties necessary to the fullness of our being and the maturity of our years' had atrophied.

At the time, Jean-Jacques seemed to take it all in his stride. There is not a word in his letters to show he was resentful. It was only to a third party that he confided, three years later, how he had really felt: 'M. de Mirabeau adopted such a bizarre tone . . . that it took all my faith in the friendly nature of his advances not to be shocked.' But if the Marquis— remarkably perspicacious for he only knew him from his writings supplemented by hearsay—had spoilt his tribute to Jean-Jacques's heart by his insight into his character, his famous son would soon more than make up for it. Even before the Revolution built the fallen hero a new pedestal, the younger Mirabeau was already extolling him as not only 'one of the greatest writers that ever lived' but also as 'perhaps the most virtuous man that ever was . . . worthy of all our respect on account of his morals and his inflexible courage . . . the apostle of virtue'.

This phoenix-like resurgence of Saint Jean-Jacques was all the more remarkable, all the more striking proof of the tenacious resilience of an established reputation, in that he had done nothing in the intervening years which could account for it. Neither his writings nor his actions, since he had lost his halo in the scuffle with Hume, had been such as to whisk it back onto his head; quite the contrary, they can at most inspire pity, and that only in hearts charitable enough to leave the quality of mercy so unstrained that it floods out all sentiments of revulsion, in minds big enough to see only madness where the less indulgent* see the manifestations of that '*triste caractère*' his beloved Comtesse came to know, or in spirits humble enough to say, 'There, but for the grace of my genes, go I.'

*

The tone for the last act in the tragi-comedy was set in its very opening, the flight from England where fourteen months earlier he had arrived in

---

* One of these, a literary critic of the last century who was a great partisan of Grimm, refused 'to describe malice, cunning and base suspiciousness as pathological symptoms'.

triumph. In the grip of that type of intermittent paranoia whose victims, suffering cycles of mental health and illness, are known in modern psychiatric parlance as cyclothymes, he had persuaded himself he was in physical danger from Hume's legions. To escape it, he was ready to eat quantities of humble pie. If only, he wrote to the minister whom Hume had approached for the pension, if only he were allowed to leave the country where he had become 'the object of ridicule and execration', he would 'never again say or write a single word' against Hume or England, nor even try to justify himself to posterity by publishing his memoirs whose manuscript he would surrender to the minister. (He had in fact seen to it that it was safely out of the country.) What was more, he would publicly take back everything he had ever said about Hume, he would explain that it was only 'my embittered temper, disposed to distrust and umbrageousness by my never-ending misfortunes,' that had allowed the 'inconsiderate' complaints to escape from his pen. And to back up these promises he offered no less than four types of security: the minister would have his letter; he, Jean-Jacques, would be happy to write another, even more binding; he would accept the King's pension which would make it utterly impossible for him 'ever to speak ill of his subjects without seeming so vile that no one would believe him'; and finally, the best guarantee of all, there was 'my well known character of fifty-six years' standing'.

It was a pathetic document, indeed, and, according to reports of contemporaries, followed by even more pathetic scenes when Jean-Jacques reached Dover and behaved very oddly, accusing Thérèse of wishing to poison him, rushing out of a dinner party and locking himself into a cabin aboard ship, haranguing passers-by in French. But what inclines one even more to pity than the moments of apparent insanity are those in which he realized he suffered from hallucinations. 'I like to think,' he wrote on one of these occasions, 'that I am no longer in my right mind. I see such sinister plots and such abominable people that, for the honour of humanity, I prefer to believe I am raving . . . I begin to fear that, having suffered so many real misfortunes I sometimes see imaginary ones that affect my brain.' At such times he occasionally seemed to catch a glimpse of the real Jean-Jacques. That had been the case when he wrote his letter to the minister. For the promise to exculpate Hume of treachery by inculpating himself of morbid distrustfulness was followed by the assurance: 'I would only be speaking the truth as, owing to this unhappy tendency, which is the product of my disasters and has now put the crowning touch to them, I have harboured only too many unjust suspicions.'

Even in such moments, however, he could not bear to look himself full in the face. The blame for his degrading distrust had to be shifted to his misfortunes. He was quite willing to admit that he carried it to 'deplorable extremes'. But he was to be pitied rather than censured: 'For forty years I was the most trusting of men and my trust was never once betrayed. No sooner had I taken up the pen than I found myself in another universe among very different beings in whom I continued to put the same trust and who have cured me of it in such a terrible manner that I have been driven to the other extreme . . . Unparalleled misfortunes and wickedness where I had least expected it, have made me distrustful and ready to believe the worst.' It is the old, ever-present theme of 'not really my fault', the flaw that spoils the effect of all his confessions and all his admissions of being less than nature's goodness incarnate.

But it is not only this that makes it so difficult to keep one's compassion up to the mark. To feel it deeply, to sympathize with another person's sufferings in the sense of sharing them, as is the literal meaning of the word, they must seem real. And as already suggested there is good reason to doubt whether a man so inconstant, so feeble, so childish, so forgetful of what he felt or thought or said a moment earlier, a man whose passions —again by his own admission—were as easily extinguished as they were ignited, was capable of deep feeling. Indeed, one has his own word for it that his tears dried as quickly as they welled up: 'His heart thirsting for happiness cannot retain any painful impression . . . No distressing thought can occupy him for long . . . Even in the greatest disasters of his unhappy life he passes quickly from extreme sadness to the purest joy . . . He feels his miseries acutely for a moment and then forgets them . . . Heaven had endowed him with a happy nature . . . a lively temperament that safe-guards him from melancholy and listless apathy . . . a natural instinct that makes him flee saddening thoughts and concentrates on the most agree-able things around him.'

There is ample proof of the truth of these assertions. Thus when he told the minister that he was 'practically out of his mind with misery' over the treacherous Hume, Davenport had seen him 'in the best of humour and health'. Two days before he completed the indictment, ending with the pitiful picture of himself as either 'the most unfortunate of mankind' or 'the most culpable', and with an expression of surprise that he had not 'died of grief in the writing of it', he had been telling his friend Dupeyrou how much he was enjoying himself: 'Do not worry about me, this place suits me very well indeed . . . I am happy in my refuge, indeed, I have never . . . followed my fancy more freely all day long.' Again, when he could stand life with Davenport's hellish servants no longer and decided to flee the country altogether, the local parson who met him when he was on the way to Dover found him 'cheerful, good humoured, easy and enjoying himself perfectly well, without the least fear or complaint of any kind'.

Seen in this context the outbursts of grief hardly rend one's heart more painfully than does a child's sobbing fit; in fact, rather less so. For by his own admission he took a voluptuous pleasure in the tears he shed at the spectacle of his own misfortunes, rendered all the more moving by the *littérateur*'s professional skill in dramatizing them. He had given a fine example of this art in the peroration, the grand finale of his letter indicting Hume. And he did so again with the ending of his letter to the minister: 'You see before you an unhappy man reduced to despair, uncertain only of the manner of his demise. You can call this sufferer back to life, you can be his saviour, and make the most wretched of men the happiest of men ... I see my last hour approaching, I am determined, if I must, to go and face it, to die or to be free. There is no middle way.'

*

But if, therefore, one need not take his despair too tragically, if most of those who knew him in the last years of his life found him, in the words of one of them, 'vigorous and gay', it was also because his childlike inability to feel anything deeply went hand in hand with an endearing buoyancy of spirit. It stood him in good stead. For life was by no means always easy in the days following his great *débâcle* and the flight from England that it occasioned. Though the news of his fall from grace in Paris society had apparently not reached the provinces—in Amiens where he stopped *en route* to Mirabeau's house, he was 'much sought after and fêted', according to a memoralist of the period, and in Grenoble, visited a year later, 'he entered the city in a procession made up of members of the bar, the judiciary, the garrison, the bourgeoisie and the people'—all this notoriety was a mixed blessing. There was, after all, still a warrant out for his arrest. He dared not return to Paris nor even go about under his own too-famous name, which he changed to Renou.

As always, a place to rest his greying head was the least of his worries. After the countesses, marchionesses and duchesses whose honoured guest he had been, this time it was no one less than the King's cousin, the Prince de Conti, who insisted on putting him up at one of his châteaux. But though this royal host was ready even to sack servants that displeased Jean-Jacques (who had started complaining about them within three weeks of his arrival), though the Prince told him that the only reason why he had not done so already was that 'you told me not to, but it will be done the moment you allow it'—he could not wait to be on the move again. It was partly because of the 'disdain' he suffered from the princely flunkeys who had done their utmost, so he wrote a year later in another bread-and-butter letter à la Jean-Jacques, 'to make me hateful and contemptible in the eyes of everybody'. But he also wanted to go—or so he claimed, for the intention seems belied by his actions on leaving the château—so as to stand trial in Paris, an idea which naturally did not appeal to the royal protector of a writer who, according to him (though not in the view of Mirabeau and others running no risk of being compromised), was still very much a wanted man.

The time he spent at Conti's château had been all the unhappier owing to the loss of yet another precious friend, Dupeyrou, whose reaction to having his face bathed in Jean-Jacques's kisses and tears had been even more sinister than that of Hume. As he was given the treatment—'I threw myself at him, glueing my face to his, inundating it with tears and uttering choked cries'—at a time when a bout of delirious fever had left him half-comatose, he had shown himself less than appreciative of his friend's turbulent bedside manner. In fact, if Jean-Jacques's account of the dramatic scene—the only one in existence—is to be believed, he had behaved abominably: 'The barbarian dared to accuse me of having selected the moment of his greatest weakness to finish him off with this commotion.' No wonder Jean-Jacques was upset. To be charged with murderous intent of a villainous cunning without parallel in the history of mayhem, was hardly a heart-warming response to the agonized solicitude he had shown for his friend's health. It was at best a very poor joke and at worst a dreadful accusation which, needless to say, is how Jean-Jacques took it. And so, from this moment the friend, whose arrival three weeks earlier had given him 'the purest and the greatest joy ever' and whom he called his 'one and only remaining friend', was his friend no more. In that 'most fatal dreadful night', he told the Prince in a long and 'strictly confidential' letter, 'I felt all my esteem, all my attachment, all my tenderness for him being snuffed out to the last spark. Since then I see only the baseness in his soul'.

In fact, even before then, ever since Dupeyrou had fallen ill and Jean-Jacques had been desperately trying to save his life with various unlikely potions, he had been sure his friend thought he was trying to kill him, at that time with the more conventional technique of old-fashioned poison. However, nobly containing his 'indignation', he had beseeched him with 'the tenderest effusions' to 'pour out his heart'. But all in vain; 'deaf to the most moving voice of friendship and sentiment he only gave obscure, equivocal, deceitful answers . . . that were belied by his look and his manner.' When finally the exhausted patient responded to his friend's treatment of last resort, tears and kisses and choking cries, with the outright accusation that he was trying to kill him by upsetting him emotionally, that was only the final proof Jean-Jacques needed to see the baseness of the other man's soul.

He saw none in his own, capable of attributing the vilest suspicion (such as he himself had harboured *vis-à-vis* Hume) to his dearest friend. It is true that a week later he was quite happy to tell the Prince he had been 'unjust' (Dupeyrou had explained that, if in his delirium he should have said something about poisoning, it must have been because Jean-Jacques had been regaling him with stories about the attempts people in England and at the château had made to treat him to a dose of hemlock). But not a word of contrition passed his lips, quite the contrary. When Dupeyrou, apparently unable to see him as a mental case who could not be held accountable, complained bitterly of his 'cruel', 'inhuman', 'humiliating judgment' of him, Jean-Jacques was much offended; 'reproaches and complaints were the last thing I expected . . . gratitude does not seem to be your strong point'. Though he ended his letter (they were still not on speaking terms, each keeping to his room) with 'let us be friends', he meanwhile told another correspondent: 'You don't know how much I am to be pitied . . . Since his arrival here he has not uttered a word of friend-ship or honesty or gratitude, while I do all I can to amuse him just as I did to restore him to health.' All this was of course 'strictly confidential'; 'I know your discretion, I feel the need to unburden myself and I am sure I could not choose anyone better.' It will perhaps no longer surprise that the trusted recipient of this letter was a faithful young admirer of ten years' standing whom he had urged Dupeyrou to avoid only a short time before: 'Everything he says, all his manoeuvres have shown what he really is about and believes so well hidden, this Coindet who thinks himself so subtle and is nothing but a coxcomb.'

It would all be less depressing, the correspondence of this period would not make quite such wretched reading, if it showed its hero to be only the pitiful victim of paranoia, 'always a martyr', as a despairing Dupeyrou was to exclaim, 'to your own distrust, the artisan of your own sorrows'. But, alas, it also shows once more the '*triste caractère*' of the man, as double-tongued as he was hard-hearted. Just as with Madame d'Epinay and with Hume, so with the 'coxcomb' Coindet, he first blackened his friends behind their back. 'I pretend to see nothing,' he had confided to Dupeyrou when he warned him against the young man (as well as against the Marquise de Verdelin, who had long been one of his most loyal and generous supporters); 'with my heart choking within me I return every one of their caresses, they dissimulate to ruin me, I dissimulate to save myself.' What with the sudden but temporary returns of trust you could no more rely on him than on a weathercock which most of the time did not even show which way the wind was blowing. 'Won't you tell me,' young Coindet asked piteously not long after he had been entrusted with Jean-Jacques's private thoughts about Dupeyrou, 'won't you tell me what causes your coldness? ... Six weeks ago your letters were so very different ... No one in the world loves you more tenderly ... I cannot bear to live like this, my heart is heavy with sighs, my eyes often fill with tears.' But Jean-Jacques was not interested in any tears but his own. Since not one of his friends, he replied, had offered any help in his distress he had decided to break off all useless relationships, 'yours not excepted'.

As for Dupeyrou, who more than once tried to re-establish the old intimacy, he, too, found Jean-Jacques's loving heart locked and barred: 'There had been a time when nothing would have given me greater happiness than to be with you, but if things have changed that is surely not my fault ... You want us to go back, I'm not so sure I feel like that ... You urge me to pour out my heart, asking me to treat you wholly as a friend or wholly as a stranger ... But you pride yourself on never pouring out yours ... You propose we should forget what you call our childish-nesses, and there is nothing I would like better. But the thing cannot be done by me, you are the one who remembers and you must do the for-getting which up to now you have not been very good at.' True to his most inviolable maxim of never rekindling old friendships he had, so he told a fellow-countrywoman, 'detached' himself from Dupeyrou, 'per-suaded that no durable relationship was possible between two hearts, one the frankest and the other the most secretive that had ever existed ... I avow that, as I compare myself with others, I grow daily more proud of myself'.

*

To fall in love with oneself, Oscar Wilde said, is the beginning of a life-long romance. In Jean-Jacques's case it became so passionate, so all-consuming, that in the end it cost him nearly every one of his friends and he was left, in the opening words of his last book, 'alone on the earth', the innocent victim of 'the most terrifying baleful plot ever hatched', as he put it in the *Confessions*. In the brief moments when he consigned these—and many far more delirious ravings—to paper, hundreds of pages written in Paris where he felt it safe to return three years after his flight from England, he was clearly mad. And what had driven him to such a state was this life-long love-affair of his. Love makes blind and none was made blinder to the real nature of the loved one than Jean-Jacques. Hence his hallucinations. Persuaded that he was on the whole the best of men, or at any rate determined to see himself in this comforting light, he was bound to regard all dissenters as '*des méchants*', refusing to obey the moral imperative enjoined upon us by Lord Tennyson's dictum: 'We must needs love the highest when we see it.' Only jealousy could account for their inability to do so. Jealousy was at the bottom of the plot which dated from the time, so he explained in the *Dialogues*, 'when his friends saw this man, so gentle and simple, suddenly taking flight and achieving a repute they could not hope for . . . The contempt they affect is only a transparent veil for the esteem they feel tearing at their heart and for their ill-concealed rage . . . His superiority is the great source of their hatred'.

It is a conviction he expresses again and again throughout his auto-biographical writings and in which he was encouraged by admirers like the Marquise who wrote to him: 'Your superiority is a crime in the eyes of these gentlemen.' And, indeed, there is little doubt that in many cases the animosity he aroused among his colleagues was at least partly inspired by jealousy. What he found 'less easy to explain' was that they had managed to win the public to their side. In fact, it took him four years to write the book, setting out in minute detail the exceedingly subtle and vicious techniques of deceit with which the original plotters like Diderot and Grimm, always working underground, had persuaded the whole of France and, indeed, of Europe to join in the plot, until he was left 'without a brother, a neighbour or a friend, the most sociable and the most loving of men outlawed by unanimous agreement'.

Such delusions, as pitiful as they were painful, were the price he had to pay for the orgiastic delights of the life-long romance; in his doting eyes the loved one was of such boundless fascination that all the world's, even if now everywhere green with malevolent jealousy, remained riveted on him. 'He was ill,' so the Comtesse d'Houdetot said of him in later life, 'with excessive amour-propre.' Far from having gone 'mad with virtue', as one of his best-known modern biographers* suggests, he went mad with self-love. There had to be a wicked plot fomented by jealous fellow-writers since otherwise their cooling off might raise doubts as to whether he was really nature's goodness incarnate. And the plot had to be universal and mysterious, operating underground, since otherwise 'the profound universal silence all around me, as impenetrable as the mystery it covers', might seem to signify that he was no longer the talk of the town.

Which, indeed, he soon ceased to be during these last eight years of his life, back in Paris. True, even though he had lost most of his following in the salons, he remained enough of a curiosity for his return to attract some attention. 'For the first few days,' Grimm reported 'it furnished a subject of conversation.' He was still enough of a social catch to be invited out; 'he goes out in society quite a lot.' And till the end of his days he continued to recruit new hero-worshippers to take the place of the old who had done so much to drive him off his head with their measureless idolatry. A typical case in point was the diplomat and field-marshal, the

* Jean Guéhenno.

Prince de Ligne, who was speechless with ecstasy at the privilege of an unexpected visit from Jean-Jacques: 'I could not believe my ears when M. Rousseau was announced.' Returning the call, he remained 'reverently silent, gazing in the eyes of the author of *La Nouvelle Héloise*'. And six weeks before the latter's death, at the time when Jean-Jacques accepted the invitation of the Marquis de Girardin on whose estate at Ermenon-ville he died, the Prince, too, pressed his hospitality on him: 'If you accept my offer I shall come and fetch you myself and take you to the Temple of Virtue; that will be the name of your dwelling place.'

But as an observer of the Paris scene noted, he did not stay long in the public eye: 'When he first arrived and showed himself in a café, people came to gape at him. Now he could walk up and down the Grand Avenue of the Tuileries without anyone noticing.' Most people had other things to talk about than a famous writer who, except for a potboiling Dictionary of Music, no longer published anything* (largely because that was the condition on which the authorities were prepared to forget about the warrant for his arrest). The nearest he came to acquainting the public with the writings of his last twelve years, nearly all devoted to that ever-fascinating subject, himself, was when he read part of the *Confessions* to a few selected audiences. Judging by the reaction of some of his listeners the public relations exercise proved far from unsuccessful. One of them relates how after the passage about his children being sent to the Found-ling Hospital, 'some of us took his hands in ours, kissed them and tried to comfort him. He wept and we wept burning tears with him'. Another, a well-known poet, exclaimed: 'What a work! . . . He avows his good quali-ties with a noble pride and his faults with an even nobler honesty. He drew tears from our eyes with the pathetic picture he painted of his mis-fortunes and his weaknesses, all the storms suffered by his sensitive heart . . . These memoirs are divine . . . a master-piece of genius, sim-plicity, candour and courage.' The five grandees, to whom he gave a reading on another occasion, seemed embarrassed rather than impressed. When he had finished, he relates, 'everyone was silent'. And his former admirer, Madame de Boufflers, who was not present but read the book when it was published after his death, was revolted and called them 'infamous memoirs like those of a farmyard worker or even lower, dis-agreeable as well as tedious, thoroughly insane and spiteful in the most disgusting manner, I cannot get over it that I used to make a cult . . . of this filthy animal'.

It was perhaps less than just or charitable to her former idol who at the time of the readings had already given more than one sign of the madness

---

* His operetta, however, was again put on at the Opéra which also produced another work of his that had not yet reached the stage.

to which she and her like had certainly contributed by their idolatry. Thus he had opened the proceedings by saying: 'The task to which I call you is the noblest mortals can fulfil on this earth, for it is to decide forever whether my name, which must live, will go down to posterity covered with obloquy or with glory.' And this was only one of the several occasions on which the public had a glimpse of the pitiful condition to which he had been reduced.

There was the time when, describing himself as 'an ill-fated stranger without a defender on earth, outraged, mocked, defamed, betrayed by a whole generation', he tried to entrust the manuscript of the *Dialogues* to 'Providence, protector of the oppressed', by leaving it on the altar of Notre Dame which, however, proved inaccessible. There was the time when he went canvassing in the street for his one-man party, handing out circulars addressed to 'Every Frenchman who still loves justice and truth'. But such attacks were few and far between. Most of the time, supplementing his modest income from annuities with his old trade of music-copying, going for country-walks to botanize, writing letters, he was of perfectly sound mind, so much so that the Foreign Minister did not hesitate to recommend him to Polish leaders for the task of drafting the new constitution that turned out such a charter for rabid nationalism.*

*

Left alone in the world, 'detached from all men', so he wrote when two years before his death he sat down to compose his last work, there was only one thing he still wanted to do, and that was to get to know himself: 'Who am I? That is what remains for me to study.' He had, of course, been doing nothing else, written almost exclusively about himself ever since he left Switzerland ten years before. Perhaps, however, it was just as well he decided to have another try. For the earlier efforts to get to know himself had proved singularly unsuccessful. Though in his auto-biographical writings there are moments of sudden insight that seem full of promise, it nearly always proves a false dawn. 'His dominant vice,' so runs one of these passages, 'is to be more occupied with himself than with others.' No man on earth, so runs another, 'ever took less interest in the affairs of others and in things that do not affect him.† It sounds

---

* It also breathed a very prudent, anti-revolutionary spirit; he counselled 'extreme circumspection' in introducing changes and in particular warned against emancipating the serfs before 'they had become worthy of their freedom and could support it'.

† One recalls his reprimand to the lady who had referred to the news of the day in her letters and who was told never again to bore him with such things. In fact, reading the correspondence, one would hardly realise there was a world outside where quite a few things happened in Jean-Jacques's time. Nor was he interested

like a belated recognition of his monumental egocentricity. But it is nothing of the kind since he goes on to prove, to his own satisfaction, that his opposites, 'those who are more occupied with others than with themselves, are the wicked ones . . . they are all egoists, he is not at all'.

It is the same with his admissions of being too feeble to be virtuous. As often as not, he undoes their effect by claiming his heart to be so far 'above the judgment of men' that he did not need to make the effort to be virtuous. For him to act virtuously was only doing what comes naturally; 'goodness, compassion, generosity . . . are not duties to him but needs of his heart which he satisfies more for his own happiness than for humanity.' What had made him flee the society of men was that he had found among them 'neither rectitude nor truthfulness, nor any of the sentiments he believes innate in their hearts because they are in his'; what had put him at such an 'enormous disadvantage' with other men was his 'inability to dissimulate'. As he said in a letter to yet another friend he had first clasped to his bosom but, as usual, was soon to accuse of treachery ('You are only a vile knave, worthy of all the contempt you have for me) his great misfortune had been that 'I have so long judged others by myself'. Never did he speak a truer word, witness the vile suspicions he had attributed to Dupeyrou, the duplicity he had attributed to Hume, the vindictive all-consuming hatred he attributed to his enemies, in the very descriptions of which he revealed the mastery this sentiment had gained over his own loving heart.

It was not until the last two years of his life that he seems to have had flashes of insight momentarily illuminating at least one or two of the dark corners of that heart which he so proudly called 'transparent as crystal'. It was only in the *Rêveries* that he occasionally dropped the old tone of bombastic self-praise. Acknowledging that 'the maxim "Know thyself" was not as easy to follow as I had thought', he blithely announced, 'I have had to modify the opinion I have long held of my own virtue considerably . . . With a feeble heart . . . one can at best preserve oneself from vice but to dare profess great virtues would be arrogant.' But the conversion to moral modesty was no more serious, in the sense of being durable, than any other attitude or idea he ever adopted. The very cheerfulness with which the man who had paid the price of madness for his self-love, announced that at the age of sixty-five he had discovered this fatal flaw in his make-up, is typical of his inability to be really in earnest about anything. The discovery, he said, had come 'very late in the day . . . but it

in other people's ideas, as Mirabeau found to his cost when he tried to get him to read some of his writings. 'I have read your book,' Jean-Jacques replied, 'because you wanted me to . . . But I have always found it very tiring to follow the thought of others.'

was never too late to learn . . . to be modest and less presumptuous'. Indeed, the context shows it to be only another example of Jean-Jacques, even when of sound mind as he is generally supposed to have been in the closing phase of his life, throwing down on paper whatever passed through his mind at any given moment, 'wholly oblivious,' as he himself admitted, 'of what he had written before.' For the good resolution to be less presumptuous forms part of a chapter full of the usual trumpeting about 'the proud loftiness of soul', 'the unparalleled good faith and love of truth' he had shown in the *Confessions*, and it was followed by the usual claims to being, if no longer the best of men, at any rate the least bad, which would seem to come to much the same thing: 'I doubt whether any man in the world has really done less evil than me.'

*

It was this man who, eleven years after his death at the age of sixty-eight, was hailed as the great moral teacher in whose virtuous spirit the men of 1789 would try to build the good society. 'There is a great dispute among their leaders,' said Burke, 'which of them is the best resemblance of Rousseau . . . Him they study, him they meditate . . . He is their standard figure of perfection. To this man and this writer . . . the foundries of Paris are now running for statues with the kettles of their poor and bells of their churches.' The great orator was hardly exaggerating. 'Divine man,' cried Robespierre, 'I have seen you in your last days. And this memory is to me a source of proud joy. I have contemplated your august traits. I have understood all the sorrows of a noble life devoted to the cultivation of truth.' 'It is to Rousseau,' exclaimed the President of the National Convention on the occasion when all of its members had marched behind the dignitaries carrying Jean-Jacques's ashes to the Pantheon, 'it is to Rousseau we owe the salutary regeneration that has worked such happy changes in our morals, our customs, our laws, our spirits and our habits.' Plays were put on dramatizing Jean-Jacques's life and death, with his last noble host praying in despair: 'Oh my God, such a being on earth is your most perfect image. Why must you take him away from us, why can you not let his days equal the number of his virtues?' It set the audience weeping copiously, so reported the leading newspaper of the day, 'one sheds tears but they are the sweet tears with which one daily drenches the writings of Jean-Jacques'. No wonder Burke, with his less than fervent admiration for the man, was baffled: 'If an author had written like a great genius on geometry, though his practical and speculative morals were vicious in the extreme, it might appear that in voting his statue they honoured only the geometrician. But Rousseau is a moralist or he is nothing.'

He was indeed, and no one had insisted on it more often, no one had been more uninhibited in claiming that his vocation was to be an example to mankind. 'If only you knew,' he wrote to an admirer who had extolled his literary merits, 'if only you knew how much more precious to me is the reputation of a good, just and truthful man I had for forty years and never deserved to lose.' He need not have worried. His hope that posterity would see him as he saw himself proved no pipe-dream. For it was indeed as the best of men, in the role of a moral hero, that all parties in the early days of the Revolution invoked his name. It was not as a political authority (few had then read *The Social Contract*) but as the moralizing author of *La Nouvelle Héloise* and *Emile* (even fewer were acquainted with the *Dialogues*, the *Rêveries* and the *Confessions*) that they harnessed him to their respective wagons. The apparently indestructible prestige he owed to his status as a self-made saint was the shining prize for which they contended. No one, not even Jean-Jacques, could have asked for more. If for the men of 1789 bliss was it in that dawn to be alive, for Jean-Jacques, beholding the longed-for canonization from regions beyond reach of the upheaval his timorous spirit abhorred, to be dead must have been very heaven.

Epilogue

'THE defects of great men,' Disraeli once said, 'are the consolation of dunces.' As will have become clear, few have more of this ignominious balm to offer than the writer who, if fame is any yard-stick, must be reckoned among the greatest of all time. If the authoritative *Encyclopaedia Britannica* is to be believed, his influence in the history of literature is 'unrivalled'. In the opinion of the *Cambridge Modern History* he did no less than to alter 'the whole bearing of man towards the world . . . A new breath of spring passed into his being'. According to the editor of his *Correspondance*, a work of infinitely painstaking scholarship, whose twenty-one volumes covering the first fifty-two years of his life still leave many more to come, he occupies a 'strategic position in the history of Western civilisation'. 'No oeuvre in any literature,' maintained the Nobel prize-winning philosopher Bergson, 'has exercised an influence comparable with that of Jean-Jacques Rousseau's.' His pen, the historian Lord Acton has said, 'produced more effect than Aristotle or Cicero or St. Augustine or St. Thomas Aquinas.' The Englishman's French colleague, the celebrated Michelet, held that he had changed the world's climate: 'Since his ardent utterance pervaded the atmosphere it is as if a zephyr has passed over the world, the earth has begun to bear fruits it never knew before.' More specifically, so declared one of the foremost historians of French literature, Gustave Lanson, he had 'given men back their self-respect'. A famous writer and biographer of our time, André Maurois, went even further when he wrote that 'nearly all men, not only of the eighteenth century, have been formed by him; this master of tenderness and sentimental reverie taught Napoleon to love, perhaps even Goethe and Stendhal'. The equally renowned anthropologist, Claude Lévi-Strauss, hailed him ecstatically as 'our master and our brother . . . every page of this book (*Tristes Tropiques*) could have been dedicated to him, had it not been unworthy of his great memory'. The famous psychologist Havelock Ellis gave him credit for having 'renovated life, effected a spiritual revolution comparable to that effected by Christianity'. And his detractors are as ready to acknowledge his importance as his admirers (respectively known to the industry as 'Rousseauphobes' and 'Rousseau-istes', the suffixes being yet another distinction few other writers can claim). Thus the famous English churchman of the 1930s, Dean Inge, said that 'his influence has perhaps been more pernicious than that of any other man who has ever lived'. The French academician Jules Lemaître held that he had 'transformed history and literature' and that 'thanks to human credulity and stupidity no man had ever done more harm to man-kind than the writer who, it seems, hardly knew what he was writing'. For François Mauriac 'the modern era is rooted in his lies . . . He is not dead like so many other writers of the past, he is Romain Rolland, Proust, Gide . . . It has taken a century and a half for his poison to accomplish its work'.

Even if it were all only half true—nothing is less scientific than the mea-surement of a writer's influence and none, of course, are less inclined to underrate it than members of the writing profession—it would still present the student of Jean-Jacques's life and work with a baffling prob-lem. How could a character so feeble, a thinker so incoherent, a *littérateur* whose prose is so patchy, have earned world-wide recognition as a figure of great historical importance? Such is the contrast between, on the one hand, the towering Jean-Jacques one sees when first faced with the enormous number of books devoted to him, and, on the other hand, the man and the writer one has come to know at the end of one's labours, that one is left feeling wholly bewildered. It is not so much because the giant he appeared to be on the library's shelves turns out to be a moral pygmy. Karl Marx was no saint either, in many ways as repellent a character as Jean-Jacques. If, studying him, one never has that feeling of an almost ludicrous disproportion between the public image and the man, it is partly because there is nothing feeble or infantile about the ferocious egotism and contempt for his fellows Karl shared with Jean-Jacques. His faults were on the same heroic scale as the single-mindedness of his dedication to his work. Jean-Jacques, really interested only in himself, had no such great all-absorbing cause to give him the courage of his vices, render him oblivious or contemptuous of them. Again, in Marx's case, the work so overshadows the man that his character is hardly visible in it or at any rate seems irrelevant to its greatness. Indeed, insofar as his writings do reflect his nature at all, they show a forcefulness that cannot but add to the respect inspired by their intellectual qualities. In the case of Jean-Jacques's oeuvre, or rather that part of it that has survived, the *Con-fessions*, the work and the cause *are* the man, morally a self-confessed weakling and intellectually so indecisive that, as Madame de Staël's lover, Benjamin Constant, has well put it, 'he thrashes about among a thousand contrary ideas as in a dark night lit up by frequent flashes of lightning'.

Could such a man, with such an oeuvre, really have 'transformed history and literature'? Where is the evidence for all the huge claims to influence put forward on his behalf? The greatness, in the sense of effect on history, of men like Buddha, Jesus, Mahomet, Luther or Marx, can be roughly quantified by reference to the number of their self-identifying followers. And it is the same with men like Galileo or Newton or Darwin to whom the whole world acknowledges its debt. But who shall say how many divisions has Jean-Jacques? Could it be that all these contentions about his unrivalled influence belong properly in the realm of mythology rather than that of history? What evidence is there other than that of the *post hoc, propter hoc* type, according to which the fact that the Revolution and Proust and Gide came after Jean-Jacques, is proof that they were strongly influenced by him or even, but for him, would not have happened or not have written as they did? And do all those statements about his having altered the climate of the world, or passing a new breath of spring into man's being, perhaps form part not so much of the discipline of history as of the bastard art of *'histoire romancée'*?

How few are the witnesses ready to acknowledge his influence. It is true that in his own lifetime there were a number who testified to the debt they owed him as a moral and religious teacher. But there are not nearly enough of them—their letters are to be counted in dozens rather than in hundreds—to credit him, as so many have done, with having led the society of his day back into the straight and narrow paths of god-fearing virtue. He himself—one recalls his sour preface to *La Nouvelle Héloise*—had no illusions about that. Perhaps the most one could say, therefore, is that he made the idea of romantic and virtuous love fashionable for a while in that tiny set that creates fashions without necessarily paying more than lip-service to them. What reason is there to believe that the virtuous conduct of the repentant Julie was any more representative of the morals adopted by his readers than the wicked goings-on of the villainous Vicomte de Valmont and his accomplice, portrayed twenty years later in Choderlos de Laclos's *Les Liaisons Dangereuses*? Among a thousand novels published within the first twenty years after the appearance of his best-seller, Daniel Mornet, one of the most authoritative literary historians of the period, found only fifty that clearly bear the marks of its influence.

As for the claim that he awakened his generation to the delights and insights to be obtained by cultivating sensibility, there are again few witnesses to support this thesis. Nor is it easy to substantiate the contention, so often advanced, that he was the first to open the eyes of his contemporaries to the beauties of nature. At least a decade before he sang their praises, there had been the beginning of a return to nature (just as two decades earlier there had sprung up a moralizing literature denouncing the life-style and the values of the salons). 'People took pleasure,' so writes Mornet, 'in country-walks, in spring flowers and in sunsets, country houses rapidly multiplied . . . There were Frenchmen who had grown tired of the geometrical patters of Le Nôtre . . . garden-architects, essayists and even poets celebrated landscapes where men had not dared to interfere with nature.' And so, as regards the cult of sensibility and the cult of nature, perhaps the most one could say is that Jean-Jacques's influence had been that of a contributor to a movement already well on the way and that had its origins in England, whose poets and novelists were much read in France. How powerful his contribution was cannot possibly be established, though one may perhaps doubt whether it was such as to warrant the tribute paid to him by an author who, in the first decade of this century, thanked him for having 'thrown us into your maternal arms, O Nature', and went on to exclaim: 'So come back to him, anxious spirits, thirsting hearts, souls in distress. He will teach you to get a grip on life again, to understand, to feel, to will, to act, to live, that is to say, to be happy!'

*

If it is not as easy as one might think to make out a strong case for Jean-Jacques having wrought a revolution in the mores and the tastes of his time, it is even more difficult to substantiate the claim that he was at least partly responsible for the great upheaval of 1780.* True, there is no lack of contemporary witnesses ready to support it. More than one speaker in the National Assembly hailed him as the 'precursor of this great Revolution' and *The Social Contract* as its 'charter'. But the evidence presented in Joan MacDonald's recent study of Jean-Jacques's role in the great events of those days, shows it to have been by no means a dominant one, let alone that of a catalyst. Judging by the official record, the *Journal des Débats et des Décrets*, no one even mentioned his name during the debate on the Declaration of the Rights of Man. Nor does it appear at any time in the two eventful months that followed the action of the Third Estate in declaring itself to be the National Assembly. It also rarely crops up in the political pamphlets published in the years 1789–1791. In the 1,114 scrutinized by Miss MacDonald there are only thirty-nine references to Jean-Jacques and out of those only twelve deal with *The Social*

---

* The Revolution was a foregone conclusion, so wrote a contributor to a symposium published in 1890, it was destined to 'emerge from Jean-Jacques's entrails' as soon as he had 'opened the world's eyes to his bleeding heart, let the world hear the cries wrung from it by the spectacle of the people's sufferings, the frivolity of the voluptuous rich, the harshness of the potentates, the cruelty of the tyrants'.

Contract. By far the least-read of his books, only one new edition of it had been published since its first appearance in 1762. Out of 248 mentions of Jean-Jacques's works unearthed in journals covering the period 1762–1789 only eight were found to refer to this book.

When he was acclaimed by the revolutionaries it was not, therefore, as the architect of the new order but as '*le bon Jean-Jacques*', the martyr in the cause of truth and justice, the example to mankind he had set out to be, the embodiment of the virtues that would enable them to build the good society, the alter ego of those two popular paragons, Julie and Emile. Very few knew he was the antithesis of these two characters. When Robespierre's henchman St. Just listed the numerous virtues of 'revolutionary man', he made no secret of it that he had taken Jean-Jacques as his model. It was to honour a mythical figure that the Assembly had voted his statue.

But it was not only because of the holy vestments with which he had been fitted out that he became one of the Revolution's patron saints, once it had been unleashed by forces rather more powerful than a versatile scribbler whose excursion into statecraft only came to be widely known when these forces had already taken control of events. If his statue was voted by general acclaim it was also because his political stock in trade was so diversified that it had something to suit every taste. Thanks to the 'superb chaos' of the thousand contrary ideas Benjamin Constant spoke of, anyone, whether reactionary or radical, could invoke his authority for the political fancies of his choice. In the early days of the Revolution the aristocrats made as much of him as the most radical members of the Third Estate. That is why it is so difficult to maintain that his political thought had a measure of influence on the course of events. As Miss MacDonald has said, 'It is necessary to distinguish between the cult of Rousseau and the influence of his political thought.' Besides, how can a man's thought be said to be influential if he has not any because he has too many, if he has not got a body of thought but only a ragbag of passing fancies? Admittedly it can be argued that some of the ideas Robespierre tried to put into practice during his brief reign were clearly taken from Jean-Jacques's comprehensive stock. But if the Seagreen Incorruptible could claim he was acting in his spirit, so did those whose heads he chopped off and who could invoke the Master's condemnation of bloodshed in the cause of Public Safety as 'one of the most execrable rules tyranny ever invented'.

Though, as Miss MacDonald's study has shown, the moderate or conservative elements who invoked Jean-Jacques's writings for their cause, were less guilty of 'blatant misrepresentation' than the radicals, it is the latter who emerged victoriously from the battle for his name. The myth of the saintly Jean-Jacques which public opinion cherished in the dawn of freedom had been superseded at the time of its sunset by the myth of the red-handed Rousseau. The unifying image of 'the best of men', revered by all, had made way for the divisive one of 'revolutionary man'. And it is this that has perhaps done more than anything else to keep his memory alive during the two centuries in which the battles of the 1790s were so often fought all over again, whether in the streets or in the debating chamber or on the printed page. It was to this never-ending misuse of his name as a counter in the political game that he owes much of the unflagging interest reflected in the immense output of the Rousseau-industry that is so easily mistaken for a measure of his greatness, his role in history. But it is not only because of this that his name lives. It is also, perhaps even more, because his experiences, his character and, last not least, chance made him such a loud-voiced and much-publicized exponent of that resentment of the restraints imposed on 'natural man' by civilized society that strikes a chord in so many hearts.

*

There remains the question of how real has been his influence on literature, which he is so often said to have 'transformed'. Once more, witnesses to confirm it are few and far between, the men of letters who have acknowledged their debt to him can be counted on the fingers of one or two hands. It is true that among them there are some who, by virtue of their own standing as front-rank philosophers and writers, may have transmitted his influence to much larger numbers. Such were Kant (who owed him the notion that in morals all men are equally knowledgeable and who said that Rousseau's insistence on the limitations of the reasoning faculty had 'made me see my error'), Tolstoy (for whom 'Rousseau and the Gospel had been the two great and salutary influences') and George Eliot (in whom he had awakened 'new perceptions'). But even those countless academics who never stop composing theses on the influence of the influence of the influence of their favourite author, rarely feel able to quantify the end-product.

It is true also that an impressive array of famous names can be mobilized to testify to their admiration for Jean-Jacques: Madame de Staël, Byron, Shelley (who called him 'a sublime genius'), Stendhal (for whom he was 'the noblest soul and the greatest genius that ever was'), Schiller, George Sand, Tocqueville, Schopenhauer, Sainte-Beuve, Ruskin, Carlyle (who managed to include him among his heroes because 'with all his faults he is wholly serious') and many others. But to admire is not necessarily to be influenced.

However, in view of the agreement among nearly all literary historians that Jean-Jacques has been uniquely influential in the development of letters, it would be the height of presumption for an outsider to cast doubt on its validity, to suggest that this, too, is perhaps but a myth just as was his moral eminence, so widely taken for granted until the Left's appropriation of the prestige attaching to it forced the Right to start examining the saint's credentials. What one could perhaps do without adding arrogance to ignorance is to ask what it is in Jean-Jacques's writing that enabled him to achieve his strategic position in the history of literature. Unfortunately the question is no sooner posed than one is confronted with a new problem as baffling as the first. How could so inordinately patchy a work as the *Confessions* have gained its author this commanding position? For by common consent it is almost entirely to this book (and a few pages of the *Rêveries d'un Promeneur Solitaire*) that he owes it. The *Confessions* are almost unanimously judged to be his masterpiece, the seminal classic that, so Lytton Strachey put it, 'started the vast current in literature and sentiment which is still flowing'. And the claim the Englishman made for it in 1911 is as nothing compared to that advanced by American scholars of our day who see 'the unfolding of civilization retraced' in this work of 'ageless beauty'.

Considering its nature as the proverbial curate's egg, whose many exceedingly unappetizing parts have become sufficiently visible in these pages, its good parts must be very, very good indeed to have made such an impact on the world of letters and through it—or so this world perhaps too readily assumes—on the world of ordinary men. Indeed, looking at the work as a whole one cannot help but feel that even more unprecedented than the influence it is said to have exercised, is the indulgence its merits have won its author. Have the world's *litterati* ever, before or after, conferred the status of an immortal, seminal masterpiece on a work so uneven, so flawed by its multiple motivation, so disfigured by the dreadful blemishes it owes to the fact that '*le style c'est l'homme*'?

Only two things can account for their readiness to do so in the case of the *Confessions*. One is that self-expanding nature of a reputation for greatness so often remarked upon in these pages. Once established, it is apt to gain its beneficiary a deference, a respect or at the very least a benefit of the doubt, that do a great deal to obscure or gloss over his shortcomings. A typical example of this attitude is provided by the author* of a scholarly study surveying the vast literature about Jean-Jacques. Referring to 'the contradictions in the expressions of Rousseau's thought', he claims it is the reader's duty to do for him what he cannot do himself, express his 'essential ideas' clearly: 'Rousseau has always admitted that he could not compose properly or that he was too lazy to do so; one must

* A. Schinz.

do it for him.' In the same helpful spirit other Rousseauiste scholars invoke the 'deeper level', so popular with some dramatic critics, to make sense out of the 'superb chaos'. Thus Lytton Strachey: 'The true gist of his meaning seems to be only partially revealed . . . He himself was never really aware of the fundamental notions that lay at the back of his thought.' Thus one of the three editors of the Pléiade edition of his collected works: 'His truth, his unity, is not to be looked for always on the level of clear, distinct ideas, but at an underlying deeper level.' Thus, too, the American academic* who claims that Jean-Jacques's apparent contradictions are now seen 'as truth-giving tensions which reveal deeper truths about human nature'.

Sometimes also the awe inspired by the reputation for greatness or, more simply, the respect felt for success, finds expression in attempts, not so much to unify the great man's thought as to romanticize it. The genre of '*vie romancée*' is extended and perfected to include the hero's '*pensée romancée*'. That is what all those have done who present the 'illumination' on the road to Vincennes which, as already noted, he had completely forgotten a few months later, as the development for which all his past had been preparing him and which shaped the rest of his intellectual life.

As for the moral benefits the great—and particularly those in the field of the arts—derive from the awe they inspire, there is not only the customary exemption from the standards by which ordinary human beings are judged but also the psychological white-washing. A good example of the former was provided by one of Jean-Jacques's latest and best known European biographers,† who wrote that 'nothing could defile him as his innermost self was beyond degradation'. An equally good example of the latter is to be found in a recent work by his foremost American biographer‡ of today. It is all the more striking as his is indeed in many ways a masterly and certainly not a Rousseauphile study. Yet its author felt bound to exculpate Jean-Jacques—though in a curiously ambivalent manner—from any 'viciousness or villainy . . . his acts resulted from paranoid sensitivity or from panic or cowardice and took the typical coward's form, the deceit and duplicity which . . . were so intimate a part of his character'. In particular his behaviour in the affair with the Comtesse, which might be thought caddish by those who 'did not know him', was not in fact caddish at all: 'The truth is that he was trying . . . to exorcise the guilt he had been impelled first to incur and then to catharize.'

If respect for success is a partial explanation for the praises heaped on the *Confessions*, another can be found in the fact that the good parts are indeed not only very good, of the same delightful quality illustrated earlier with a few passages from *Emile*, but also, as already remarked on that

* M. Einaudi.   † Jean Guéhenno.   ‡ L. G. Crocker.

occasion, breaking fresh ground, sounding a note that was new in his time. They fill pages familiar to every schoolboy in the French-reading world: about 'going to bed with the larks' after having sat up all night reading; about a blissful day of love-lost innocence spent on an outing with two young girls; about the happy days in 'Maman's' rural retreat, Les Charmettes ('I rose with the sun, and I was happy; I went for walks, and I was happy; I saw Maman, and I was happy; I left her and I was happy; I strolled through the woods and over the hills, I wandered in the valleys, I read, I lazed, I worked in the garden, I picked the fruit, I helped in the household, and happiness followed me everywhere'); about his being reminded of these good old times by the sight of some periwinkles thirty years later; about the gentle joys of domesticity in the early phase of life with Thérèse in a fourth-floor flat in Paris.

It all makes delightful reading even today. But how little of it there is. What a tiny proportion these passages form of the six hundred pages of the *Confessions*. And how haphazardly are they intermingled, sometimes even on the same page, with those where the lyrical poet makes way for the bragging public relations officer, the shifty lawyer, the bombastic rhetorician, the petty gossip-monger, the posturing horror-comic, the whining egomaniac, to say nothing of the pitiable paranoid who has left his mark even on the part written before he became dominant. If it is to the poetical and lyrical passages of the *Confessions* (and the *Rêveries* where the proportion between the delightful and the awful or pitiful is not much better), if it is to them that Jean-Jacques owes his towering reputation, how minute is its base compared with that of any other celebrated writer one cares to mention.

Fortunately for the pyramid's stability it is propped up by Jean-Jacques's undeniable qualities as an innovator in a rather more important field than that of condolence and bread-and-butter letters. Though he was not the first to concentrate on the study and the exhibition of self—Montaigne had already done so two centuries earlier—Jean-Jacques's approach to the subject was novel indeed. The Frenchman had looked inward to try and understand 'human nature in general' of which he felt himself to be representative, 'made of the common clay'. The Citizen of Geneva made it clear in the first page of his *Confessions* that what he was interested in was the unique qualities of the self: 'The man I shall portray is myself . . . unlike anyone I have ever met . . . like no one in the whole world.' It was this kind of introspection and exhibition that was novel, opened up a whole new field to literature.

Of course, once again there is no telling whether it would really have been left uncultivated if Jean-Jacques had never put his hand to the hoe. It is such a tempting field that others might well have taken to it if Jean-

Jacques had left it unexplored, or if his experiment had not been invested with such glamour because of the celebrity already attaching to his name: no better example of the *post hoc, propter hoc* fallacy than that provided by the well-known nineteenth-century historian E. Faguet who, no admirer of the genre Jean-Jacques launched, holds him responsible for 'the most ungracious, boring literature, the display of the self, the cult and the apotheosis of the self, which doubtless would never have existed without him, for the simple reason that before him it had not dared to exist'. But that he did launch it, that in this field he was a true innovator, cannot be denied.

Whether that makes him the Father of the Romantic Movement, as he has so often been called, is a question that cannot even be adumbrated here, if only because the term is used to cover such a multitude of disparate things. In so far as he went further than any of his contemporaries and predecessors in exalting sensibility (which, being all one's own, sets men apart) over reason (in which they can recognize one another), he can certainly be said to have put himself at the head of the Romantic rebellion against the Classical tradition. But there are many ideas, sentiments and values usually associated with Romanticism which he did *not* cherish. His preferred landscape was not the lonely crags or the towering peaks of his native land but the gentle lakeside. He dreamt not of ruined abbeys and ghostly tombs but of a chalet with green shutters, a cow in the field and a duck in the duckpond. He saw the good life not as did Byron or Shelley but as achieved by his Julie in the bourgeois domesticity of life with her elderly husband. He did not exalt passion above what the later Romantics called vulgar or banal virtue, but in the end opted for the traditional morality.

That, finally, is also one of the reasons why he should be acquitted of the charge brought against him by those who debit him with the world record for 'pernicious influence'. Apart from the gratuitous nature of such sweeping assertions, for which no more evidence can be produced than for those of his admirers, it is based on a selective reading and, therefore, a distortion of his works. As has been shown, one can find in it exhortations to clear-eyed self-denial as well as invitations to self-deceiving self-indulgence, the traditional moralist's stern sermons as well as the sophist's sweet siren-songs. If it should be these that have found the widest audience, that is hardly the fault of Jean-Jacques. If the *Confessions*, that show him, in a few places, at his best as a writer and throughout at his worst as a man, should be the only work to have survived, that is a reflection rather of the values cherished by those who hold it to be his main claim to greatness.

*

Taking leave at last from the most controversial writer ever, still the subject of heated controversy between those to whom his temperament appeals and those whom it appalls, I would crave indulgence for ending in the first person with a confession of my own; the historian I respect above all others, my father, is among those who credit Jean-Jacques with 'immense influence', and it is only because, alas, I no longer need fear being put in my place that I have dared question its reality. May I be allowed, by way of penance, to leave the last word to him: 'With Rousseau,' so he wrote, 'triumphed the anti-stoical life-style', with him came the end of 'the aristocratic culture which does not advertise its sentiment but remains sober and reserved in its manner of expression, stoical in its general attitude.'

SELECT BIBLIOGRAPHY

Works by Jean-Jacques Rousseau
Oeuvres Complètes, 4 vols, édition Pléiade, Paris, 1959.
The Confessions, translated by J. M. Cohen, Penguin, London and Baltimore, 1953.
Emile, translated by Barbara Foxley, Everyman's Library, London, 1911.
The Social Contract, translated by Maurice Cranston, Penguin, London and Baltimore, 1968.
The Social Contract and the Discourses, translated by G. D. H. Cole, London, 1973.
La Nouvelle Héloise, translated and abridged by Judith H. McDowell, London and University Park, Penn., 1968.
Correspondance Générale collationnée sur les originaux, annotée et commentée par Théophile Dufour, 21 vols, Paris, 1928–1934.
Correspondance Complète, édition critique établie et annotée par R. A. Leigh, 21 vols, Geneva, 1965–1974.

Biographies
Sir Gavin de Beer, *Jean-Jacques Rousseau and his world*, London, 1972; New York, 1973.
Jacques Borel, *Génie et Folie de Jean-Jacques Rousseau*, Paris, 1966.
L. Brédif, *Du caractère intellectuel et moral de Jean-Jacques Rousseau*, Paris, 1906.
Lester G. Crocker, *Jean-Jacques Rousseau*, 2 vols, New York, 1968/1973.
Louis Ducros, *Jean-Jacques Rousseau*, 3 vols, Paris, 1908.
E. Faguet, *Vie de Rousseau*, Paris, 1912.
F. C. Green, *Jean-Jacques Rousseau*, London and New York, 1955.
R. Grimsley, *Jean-Jacques Rousseau*, Cardiff and Mystic, Conn., 1961.
Jean Guéhenno, *Jean-Jacques Rousseau*, 2 vols, translated by John and Doreen Weightman, London and New York, 1966.
Jules Lemaître, *Jean-Jacques Rousseau*, translated by J. Mairet, London, 1908.
Frederika MacDonald, *Jean-Jacques Rousseau*, 2 vols, London, 1906.
Saint Marc Girardin, *Jean-Jacques Rousseau*, 2 vols, Paris, 1875.
Daniel Mornet, *Rousseau, l'homme et l'oeuvre*, Paris, 1950.
J. F. Nourisson, *Jean-Jacques Rousseau et le Rousseauisme*, Paris, 1903.
Ernest Seillière, *Jean-Jacques Rousseau*, Paris, 1921.
J. Starobinski, *La transparence et l'obstacle*, Paris, 1957.

General
Irving Babbitt, *Rousseau and Romanticism*, Boston, 1928.
C. L. Becker, *The heavenly city of the 18th century philosophers*, New Haven, 1935.
C. B. A. Behrens, *The Ancien Régime*, London and New York, 1967.

Jules Bertaut, *La vie littéraire en France au 18ᵉ siècle*, Paris, 1954.

W. Boyd, *Emile for today*, London, 1956.

Crane Brinton, *History of Western Morals*, London, 1955; New York, 1959.

A. Brulé, *Les Gens de lettres*, Paris, 1929.

Ferdinand Brunetière, *Manuel de l'histoire de la littérature Française*, Paris, 1898.

H. Buffenoir, *Le prestige de Jean-Jacques Rousseau*, Paris, 1909.

Sir Edmund Burke, *Letter to a Member of the National Assembly*, London, 1791.

H. Carré, *La Noblesse Française et l'opinion publique au 18ᵉ siècle*, Paris, 1920.

E. Cassirer, *The question of Jean-Jacques Rousseau*, New York, 1954.

J. Charvet, *The social problem in the philosophy of Rousseau*, London and New York, 1974.

L. Clarétie, *Rousseau et ses amis*, Paris, 1896.

L. G. Crocker, *The embattled philosopher*, East Lansing, Mich., 1954; London, 1955.

D. Diderot, *Letters to Sophie Volland*, translated by Peter France, London and New York, 1972.

C. P. Duclos, *Considérations sur les moeurs de ce siècle*, London, 1784.

L. Ducros, *La société Française au 18ᵉ*, Paris, 1922.

G. Duhamel, *Les Confessions sans pénitence*, Paris, 1941.

M. Einaudi, *The early Rousseau*, Ithaca, N.Y., 1967.

Havelock Ellis, *From Rousseau to Proust*, London, 1936.

M. B. Ellis, *Rousseau's Venetian Story*, Baltimore, 1966.

Madame d'Epinay, *Memoirs and correspondence*, translated by J. H. Freese, London, 1899.

E. Faguet, *Les amies de Rousseau*, Paris, 1912.

— *Rousseau artiste*, Paris, 1913.

— *18ᵉ siècle: études littéraires*, Paris, 1890.

Claude Ferval, *Jean-Jacques Rousseau et les femmes*, Paris, 1934.

C. A. Fusil, *L'anti-Rousseau ou les égarements du coeur et de l'esprit*, Paris, 1929.

Peter Gay, *The Party of humanity*, New York, 1963; London, 1964.

J. Grand Carteret, *Jean-Jacques Rousseau jugé par les Français d'aujourd'hui*, Paris, 1890.

F. Gribble, *Rousseau and the women he loved*, London, 1908.

Ch. Guyot, *Un ami et défenseur de Rousseau, Pierre Alexandre Dupeyrou*, Neufchâtel, 1958.

C. Kunstler, *Vie quotidienne sous Louis XV*, Paris, 1953.

G. Lanson, *Histoire de la littérature Française*, Paris, 1912.

Joan MacDonald, *Rousseau and the French revolution*, London and New York, 1965.

P. M. Masson, *La réligion de Jean-Jacques Rousseau*, 3 vols, Paris, 1916.

F. Mauriac, *Trois grands hommes devant Dieu*, Paris, 1930.

— *Mes grands hommes*, Paris, 1949.

A. Maurois, *Sept Visages de l'amour*, Paris, 1946.

F. Michelet, *Histoire de France au 18ᵉ siècle*, Paris, 1863–67.

D. Mornet, *Le romantisme en France au 18ᵉ siècle*, Paris, 1912.

— *Pensée Française au 18ᵉ siècle*, Paris, 1926.

A. Noyes, *Voltaire*, London, 1936.

R. R. Palmer, *The world of the French Revolution*, London and New York, 1971.

M. Pélisson, *Les hommes de lettres au 18ᵉ siècle*, Paris, 1911.

R. Picard, *Les Salons littéraires et la société Française 1610–1789*, New York, 1943.

R. O. Rockwood, *Carl Becker's heavenly city revisited*, Hamden, Conn., 1968.

J. Roussel, *Jean-Jacques Rousseau en France après la révolution*, Paris, 1972.

M. Roustan, *Les Philosophes et la société Française au 18ᵉ siècle*, Lyon, 1906.

George Sand, *Quelques réflections sur Jean-Jacques Rousseau*, Paris, 1841.

E. Scherer, *Melchior Grimm*, Paris, 1887.

A. Schinz, *Etat des travaux sur Jean-Jacques Rousseau*, Paris, 1941.

Louis Philippe de Ségur, *Mémoires*, 3 vols, Paris, 1824.

E. Seillière, *Le mal romantique*, Paris, 1903.

Société Jean-Jacques Rousseau, *Annales*, Geneva, 1905–1971.

G. de Staël, *Lettres sur les écrits et le caractère de Rousseau*, Paris, 1778.

Lytton Strachey, *Landmarks in French literature*, London, 1911.

M. G. Streckeisen-Moultou, *Jean-Jacques Rousseau, ses amis et ses ennemis*, Paris, 1864.

'Studies in Voltaire and the 18th century', vol. 22, *Rousseau's contemporary reputation*, by S. S. B. Taylor, Geneva.

H. A. Taine, *The Ancien Régime*, translated by J. Durand, London, 1876.

Alexis de Tocqueville, *On the state of society before the Revolution*, translated by H. Reeve, London, 1856.

G. Vallette, *Jean-Jacques Rousseau Génévois*, Paris, 1911.

M. Villemain, *Cours de littérature Française*, Paris, 1855.

Arthur Young, *Travels in France, 1787–89*, London, 1899.

INDEX